Promoting the
General Welfare

Promoting the General Welfare

NEW PERSPECTIVES ON GOVERNMENT PERFORMANCE

Alan S. Gerber
Eric M. Patashnik
editors

BROOKINGS INSTITUTION PRESS
Washington, D.C.

Copyright © 2006
THE BROOKINGS INSTITUTION
1775 Massachusetts Avenue, N.W., Washington, D.C. 20036
www.brookings.edu

Library of Congress Cataloging-in-Publication data

Promoting the general welfare : new perspectives on government performance /
Alan S. Gerber, Eric M. Patashnik, editors.
    p.   cm.
Summary: "Analyzes government's ability to "promote the general welfare" in the areas of health, transportation, housing, and education. Then examines two tools to improve policy design: information markets and laboratory experiments. Concludes by asking how Congress, the party system, and federalism affect government's ability to solve important social problems"—Provided by publisher.
Includes bibliographical references and index.
Papers originally presented at a conference held at the University of Virginia in November 2004.
    ISBN-13: 978-0-8157-3120-7 (cloth : alk. paper)
    ISBN-10: 0-8157-3120-5 (cloth : alk. paper)
    ISBN-13: 978-0-8157-3121-4 (pbk. : alk. paper)
    ISBN-10: 0-8157-3121-3 (pbk. : alk. paper)
1. Public welfare administration—United States—Evaluation—Congresses.
2. Public administration—United States—Evaluation—Congresses. 3. United States—Social conditions—1980—Congresses. 4. United States—Politics and government—2001—Congresses. I. Gerber, Alan S. II. Patashnik, Eric M. III. Brookings Institution.
    HV95.P7375 2006
    361.60973—dc22   2006028091

9 8 7 6 5 4 3 2 1

The paper used in this publication meets minimum requirements of the American National Standard for Information Sciences—Permanence of Paper for Printed Library Materials: ANSI Z39.48-1992.

Typeset in Adobe Garamond

Composition by Cynthia Stock
Silver Spring, Maryland

Printed by R. R. Donnelley
Harrisonburg, Virginia

Contents

Part III. New Tools for Problem Solving

Part IV. Political Institutions as Problem Solvers?

Part V. Conclusion

Preface

This book originated in a three-month-long conversation between the editors about the implications of a remarkable study that was published in the *New England Journal of Medicine* in 2002. The study reported that a common operation for arthritis of the knee improves knee function no better than a sham procedure in which patients were sedated while surgeons pretended to operate. Those who received the placebo surgery reported as much pain relief as those who had the real operation. We were curious how this operation became so popular if it does not work and wondered how physicians, health insurers, and government policymakers would respond to the results of the *NEJM* study.

What we learned dismayed us. As we report in chapter 3, it is relatively common for surgical procedures to diffuse into clinical practice on the basis of little or no rigorous evidence. Once a procedure becomes popular, there are few incentives to use scientific methods to determine its effectiveness. As a society, we have largely delegated to physicians and health insurance firms responsibility for discovering the risks, benefits, and costs of alternative medical treatments and for ensuring that research findings are quickly translated into clinical practice. There are, however, good reasons to doubt that doctors and insurers are up to this job. While health services experts have long noted that the effectiveness of many treatments has not been demonstrated, problems in the evidentiary basis of medical care barely register on the national policy agenda. All Americans have an interest in a medical system that generates and uses high-quality information, but it appears that this vital common interest is not adequately being served.

The more we reflected on informational problems in the health care sector, the more we wondered about government's performance in other policy areas. The U.S. Constitution foresees a role for the government to "promote the general welfare," but how well does government carry out this task? This book brings together leading political scientists and economists to consider this important subject. Taken together, the chapters in this volume suggest that opportunities to promote the common good are frequently missed in modern American government, but the book also carries a more hopeful message. By identifying possible solutions to the problems created by weak incentives, poor information, and inadequate institutional capacity, *Promoting the General Welfare* suggests how government performance might be improved.

It is a pleasure to acknowledge the institutions and individuals that have supported this project. Most of the chapters in this book were originally presented at a conference held at the University of Virginia in November 2004. The conference was cosponsored by the Bankard Fund for Political Economy at the University of Virginia and by the Center for the Study of American Politics at Yale University. We are grateful to Donald Green, director of Yale's Institution for Social and Policy Research, for additional financial support. We also wish to acknowledge the support of Sid Milkis and David Mills. We wish to thank Martha Derthick and William R. Johnson, for providing comments on the original conference papers. Larry Bartels and John Donahue made important intellectual contributions to the project. Jesse Rhodes and Daniel DiSalvo provided administrative and research support. Pam Greene prepared the conference papers for publication. We also wish to thank our editors at Brookings Institution Press: Christopher Kelaher, Janet Walker, Joseph Parsons, and especially Mark Kwak. Finally, we wish to thank the external reviewers for Brookings Institution Press. Their comments led to many substantive and stylistic improvements.

PART I

Introduction

1

Government Performance: Missing Opportunities to Solve Problems

ALAN S. GERBER AND ERIC M. PATASHNIK

Journalists, activists, and other policy actors have strong incentives to publicize and stir up political conflict. Newspapers frame stories about complex issues around personality battles among the players. Political activists with parochial interests claim to be on the front lines of a "cultural war" that will determine the fate of the nation.[1] And candidates for public office go to great lengths to differentiate themselves from their allegedly extremist opponents.

Lost in the political system's focus on conflict and controversy is the tremendous common ground—among ordinary citizens and political elites alike—over government's role in contemporary American society. No prominent leader or influential social group today advocates a wholesale shedding of the federal government's responsibility in any major area of public policy. Regardless of whether Democrats or Republicans are elected to office, the government will continue to protect the environment, assist senior citizens with health care costs, and maintain the world's most formidable military. Although the media tend to magnify the differences between opposing sides on policy issues, the reality is that even ideologically charged clashes typically take place within certain boundaries.

Consider a contentious issue such as Social Security reform. Important social values are undeniably at stake in choosing among pension reform alternatives. Liberals and conservatives have very different reform ideas. Yet, as political scientist Hugh Heclo points out, not even the most radical privatization plan calls for a total government withdrawal from the problem of retirement security. First, there is a general consensus against relying solely on "do-it-yourself" pension arrangements. The public *expects* the government to address the problem of financial security in old age. Second, there is no "government-less private sector in sight to withdraw to."[2] Even the most "private" individual market plan would require an extensive framework of government rules to govern withdrawals, borrowing, and investment choices. Most plans would also include new subsidies for the poor.

This pattern repeats itself across the full scope of governance. Policy alternatives are debated, often quite vehemently, but the essential role of government as supplier of public goods and guarantor of public health and safety is *not*. Total government expenditures in the United States accounted for 30.9 percent of gross domestic product in fiscal year 2004.[3] This aggregate level of government activity has been remarkably constant in the face of large-scale economic, social, and political developments since the 1970s.[4] It is highly unlikely that the United States will soon develop a government as large as Sweden's, but it is equally unlikely that the federal government will shrink back to the size it was prior to World War II and the Great Depression.

If activist yet limited government is a widely desired and, in any event, permanent fixture of modern American society, government performance matters greatly. Can the government identify and solve collective problems? Does the government possess the political incentives, institutional capacity, and analytic tools to weigh social benefits and costs and generate useable information about problems, preferences, and policy priorities? What are the major causes of government performance troubles? When all is said and done, can the government promote the general welfare?

This book offers new perspectives on government performance. The essays in the volume address the topic by examining both the government's performance in specific policy areas and the capacity of key political institutions to identify and solve important societal problems. The first group of essays demonstrates that the government is failing to tackle significant problems in key arenas of domestic policymaking, including health (Alan Gerber and Eric Patashnik), transportation (Clifford Winston), housing (Edgar O. Olsen), and special education (Jay P. Greene). These cases are both illustrative of the tasks performed by modern American government and designed to stimulate thinking about government performance. They do not, however, represent all the important tasks government does or might undertake. We chose to study these policy areas not only because they are substantively important, but also because they demonstrate the pervasiveness and significance of market and government failures and the incompleteness of existing explanations of the sources of government underperformance. These case studies underscore the need for fresh thinking about the reasons for government underperformance and are complementary to other studies that formally test hypotheses by considering the effect of variation in independent variables across cases or over time.[5]

It is helpful when policy analysts not only address problems that decision-makers have placed on the agenda, but also speak up for the general public and other diffuse interests that lack adequate representation in the political process. As David L. Weimer and Aidan R. Vining explain in chapter 2, prominent among those interests deserving greater voice is efficiency. The concept of efficiency takes a variety of forms. In practice, many policy analysts use the concept of potential Pareto improvement. The relevant test is whether a policy change produces sufficient social benefits that winners could theoretically compensate losers and still come out ahead. This concept of potential efficiency (formally known as the Kaldor-Hicks criterion) is not uncontroversial. Its implementation requires the ability to measure gains and losses in a common metric. Moreover, in practice, the transfer payments needed to compensate losers may not be made. Nevertheless, the Kaldor-Hicks criterion gives analysts a powerful diagnostic lens for seeing potential opportunities to improve on the status quo. Weimer and Vining forcefully argue that efficiency should not necessarily override other social values, such as equity and human dignity, but it deserves much greater respect than it often receives in the democratic process.

The second group of chapters examines novel institutional mechanisms for improving government performance, including the use of laboratory experiments as a tool for policy design (Charles A. Holt, William M. Shobe, and Angela M. Smith) and the creation of information markets (Robin Hanson). The chapters explain how new analytic tools can promote more informed decisions and the conditions under which their use is likely to be compatible with the incentives of policymakers. The point of these chapters is not that such methods can identify the "right answers" to complex problems such as the prevention of terrorist attacks, but rather that they may help policymakers evaluate alternatives and reduce the uncertainty under which they must make high-stakes decisions.

In the third part of the book, the authors step back from the details of specific policy debates and assess the overall performance of three foundations of American government: Congress (chapters by David R. Mayhew and

Sarah A. Binder), the political party system (Morris P. Fiorina), and federalism (Mark Carl Rom and Roberta Romano). These contributors evaluate whether electoral incentives and institutional rules give politicians an adequate motivation to support public policies that are in the broad national interest. Several of the chapters raise disturbing questions about whether recent political developments have led to a decline in the amount of problem-solving activity in government. In the concluding chapter, Eugene Bardach critically reviews the arguments and assumptions of the individual essays, pointing out the strengths and limitations of the two major contending disciplinary perspectives (economics and political science) on government underperformance. He argues that economists' studies of the relative efficiency of specific policies are very useful in assessments of government performance, but that it is also important to understand the political and institutional conditions that promote or hinder effective government problem solving. Bardach suggests that this is a research area to which political scientists could bring special insights, and he urges the political science profession to devote far more energy to studying this topic.

Although we are sympathetic to Bardach's advice, we also recognize that any effort to persuade political scientists to direct more attention to the overall quality of government performance is an uphill battle. Most political scientists today view politics as a zero-sum game in which values and scarce resources are allocated among contending social groups. Since the 1930s, the fundamental political science research question—following the pioneering work of Harold D. Lasswell—has been "who gets what the government has to give?"[6] Relatively few political scientists investigate the political requisites of effective problem solving or the conditions under which government promotes (or frustrates) the efficient operation of society as a whole. As table 1-1 shows, the ratio between the level of attention given to distributive issues and that paid to efficiency in leading political science journals is almost four to one. It is not surprising that the situation is reversed in top economics journals—economists publish nearly three articles on efficiency for each article on distributional issues.

Recent developments in political science are only likely to reinforce these basic patterns. Under the leadership of Theda Skocpol, the American Political Science Association has published major reports on the impact of economic inequality, race, and ethnicity on democratic governance.[7] Some of the discipline's most distinguished scholars have strongly criticized the profession for devoting *too little* attention to "the distribution of political power and influence."[8] We applaud this important commitment but also see an unmet

Table 1-1. *Attention Paid to Distributional Issues and Efficiency Concerns, Leading Political Science and Economics Journals, 1980–2002*
Number

Discipline	Distributional issues	Efficiency concerns
Political science	149	39
Economics	45	123

Methodology: J-STOR search of abstracts of articles appearing in the following journals over 1980–2002 period: *American Political Science Review, American Journal of Political Science, Journal of Politics, American Economic Review, Journal of Political Economy, Journal of Economic Perspectives.* Coverage of distributional issues was measured by counting number of article abstracts that contained the following terms: distributional, distributive, redistribution, redistributive, or justice. Coverage of efficiency concerns was measured by counting number of article abstracts containing the terms efficiency or Pareto (but excluding those containing the terms informational or cognitive to eliminate articles focusing on technical or narrow meanings of the term efficiency only indirectly related to the overall quality of government performance).

need for a research agenda that assesses the political system's capacity to identify and solve problems that are not essentially distributional in nature.

In this introductory chapter, we frame some new arguments about the politics of government underperformance. Drawing on the individual chapters, we shall argue that a critical attribute of American government is the degree to which social problem solving and efficient policy design emerge as a by-product of democratic politics, which we take to be "that institutional arrangement for arriving at political decisions in which individuals acquire the power to decide by means of a competitive struggle for the people's vote."[9] This "Schumpeterian" perspective on government performance stands in contrast not only to idealistic models of democratic deliberation, in which the people directly get to decide public policy matters, but also to more realistic "public-choice" theories in economics. Because the classic public choice theories have contributed a great deal to our understanding of public sector underperformance, we begin by discussing these theories.

Public Choice Theories and Government Failure

Public choice scholars argue that politics, like markets, is organized around the pursuit of self-interest. The decisions public leaders make depend largely upon the pressures they face from social actors. Hence, public choice scholars have traditionally emphasized the role of interest groups and have neglected other actors in the political process.[10] There is considerable disagreement among public choice theorists about whether pressure group influence leads to efficient outcomes.[11] "Virginia School" public choice scholars, such as Gordon Tullock and James Buchanan, are quite pessimistic about this.[12] For the Virginians, government is not an institution that promotes social welfare by producing public goods and overcoming externalities. Rather, government officials use their monopoly on the coercive power of the state to extract wealth, which is redistributed to favored "rent-seeking" groups.[13] In contrast, the "Chicago School," associated with widely influential economists such as Gary Becker, is much more sanguine about the possibility of efficient governance. Like the Virginians, Chicago School theorists recognize that compact groups may function as cartels and that diffuse interests may be poorly represented in the political process. Groups that are able to overcome the free-rider problem will be more able to win favors from politicians in exchange for political support.[14] Chicago School theorists, however, are as skeptical of claims about destructive monopoly power in political markets as they are about assertions of destructive monopoly power in economic markets. Chicagoans believe that political competition limits the social costs of rent-seeking behavior, very much as the 1950s "pluralist" theorists in political science once claimed that interest groups check and balance one another. According to Becker, a particular interest group can gobble up only so much wealth before it triggers a political countermobilization or undermines the economic production that makes its subsidies possible. Because inefficient policies reduce the surplus available for distribution (an outcome no one wants), there should be strong pressure toward efficiency.[15] Yet we know empirically that inefficient policies (such as farm subsidies) can last for long periods of time. If the Virginia model is too pessimistic, the Chicago model can lead to Panglossian conclusions.[16]

For all their differences, the Virginia School and the Chicago School share some fundamental analytic assumptions. Both seriously downplay the importance of competition *among public officials or candidates* in a representative democracy and the myriad ways that political elites seek to build public support for their platforms, proposals, and pet ideas. In classic public choice models, the government is a "black box." At best, politicians are brokers who exist to do client groups' bidding. This portrait is misleading. U.S. politicians are also *sellers* of problem definitions and proposed policy solutions who may be entrepreneurial in searching for market niches for their products. The creative problem-defining and problem-solving role of politicians must be taken into account in any effort to understand and evaluate what government does or how well it performs.[17] As Richard Posner observes, the most interesting politicians are the ones who seek to create (to satisfy at a price) new demands among the public. "The consuming public did not know that it wanted social security, conscription, public education, an independent central bank, an interstate highway system, a Presidency open to divorced or Catholic persons, the North Atlantic Treaty Organization, or the auction of rights to the use of the electromagnetic spectrum before those things were proposed by political entrepreneurs, as distinct from run-of-the-mill politicians."[18]

In sum, traditional public choice theories of government failure—for all their important insights—often rest on a simplified view of the political process. The public choice literature tends to focus on sins of commission (the myriad ways that government blunders). Less noticed are the government's sins of *omission*. If government fails to seize opportunities to improve social welfare that are technically feasible and for which supportive political coalitions are potentially assemblable, it is not serving the citizenry, its constituency. Many government performance problems are extremely subtle. The same litany of concerns (for example, rent seeking, bureaucratic waste and abuse, pork barrel spending) receive seemingly endless attention. Yet these are not necessarily the worst policy distortions.[19] Less obvious but far more serious government performance problems include the failure to bring relevant information to bear on complex problems; the undersupply of political entrepreneurship in areas where diffuse constituencies lack representation; the unwillingness of policymakers to experiment with new approaches when old ones are not working; and, above all, the maximization of the *appearance* of problem solving rather than the successful execution of its reality.

A Schumpeterian Perspective on Government Failure

These governance failures can be best understood from a Schumpeterian perspective. In the starkest version of this model, there are only two sets of actors: politicians, whose sole motivation is to win office, and voters, who evaluate the politicians and cast votes. Good public policy will emerge if politicians have the capacity to *produce* good public policies and voters adequately *reward* politicians who offer it. These conditions sound easy to satisfy, but they might not be.

If politicians are to produce good public policies, they must first be able to recognize them. This may be a demanding requirement. As Edgar Olsen argues in chapter 5, despite substantial evidence that vouchers are a superior method for delivery of subsidized housing benefits, the shift away from project-based assistance is occurring at an unjustifiably slow pace. Olsen argues that one reason vouchers have not diffused more rapidly is the failure of housing policy experts (as against industry lobbyists) to make sufficient efforts to communicate with congressional staffs and the negligible inducements provided by the academic reward system for scholars to allocate time to this important public service. The professional return on conducting studies relevant to current policy debates typically comes only from writing journal articles that no one in power will read.[20]

Politicians may not only be ignorant of the costs and benefits of alternative policy solutions. They may also fail to employ the best methods for analyzing policy options rigorously, such as the experimental approaches described by Holt, Shobe, and Smith in chapter 8, either because they are unaware of these methods or because they are uncomfortable with them. The potential return from experimentation is large in policy areas where the outcomes are important, and our knowledge of what works is poor because of weak studies and the presence of actors with a stake in preserving the existing system. A good example is K–12 public education. We know embarrassingly little about the best way to teach children, in part because teachers unions have blocked direct assessments of teacher and school performance. To be sure, there are many education theories and studies, but precious little high-quality scientific evidence. Despite the potential benefits of such studies, experimentation has been regarded as an anathema in education research because we cannot treat children like "lab rats." As Eric A. Hanushek points out, the irony is that "schools experiment on children all the time. They just do so in a nonsystematic way and seldom evaluate the experiments so that we can learn from them."[21]

Elected officials may be genuinely offended by novel policy analytic tools that seem to challenge widely held cultural taboos, such as the proposal to create an information market in which actors would bet on the likelihood of specific geopolitical events taking place. As Robin Hanson argues in chapter 7, decision markets could generate potentially useful policy-relevant information at extremely low cost, but their creation requires politicians to cross perceived moral boundaries, something they are often unwilling to do.

There may be other reasons why politicians fail to recognize opportunities for policy improvements. Posner, in his provocative recent book on the dangers posed by a variety of catastrophic threats, observes that governmental responses to the possibilities of mega-risks such as bioterrorism and nuclear winter are often grossly inadequate because people struggle to think sensibly about low-probability threats.[22] A central problem is that politicians have very short time horizons. Their focus on near-term risks may cause them to neglect more remote ones that could be far more serious. Moreover, people, politicians included, are captives of their experiences. When horrific events have not occurred before (like the risk of 9/11, *before* 9/11 happened), it is difficult to imagine them.[23]

Zero Credit Policymaking

Another reason politicians may fail to produce good public policy is because problem solving may offer small political returns. If problem solving is an unintended by-product of political competition rather than something pursued for its own sake, and if politicians are motivated to do what wins elections, a tension exists in our system of collective choice. From the standpoint of social welfare, a policy should be adopted if the benefits are greater than the costs, whereas from the standpoint of a politician, a policy should be adopted if the political benefits to the politician are greater than the political costs. Good policies that have large *social* but small political benefits may not find a political sponsor.

Proposing creative, thoughtful solutions to important policy problems may not be the most straightforward way to generate political support. As David R. Mayhew explains in chapter 10, there may be severe disagreement over whether some objective societal condition constitutes a "problem" that requires governmental intervention. Even if people agree that a problem exists, there may be disagreement over the best course of action. A Schumpeterian legislator who wishes to do good for society while doing well for herself first needs to frame the problem in a way that brings the public along yet also makes sense from the standpoint of the instrumental rationality needs of political executives and bureaucrats. She must then "deliberate, bargain, and compromise in a fishbowl setting in a fashion that can swerve both publics and experts toward emergent solutions" (Mayhew, p. 223). All this requires tremendous political effort and creativity.

Sometimes good policy choices will be available but public support for them will be absent because of misconceptions and ignorance. Politicians-cum-problem solvers then must seek to *create* public demand for the new solutions. This is not just difficult but also electorally risky. If a politician pushes a policy idea that conflicts with what voters currently believe, or that is simply difficult for nonexperts to understand, voters might conclude the politician is a courageous truth teller and change their minds. Yet it is also possible (and perhaps *more* likely) that voters will instead remain skeptical about the proposal and become somewhat skeptical about its advocate as well. There are good reasons for voters' skepticism. Sometimes politicians are well meaning but out of step with their constituents. Sometimes they really are snake oil salesmen. When an uninvited visitor comes knocking with promises to help, it is not crazy that the first instinct of many people is to slam the door. One thing is certain: the opponents of the policy change can be counted on to pounce if they sense an opportunity to denigrate the proposal and thereby undermine the policy innovator's public standing.[24]

Despite these strong disincentives, suppose a politician *does* try to shift public opinion. This effort at persuasion might be viewed as making a risky investment that may or may not pay off. But what if the attempt to build public support for a new policy approach begins to work? In a commercial setting, such an investment often enjoys legal protections such as patents and trademarks. In a political setting, however, there is nothing to stop an opportunistic opponent who observes the changes in public opinion produced by a rival's hard work from proposing a substantively similar proposal of his own. If this effort at political mimicry is successful, the policy innovator will capture, at best, a small share of the credit for the results of his efforts. Worse, the second politician, by hanging back until political conditions become more favorable and observing how opinion unfolds, may generate more support for his alternative scheme, a copycat plan better tailored to public opinion. In the ruthlessly competitive world of democratic politics, the policy innovator could end up worse off for his effort.

In their chapter on the reaction of the government to the publication of a landmark study demonstrating that a common surgical procedure works no better than a placebo operation, Gerber and Patashnik conjecture that correcting popular misconceptions about the quality of medical evidence in the United States today is an example of what they term a "zero credit" policy, meaning a government intervention or activity that offers no captureable political returns even though it has large net social benefits. Patients are strongly inclined to trust their doctors' views about the care they need, and any effort to build support for more rigorous, third-party investigation of the benefits, costs, and risks of surgical practices would require challenging this deeply help popular belief. If this effort began to gain legislative traction, it is likely that all politicians would be willing to support some policy to address the problem, making it impossible for the original entrepreneur to differentiate herself from other politicians, including campaign opponents. If policy innovators anticipate that the political benefits from proposing novel solutions to public problems will be quickly appropriated, the effect will be to discourage the entrepreneurial investments in the first place.

This is not to say that *no* such political investments will be made. Political entrepreneurs who are willing to invest their time and energy on behalf of general interest reforms clearly do exist. Consider the case of airline deregulation. In the 1970s, the federal government controlled the fares airlines could charge and what routes they could fly. Airline service was generally excellent, but ordinary Americans could not find affordable flights to take them where they wanted to go. Although professional economists argued that the freeing of market forces would be highly beneficial for air passengers, the millions of potential winners from airline deregulation were largely unorganized. In contrast, the major airlines that benefited from anticompetitive regulations were mobilized. Nevertheless, in 1978 Congress passed a major airline deregulation bill in the face of strong industry opposition. Key to this reform victory was the entrepreneurial activity of both visible and less visible policy actors, including Alfred Kahn (a professional economist who headed the independent commission that regulated the airline industry), Senator Ted Kennedy (who saw in airline deregulation the potential to enhance his standing with the burgeoning consumer movement), and one of Senator Kennedy's (then unknown) legislative aides, a young Stephen Breyer.[25] Airline deregulation, together with cases such as the creation of an efficient market trading system to control the sulfur dioxide emissions that cause acid rain, demonstrates that general interest reform *is* possible.[26] But the level of entrepreneurial investment in collective problem solving (as against posturing or position taking) may be inadequate given the social return.

Politicians' willingness to invest in the development of good policy solutions is further inhibited by the short time horizons of voters, who generally reward current performance without regard to long-term consequences.[27] This gives politicians a perverse incentive to focus on policies with short-term benefits and long-run costs (for example, the Medicare prescription drug bill) and ignore solutions with short-term costs and long-run benefits (for example, flood preparedness steps in New Orleans).

Organizational myopia is not unique to government. The owners of private firms worry that managers will focus only on short-term performance to the neglect of future prospects. One of the ways that owners encourage their agents to take the long view is to tie compensation in part to the performance of the company's stock or give officers restricted stock that can be exercised only after some future date. Stocks and debt securities developed as a way to raise capital, but their trading produces an important informational by-product. If the stock market is efficient, stock prices are reliable measures of each firm's expected future earnings. Decisions taken today that improve the expected future earnings of the company are therefore reflected in the stock price prior to their realization. If, for example, a pharmaceutical company announces positive results from a new drug trial, its stock price should rise because future sales of the new product can be expected, even though the positive clinical result may cause the firm to incur large "losses" over the next few years in the form of development and marketing costs. In politics, however, the payoffs from good decisions are rarely "capitalized" by the voters. Voters may punish politicians for raising taxes, even if future benefits from the resulting expenditures will be large. Indeed, recent scholarship suggests that voters may punish politicians for events clearly beyond their control, such as natural disasters or swings in commodity prices on world markets.[28]

How might voters be encouraged to reward and punish politicians today for the effect of their decisions on the future? One possibility is to rely on decentralized information-generation mechanisms, such as financial markets. Information is produced as a natural by-product of market trading. As Hanson explains in chapter 7, securities can be designed to generate information about whether a policy being considered for adoption is expected by interested observers to produce certain effects in the future. The example he uses is whether national health outcomes will improve by a certain amount over a specific time period if a national health insurance bill is passed today. The information generated by purchases and sales of this proposed "health policy security" could potentially elevate the political debate over whether the proposal should be adopted.

One limitation of this kind of decision market as a mechanism for promoting electoral accountability is that the value of the security depends upon a specific government action (for example, passage of national health insurance) rather than on the election of particular candidates. Yet voters in a Schumpeterian democracy like the United States do not make direct policy decisions. Their role is to choose the leaders who in turn decide public policy.

Building on Hanson's arguments regarding the informational benefits of policy markets, we suggest the construction of decision markets with the explicit goal of producing information geared to the needs of voters when selecting among candidates.[29] Voters currently lack clear, unbiased information about the past and expected future performance of incumbent politicians and potential replacements. To help address this problem, we propose establishing securities called "Voter Information Shares." The value of these securities would be based upon the average outcomes during specified periods on economic or social performance measures such as economic growth, budget deficits, tax rates, unemployment, inflation, and poverty. There would be at least two types of Voter Information Shares for each outcome measure, one conditional on the Democratic candidate winning the presidency and one conditional on the Republican candidate winning the presidency.[30] For example, there might be a security whose value is determined at the end of 2012, with a value equal to zero if a Republican is elected president in 2008, and a value equal to the average economic growth rate from 2009–12 if the Democratic Party nominee is victorious in 2008. Voters could compare the corresponding Democratic and Republican securities prices and take them into account when deciding whom to support. While these remarks are obviously exploratory, and there are both technical challenges and incentives for manipulation to overcome, a well-designed market for Voter Information Shares might provide voters with useful information about expected officeholder performance.

Viewing policymaking as an unintended by-product of elite competition for votes captures some essential features of democratic politics, yet it is obviously simplistic. The chapters in this book therefore offer a more realistic account of policymaking in modern American government by incorporating the roles of both interest groups and political institutions. Interest groups may offer rewards and punishments to supplement those offered by voters, and the policy information they provide may enlighten, embolden, confuse, or paralyze politicians. As the chapters by Clifford Winston, Jay Greene, and others show, interest groups are responsible for many gross policy distortions, though they clearly play constructive information- and preference-aggregation roles as well.[31]

Political institutions similarly both foster and hinder governmental performance. Roberta Romano's chapter demonstrates that, in the case of public policy toward corporate governance structures, federalism indeed functions as a "laboratory of democracy" that generates efficient policy solutions. The financial incentives for states to create a favorable business climate are very strong. Yet Mark Carl Rom cautions in his chapter that this laboratory may function effectively only under very limited policy conditions and that differences in state preferences and goals often discourage policy learning. These two chapters offer fresh data and arguments to the longstanding debate about what programs and policies are most efficiently delivered at each level of American government.

The chapters by Sarah Binder, David R. Mayhew, and Morris P. Fiorina offer a mixed portrait of the problem solving capacities of Congress. Contrary to popular belief, Congress *is* capable, at least at times, of passing bills that serve the general welfare. Nevertheless, the incentives for effective problem solving in the House and Senate today are often quite weak, and the organizational and analytic capacities needed to promote the larger view are often missing. As Fiorina's chapter argues, too often party polarization and electoral competition undermine the incentives for collective responsibility. Both Fiorina and Mayhew argue that political scientists' traditional belief that strong parties improve government performance by presenting voters with clear choices may need to be revised. The congressional parties are more cohesive and unified today than they were in the 1950s, yet public trust in the federal government is much lower. The institutional design challenge is to encourage more cooperation across party lines, and carve out a space for nonpartisan problem solving, without sacrificing the vital organizational roles that parties continue to play.

Binder suggests that although there is no guaranteed path to success, control of the policy agenda is essential. Coalition leaders must structure the procedural rules of the game to limit the blocking power of narrow groups, and they must frame socially efficient policies in ways that are attractive to both rank-and-file politicians and mass publics. Both Binder and Mayhew agree that information flows are critical, though they emphasize different approaches. Binder suggests that lawmakers may sometimes need to operate under a political veil if they are to be free to impose costs on narrow groups to serve the broad public interest, whereas Mayhew believes the potential of C-SPAN and other modern information-transmission technologies to educate the public about what their leaders are up to should be better exploited. As Eugene Bardach points out in his chapter, the conditions under which transparency promotes (or hinders) efficient governance is an important empirical consideration that requires careful attention.

Taken together, the essays in this volume suggest that opportunities to promote the common good are frequently missed in modern American government. A central challenge for researchers and institutional reformers is to find ways to make seizing these opportunities more rewarding for politicians.

Notes

1. Morris P. Fiorina, *Culture War? The Myth of a Polarized America* (New York: Pearson Longman, 2005). See also Fiorina's chapter in the present volume.

2. Hugh Heclo, "A Political Science Perspective on Social Security Reform," in *Framing the Social Security Debate: Values, Politics, and Economics,* edited by R. Douglas Arnold,

Michael J. Graetz, and Alicia H. Munnell (Washington, D.C.: National Academy of Social Insurance, 1998), pp. 65–88, at 69.

3. In fiscal 2004, federal government expenditures accounted for 19.8 percent of GDP, and state and local government expenditures accounted for 11.0 percent of GDP. Office of Management and Budget, *The Budget for Fiscal Year 2006: Historical Tables* (Washington, D.C.: Government Printing Office, 2005), table 15.3, p. 304.

4. In 1974 total U.S. government expenditures accounted for 28.9 percent of GDP; in 1984 the figure was 31.7; and in 1994, 31.9 percent. Ibid.

5. More recent scholarship has begun to examine the conditions under which governments make Pareto inefficient policy choices. For example, in his important recent manuscript Timothy Besley stresses the role of ignorance, costly rent-seeking, poor selection of policymakers, and intertemporal political and policy linkages. See Timothy Besley, "Principled Agents? The Political Economy of Good Government," typescript, October 2005, London School of Economics and Political Science. See also Timothy Besley and Stephen Coate, "Sources of Inefficiency in a Representative Democracy: A Dynamic Analysis," *American Economic Review,* vol. 88, no. 1 (1998): 139–56.

6. See Harold D. Lasswell's classic *Politics: Who Gets What, When, and How* (New York: McGraw-Hill, 1936).

7. See American Political Science Association Task Force on Inequality, "American Democracy in an Age of Rising Inequality," *Perspectives on Politics,* vol. 2 (December 2004): 651–66.

8. Lawrence R. Jacobs and Theda Skocpol, "Restoring the Tradition of Rigor and Relevance to Political Science," *P.S.: Politics and Political Science* (January 2006): 27–31, at 29.

9. Joseph A. Schumpeter, *Capitalism, Socialism, and Democracy,* 3d ed. (New York: Harper, 1950), p. 269. For a defense and insightful exposition of Schumpeter's theory of democracy, see Richard A. Posner, *Law, Pragmatism, and Democracy* (Harvard University Press, 2003), pp. 158-212.

10. Posner, *Law, Pragmatism, and Democracy,* p. 386.

11. For an excellent review of the two main paradigms of public choice theory, see William C. Mitchell and Michael C. Munger, "Economic Models of Interest Groups: An Introductory Survey," *American Journal of Political Science,* vol. 13, no. 2 (1991): 512–46.

12. See, for example, Gordon Tullock, *Rent Seeking* (Aldershot, U.K.: Edward Elgar, 1993).

13. In some models, politicians do not transfer the rent they collect to interest groups but rather keep it for themselves. See, for example, Fred S. McChesney, *Money for Nothing: Politicians, Rent Extraction, and Political Extortion* (Harvard University Press, 1997); on "budget-maximizing" bureaucrats, see William A. Niskanen, *Bureaucracy and Representative Government* (Chicago: Aldine Press, 1971).

14. George Stigler, "The Theory of Economic Regulation," *Bell Journal of Economics and Management Science,* vol. 2 (1971): 3–21; see also Mancur Olsen, *The Logic of Collective Action* (Harvard University Press, 1965).

15. Gary Becker, "A Theory of Competition among Pressure Groups for Political Influence." *Quarterly Journal of Economics,* vol. 98, no. 3 (1983): 371–401.

16. See Roger Noll, "The Economic Theory of Regulation a Decade after Deregulation," *BPEA: Microeconomics* (1989), p. 57.

17. On the need to take seriously the political autonomy of U.S. lawmakers, see David R. Mayhew, *America's Congress: Actions in the Public Sphere, James Madison to Newt Gingrich* (Yale University Press, 2000).

18. Posner, *Law, Pragmatism and Democracy,* 194.

19. Pork barrel projects, for example, do not constitute a significant share of federal spending and can be useful for building winning coalitions for general interest legislation. See John W. Ellwood and Eric M. Patashnik, "In Praise of Pork," *Public Interest* (Winter 1993), pp. 19–33; Diana Evans, *Greasing the Wheels: Using Pork Barrel Projects to Build Majority Coalitions in Congress* (Cambridge University Press, 2004); see also Sarah Binder, "Can Congress Serve the General Welfare?" present volume.

20. One suggestion is that universities—particularly public policy schools—consider providing incentives for scholars "to follow through on research by effectively introducing it into the policy process." Eric A. Hanushek, "Policy Analysis: Is It, or Could It Be, the Fifth Estate?" 2005 Spencer Foundation Distinguished Lecture in Education Policy and Management, originally delivered at the Association for Public Policy Analysis and Management Fall Research Conference, Washington, D.C., November 3–5, 2005, at p. 16.

21. Ibid., p. 10.

22. Richard A. Posner, *Catastrophe: Risk and Response* (Oxford University Press, 2004).

23. National Commission on Terrorist Attacks upon the United States, *The 9/11 Commission Report* (New York: W. W. Norton, 2004).

24. Putting aside its substantive merits, the recent effort by President Bush to gain support for Social Security privatization is instructive. The proposal initially enjoyed only mixed support; trying to move public opinion toward privatization did not just divert time and energy away from other domestic priorities but also appeared to lower the president's standing more generally among an increasingly skeptical public. This episode illustrates the danger of trying to change people's minds.

25. Martha Derthick and Paul Quirk, *The Politics of Deregulation* (Brookings, 1985).

26. See Eric M. Patashnik, "After the Public Interest Prevails: The Political Sustainability of Policy Reform," *Governance,* vol. 16 (2003): 203–34.

27. Edward Tufte, *Political Control of the Economy* (Princeton University Press, 1973).

28. Larry M. Bartels and Christopher H. Achen, "Blind Retrospection: Electoral Responses to Droughts, Flu, and Shark Attacks," paper presented at the Annual Meeting of the American Political Science Association, Boston, August 29–September 1, 2002.

29. In previous writings, Hanson has suggested the creation of securities similar to those we discuss here. In 1996 Hanson posted a web page about decision markets that included the example of a security that would allow people to bet whether the nation would be more likely to go to war under a president Clinton or Dole. See http://hanson.gmu.edu/policymarkets.html (August 7, 2006). In a 1999 article, Hanson discussed examples of military casualties conditional on the president's party, and of stock prices conditional on the party controlling Congress. See Robin D. Hanson, "Decision Markets," *IEE Intelligence Systems,* May/June 1999, pp. 16–20.

30. Third-party candidates might promote confidence in their electoral prospects if a bundle of securities associated with their candidacies were traded. This would also help remove barriers to entry in the electoral process.

31. A prominent line of political science scholarship argues that public policies may give rise to interest groups that then resist policy changes in their domain. See, for example, James Q. Wilson, *Political Organizations* (New York: Basic Books, 1973), and Paul Pierson, *Dismantling the Welfare State?* (Cambridge University Press, 1994).

2

Policy Analysis in Representative Democracy

David L. Weimer and Aidan R. Vining

An enlightened philosopher-king would assess how alternative policies affect the welfare of society before choosing among them, but even a rapacious "stationary bandit" would almost certainly assess how alternative policies would affect the actual willingness and capacity of society to be taxed before making policy choices.[1] At either extreme of this dictatorial spectrum, identifying relevant social values, crafting alternative policies, predicting the consequences of the policies, and assessing them in terms of the identified values—the craft of policy analysis—would be useful. A fundamental advantage of representative government, what some would argue is *the* fundamental advantage,[2] is that it allows the polity to eject stationary bandits as well as philosopher-kings (who, anyway, almost always become unenlightened) peacefully. Representative government, however, offers even more. It provides incentives for the articulation of interests and mechanisms for their influence on the choice of public policies. If all the interests of people are fully articulated and effectively represented, then the role of policy analysis primarily is one of design and prediction: specifying the necessary details of policy alternatives that arise in the political process and predicting their effects relevant to the interests of people in society. Yet interest articulation is incomplete, and interest representation is imperfect and, indeed, cannot be perfected.[3] Consequently, policy analysis in representative government can play a valuable role, not only in specifying and predicting the consequences of alternative policies, but also in speaking for those interests in society that lack adequate articulation or representation in the arenas of collective choice. Most prominent among the interests deserving greater voice is efficiency.

Efficiency simply means getting the most value for people from the resources available. It includes technical efficiency, which means producing things of value in ways that involve giving up the smallest amounts of other things of value. More generally, however, it concerns the allocation of resources among competing uses to generate the greatest aggregate value. One can intuitively think of a policy as promoting efficiency if, summing across all members of society, the benefits obtained exceed the costs incurred. The policy achieves efficiency if no other policy can be identified that offers a larger excess of benefits over costs. It is clear that any policy that would create greater costs than benefits is inefficient. For example, a policy that would inflict $300 million in costs but only $200 million in benefits would reduce, rather than increase, efficiency.

Why do representative governments often choose inefficient policies? The argument that efficiency receives too little weight in representative government has the following logic:[4] First, elected representatives, such as legislators, desire to at least some extent to be reelected or advance to higher office. Thus, representatives base their decisions on not just their conceptions of the good society, but also on how their decisions will affect electoral support from their current or desired future constituencies. Second, it is costly for constituents to monitor and influence representatives. Even participation as simple as seeking out the position of one's representative on a particular issue and writing a letter urging a particular action is costly in terms of time. Some may even find voting too costly. Those who do vote may rely heavily on shortcuts, such as party affiliation, ideological labels, or simple heuristics,[5] rather than full assessments of incumbents' records (retrospective voting) or candidates' platforms (prospective voting). Third, those with high stakes in policy issues (concentrated interests) or those representing organized interests are more likely to find it worthwhile to monitor and lobby representatives than those with low stakes (diffuse interests) who are not already organized. Lobbying may simply inform representatives of some of the costs and benefits of relevance to at least some of their constituents; it may also involve promises of electoral support or threats of electoral opposition. Fourth, as a result of the differential monitoring and lobbying, policies favorably affecting concentrated and organized interests tend to receive more support from representatives than policies favorably affecting diffuse and unorganized interests.

Consider, for example, that the benefits provided by the longstanding U.S. program to restrict sugar imports to the relatively small number of domestic sugar cane and sugar beet growers, sugar beet processors, and producers of alternative sweeteners fall short of the costs it inflicts on sweetener consumers by more than $500 million per year.[6] This inefficiency persists because large benefits accrue to a small number of firms that have a strong incentive to lobby to protect the program, whereas small costs accrue to each of a large number of sweetener consumers who are individually unwilling to bear the costs of lobbying against the program. Lobbying by sweetener users has the characteristics of a public good: no sweetener user can be excluded from the benefits of lobbying (lower prices if the sugar program were eliminated) and the realization of the benefits by one user does not detract from the benefits of other users. As a consequence of these public good incentives, there is too little voluntary supply of the good in question, lobbying. The public good nature of lobbying to end the sugar program would be mitigated to some extent if there were an organization of sweetener users whose members would agree to be taxed by the organization to provide lobbying—say, as gun enthusiasts who join the National Rifle Association primarily for information about their hobby—allow some of their dues to be used for lobbying.

A variety of other factors also tend to push representative government away from pursuing efficient policies. Geographically based constituencies encourage representatives to place greater weight on the costs and benefits received by residents and businesses in their districts than on those incurred in the rest of the country.[7] Electoral cycles encourage representatives to place excessive weight on immediate gains relative to future losses.[8] Institutional arrangements to guard against tyranny of the majority, such as bicameral legislatures, executive vetoes, federalism, and judicial review, tend to make all policy change, including that to enhance efficiency in the face of changing technologies and preferences, difficult,[9] and voters may actually vote in an effort to avoid radical change through divided government.[10] People care about many issues, including some that may trump concern about candidates' records and platforms relevant to resource allocation. The tendency of people to treat losses and gains asymmetrically[11] creates a bias against change—politicians and interest groups are especially effective in political campaigns at playing upon voters' fears concerning change that they perceive as imposing losses.[12] Further, change requires prediction, which is always imperfect, and thereby often involves greater uncertainty that risk-averse people may wish to avoid.[13]

Because efficiency tends to receive too little attention in representative government, policy analysts can contribute to a better balancing of social values in political deliberations by assessing the efficiency of both the status quo policies and the alternatives to them. The argument is not that efficiency should necessarily override other social values, such as equity and human dignity, but rather that efficiency should be considered seriously.[14] As we note later in our discussion of multiple goals, even when some non-efficiency goal is appropriately the primary end sought, it is desirable to consider the efficiency of alternative means of achieving it.

Normative theorists raise two other types of concern about the role of policy analysis. First, they worry that policy analysis itself may threaten key procedural values in the polity, such as democratic deliberation.[15] To the extent that a technocratic elite exercises influence over policy, the argument goes, citizens have less opportunity to discover and choose through public discourse policies that promote authentic values. We would argue, however, that this line of argument relies on a naive view of political institutions—the Nirvana fallacy of comparing ideal types rather than real alternatives. Rather than policy analysis displacing public discourse, it is the incentives operating within representative government that keep public discourse from being prominent in civil society. Even when these incentives can be countered to open up the public sphere to broader participation, those without a specific interest may still prefer to spend their time in personal, family, or local community pursuits—after all, those who enjoy spending time in meetings are probably very far from a representative sample of the population. Policy analysts almost certainly facilitate meaningful public discourse by crafting concrete policy alternatives that can be systematically discussed and by predicting consequences that might otherwise be neglected or left vague in terms of magnitude.[16] Further, good policy analysis recognizes that people often care deeply about procedural values, and therefore these values should be part of any analysis, especially in the design of institutional arrangements.

Second, policy analysts may be too influential in promoting the particular value of efficiency.[17] There is not a great deal of empirical evidence to support this concern, but, as we discuss below, one way to respond to this concern is to address other substantive goals forthrightly when it is legitimate to do so. We believe, however, that the more serious concern in most policy contexts is whether efficiency as a social value will receive any serious attention in policy choices. After all, in view of the forces within representative government pushing toward too little concern for efficiency, how is it that policy analysts can be influential at all?

All is not lost. One line of argument for effectiveness assumes that some representatives care about promoting the good society as well as their own electoral interests.[18] Information about potential gains and losses in efficiency of a policy proposal credibly presented by policy analysts may influence their decisions. The decisions of legislatures to delegate authority over some policy areas to regulatory agencies might be viewed as an effort to protect themselves from the pressure of interest groups;[19] subsequent requirements by the executive to force regulators to consider costs and benefits of major decisions also show some general regard for the importance of efficiency.[20] The creation by legislatures of nonpartisan organizations to provide assessments of the costs and benefits of proposed legislation, such as the California Legislative Analyst's Office or the Congressional Budget Office, also indicates a general regard for efficiency.[21] The institutionalization of policy analysis by politicians may even enable those same politicians to advocate for particular interests knowing that the more credible voice for efficiency will help stop the worst of the pandering from affecting policy.[22]

Another line of argument for the potential influence of assessments of efficiency by policy analysts recognizes that such information may alert politicians to the existence of latent interests that might be mobilized to electoral advantage. Information about the costs and benefits of alternative policies may enable skillful politicians to influence voters who would not be willing to engage in more costly lobbying. It may also help identify opportunities for compensating those who lose from more efficient policies by establishing the magnitudes of losses and gains as the starting point for negotiations over compensation.

We believe that policy analysis, including that which informs representatives about the relative efficiency of alternative policies, does have some influence. Yet, analysis is rarely dominant and may have to be repeated many times before it has a clear impact on policy.[23] Nonetheless, it plays a positive role in countering the tendencies of representative government to give too little weight to efficiency.

How do policy analysts assess efficiency? In the sections that follow, we sketch an answer to this question. We begin by providing a clearer explanation of efficiency and by explaining how it is achieved by markets under certain assumptions. We then sketch violations of these assumptions—market failures—that provide rationales for possible government intervention. Next, we sketch government failures, of the sort we have already introduced, as inefficient interventions, including failures to correct market failures appropriately. After showing how these trade-offs between market and government failures can be used to frame policy problems, we consider some examples of the sorts of generic policy instruments that can be used to improve efficiency.

Efficiency

The concept of efficiency takes a variety of forms: Pareto efficiency as the deep conceptual foundation, potential-Pareto efficiency as the guide to practical application, and the net benefit rule as the actual basis for assessment. We very briefly address each of these in turn. [24]

An allocation is Pareto efficient if it is not possible to make someone better off without making anyone else worse off. A Pareto improvement is a change in allocation that makes at least someone better off without making anyone else worse off. An allocation is Pareto efficient when no Pareto improvements are possible. Pareto efficiency has great appeal in that it does not require an assessment of how much more people prefer one allocation or another. A Pareto improvement harms no one but helps someone else. How could it not be desirable? Taking the initial allocation from which possible Pareto improvements are considered as a valid starting point, and ignoring the distribution of the final allocation (in other words, ignoring concerns about equity), the answer for those who are not malevolent must be that such improvements are desirable.

Pareto improvement, however, is too stringent a standard for practical application. Even policies that offer great aggregate gains are likely to harm some people—for example, removing sugar quotas would make sugar-beet growers worse off. A more practical standard for assessing efficiency is potential Pareto improvement: Are the gains from the policy change sufficiently large so that, with costless redistribution, it would be possible to compensate fully all losers without exhausting all the gains? This is a casual statement of the so-called Kaldor-Hicks criterion, which guides applied welfare (normative) economics.

The application of the Kaldor-Hicks criterion requires the measurement of gains and losses in a common metric, such as dollars, pesos, or whatever the unit of currency used in an economy. Each person in society is assumed to have some willingness to pay for any policy change. We could imagine determining the maximum amount people who gain from the policy could be made to pay so that they would just be indifferent between having the policy change and paying the money on the one hand and not having the policy change on the other. We could also imagine determining the minimum amount that could be paid to people who lose under the policy so that they would be just indifferent between having the policy change and receiving the payment on one hand and not having the policy change on the other. Summing these amounts algebraically across all people yields the net benefits of the policy. If the net benefits are positive, then it would not take all of the gains of winners to pay the losers so that they were all indifferent between having and not having the policy. If the net benefits were negative, however, then it would take more than the gains of the winners to make the losers indifferent. Only policies with positive net benefits should be adopted if efficiency is the goal. If policies are mutually exclusive, then choosing the one offering the greatest net benefits is efficient.

Cost-benefit analysis employs a variety of methods to estimate willingness to pay. If the effects of a policy can be modeled as changes in the quantities produced and consumed in operational markets, then the aggregate willingness to pay can be estimated as the change in social surplus it produces, where social surplus is the difference between the benefits of the change and the social costs of the change, information that can be derived from supply and demand schedules. If the effects do not occur in operational markets, then economists resort to a variety of other methods to make inferences about aggregate willingness to pay.[25] One of the fundamental theorems of welfare economics is that, under a number of specific assumptions about the nature of consumer preferences and production technologies, market allocation maximizes social surplus. In other words, market allocation is efficient— even with compensation, if it would not be possible to find an alternative allocation that made someone better off without making anyone else worse off.

Market Failures

The assumptions underlying the welfare theorem of market efficiency, however, are often violated. In these circumstances, market allocation is inefficient in the sense that alternative allocations could increase net benefits. Violations of the assumptions are commonly summarized as market failures. A market failure provides a necessary but not a sufficient condition for a policy intervention to be efficient. It is necessary because in its absence there would be no possibility for finding a more efficient allocation; it is not sufficient because it may not be possible to find a feasible intervention that would actually produce a more efficient allocation.

There are four commonly recognized market failures: externalities (a divergence between private and social costs or benefits), public goods (the presence of nonrivalry in consumption, nonexcludability in consumption, or both), natural monopoly (declining average cost of production over the relevant range of demand), and information asymmetry (a difference in the information available to the parties to a transaction).[26] We have already introduced one illustration of the public goods problem in connection with the undersupply of lobbying by diffuse interests. As these market failures are well-known, we will only briefly illustrate how one of them, externalities, can be used to frame public policy problems.

Externalities arise when consumers or producers, broadly defined, fail to bear the full costs or benefits of their actions. For example, someone talking loudly on a cell phone inflicts costs on others nearby who do not wish to hear the conversation. One could imagine the others being willing to pay a sufficient amount to silence the cell phone talker—hence, doing so would be efficient. Yet this may not happen because there is no mechanism in place for the others to coordinate their payments. In other words, there is no market for silence on the bus. Indeed, externality problems are also referred to as problems of missing markets.

Negative externalities often serve as the rationale for environmental regulations. For example, manufacturers who release toxic wastes into waterways inflict costs on other users of the waterways such as swimmers and fishers. If property rights to the waterway were sufficiently well defined, then a market for use of the waterway might develop so that a price would arise for dumping toxic waste into the waterway that reflected its marginal value to the manufacturers and its marginal cost to other users. In the absence of clear property rights, or even with clear property rights but high transaction costs among potential participants, the market will be missing and an inefficient level of toxic release will result.

Positive externalities also serve as the rationale for public policies. For example, people who are vaccinated not only reduce their own risks of the infectious disease but also reduce the risk to the rest of the population. From an efficiency perspective, too few people will choose to be vaccinated because at least some will ignore the benefits that spill over to others. Thus, it is probable that public policies designed to increase the vaccination rate against viruses or bacteria that cause serious disease will increase efficiency.

Government Failures

Just as imperfect markets fail to produce efficient allocations, the imperfect processes of collective choice (another name for government) can also result in inefficiency. Our introductory discussion of representative government described how the various dynamics of representation can generate inefficient policy choices. Other characteristics inherent in sovereignty, bureaucratic supply, and decentralized government can also result in inefficiency.[27]

National-level regimes claim sovereignty and maintain armies and police forces to back up their claims. They impose rules governing the actions of those under their jurisdictions. Nevertheless, they face the problem of credibly imposing rules on themselves—any rules they set may be changed, either by the current government or one in the future.[28] Indeed, for a government to be responsive, one of the commonly employed criteria for assessing representative governments, it must be able to change policy. In the U.S. context, one Congress cannot bind the next. The inability to make credible commitments to long-term policies may, however, foreclose socially valuable investments. For example, price controls and mandatory allocations employed in the 1970s to oil stocks held by U.S. refineries raise concerns about the security of private stocks and have resulted in refineries holding too few speculative stocks from the perspective of security against oil price shocks.[29] Norms of compliance to constitutional principles may help strengthen credibility for some types of policies, such as protections of basic personal rights. Yet they may not be very effective in giving credibility to policies that can be modified without clear constitutional implications. As Joseph Stiglitz illustrates, drawing on his service on the President's Council of Economic Advisors, the inability to make commitments to future policies often precludes the credible delivery of compensation that might allow for Pareto-improving repeal of inefficient policies.[30]

Government bureaus often directly supply goods and services, commonly because a market failure leads to no, or too little, private sector supply. Unlike private firms that sell their output at market-determined prices, bureaus typically provide their output at zero or some administratively set price. Hence, the value of the output of the bureau must be imputed rather than simply observed in (competitive) market prices. Unlike private firms in competitive markets that have profit and survival incentives to be technically efficient, bureaus have much weaker incentives to produce at minimum cost because any savings are likely to be reclaimed by budgetary sponsors and survival is likely to be guaranteed. Further, when bureaus have a monopoly over supply, they force dissatisfied clients to rely on the relatively expensive exercise of political voice rather than the less costly exit to an alternative supplier. In response to these weaker incentives for efficiency, as well as to reduce the risks of the use of bureaus for partisan political ends, bureau designers typically impose various ex ante controls on bureau managers, such as civil service constraints governing employment practices and line item budgets to restrict discretion in the use of resources. Ex ante controls, along with the absence of independent access to capital markets, make it relatively more difficult for bureau managers to innovate than their private sector counter-parts. For all these reasons, bureaus often achieve neither technical nor allocative efficiency.

Decentralized government—or, more accurately, multiple governments—offers a variety of advantages. Multiplicity may be either vertical (some version of federalism and separation of powers), horizontal (decentralized governance to states, counties, municipalities, etc.), or both. As already noted, separation of powers helps guard against tyranny by the majority. Federalism allows for differences in tastes to be reflected in the goods and services provided by different governments. It also facilitates a sort of competition among parallel levels of government by allowing people to "vote with their feet" in choosing where they live and do business. There are corresponding disadvantages, however. Separation of powers not only provides veto points to protect electoral minorities, but also possibly helps preserve no-longer-efficient policies. It also establishes authorities that can interfere with the implementation of adopted policies. Federalism creates incentives for parallel jurisdictions to adopt policies that attract residents who demand less than average in government services and pay higher than average taxes. It also raises coordination problems for dealing with market failures whose geographic footprints do not match jurisdictional boundaries.

Government failure does not have as direct a link to inefficiency as does market failure. Inefficiency is a *necessary* result of market failure. It need not be a necessary result of government failure, though representative government, bureaucratic supply, and decentralization all can contribute to inefficiency that manifests itself in government failing to respond to market failures, inappropriately responding to market failures, or creating market failures where none would exist in the absence of government intervention. The theories of market and government failure enable policy analysts to frame public policy problems in terms of the extent and sources of inefficiency; however, theory on how to tradeoff, or balance, market versus government failure is not well developed. If it were, then policy analysis would primarily be a science. Instead, it is a craft. The next section presents some craft heuristics.

Assessing Public Policy Problems

Assessing public policy problems effectively usually involves at least two tasks. One task is to understand why someone, particularly a client for a professional policy analyst, is concerned about some condition: Have circumstances become worse? Are they being perceived as worse? Have opportunities for possible improvement been identified? Once a condition has been put in perspective, and identified as something that one can do something about, the second task of the analyst is to frame the problem in terms of market and government failures. Doing so helps identify a rationale for potentially changing public policy, and it also points to possible generic policy designs that could be employed.

We sketch here a pragmatic procedure for framing market and government failures.[31] We believe that it is useful for those (many) policy problems that are not exclusively concerned with redistribution or with raising government revenues. We initially describe the procedure on the assumption that efficiency is the only social goal of policy. Later we argue that it is also a useful analytic starting point even when multiple social goals are relevant. Also, we discuss the procedure in terms of analyzing some current policy; it can also be applied to proposed policies, though relative to analyzing policies in place, more reliance has to be placed on prediction rather than observation.

The starting point for the analysis is to ask whether there is an operational market in place. The answer may not be clear-cut—whether there is an operational market is somewhat arbitrary, because actual markets form a complex continuum from free, completely unfettered markets (perhaps even without the foundation of formal property rights defined and enforced by government) to the complete absence of markets (perhaps pervasively throughout an economy). Nonetheless, a reasonable approach is to answer yes if prices legally exist as signaling mechanisms (no matter how extensively regulated). If prices are not legally permitted, for example, if only black market transactions take place, then answer no.

If there is an operational market, then a sequence of questions should be asked: First, is this operational market subject to market failure? If this market is subject to market failure, then there is a prima facie case for government intervention on efficiency grounds. If there is no government intervention in this circumstance, then this could be considered evidence of a form of passive government failure—government has not addressed the market failure. Passive failure may stem from the government's lack of capacity to diagnose market failures correctly or because of the influence of organized interest groups that successfully block efforts to correct market failure. For example, the government may either fail to recognize some industrial emission as an externality problem because of lack of extant scientific knowledge or, recognizing it, fail to intervene because a polluting industry is able to lobby successfully to block taxes or other policies that would internalize the externality. Second, if there is government intervention, has it actually addressed the specific market failure identified? If the extant intervention does not address the failure, then there is prima facie evidence of government failure. If the observed market is *not* subject to market failure (i.e., a market is making efficient allocations), has there been government intervention? If there is government intervention, then there is prima facie evidence of government failure, at least from the perspective of efficiency.

If there is not an operational market, then a sequence of questions should be asked: First, if there were an operational market, would it be subject to market failure? In these circumstances, the analysis must draw upon the theory of market failure, evidence available from other jurisdictions (for example, other cities, states, and countries), or analogous problems. Second, if it would be subject to market failure, does the current government intervention appropriately address the posited market failure? If the intervention is appropriate, then the relevant question becomes whether intervention can be improved through better implementation or management. If the intervention does not solve the posited market failure, then there is a complex policy problem. A market would not operate efficiently, but the extant government intervention does not address the market failure appropriately. Specific evidence indicating the cause of government failure, such as interest group rent seeking, further bolsters the case. This line of analysis naturally leads to the examination of generic alternatives to the current policy.

Figure 2-1 provides a summary of the possible results of this kind of efficiency-only analysis. As a simplifying assumption, the typology treats both market failure and government failure as dichotomous. The northwest quadrant of no market failure and no government failure (equivalent in this case to no government intervention) can be considered the case in which both the market and government are working effectively—no intervention is called for and no intervention is undertaken. The case of market failure and no government failure is shown in the northeast quadrant. Current policy is an efficient intervention; for example, a policy that ensures the internalization of an externality at the lowest aggregate net social cost. The southwest quadrant is the case of no market failure and the presence of government failure (in this quadrant, government failure is necessarily active). The policy prescription here would require the withdrawal of government, whether through privatization, deregulation, or other means. Clifford Winston, in his chapter on transportation in this volume, advocates such policy prescription for at least some forms of urban transportation.[32] The southeast quadrant of market failure and government failure is the workaday world of most policy analysts.

Figure 2-1. *Market Failure and Government Failure*

| | | Market failure? | |
		No	*Yes*
Government failure?	*No*	Market works; leave it alone	Intervention appropriate; preserve it
	Yes	Any intervention inappropriate; return to market	Particular intervention inappropriate; redesign policy

This is hardly surprising. Politicians and interest groups are more likely to be able to sell their favored (inefficient) intervention, in those policy arenas where there are demonstrable market failures and there is a general appetite for some form of government action. In this volume, Alan Gerber and Eric Patashnik, in their detailed case study of arthroscopies, describe just such a complex mix of market failure (the public good nature of information about the efficacy of surgical procedures and information asymmetry between surgeons and patients, which leads to too little being known about different types of surgery and too many dubious surgeries being preformed) and government failure (the disproportionate influence of professional organizations that leads to the risks and benefits of surgery being less-well-known than those for drug treatment).[33]

Multiple Goals

Policy analysis is relatively simple if the only goal is efficiency. In the absence of market failure, government intervention will almost always be inefficient. Multiple goals, however, make such a simple policy analysis inappropriate. It may be worth bearing some inefficiency in order to achieve other social goals. Most important, decisionmakers, responding to people's concerns about equity, usually care about the distributional consequences of policies, whether in terms of socioeconomic, racial, or other status characteristics.

It is worth noting, however, that efficiency and equity do not always involve a trade-off. In the presence of market failures (that is, in the northeast and southeast quadrants of figure 2-1) redistributive policies may be efficiency enhancing.[34] Indeed, policies that tightly target disadvantaged racial or socioeconomic groups may be *more* efficient, with higher net present values, than alternative policies that are not so targeted. For example, consider a program that substantially reduces class sizes in schools. It might very well be that the program offers positive net benefits only in schools with disproportionate numbers of children from low-income families—the marginal gains from the small class size are much greater for these children than for children from more advantaged backgrounds. In this case, the well-targeted program is efficient, whereas the more general one is not.

Yet, in some policy contexts, the absence of market failure does not preclude desirable government intervention when other goals are sufficiently important to accept losses in efficiency. Nonetheless, even in situations in which representatives wish exclusively, or primarily, to pursue some other goal, such as assistance to the poor or national defense, consideration of efficiency is socially desirable because it can help identify better choices among the possible means for advancing that goal. For example, imagine that the primary purpose of a policy is to raise the disposable income of the poorest families. If we identify two policies that would produce identical gains for this target population, then it would be sensible to choose the one that involved the lowest cost so that society would have more resources available for other uses. Or, thinking of expending some fixed budget on reducing poverty, one would want to choose the use of the funds that would produce the greatest gains for the families.[35] The chapter in this volume by Edgar Olsen illustrates this point with respect to the housing market, demonstrating the relative inefficiency of project-based assistance: "It would be possible to serve current [low-income] recipients equally well, serve many additional families, and reduce taxes by shifting resources from unit-based to recipient-based assistance."[36] Similarly, in this volume Jay Greene argues that reforming special education funding would target funds much more tightly on students with real and serious disabilities and thereby improve social returns. Efficiency thus enters an analysis by the "back door," so to speak. The same logic applies generally to policy analyses that have a single goal apart from efficiency.

With more than two goals, however, policy analyses must generally adopt qualitative assessments rather than the unambiguous rankings in terms of efficiency, if it is the only goal, or cost-effectiveness if it and only one other goal are relevant. The Congressional Budget Office, for example, routinely considers policy problems where it posits three goals: efficiency, distributional impacts, and the impact on government revenue.[37] Multiple goals raise issues of commensurability that require more judgmental trade-offs in ranking or valuing policy alternatives. Multiple goals make it less likely that analysts will be able to, or have clients receptive to, monetization or other quantification, thus reducing the likelihood that analysis will identify a clearly dominant policy alternative.[38] Nonetheless, good analysis makes clear the nature of the trade-offs among the goals that decisionmakers face in choosing among alternative policies.

Policy Instruments

Framing policy problems as market and government failures often provides a starting point for identifying policy alternatives worthy of comparison to the status quo. For example, negative externalities might be internalized through taxes that align private and social costs or reduced in magnitude through regulation of outputs or processes. In such cases, these generic policy alternatives provide only the broad outlines for design—a well-crafted alternative must be sufficiently concrete for its consequences to be predicted.[39] Nonetheless, consideration of generic policies relevant to market and government failures often helps analysts identify alternatives that might otherwise be neglected.

Generic policies can be categorized in a number of ways. Political scientists have often adopted a positive theory perspective on generic instrument choice, whereas economists have tended to formulate normative typologies.[40] Elsewhere, we have grouped generic policies into five major categories: (1) freeing, facilitating, and simulating markets; (2) using taxes and subsidies to alter incentives; (3) establishing rules (this category is broader than, but includes, regulation) (4) supplying goods through nonmarket (governmental) mechanisms; and (5) providing insurance and cushions.[41]

As an illustration, consider the first category of policies among the five just outlined. The first subset of interventions (deregulation, legalization, privatization) frees markets to work. They respond directly (from a normative perspective) to the problem identified in the southwest quadrant of figure 2-1: inappropriate government intervention into otherwise efficient markets. Privatization, for example, has been widely advocated and implemented around the world for industrial sectors that sell in competitive, or at least reasonably contestable, markets.[42] This wave of privatization has tended to confirm that, in the absence of market failures, private organizations can more efficiently supply goods previously supplied by government bureaus.[43]

The second subset of instruments within this category, the facilitation of markets by the creation of property rights and new marketable goods, seeks to create markets where they are otherwise missing. If the facilitated market achieves an efficient result, then this intervention falls into the northeast quadrant of figure 2-1. Opportunities for facilitating markets often arise because of changes in technology that create new goods or changes in tastes that create substantial demands for goods not previously recognized. For example, growing concerns about acid rain during the 1980s lead to calls for reductions in the quantity of sulfur dioxide emitted from power plants. The Clean Air Act Amendments of 1990 facilitated a market for sulfur dioxide emissions by creating permits to emit that could be traded among utilities.[44] The resulting permit prices signal to utilities the marginal value of reducing emissions by one unit that they can compare to the marginal cost of doing so. The efforts of the utilities to minimize their own costs result in reaching the target level of emissions efficiently.

The third subset of instruments simulates market allocation through auctions. Governments often allocate goods through administrative mechanisms that do not necessarily guarantee that the goods go to those who value them most—hence a result in the southeast quadrant of figure 2-1. For example, until recently the Federal Communications Commission (FCC) selected among applications for use of electromagnetic spectrum in ways that did not necessarily maximize the value of the uses. In the mid-1990s, however, the FCC effectively employed a sophisticated auction to allocate spectrum for personal communication devices.[45] Charles Holt, Angela Moore, and William Shobe in this volume provide a number of examples of the effective use of auctions to simulate markets.[46]

The second category of generic policies—using taxes and subsidies to alter incentives—has also been widely advocated over the past two decades. For example, vouchers have been advocated as a mechanism to control various forms of government failure, especially those related to bureaucratic supply.[47] Jay Greene persuasively argues that funding special education needs by vouchers that go directly to parents, rather than by payments to school districts, would eliminate many of the perverse incentives that the current funding regime fosters.[48]

It is important to emphasize that generic policy instruments only provide the starting point for crafting policy alternatives. Much detail has to be specified to make it possible to predict their consequences and thus make meaningful comparisons to current policy. For example, the FCC auction of spectrum for personal communication devices requires more than 130 pages of regulatory rules to implement in a way that avoided problems observed in similar auctions in Australia and New Zealand and undesirable manipulations discovered during experimental testing.[49] Moving from generic instruments to well-crafted policy alternatives is an important task for the policy analyst.

Conclusion

Policy analysts play diverse roles in representative government—the general recognition of these diverse roles is what Beryl Radin refers to as policy analysis coming of age.[50] In addition to providing credible predictions of the consequences of alternative policies, policy analysts can help facilitate the enlightenment function of social science research by connecting it to public policy issues;[51] they can speak for otherwise silent losers—the unaware, unorganized, and even the unborn;[52] they can help in the interpretation of issues and the justification of actions;[53] they can introduce policy ideas that may resurface to motivate viable policy alternatives sometime in the future[54] when circumstances open "policy windows" favorable to their consideration;[55] and policy analysts can contribute to the gradual accumulation and interpretation of evidence that may lead even relatively sable advocacy coalitions of interests to reconsider favored means and even desired goals.[56] We have emphasized one particular role: giving a stronger voice to efficiency than would otherwise be the case in representative government.

We have sketched a way to bring efficiency into policy analysis. It begins with an assessment of the market and government failures that may be leading to inefficiency. Although our brief and stylized presentation rested largely on logical argument, recognizing various undesirable conditions as matching the elements of market and government failure, the actual conduct of policy analysis usually requires efforts to assess the magnitude of the resulting inefficiency. Associated with various market and government failures are generic policy instruments that often serve as a starting point for crafting specific policy alternatives. In practice, however, alternatives come from a variety of sources—interest groups, scholars, and the creativity of policy analysts. The full set of consequences of alternatives should be assessed, in terms of not just efficiency, but also all the social values they affect. Only then can the analysts, making an explicit comparison of value trade-offs, responsibly make a recommendation. The forces at play in representative government often frustrate such recommendations, at least in the short run. Nonetheless, sometimes they are influential and contribute to a better society.

Notes

1. Mancur Olson, "Dictatorship, Democracy, and Development," *American Political Science Review*, vol. 87 (September 1993): 567–76.

2. William H. Riker, *Liberalism against Populism* (New York: Freeman, 1982).

3. At the most fundamental level, no fair social choice rule can guarantee a coherent social ordering of more than two alternatives. Kenneth Arrow, *Social Choice and Individual Values,* 2d ed. (Yale University Press, 1963).

4. This is the basic logic behind models of rent seeking, in which concentrated interests attempt to use government to create barriers to competition that generate rents, or economic profits. See James M. Buchanan, Robert D. Tollison, and Gordon Tullock, eds., *Toward a Theory of the Rent-Seeking Society* (Texas A&M University Press, 1980). Also see James Q. Wilson, ed., *The Politics of Regulation* (New York: Basic Books, 1980).

5. Because it is costly to assess the performance of incumbents, the heuristic may be quite crude: reward incumbents for good times and punish them for bad, no matter what the possible extenuating circumstances. See Christopher H. Achen and Larry M. Bartels, "Blind Retrospection: Electoral Responses to Drought, Flu, and Shark Attacks," paper presented at the Annual Meeting of the American Political Science Association, Boston, August 29–September 1, 2002.

6. John C. Beghin, Barbara El Osto, Jay R. Chernow, and Sanarendu Mohanty, "The Cost of the U.S. Sugar Program Revisited," *Contemporary Economic Problems*, vol. 21 (January 2003): 106–16.

7. See, for example, Barry R. Weingast, Kenneth A. Shepsle, and Christopher Johnsen, "The Political Economy of Benefits and Costs: A Neoclassical Approach to Distributive Politics," *Journal of Political Economy*, vol. 89 (August 1981): 642–64.

8. The seminal work is William D. Nordhaus, "The Political Business Cycle," *Review of Economic Studies*, vol. 42 (April 1975): 169–90. For a more recent overview, see William R. Keech, *Economic Politics: The Costs of Democracy* (Cambridge University Press, 1995).

9. James Madison addresses the separation of powers as a guard against tyranny by the majority in Numbers 47 to 51 of the *Federalist Papers* (New York: New American Library, 1961), pp. 300–25. For a generalization of the implication of the separation of powers, see George Tsbelis, *Veto Players: How Political Institutions Work* (Princeton University Press, 2002).

10. Morris P. Fiorina, *Divided Government* (New York: Macmillian, 1992).

11. Daniel Kahneman and Amos Tversky, "Prospect Theory: An Analysis of Decision under Risk," *Econometrica*, vol. 47 (March 1979): 263–91.

12. William H. Riker, *The Strategy of Rhetoric: Campaigning for the American Constitution* (Yale University Press, 1996).

13. Raquel Fernandez and Dani Rodrik, "Resistance to Reform: Status Quo Bias in the Presence of Individual-Specific Uncertainty," *American Economic Review*, vol. 81 (December 1991): 1146–55.

14. Policy analysis almost always involves tradeoffs among competing goals. For introductions to policy analysis, see Eugene Bardach, *A Practical Guide for Policy Analysis: The Eightfold Path to More Effective Problem Solving*, 2d ed. (Washington, D.C.: CQ Press, 2005); Duncan MacRae Jr. and Dale Whittington, *Expert Advice for Policy Choice:*

Analysis and Discourse (Georgetown University Press, 1997); David L. Weimer and Aidan R. Vining, *Policy Analysis: Concepts and Practice*, 4th ed. (Upper Saddle River, N.J.: Prentice Hall, 2004).

15. See, for example, John S. Dryzek, *Discursive Democracy: Politics, Policy, and Political Science* (Cambridge University Press, 1990).

16. David L. Weimer, "Enriching Public Discourse: Policy Analysis in Representative Democracies," *Good Society*, vol. 11 (Winter 2002): 61–65.

17. See, for example, Peter G. Brown, "The Failure of Market Failures," *Journal of Socio-Economics*, vol. 21 (Spring 1992): 1–24, and Steven Kelman, "Cost-Benefit Analysis: An Ethical Critique," *Regulation* (January/February 1981): 33–40.

18. Mark Moore argues that even imperfect statesmen sometimes produce public-spirited outcomes that we would recognize as the product of statesmanship. Mark H. Moore, "Statesmanship in a World of Particular Substantive Choices," in *Bureaucrats, Policy Analysts, and Statesmen*, edited by Robert A. Goodman (Washington, D.C.: American Enterprise Institute, 1980), pp. 20–36.

19. Morris P. Fiorina, "Legislative Choice of Regulatory Forms: Legal Process or Administrative Process," *Public Choice*, vol. 39, no. 1 (1982): 33–66.

20. Executive Order 12291 (President Reagan, 1981) and Executive Order 12866 (President Clinton, 1994).

21. David L. Weimer, "Institutionalizing Neutrally Competent Policy Analysis: Resources for Promoting Objectivity and Balance in Consolidating Democracies," *Policy Studies Journal*, vol. 33 (May 2005): 131–46.

22. Patrick J. Wolf, "Neutral and Responsive Competence: The Bureau of the Budget, 1939–1948 Revisited," *Administration and Society*, vol. 31 (March 1999): 142–67.

23. See, for example, the role of the accumulation of studies questioning the need for fare and route regulation of airlines. See Martha Derthick and Paul J. Quirk, *The Politics of Deregulation* (Brookings, 1985), pp. 246–52.

24. For a fuller development of the underlying concepts, see Anthony E. Boardman, David H. Greenberg, Aidan R. Vining, and David L. Weimer, *Cost-Benefit Analysis: Concepts and Practice*, 3d ed. (Upper Saddle River, N.J.: Prentice Hall, 2006), pp. 26–50.

25. For example, when there is no market demand curve for a good such as a park, economists may infer one by recognizing that people bear different costs in traveling different distances to the park (travel cost method). When no market exists at all, which is the case for many public goods, economists pose hypothetical valuation questions in surveys of random samples of the relevant population to make inferences about the population's willingness to pay (contingent valuation surveys).

26. For a more detailed development of these traditional market failures, as well as other limitations of welfare economics framework, see Weimer and Vining, *Policy Analysis*, chap. 5 (pp. 71–112) and chap. 6 (pp. 113–31).

27. See Weimer and Vining, *Policy Analysis*, chap. 8 (pp. 156–91), for a fuller development.

28. Some see the problem governments face in creating property rights with a high credibility of persistence as the central problem of political economy. William H. Riker and David L. Weimer, "The Economic and Political Liberalization of Socialism: The Fundamental Problem of Property Rights," *Social Philosophy & Policy*, vol. 10 (Summer 1993): 79–102.

29. George Horwich and David L. Weimer, *Oil Price Shocks, Market Response, and Contingency Planning* (Washington, D.C.: American Enterprise Institute, 1984), p. 113.

30. Stiglitz also notes that this government failure, the inability to make binding contracts, can be thought of as a form of the problem of incomplete contracting (missing markets as discussed in the previous section) that underlies many market failures. Joseph Stiglitz, "The Private Use of the Public Interests: Incentives and Institutions," *Journal of Economic Perspectives*, vol. 12 (Spring 1998): 3–22.

31. This procedure is more fully explained in Weimer and Vining, *Policy Analysis*, chap. 9, pp. 204–08; a simple example is provided on pp. 192–203.

32. Clifford Winston, "Urban Transportation," present volume.

33. Alan S. Gerber and Eric Patashnik, "Sham Surgery: The Problem of Inadequate Medical Evidence," present volume.

34. For a discussion of this, see Philippe Aghion, Eve Caroli, and Cecilia Garcia-Penalosa, "Inequality and Economic Growth: The Perspective of the New Growth Theories," *Journal of Economic Literature*, vol. 37 (December 1999): 1615–60; and Mark Rogers, "A Survey of Economic Growth," *Economic Record*, vol. 79 (March 2003): 112–35.

35. As an example, see Edward M. Gramlich and Michael Wolkoff, "A Procedure for Evaluating Income Distribution Policies," *Journal of Human Resources*, vol. 14 (Summer 1979): 319–50.

36. Edgar O. Olsen, "Achieving Fundamental Housing Policy Reform," present volume.

37. See "Goals/Alternatives Matrices: Some Examples from CBO Studies," in Weimer and Vining, *Policy Analysis*, chap. 15, pp. 363–79; MacRae and Whittington, *Expert Advice for Policy Choice: Analysis and Discourse*, also focus their text around a multigoal framework.

38. For a discussion of multiple goals, monetization and related issues, see Aidan R. Vining and Anthony E. Boardman, "Metachoice in Policy Analysis," *Journal of Comparative Policy Analysis: Research and Practice*, vol. 8 (March 2006): 77–87.

39. See David L. Weimer, "The Current State of Design Craft: Borrowing, Tinkering, and Problem Solving," *Public Administration Review*, vol. 53 (March 1993): 110–20.

40. For a review of policy instrument choice, see Michael Howlett and M. Ramesh, "Patterns of Policy Instrument Choice: Policy Styles, Policy Learning and the Privatization Experience," *Policy Studies Journal*, vol. 12 (Spring/Summer 1993): 3–25.

41. See Weimer and Vining, *Policy Analysis*, chap. 10, pp. 209–60.

42. Aidan R. Vining and David L. Weimer, "Government Supply and Government Production Failure: A Framework Based on Contestability," *Journal of Public Policy*, vol. 10 (January–March 1990): 1–22.

43. For a review of the empirical evidence, see William Megginson and John Netter, "From State to Market: A Survey of Empirical Studies on Privatization," *Journal of Economic Literature*, vol. 39 (June 2001): 321–89. See also Aidan R. Vining and David L. Weimer, "Economic Perspectives on Public Organizations," in *Oxford Handbook of Public Management*, edited by Ewan Fairlie, Laurence E. Lynn Jr., and Christopher Pollitt (Oxford University Press, 2005), pp. 209–33.

44. For an overview with specific attention to issues of equity in the initial allocation of permits, see Leigh Raymond, *Private Rights in Public Resources: Equity and Property Allocation in Market-Based Environmental Policy* (Washington, D.C.: Resources for the Future, 2003).

45. For an overview, see R. Preston McAfee and John McMillian, "Analyzing the Airwaves Auction," *Journal of Economic Perspectives*, vol. 10 (Winter 1996): 159–75.

46. Charles A. Holt, William Shobe, and Angela M. Smith, "An Experimental Basis for Public Policy Initiatives," present volume.

47. See C. Eugene Steurele and others, eds., *Vouchers and the Provision of Public Services* (Brookings, Committee for Economic Development, Urban Institute Press, 2000).

48. Jay P. Greene, "Fixing Special Education," present volume.

49. McAfee and McMillan, "Analyzing the Airwaves Auction," p. 160.

50. Beryl A. Radin, *Beyond Machiavelli: Policy Analysis Comes of Age* (Georgetown University Press, 2000).

51. Carol H. Weiss, "Research for Policy's Sake: The Enlightenment Function of Social Research," *Policy Analysis*, vol. 3 (Fall 1977): 531–45.

52. Weimer and Vining, *Policy Analysis*, pp. 152–53.

53. Nancy Shulock, "The Paradox of Policy Analysis: If It Is Not Used, Why Do We Produce So Much of It?" *Journal of Policy Analysis and Management*, vol. 18 (Spring 1999): 226–44.

54. Patricia Thomas, "The Use of Social Research: Myths and Models," in *Social Science Research and Government: Comparative Essays on Britain and the United States*, edited by Martin Bulmer (Cambridge University Press, 1987), pp. 51–60.

55. John W. Kingdon, *Agendas, Alternatives, and Public Policies* (Boston: Little, Brown, 1984).

56. Paul A. Sabatier and Hank C. Jenkins-Smith, "The Advocacy Coalition Framework: An Assessment," in *Theories of the Policy Process*, edited by Paul A. Sabatier (Boulder, Colo.: Westview Press, 1999), pp. 117–66.

PART II

Documenting Government
Performance Failures

3

Sham Surgery: The Problem of Inadequate Medical Evidence

ALAN S. GERBER AND ERIC M. PATASHNIK

In a well-functioning health care system, doctors would operate on patients only when there is a strong medical basis for doing so. Researchers would use rigorous methods to evaluate whether specific operations are safe and effective for specific conditions. If scientific evidence emerges to suggest that a surgical procedure is not working as expected, physicians and other health care actors would investigate. Once the truth is discovered, the information would be disseminated to practitioners. In sum, medical treatments would be based on current scientific evidence and important gaps in knowledge would be rapidly identified and filled.

We explore the performance of the medical system along these important dimensions by examining a particular case, the use of arthroscopic surgery to treat osteoarthritis (OA) of the knee. The case of this common surgical

The authors wish to acknowledge the comments of J. Bruce Moseley, Nelda Wray, David Felson, Iain Chalmers, Bernard Patashnik, Eugene Bardach, Jacob Hacker, Alan Cohen, Ruth Hanft, John W. Ellwood, William R. Johnson, and the faculty and fellows of the Scholars in Health Policy Program at the University of California–Berkeley. We acknowledge financial support from the Yale Center for American Politics and the Bankard Fund for Political Economy Research. Nathan Jones and Jesse Rhodes provided superb research assistance.

procedure illustrates three overlapping problems. First, too little scientific research is conducted on whether surgical procedures are effective. Our level of investment in research on the effectiveness of medical interventions seems much too low given the stakes for public health. Second, the quality of evidence presented in medical journals to demonstrate the effectiveness of surgical innovations is often poor. Many studies are based on anecdotal case series evidence, and randomized controlled trials are rarely used to evaluate surgical procedures. Finally, credible information about the efficacy of surgical procedures, even when available, seems not to be swiftly incorporated into clinical practices. Procedures may diffuse into clinical practice before they are scientifically evaluated. Once a surgery becomes popular, physicians may keep performing it, even after evidence emerges suggesting that it does not work.

These claims will come as no surprise to many students of modern medical practice. That much of conventional clinical medicine has not been scientifically validated is an open secret among health researchers, but the mainstream media has only recently begun to bring this problem to the attention of the public. Many Americans were surely troubled by a 2006 *Business Week* cover story reporting that "from heart surgery to prostate care, the medical industry knows little about which treatments really work."[1]

The arthroscopy case offers a window into the problem of inadequate medical evidence.[2] During the past several decades, millions of Americans have undergone arthroscopies to reduce the pain of osteoarthritis and delay or eliminate the need for a total knee replacement. The procedure typically costs between $2,500 and $5,000. Although precise data on the number of these surgeries performed annually on patients with this condition are unavailable, a reasonable lower estimate is 100,000. This translates into hundreds of millions of dollars a year to Medicare, the Veterans Administration, and private insurers.[3]

About half of all patients typically say they feel better after their arthroscopies, but some experts have doubted that the operations are beneficial. In the mid-1990s, a medical research team led by J. Bruce Moseley, a board-certified orthopedic surgeon at Baylor College of Medicine and the team physician of the Houston Rockets and of the 1996 U.S. Olympics Basketball "Dream Team," and Nelda P. Wray, a physician and health services researcher at the Veterans Administration in Houston, decided to test whether the surgery was effective. The Moseley-Wray team conducted a rare randomized placebo-controlled clinical trial of a surgical procedure, in which some patients underwent fake operations designed to mimic the real interventions. Patients assigned to the placebo arm received only incisions while they were asleep. Tests of knee function showed that the operations had not helped, and those who had only the placebo incisions reported as much pain relief as those who had the real procedures.[4] In short, a surgical procedure performed on hundreds of thousands of patients each year to ease the pain of arthritic knees worked no better than a fake operation.

How is it possible that millions of Americans have had knee surgery in the absence of hard evidence that the procedure is superior to a placebo? Why did it take so long for the medical profession to generate this information? What does the arthroscopy case suggest about the capacity of American government to promote citizens' shared interest in effective medicine?

We argue that the weak evidentiary basis of medical procedures such as arthroscopy for knee arthritis is a product of the simultaneous presence of market failures and government failures in the health care sector. Neither the profit motive nor existing public policy mechanisms are sufficient to provide an adequate incentive for the creation and diffusion of reliable information about whether medical procedures work as advertised. Medical researchers have called for more rigorous evaluation of surgical procedures at least since the 1970s, yet the issue barely registers on the political agenda. Our pessimistic conclusion is that this problem is not self-correcting.

The remainder of the chapter proceeds as follows. We first discuss the state of medical knowledge prior to the landmark sham surgery study. We describe how the orthopedic community mostly ignored clear warnings that the arthroscopic surgery might not be effective. We then review the study's findings, describe what responses they prompted from the medical community and policymakers, and explain why these responses were almost certainly suboptimal. Finally, we take up the key puzzle of why surgical procedures are routinely subjected to less rigorous evaluations than are drugs and medical devices, locating the answer in the inability of surgeons to capture the economic returns from effective innovations and in the relative weakness of the incentives for political entrepreneurs to address this market imperfection.

Arthroscopic Surgery for OA of the Knee

About 12 percent of those aged sixty-five and over experience frequent knee pain from OA.[5] When anti-inflammatory medication and physical therapy fail to relieve symptoms, doctors may recommend two forms of arthroscopic knee surgery: lavage and debridement with lavage. Lavage (French, "to wash") is a procedure in which the knee joint is thoroughly washed out. Debridement (a French word related to "debris") "cleans up" the knee by cutting away loose tissue, trimming torn and degenerated meniscus (the shock-absorbing cartilage in the knee joint), and smoothing out the remaining meniscus. These procedures originated in the medical practices of the 1930s and 1940s but did not take off until the development of fiberoptics in the 1970s.[6] By the mid-1980s, arthroscopy for OA of the knee had become extremely popular. Arthroscopies are typically performed under general anesthesia and require a recovery period during which the patient experiences pain and decreased mobility. Although serious complications from the procedure are rare, debridement may have a negative effect on the outcomes of a subsequent total knee replacement.[7]

The Weak Evidentiary Basis of the Procedure

The spread of arthroscopic surgery for OA began as surgeons reported their experiences with arthroscopic surgery at scientific conferences and in journal articles. Colleagues became excited about the procedure and started performing it on their patients. These clinical experiences, rather than scientifically rigorous evaluations or a good theoretical understanding of the mechanism behind alleged treatment effects, provided the basis for the widespread adoption of the procedure in the United States.

A review of the relevant medical literature before Moseley and Wray's 2002 article highlights the weak evidentiary basis of this surgery. Although there had been reports on operations similar to lavage and debridement several decades earlier, the first modern study of arthroscopy for OA of the knee was published in 1981. Norman F. Sprague III debrided the joints of patients for whom other therapies had failed.[8] The outcome measure was pain and a subjective measure of functioning. About fourteen months after the surgery, patients were asked to compare their current level of pain and functioning to their recollection of what they had experienced before the operation.[9] Approximately 75 percent of the patients said their pain and functioning had improved or stayed the same. This early study had two major design weaknesses that persisted in subsequent research. First, the research design did not permit the effect of the surgery to be distinguished from the natural history of the disease or from a placebo effect. Placebo effects are especially common when a subjective measure, such as pain, is the target of the treatment. Second, the assessment was not "blinded." Those conducting the evaluations knew what procedures individual patients had received. Sprague's study was actually based on patients' self-reported experiences, though a similar problem would arise if third-party evaluators knew each patient's treatment history. Unblinded assessment is an established source of bias.

At least twenty-five additional studies evaluating the effectiveness of lavage and debridement with lavage were published during the next twenty years.[10] Like Sprague, most of these follow-up studies relied on retrospective evaluations of the surgery using either patient charts or follow-up interviews—methodologies that tend to produce biased results. In a typical example, Yang and Nisonson (1995) evaluated 105 postoperative knees by using a 12-point scale that included both subjective measures and measurements of range of motion. Sixty-five percent of patients scored 9 or higher, the cutoff the authors selected to determine which knees should be labeled "good" or "excellent." The 65 percent "success rate" was taken as supportive of the use of arthroscopic surgery. The Yang and Nisonson study lacked a control group to assess the benefit from the intervention. The physician who conducted the case evaluations knew whether individual patients had been operated on.

The pre-Moseley literature did contain some randomized trials. A few well-designed randomized clinical trials were conducted to gauge the effectiveness of one of the two arthroscopic surgeries, lavage without debridement.[11] In contrast to most of the case series evidence, these studies failed to produce convincing evidence that lavage was beneficial. With a much larger number of case histories reporting positive effects from the procedure, however, these negative findings were downplayed. No randomized trial prior to Moseley and colleagues (2002) evaluated debridement versus a placebo version of the operation.

Doubts about the Effectiveness of the Procedure

Some physicians did question whether or how arthroscopy benefited patients with OA. If there is a strong theoretical argument for how an operation produces benefits, the need for empirical support is reduced. There was, however, no broadly accepted theoretical mechanism to explain how arthroscopic surgery helped patients. Several hypotheses were offered to explain the positive findings reported in the typically nonrandomized, unblinded clinical studies. Some researchers pointed out that the arthritic joint contains irritating debris and enzymes. It was suggested that flushing out these sources of irritation might reduce pain.[12] Debridement was said to reduce pain by reducing "mechanical problems" of the knee such as "catching" or "popping" and improving the distribution of weight on joint surfaces.[13] These explanations were recognized as quite speculative. Many studies reporting positive clinical findings were at a loss to explain them. In one review article generally supportive of the surgery, for example, Hanssen and colleagues acknowledged that "the mechanism of pain relief following arthroscopic treatment of OA is obscure."[14]

Questions about the use of arthroscopy for patients with knee arthritis were raised at medical conferences and in professional journals. In a symposium ("Uses and Abuses of Arthroscopy") conducted at the 1992 annual meeting of the American Academy of Orthopedic Surgeons (AAOS) and an article reprinted in one of the leading journals in the field, practitioners and researchers openly discussed both the state of knowledge regarding arthroscopic surgery and how the financial incentives of the health care system might distort the decision to recommend surgery. The symposium was noteworthy for its blunt language regarding a common orthopedic procedure. Dr. John Goodfellow, a former president of the British Orthopedic Association, mocked the use of arthroscopic surgeries for OA and suggested they might be "pseudotreatments." He commented that "no one has performed the double-blind controlled trial that would be necessary to distinguish between the placebo effects of any operation and the direct benefits of debridement."[15] Despite the obvious and recognized need for rigorous investigation to determine whether the procedure worked, there was no sense of urgency. The lack of hard evidence for the procedure's effectiveness was apparently more a regrettable condition than a pressing problem for physicians and researchers to solve.

This troubling situation—in which the lack of hard evidence for the use of a procedure is a poorly kept secret among practitioners—is not unusual in American medical practice. Many popular surgical procedures rest on surprisingly weak evidence.[16] This is especially common for procedures that are intended to provide symptomatic relief rather than prolong life. Examples include procedures done to relieve lower back, neck, spine or neurological pain, tendonitis, and impingement in the shoulder. Questions have recently been raised about vertebroplasty, a procedure in which a form of hot cement is injected into the broken spinal bones of patients with OA. It is not clear whether this procedure works or whether it simply has a placebo effect.[17] Another widely reported example of a suspect operation is "spinal fusion surgery," in which a bone graft is used to fuse together two vertebrae in an attempt to relieve lower back pain from degenerated discs. During the past decade, patient traffic has quadrupled to 125,000 procedures annually at a cost of $30,000 per operation. Recently, there has been a move to further expand the indications for the operation. The operation can have serious side effects, including blindness and paralysis. Yet the evidence that spinal fusion surgery, which has a high rate of dangerous complications, works well for back pain is "essentially nonexistent."[18]

Pioneering Sham Surgery Study

The publication of the landmark study "A Controlled Trial of Arthroscopic Surgery for Osteoarthritis of the Knee," in the July 11, 2002, issue of the *New England Journal of Medicine,* presented the findings of an experimental study that subjected a questionable procedure to rigorous scientific analysis. The article reported the results of a double-blind clinical trial in which Houston Veterans Administration hospital patients were randomly assigned to receive lavage, debridement with lavage, or "sham surgery." One of the study's lead authors, surgeon J. Bruce Moseley, had long been skeptical of debridement and lavage. "I just didn't quite understand why people were reporting so much benefit when seemingly there wasn't very much done," he said.[19] Nelda Wray, the coleader of the research team, thought the placebo effect might be responsible for patients feeling better after the operation. The two researchers agreed that a sham surgery clinical trial was the best way to test whether the procedure had any benefit beyond a possible placebo effect.[20] Participants in the trial were told that they might receive only placebo surgery and had to give their informed consent. The researchers created a placebo arm that mimicked the sight and sound of the actual procedure and included both sedation and an incision. For ethical reasons, patients in the sham surgery group were not placed under general anesthesia (they instead received a short-acting tranquilizer that caused them to fall asleep). Special care was taken to ensure that patients understood that they might receive sham surgery. Subjects were required to transcribe the informed consent form prior to signing it. Subjects receiving the real procedures and those receiving the fake operations were equally likely to guess they were in the placebo group.

Moseley performed all the procedures himself and did not know until he opened a sealed envelope when patients were wheeled into surgery whether the patient would receive a real or fake operation. The effects of the procedures were assessed through measures of pain and subjective measures of function as well as through objective measures of function such as the amount of time it took for patients to walk thirty meters and climb up and down a flight of stairs. Measurements were obtained at several points throughout a two-year period. Evaluators did not know whether patients were in the treatment or control groups.

The results suggest that the surgeries were no better than the placebo operations. At no point during the two-year period did either of the actual surgery groups report a statistically significant improvement in pain or function versus the placebo group. The average outcome measures produced by the placebo group were statistically superior to the surgery groups at two weeks. At all other time periods, the outcomes were statistically equivalent. Although many scientific breakthroughs receive little attention from broader publics, the study's novel research design and provocative results made for arresting news copy. The study was praised in the lead editorial of the *New England Journal of Medicine*[21] and produced extensive, if short lived, media coverage. There were front page articles in the *New York Times* and the *Washington Post*, and other major newspapers.[22] The study's finding that a major procedure worked no better than a fake operation was something of a bombshell, but the results were probably not shocking to many experts. As one leading evidence-based medical research organization stated, "The results of the [sham surgery study] should not be a surprise based on the evidence from the literature. There never was any good evidence that lavage and debridement were useful things to do."[23]

Strengths and Limitations of the Study

Moseley and Wray's study was a significant advance on previous research. Whereas most prior investigations in orthopedics were retrospective caseseries studies in which surgeons simply reported their experience with a procedure, the Moseley-Wray study was a double-blinded, placebo-controlled randomized trial—the "gold standard" in research medicine. Of course, even the best scientific studies have limitations. There were some features of the Moseley-Wray research design that might cast doubt on the validity or generalizability of the findings. An understanding of the scientific basis of the criticisms is therefore necessary to assess the reactions the study generated from interested parties.

One limitation of the study's research design is that it could not determine whether the benefits of the sham surgery intervention were due to some active placebo effect (such as some psychological benefit from receiving a physician's attention) or to the natural history of patients' disease. If the decision to have surgery follows a period of unusually severe symptoms, simple regression to the mean might produce improvement over time in the absence of any medical intervention. Although there are reasons to believe the placebo effect was responsible for the improvement in patients' conditions, the issue cannot be resolved because of the study's lack of a natural history arm in which patients received neither a real nor a sham procedure.[24] However, whereas assigning the improvement in the placebo arm to its sources would be an important research finding, it has no implications for whether the arthroscopic procedures are superior to the sham surgery.[25]

A potentially more important criticism is the claim by some critics that the study used a flawed method for selecting patients for inclusion in the clinical trial. To gain entry into the trial, patients had to report knee pain. Critics argued that the orthopedic community *already* recognized before the Moseley-Wray study that patients who present with pain only are unlikely to benefit from the surgery but that there are subgroups of patients with knee arthritis for whom the procedure is efficacious, including patients with early-stage arthritis, those with normal knee alignment, and those with mechanical symptoms, such as joint "locking," "giving way," "popping," or "clicking."[26] The implication is the sham surgery study selected the wrong patients as subjects and that its findings should not fundamentally reorient orthopedic practice.

This argument is unconvincing. First, it appears to be based on a crude misreading of the study design. The study *did* include patients on the basis of a pain measure but excluded patients only if they had a severe deformity or a meniscal tear that were observed preoperatively.[27] Almost all of the patients included in the trial had *both* pain and mechanical symptoms. Mechanical problems of the knee are ubiquitous among patients with OA. In older patients with joint pain, it is nearly always possible to find some kind of mechanical symptom.[28] In follow-up correspondence appearing in the *New England Journal of Medicine*, the authors reported that 96 percent (172/180) of the patients in the study had at least one mechanical problem.[29] The study results therefore suggest that neither lavage nor debridement with lavage is an effective treatment beyond placebo for patients who present with pain and one or more mechanical problems.

In addition, the sham surgery performed as well as the actual operations on the entire sample. If there was in fact a subgroup of patients for whom the operation was effective, it might be expected that the average improvement for the treatment groups, which consist of a mix of "appropriate" and "inappropriate" patients, would be attenuated but not entirely absent; there was, however, no consistent pattern of relative improvement by the treatments versus the placebo group. Third, although there were assertions about patient selection practices prior to the Moseley and Wray study, no empirical evidence was presented regarding actual patient selection practices. One study that examined the ability of doctors to anticipate which patients were likely to benefit from arthroscopy found they performed only slightly better than chance.[30] Finally, it should be noted that even if the Moseley and Wray study can be cast aside completely, the state of the evidence merely reverts to the pre-Moseley condition; prior to Moseley there is no methodologically convincing evidence that arthroscopic surgery works for the subgroups identified by the Moseley critics.[31]

To summarize: Moseley and Wray found no evidence that arthroscopic surgery relieves pain or improves function any better than a placebo operation for patients with knee arthritis. If there were any large beneficial effects, the study would very likely have found them.[32] "Despite their current popularity, lavage and debridement are probably not efficacious as treatments for most persons with osteoarthritis of the knee," wrote David T. Felson and Joseph Buckwalter in an editorial in the *New England Journal of Medicine*. In a personal communication, Dr. Felson stated that he believes the study's findings mean that 80 to 90 percent of the arthroscopies that have been performed on patients with arthritic knees should not have been done.[33]

Medical and Policy Community's Reactions to Moseley's Findings

At first glance, the knee surgery case might seem to illustrate the U.S. research and policymaking enterprise working at its best. Moseley, Wray, and their colleagues performed a first-class study that used powerful scientific methods to address a substantively important question. The study was conducted at a Veterans Administration hospital and paid for by federal research grants. It was published in the *New England Journal of Medicine,* and its results were disseminated to the public by the *New York Times* and other media outlets. Contrary to the argument that large, bureaucratic organizations are hidebound and slow to react, key federal agencies, including the Centers for Medicare and Medicaid Services, altered their coverage policies in direct response to the study's findings.

But these first impressions are misleading. If we probe more deeply into the case, the system's performance appears troubling. The orthopedic professional associations have pressured the government to adopt a very narrow interpretation of the study's findings, which preserves surgeons' clinical autonomy and supports prior medical practices. The coverage decisions of federal health agencies have largely been in line with the associations' position. Efforts to replicate or build on the Moseley study have been absent. That the sham surgery trial was conducted in the first place depended upon individual initiative. Although doubts about the efficacy of arthroscopic surgery for knee arthritis had been raised at least since the early 1990s, the value of the procedure might never have been rigorously tested if the Moseley-Wray team had not fortuitously come along to conduct a critical sham surgery test. There were no institutions in place to make detection and investigation of questionable procedures a routine matter.

Surgeons and Professional Societies

We suspect that many individual orthopedic surgeons found it hard to believe Moseley and Wray's stunning finding the surgery had no advantage over the placebo. What orthopedic surgeons knew—saw with their own eyes—is that *their* patients clearly improved after the operation. "I've done thousands of these in people with osteoarthritic knees, and they really are better," said surgeon Robert W. Jackson, a fierce defender of the procedure.[34] These surgeons may have failed to understand that the study did not claim the procedure had no impact, only that the observed benefits are due to the placebo effect or natural history of the disease rather than the surgeon's skill.[35]

The main reaction to Moseley and Wray's study from professional associations was not confusion but hostility. The professional associations defended the practices of their members and argued that Moseley and Wray's findings should not discredit use of the procedure for patients with OA. Professional groups like the AAOS argued that Moseley and Wray had failed to examine the benefits of the procedure for various subgroups, such as those with mechanical symptoms and normal alignment, and asserted that responsible surgeons *already* practiced proper patient selection.

At one level, the resistance to Moseley and Wray's findings from the specialty associations reflects a difference in professional norms and orientations. As Wray put it, "I speak the language of science, and the orthopedists do not." In addition, Moseley and Wray's study is a direct economic threat to the specialists. "There's a pretty good-size industry out there that is performing this surgery. It constitutes a good part of the livelihood of some orthopedic surgeons. That is a reality," said Felson.[36]

Some surgeons who questioned the use of arthroscopy for patients with knee arthritis insisted it was vital to preserve insurance coverage and maintain professional autonomy. "I'm both a patient and a physician," said AAOS chief executive Dr. William J. Tipton Jr., explaining to a *New York Times* reporter that he has osteoarthritis. "My knee is buckling now, but I'm not going to have arthroscopy done. I recognize that it's not going to help." But Tipton said he would hate to see insurers refuse to pay on the basis of the Moseley-Wray study. If that occurs, he said, surgeons will complain. "This is where eyebrows are going to be raised," he said. "There's going to be a certain group of physicians who are very upset. This is another example of managed care at its lowest, with payers calling the shots. I think it's not good medicine."[37]

Federal Agencies and Private Insurers

The federal government pays for a significant share of health care provision through Medicare and other programs and influences coverage decisions in the private sector. When a state-of-the-art medical study finds that an expensive medical procedure works no better than a fake operation for most people with a common medical condition, this should be reflected in health policy decisions. Yet federal health officials have traditionally treaded uneasily on physicians' professional autonomy, especially with respect to clinical judgments about what services patients require. The founding premise of the Medicare program is that the clinical autonomy of participating hospitals and physicians would be protected. Over time, the federal government's efforts to control health care costs, along with the growth of managed care in the private sector, has resulted in some degree of erosion of physicians' clinical autonomy, but the presumption remains that doctors can best judge what treatments patients need.

Federal bureaucrats are often faulted for being slow to act in the face of new information, but federal health agencies began reviewing their coverage policies immediately after the publication of the Moseley-Wray study.[38] The final decisions of these agencies, however, followed a questionable, narrow reading of the study's findings preferred by the professional associations. Although the Veterans Administration initially recommended that arthroscopies for knee arthritis not be performed absent "clear clinical evidence of significant derangement," it subsequently announced that the Moseley-Wray study would not change the standard of practice at VA hospitals after all.[39] Both an internal review by VA officials and an expert panel on orthopedic surgery concluded that the findings of the sham surgery study were not sufficient to limit or prohibit knee arthroscopy within the VA. The main reason given for the decision not to limit coverage was that outside experts asserted that surgeons rarely perform arthroscopy solely for pain associated with OA.[40] The federal Centers for Medicare and Medicaid Services (CMS) also made policy decisions that were largely in line with the position of the orthopedic associations. Following the publication of the Moseley-Wray study— which CMS analysts believed was so important that it simply could not be ignored—the agency began a careful review of the scientific evidence to determine whether arthroscopic surgery for patients with arthritic knees should be nationally covered under Medicare.[41] The agency met with Dr. Wray, spoke with Dr. Moseley on the phone, and then held two separate meetings (in November 2002 and January 2003) with representatives of key professional associations.

The AAOS, the Arthroscopy Association of North America (AANA), the American Association of Hip and Knee Surgeons, and affiliated groups prepared a joint report to "provide CMS with clinical and scientific information" about arthroscopic procedures for patients with arthritic knees. The major conclusion of the report is that many patients with OA of the knee, especially those with early degenerative arthritis and mechanical symptoms, can be significantly helped with arthroscopic surgery.[42] All of the research studies cited in support of this conclusion, however, suffered from the basic methodological problems characterizing the research literature prior to the Moseley-Wray study. These problems were not acknowledged. Nor did the report address Moseley and Wray's response that 172 of 180 subjects in their study had mechanical symptoms or indicate that the orthopedic groups would seek to generate hard evidence to support their claims about the benefits of the procedure for population subgroups by sponsoring replications of the study.

In July 2003, the CMS concluded that coverage should be changed in response to the Moseley and Wray study and the subsequent review of the evidence.[43] The agency concluded that there was no evidence to support lavage alone for OA patients and that the procedure would henceforth be nationally noncovered. With respect to debridement, CMS determined that the procedure would be nationally noncovered when patients presented with knee pain only or with severe OA. CMS decided, however, to maintain local Medicare contractors' discretion to cover the surgery if physicians requested it for patients with pain and other indications (for example, mechanical symptoms). This policy was subsequently echoed in the coverage decisions of major private insurers.[44]

CMS was unable to present solid evidence in support of its decision to maintain coverage of debridement for the vast majority of patients with arthritic knees (mechanical symptoms being ubiquitous in the OA population). Indeed, the agency deemed the available medical evidence on the issue to be "inconclusive because of methodological deficiencies." Including the Moseley and Wray investigation, there were only four studies that addressed debridement in patients with mechanical symptoms as the indication for surgery, but three of them were case series without random assignment to control groups and using unvalidated assessment scales. The CMS acknowledged that the level of evidence supporting the usefulness of the procedure was "suboptimal" and that case series studies in general are considered method-ologically weak in their ability to minimize bias.[45] Nonetheless, CMS declined to stop paying for debridement. It argued that the three case series "consistently" pointed to improvements in outcomes. The CMS coverage analysis acknowledged the unusually high quality of the Moseley-Wray study, calling it the only "large-scale, well-designed" randomized clinical trial in the pool of evidence, but argued that the study failed to "specifically address the issue of reduction of mechanical symptoms." The fact that virtually all of the patients in Moseley and Wray's study *had* one or more mechanical symp-toms, as the authors reported in follow-up letters to the *New England Journal of Medicine* and other professional journals, went unmentioned.[46] Although CMS's official policy is to take into account the scientific quality of medical evidence, in practice its coverage decision process weighs most heavily the findings of studies published in peer-reviewed journals, even if the method-ological quality of a study is problematic.[47] CMS's coverage review process is thus based on a high degree of trust in the medical profession's ability to determine appropriate medical practices.

The AAOS welcomed the CMS's coverage decision. "The coverage deci-sion parallels the position of the musculoskeletal societies. CMS recognized that arthroscopy is appropriate in virtually all circumstances in which the orthopedic community now employs this technology," an association newsletter stated.[48] In fact, CMS did not perform an empirical investigation of actual surgical practices regarding patient selection for OA of the knee and consequently could not provide assurances regarding current surgical prac-tices. The societies recognized that the CMS decision left key coverage deci-sions in the hands of local Medicare contractors. The implementation process would therefore be critical. The AAOS promised its members that the organization would provide carriers with "specific and detailed instruc-tions to implement the coverage decision appropriately. The instructions should clearly reflect the limited application of the policy decision." Moseley and Wray have moved on to other endeavors, and no interest group exists to balance the messages that Medicare contractors will hear about the indica-tions for arthroscopy from surgeons.

Moseley and Wray's results may have been strong enough that CMS would have been justified in denying coverage of debridement for patients with OA, with an exception for those patients with anatomic abnormalities, such as one that produces locking of the joint, preventing a complete exten-sion of the knee. Ideally, CMS coverage decisions should be based on strong medical evidence, yet CMS acknowledged that the clinical evidence for benefits to subgroups came from case series studies that the agency considered to be methodologically deficient. In light of the agency's own concerns about the existing level of evidence data, one reasonable approach would have been for CMS to have made no coverage changes for the time being regarding debridement but to have announced that it would stop paying for the procedure after some time period (say, three years) unless more rigorous evidence was presented to demonstrate the procedure's benefits. This would have created a powerful economic incentive for defenders of the procedure to replicate Moseley and Wray's study.

CMS is in a difficult political position, because a decision to deny coverage for a procedure will create cases where CMS judgments substitute for those of a patient's doctor. The fact that the CMS initiated the coverage review of arthroscopy in the first place reflects well on the agency and its staff. To go further, and deny coverage of both lavage and debridement, would likely have caused the agency to come under withering attack from orthopedists and other medical specialties. It is understandable that the agency would wish to see the results of a replication study that specifically addresses the concerns raised about patient selection before taking a more aggressive coverage stance. Unfortunately, the history of research efforts in this area suggests that years will pass before another study of the quality of Moseley-Wray appears. The critical policy failure is not that the CMS continues to pay for a procedure for a (large) population subgroup in the absence of solid clinical data, but that no agency appears to have a regular system for encouraging or requiring the generation of the information necessary to determine whether the procedure actually benefits patients.[49]

The ultimate test of the impact of Moseley and Wray's study is whether the number of knee arthroscopies performed on patients with OA will decline. The data are not yet available to address this question. In future research we hope to assess if and how practice changed in response to the new research and the CMS decision. Moseley and Wray, for their part, believe that the immediate impact of the study will be small given the fiercely negative reaction it generated from the orthopedic community. They note that the CMS's coverage policy leaves plenty of wiggle room for surgeons who wish to perform debridement, because nearly all patients have some indication besides pain. Moseley reports that he is personally unaware of any surgeon who used to perform the procedure on patients with knee arthritis who has stopped doing so as a result of the study's findings; the surgeons who believed in the procedure before the study still do, and those who questioned it are still confident about their judgment.[50] The only change that may occur in the short run is that the few surgeons who used to perform lavage alone may now perform lavage with debridement, to satisfy Medicare reimbursement rules.[51] Whereas Wray stated her belief that the CMS coverage decision is problematic, she applauded the agency's willingness to initiate the coverage review and also expressed her belief that the coverage decision may have halted an emerging movement to perform lavage in doctors' offices rather than in an out-patient hospital setting.[52]

We would further speculate that surgeons who were already performing the procedure on patients with knee arthritis will continue doing so but that two factors will gradually reduce the prevalence of the surgery over time. First, physicians who do not perform the surgery themselves may stop referring patients to orthopedic surgeons to obtain it. Second, medical schools and teaching hospitals affiliated with academic institutions may revise their training protocols in orthopedics and downplay the use of arthroscopy for this condition. In sum, over time the study's findings are likely to have an impact.

Medical Researchers: Absence of Replication Studies

The publication of the landmark *New England Journal of Medicine* sham surgery study has not led the medical research community to carry out new clinical trials to repeat this research design to determine whether the findings are robust, even though many prominent orthopedic specialists have called for just this to occur. Replication studies would allow any lingering concerns about the stunning finding that arthroscopy works no better than placebo for patients with knee arthritis to be addressed in a scientifically valid way. If the *New England Journal of Medicine* study is wrong, it would seem important to find out. At the same time, if the findings are strong enough to alter clinical practice, the stakes are high enough that the study should be replicated without delay.

Yet, as of this writing, no replication studies are being carried out in the United States. The one effort to replicate features of the Moseley-Wray study that we have been able to identify is taking place in the United Kingdom, which has a single-payer health system. In 2005 the National Health Service's Health Technology Assessment Programme awarded researchers at the University of Aberdeen a $1.6 million grant to explore the feasibility of, and then carry out, a randomized trial comparing three interventions (lavage, a sham surgery procedure, and medical management) for patients with OA. Unfortunately, it appears the study will not contain a debridement arm, severely limiting the significance of its ultimate findings.[53] We see no evidence that the Mosley-Wray study has raised the methodological bar for clinical research in this area. A 2006 *Journal of Bone and Joint Surgery* study of the role of debridement in the treatment of OA of the knee, for example, concludes that the procedure works better for patients with mild arthritis than for those with severe arthritis, but it reaches this conclusion on the basis of case series evidence. The study lacked a control group and was not double blinded.[54]

Diagnosing the Problems

The problems we observe in the production and use of evidence in the case of arthroscopic surgery are not atypical. Randomized controlled trials— the most reliable way to distinguish effective procedures from ineffective ones— comprise only 3 to 9 percent of clinical study designs of surgery, despite the dramatic increase in the scope of surgical interventions and the widespread adoption of randomization in other areas of medical research.[55]

Some medical researchers have called attention to the inconsistency of regulations governing the dissemination of medical therapies. An article in *Science* magazine observed in 1978, although new drugs and devices must satisfy federal regulations that require rigorous testing in animals followed by carefully controlled testing, new surgical operations "may or may not be tested in animals, may be introduced as human therapy with or without review by a human experimentation committee and with or without a formal experimental design, and may or may not be evaluated by long-term follow-up observation."[56] A 1975 commentary in the *Journal of the American Medical Association* pointed out that a double standard exists for surgery. Drugs must undergo Food and Drug Administration (FDA) review—a requirement that is not costless but is almost certainly socially appropriate.[57] Yet no agency has been created to protect the patient from harmful and ineffective operations. This same double standard exists among journal editors and reviewers, "who regularly reject inadequately controlled medical trials and regularly publish inadequately controlled surgical trials."[58]

Ethics as Barrier to Scientific Progress?

What accounts for this double standard and for the poor state of scientific knowledge about surgical procedures more generally? The conventional wisdom is that ethical considerations preclude the use of rigorous, placebo-controlled clinical trials to study surgical interventions. Although it is morally acceptable to use placebos when evaluating a new drug, it is often thought unacceptable to do so when studying a new operation. A recent review of the medical literature identified only a handful of experts who support the use of shams in the assessment of surgical procedures,[59] even though this research approach has produced startling results on the rare occasions it has been used. [60] Opponents of sham surgery trials argue that it is too difficult to design an operation as inert as the usual sugar pill used as a placebo in drug trials.

Proponents of placebo arms in studies of surgical procedures argue that such research designs are ethically sound. Ethical reservations about sham surgery, they claim, confuse the ethics of clinical research with the ethics of personal medical therapy. Clinical trials routinely administer interventions whose risks to patients are not compensated by medical benefits but are justified by the anticipated value of the scientific knowledge that might be gained.[61] If there is no consensus among the medical community on the use of a procedure, the scientific need for blinding is pressing, participants are fully informed about the risks to the placebo control group, and the risks to subjects in the control group are sufficiently minimized, then sham surgery trials may be ethically appropriate, as the American Medical Association has recently acknowledged.[62]

The ethical argument against sham surgery studies can easily be turned on its head. As physician David H. Spodick wrote thirty years ago, "[T]he omission of adequate standards for surgical therapies should be especially surprising, since even the most essential operation involves inevitable trauma— physical, metabolic, and psychic—not to mention the risks of anesthesia. Indeed, when evaluated under comparable conditions against the outcome of alternative treatments or of no treatment, a new operation resulting in net loss to patients, or in the same degree of recovery that would have occurred spontaneously, might be fantasized as a well-intended 'assault.'" If ethics were decisive, one might reasonably expect placebo-controlled arms to be *more* prevalent in the evaluation of surgery than in the evaluation of any other kind of medical intervention.[63]

The strong taboo against the use of placebo-controls in the evaluation of surgeries does raise genuine ethical issues. For example, if fake operations make people feel better, should surgeons perform them?[64] We are skeptical, but the issue is complicated and requires careful scrutiny.[65]

It is clear that many doctors have an instinctive reaction against the use of sham surgery in medical studies. Yet one interesting empirical fact is that the ethics of medical research seems to vary markedly across different areas of clinical practice. If, as we strongly suspect, norms can survive over the long run only when they are broadly compatible with the interests of the actors whose behavior they would govern, we must ask why surgeons would permit the norm against the rigorous evaluation of surgical procedures to persist. Our strong suspicion is that if surgeons had a strong economic motivation to get to the bottom of the issue of surgical effectiveness, concerns about the ethics of sham surgery would be sidestepped in one way or another. If this conjecture is correct, those who cite ethics as the barrier to a more vigorous investigation of surgical effectiveness are mistaking a symptom for the cause. Why then would surgeons not readily accept the legitimacy of third-party scrutiny just as have pharmaceutical companies when producing drugs?

Attention to the role of market failures and government failures provides some answers to this question. If it were repeatedly and decisively demonstrated, against all reasonable methodological objections, that a surgery did not work, we expect that doctors would stop performing it and patients would not request it. Unfortunately, credible information about surgical effectiveness is generally unavailable because it is a public good. In the absence of government subsidy, we expect such information to be undersupplied and inadequately disseminated. For reasons we elaborate below, the political system has failed to correct this key market failure.

Market Failures

The core market failure stems from the public good character of information about the effects of surgical procedures.[66] Medical treatments can be classified into two distinct groups: "devices" (including drugs, equipment, and medical devices) and "strategies" (including surgical procedures as well as treatment protocols and strategies).[67] The economic incentives for producing knowledge about the effectiveness of devices and strategies are fundamentally different. Drugs and medical devices are commercial products. Manufacturers enjoy property rights and have a strong incentive to invest in the creation and dissemination of information about the usefulness of their goods. The more widespread a drug's adoption, the greater the profits reaped by its manufacturer.

In sharp contrast, surgical methods are not commercial products that can be marketed and sold like drugs and devices. Such innovations are a public good, because when a new technique is described in a medical journal, "it can be used freely by all surgeons."[68] The person who develops a new procedure generally does not enjoy patent protection and so can capture only the smallest fraction of the total returns from proving the usefulness of the new method. A surgeon who spends the time and money to invent or investigate a procedure cannot expect to recover these expenses through licensing fees or "additional business." No matter how good the surgeon is, she can only perform so many operations herself.[69]

Nor can health insurance or managed-care firms be expected to carry out evaluations of medical procedures. If an individual firm invests in clinical trials to determine whether a medical procedure is effective, the information would quickly be obtained by its business competitors. "What good would that do for us," asked a senior executive of a large health maintenance organization. "The other managed care companies could just take those findings and use them for their own benefit."[70] The effect of this "free rider" problem is to eliminate the incentive for these firms to finance and administer such evaluation studies in the first place.[71]

Government Failures

When markets fail, government intervention can provide missing incentives. Unfortunately, the federal government currently lacks the authority and capacity to protect the fundamental interests of health care beneficiaries and payers in the rigorous evaluation of surgical procedures. Unlike drugs and medical devices, surgical and other medical procedures in the United States are not subject to FDA regulation or other government review. The government's failure to address the problem of inadequate evaluation of medical procedures arises from three political factors: the diffuse benefits problem, overreliance on professional self-regulation, and weak incentives for political entrepreneurship. We discuss the last factor at some length because it is both important and underappreciated in the literature.

One reason why the government is not more active in promoting rigorous evaluation of surgical procedures is because the benefits from this intervention are widely diffused across society. As a result, there is no organized constituency to pressure the government to provide them.[72] Meanwhile, the perceived costs of more rigorous scrutiny of surgical procedures are borne by well-organized provider groups. Surgeons do not really want the government or other third parties to control the dissemination of new operations, their calls for the need for better studies notwithstanding.[73] The major goal of surgical professional associations is to preserve professional autonomy.

Again, the contrast with the pressures for drug regulation is striking. Although no drug company wants the government to block its sales, manufacturers of high-quality drugs do wish to differentiate their products from low-quality competitors. FDA review is quite useful in this regard. It creates barriers to entry that screen out low-cost quack remedies, increasing the market share of those who make useful drugs. It also expands the size of the pharmaceutical market, because consumers are more confident that drugs are safe and effective.[74] FDA or other governmental review of surgical procedures would be far less effective as a way to ensure that the returns from new methods flow only to the rightful owners of the medical innovations.

Revealingly, when surgical innovations *do* involve the use or implantation of some new drug or device that can be commercially sold, actors often seek FDA approval for marketing purposes. For example, the FDA recently approved a robotic device that enables a surgeon to perform laparoscopic gall bladder and reflux disease surgery while seated at a console with a computer and video monitor. FDA clearance was based on a review of clinical studies of safety and effectiveness submitted by the manufacturer, Intuitive Surgical, Inc.[75]

A second reason for the lack of effective government action is that the public may be putting too much faith in the capacity of doctors to self regulate, and this faith leads to political quiescence. We suspect that even among the best educated and politically active members of the general public there is a mistaken belief in the quality of the supporting evidence and the energy with which medical organizations respond to legitimate questions about medical practices. The public regards surgeons as good-faith trustees of their health. Although there has been some erosion of faith in the medical profession among the American public over time, most citizens trust their doctor far more than government or their managed-care company.[76] The public holds doctors in high regard, though many harbor suspicions that financial incentives have an important influence in what medical care they get. Despite this dose of cynicism, we expect the overwhelming majority of the public believes that if convincing evidence is presented that shows a surgical procedure is not working as expected, doctors will make a serious effort to determine the truth. The arthroscopy case suggests this faith in the medical profession is naïve. The poor evidentiary basis for some surgery thus ultimately rests in part on public complacency, which in turn is founded on the widespread yet mistaken popular assumption that professional norms ensure an energetic pursuit of best medical practices.

Weak Incentives for Political Entrepreneurship

The most important reason for the government's failure to promote evidence-based medical practices is the lack of strong incentives for political entrepreneurship. Virtually all politicians are likely to agree *in principle* about the importance of accurate information on the efficacy of surgical procedures. Yet the very fact that this position has such broad appeal could make it a loser for prospective political entrepreneurs considering whether to invest their scarce time and energy in promoting it. The politician who first calls for more rigorous evaluations of operations is a natural target for punishment by an organized group (for example, the surgeons) and would therefore potentially pay a high price for taking the initiative. If the issue began to gain political traction, however, all officeholders would feel constrained to adopt more or less the same position. This copy-cat behavior will make it hard for the pioneering entrepreneur to differentiate herself from her opponent, making it impossible for poorly informed voters to offer the appropriate political rewards. If would-be political entrepreneurs anticipate that the political gains from their efforts will be immediately appropriated, the effect will discourage the entrepreneurial activities in the first place. In sum, supporting better evaluation of surgical procedures may be an example of a "zero credit" policy, meaning a policy that offers no captureable political returns even though the policy's social benefit-cost ratio is highly favorable.

Stem cell research is the opposite case of a policy that allows partisan officials to differentiate themselves in the political marketplace. While it has received enormous publicity, stem cell research is only one of many important lines of medical research today. Moreover, stem cell studies are funded by private biomedical companies. Yet stem cell research is a highly attractive political issue for liberal and conservative activists alike who can win credit from their supporters by fighting the abortion issue by proxy.

An influential recent line of political science research concludes that even minimally informed citizens can obtain effective political representation of their interests through the use of simple cues and decision heuristics.[77] This literature grants that the public generally lacks direct knowledge about politics and policy but claims that citizens are nevertheless able to make intelligent choices among candidates and reward good performance by exploiting the information in endorsements, party labels, campaign communications, and opinion polls. Our analysis suggests this assessment is far too optimistic. The costs of subtle but massive government failures, such as the inadequate evaluation of medical procedures, may be extremely difficult for ordinary citizens to discern. High-status professional groups with high stakes in the outcome typically control the flow of relevant information. When citizens are largely ignorant (through no fault of their own) and deferential, significant general interests may be underrepresented year in and year out. This is not to say that the latent popular support for medicine that works could not be activated.[78]

Public opinion can be led.[79] It does not seem beyond the realm of imagination that a highly talented politician would be unable to bring media attention to the problem. Our claim is not that the situation is hopeless, but only that the political incentives for political entrepreneurship are much too weak in light of the potentially massive social welfare gains from reform.

Implications for Research and Practice

Our look at a common surgical operation, arthroscopy for OA of the knee, suggests that the health policy system's generation and use of scientific information about the efficacy of medical procedures is almost certainly suboptimal. Our national research investment in the evaluation of common procedures is almost certainly much too low in view of the high stakes for public health and the questionable quality of many existing studies.

The case of arthroscopy for OA of the knee suggests that not nearly enough attention is paid to evaluating the effectiveness of surgical procedures. It is especially surprising and disappointing that the reaction to the Moseley-Wray study did not include a push for immediate replication studies to confirm the findings and address remaining issues raised by critics of the research. The public welfare might be served by charging an agency or commission with the tasks of identifying common procedures with weak supporting evidence and then providing funds to support the research necessary to determine their actual usefulness.[80]

One possible implication of our analysis is the need to reform medical education. The argumentation produced in response to the Moseley and Wray study suggests that physicians do not instinctively think about issues such as natural history, placebo effects, and regression to the mean. As a result, there is a tendency for physicians to attribute all of the perceived benefits of an intervention to the medical treatment. Yet just because a patient says she feels better after a surgery does not mean that the medical intervention per se helped. It is possible that training at medical schools might wish to include a heavier dose of statistics and research methods if the goal is to produce physicians who are also, in part, evidence-based scientists with an appropriate awareness of the limits of their own professional experiences.

A second implication is the need for health policymakers and practitioners to gain a better understanding of the role of placebos and expectations in medicine. If several follow-up studies to Moseley-Wray definitely proved that all the benefits of the procedures were due to placebo effects, we doubt surgeons would continue performing them. It should be noted that we found no proponent of arthroscopy who argued that continued use of the surgery was justified by its placebo effects, but the patients in the Moseley-Wray study really did feel better. The challenge is to find new ways to capture the benefits of sham surgeries through less deceptive, costly, and risky interventions.

This chapter also raises important questions for policymakers to consider. A full-fledged policy analysis is beyond the scope of this chapter, but it is reasonable to think that increased subsidies for clinical trials of surgical procedures and the dissemination of new research findings might be appropriate. Any policy intervention would of course have to avoid the creation of collateral problems, such as so overburdening surgeons that the innovation process was chilled. Developing good general principles to guide the regulation of surgical procedures is a difficult problem. A comprehensive analysis might consider the troublesome theoretical possibility that there may be real social benefits from permitting informal and speculative investigation of novel or radically new surgical methods, even if that experimentation is so unlikely to help the individual patient that it is ethically questionable.[81] This rationale for relaxed evidentiary requirements does not apply to standard, widely practiced operations; it is difficult to see any good reason why it makes sense to neglect energetic efforts to evaluate these procedures.

Although the technical challenges to improving the scientific basis of surgery are nontrivial, the political challenges are daunting. In light of the general movement toward evidence-based medicine and the increasing budgetary pressures facing Medicare, Medicaid, and private insurers, we expect the scientific quality of surgical research to improve in the future. What gives us pause is that many people were no less optimistic thirty years ago. In the interim, millions of patients have undergone surgical procedures they did not need. Some of them might have felt better afterward, but some of them surely felt worse or even suffered serious postoperative complications. The failure to uncover ineffective procedures almost certainly forestalled the development of truly effective medical responses. There is good reason to believe the system is not performing as well as it could be.

Notes

1. See John Carey, "Medical Guesswork: From Heart Surgery to Prostate Care, the Medical Industry Knows Little about Which Treatments Really Work," *Business Week*, May 29, 2006, pp. 72–79.

2. See Alan B. Cohen and Shirley A. Stewart, "Safety and Efficacy Concerns: Medical Technology and Market Entry," in *Technology in American Health Care: Policy Directions for Effective Evaluation and Management*, edited by Alan B. Cohen and Ruth S. Hanft,

with others (University of Michigan Press, 2004), p. 275; and E. Haavi Morreim, "A Dose of Our Own Medicine: Alternative Medicine, Conventional Medicine, and the Standards of Science," *Journal of Law, Medicine, and Ethics,* vol. 31 (2003): 222–35.

3. Because medical coding of the indications for arthroscopic procedures varies greatly across orthopedic surgeons, it is virtually impossible to determine the exact number of such procedures performed each year on patients with arthritic knees as opposed to other conditions. The original Moseley-Wray *New England Journal of Medicine* article had indicated that the procedure was performed 650,000 times each year on patients with arthritic knees, but the authors now believe that figure is an upper limit. J. Bruce Moseley, personal communication, November 1, 2004.

4. J. B. Moseley, K. O'Malley, N. J. Petersen, and others, "A Controlled Trial of Arthroscopic Surgery for Osteoarthritis of the Knee," *New England Journal of Medicine,* vol. 347 (2002): 81–88.

5. David T. Felson and Joseph Buckwalter, "Editorial: Debridement and Lavage for OA of the Knee," *New England Journal of Medicine,* vol. 347 (2002): 132–33.

6. M. S. Burman, H. H. Finkelstein, and L. Mayer, "Arthroscopy of the Knee Joint," *Journal of Bone and Joint Surgery,* vol. 16 (1934): 255–68. A brief discussion of the early history of lavage and debridement can be found in S. S. Yang and B. Nisonson, "Arthroscopic Surgery of the Knee in the Geriatric Patient," *Clinical Orthopedics,* vol. 316 (1995): 50–58.

7. Arlen D. Hanssen and others, "Surgical Options for the Middle-aged Patient with Osteoarthritis of the Knee Joint," *Journal of Bone and Joint Surgery,* vol. 82, no. 12 (2000): 1767.

8. Norman F. Sprague III, "Arthoscopic Debridement for Degenerative Knee Joint Disease," *Clinical Orthopaedics and Related Research,* vol. 160 (1981): 118–23.

9. Use of subjective measures, and especially subjective measures that are based on remembering something like "pain" levels many months earlier, are unlikely to satisfy rigorous standards for reliability and validity. A number of the subsequent studies employed a prospective design and so obtained measures of pain and functionality prior to the operations.

10. For a comprehensive list of clinical studies published up to 2003, along with a brief description of their designs and main results, see appendix B, "Decision Memo for Arthroscopy for the Osteoarthritic Knee," Centers for Medicare and Medicaid, CAG-00167N. Centers for Medicare & Medicaid Services (CMS). Arthroscopy for the Osteoarthritic Knee (CAG-00167N). National Coverage Analysis (NCA) Baltimore: CMS; July 3, 2003 (www.cms.hhs.gov/ncdr/memo.asp?id=7 [July 28, 2003]).

11. K. Kalunian and others, "Visually-guided irrigation in patients with early knee osteoarthritis: a multicenter randomized, controlled trial," *Osteoarthritis and Cartilage,* vol. 8 (2000): 412–18. See also P. Ravaud and others, "Effects of Joint Lavage and Steroid Injections in Patients with Osteoarthritis of the Knee," *Arthritis & Rheumatism,* vol. 42 (1999): 475–82; and P. T. Dawes and others, "Saline Washout for Knee Osteoarthritis: Results of a Controlled Study," *Clinical Rheumatology,* vol. 6 (1987): 61–63.

12. Yang and Nisonson, "Arthroscopic Surgery of the Knee in the Geriatric Patient."

13. Joseph Bernstein and Tony Quach, "A Perspective on the Study of Moseley *et al:* Questioning the Value of Arthroscopic Knee surgery for Osteoarthritis," *Cleveland Clinic Journal of Medicine,* vol. 70, no. 5 (May 2003): 405.

14. Hanssen and others, "Surgical Options for the Middle-aged Patient with Osteoarthritis of the Knee Joint," p. 1767.

15. J. B. McGinty and others, "Uses and Abuses of Arthroscopy: A Symposium," *Journal of Bone and Joint Surgery*, vol. 74, no. 10 (1992): 1563–77.

16. This is not to say that surgery is generally ineffective. For example, major joint replacement operations, such as total knee replacement and hip replacement, are supported by convincing evidence. These operations improve quality of life and may also be cost saving, because they replace the frequent doctor visits and drug expense associated with chronic care, reduce costs by eliminating falls, and permit the patient to resume more normal activity including employment. David T. Felson, personal communication, October 27, 2004.

17. Gina Kolata, "Spinal Cement Draws Patients and Questions," *New York Times*, August 28, 2005, p. A1.

18. Ibid.

19. Stacey Burling, "Is a Knee Operation Worth It?" *Philadelphia Inquirer*, July 11, 2002, p. A1.

20. At the time of the trial, the Houston VA (unlike many other VA hospitals around the nation) did not routinely cover the procedure for patients with knee arthritis, because an excess of patient demand relative to the supply of available surgical suites forced local hospital officials to set priorities, and other surgical procedures were considered more important. The only way Houston area veterans could receive the procedure from the VA for this condition was by entering the trial. Nelda P. Wray, personal communication, October 5, 2004.

21. Felson and Buckwalter, "Editorial: Debridement and Lavage for OA of the Knee."

22. Susan Okie, "Knee Surgery For Arthritis Is Ineffective, Study Finds," *Washington Post*, July 11, 2002, p. A1; Liz Kowalczk, "Sham Surgery Aids Patients' Knees Woes, Study Finds," *Boston Globe*," July 11, 2002, p. A1.

23. "Surgery for Arthritic Knee: Roundup," *Bandolier*, (www.jr2.ox.ac.uk/bandolier/booth/Arthritis/arthrokn.html [November 1, 2004]).

24. The authors believe that the placebo effect was responsible for the improvement in part because most of the patients in the study had fairly stable symptoms at the time they entered the trial. They did not have acutely worsened symptoms that would be expected to naturally regress to the mean. J. Bruce Moseley, personal communication, December 7, 2004.

25. The study was conducted at a VA hospital, and therefore most subjects were men, but OA of the knee affects women more than men. There is, however, no medical reason to think surgery response varies according to sex. Critics did not press this argument very hard.

26. Moseley and Wray classified "popping" and "clicking," "locking," and "giving way" as mechanical symptoms for purposes of their subgroup analysis. (J. Bruce Moseley, personal communication, April 10, 2006). David Felson states that orthopedic surgeons generally regard locking and giving way as mechanical indications for arthroscopic surgery, but not popping and clicking. (David T. Felson, personal communication, March 15, 2006). We are unaware of any systematic data on surgeons' actual clinical decisions or behavior in this area.

27. As it turned out, however, some patients with a torn meniscus inadvertently entered the study. (Such patients often had false-negative magnetic resonance imaging findings.) For ethical reasons, an unstable meniscal tear found among patients in the

lavage and debridement arms was treated. Although the number of such patients was too small for firm conclusion, they did not appear to do substantially better than patients in the placebo arm. The authors believe this requires further study, but in the meantime arthroscopy should continue to be performed on those with conditions like a bucket-handle tear. J. Bruce Moseley, personal communication, November 1, 2004.

28. David T. Felson, personal communication, September 27, 2004

29. See Nelda P. Wray, J. Bruce Moseley, and Kimberly O'Malley, "Letter to the Editor," *Journal of Bone and Joint Surgery*, vol. 85, no. 2 (2003): 381; see also Nelda P. Wray, J. Bruce Moseley, and Kimberly O'Malley, "Letter to the Editor," *New England Journal of Medicine*, vol. 347, no. 21 (2002): 1718

30. G. F. Dervin and others, "Effect of Arthroscopic Debridement for Osteoarthritis of the Knee on Health-Related Quality of Life," *Journal of Bone and Joint Surgery*, vol. 85, no. 1 (2003): 10–19.

31. There is a general consensus that the procedure is appropriate for patients with an unstable meniscal tear, though Moseley and Wray believe more research is needed on this question. J. Bruce Moseley, personal communication, November 1, 2004.

32. If there are lingering doubts about whether arthroscopic surgery would be efficacious in a specific subgroup, the ethically and scientifically appropriate way to proceed world be to test the hypothesis by conducting a placebo-controlled trial in that subpopulation. Yet even if critics sincerely believe there is a subgroup that would benefit greatly from the surgery, the downward bias of the *New England Journal of Medicine* study's results would be proportional to the subgroup's share of the patients enrolled in the trial. The fact that the study found *no* benefit (and not merely a statistically insignificant benefit) implies that the magnitude of the benefits or the percentage of people helped is most likely small.

33. David T. Felson, personal communication, September 27, 2004.

34. Robert W. Jackson, "Letter to the Editor," *New England Journal of Medicine*, vol. 347 (2002): 1716.

35. Nelda P. Wray, personal communication, October 8, 2004.

36. Gina Kolata, "Arthritis Surgery in Ailing Knees Is Cited as Sham," *New York Times*, July 11, 2002, p. A1.

37. See www.vaccinationnews.com/DailyNews/July2002/StudyCastsDoubt10.htm (September 8, 2006).

38. On the truth behind popular arguments about bureaucratic problems, see James Q. Wilson, *Bureaucracy* (New York: Basic Books, 1991).

39. Gina Kolata, "V.A. Suggests Halt to Kind of Knee Surgery," *New York Times*, August 24, 2002, p. A9.

40. "VA Issues Advisory Based on Knee Surgery Study," *US Medicine Information*, November 27, 2002 (www.usmedicine.com/dailyNews.cfm?dailyID=122 [October 10, 2004]).

41. Shamiram Feinglass, personal communication, October 22, 2004.

42. The report, entitled "Arthroscopic Surgery and Osteoarthritis of the Knee: A Report for the Centers for Medicare and Medicaid Services, Coverage Analysis Group," December 2002, was endorsed by the American Academy of Orthopedic Surgeons, the American Academy of Hip and Knee Surgeons, the Arthroscopy Association of North America, the American Orthopedic Society of Sports Medicine, and the Knee Society.

43. Center for Medicare and Medicaid Services, "Decision Memo for Arthroscopy for the Osteoarthritic Knee (CAG-00167N), July 3, 2003. See note 10 above.

44. See, for example, Aetna, "Clinical Policy Bulletin Number 0673: Arthroscopic Lavage and Debridement for Osteoarthritis of the Knee," September 26, 2003; Cigna, "Cigna HealthCare Coverage Position 0032: Arthroscopic Lavage and Debridement of the Knee for the Treatment of Osteoarthritis," April 15, 2004.

45. Ibid.

46. Ibid.

47. Shamiram Feinglass, personal communication, October 22, 2004.

48. Daniel H. Sung, "Orthopedics Responds as Medicare Questions Arthroscopy for Osteoarthritis of the Knee," *American Academy of Orthopedic Surgeons Bulletin,* vol. 51, no. 4 (August 2003) (www.aaos.org/wordhtml/bulletin/aug03/fline2.htm [October 31, 2004]).

49. The CMS has recently taken some important steps to address this information problem. In November 2004, the CMS chief administrator, Dr. Mark McClellan, who is both an internist and an economist, announced that the agency would make payments for certain new expensive treatments, such as implantable defibrillators for heart patients, conditional on agreement by companies and other actors to pay for studies on whether these new methods are effective on the Medicare population. This new initiative is intended to generate medical effectiveness data that are not routinely produced by the regular FDA review process. The agency's evidence-based initiatives, however, cover only certain drugs and devices. They do not require more systematic study of pure surgical procedures. See Gina Kolata, "Medicare Covers New Treatments with a Catch," *New York Times,* November 5, 2004, p. A1.

50. J. Bruce Moseley, personal communication, November 1, 2004.

51. It is unclear whether Medicare's ruling will have any impact on clinical practice. Not many surgeons performed lavage without debridement even before the Medicare policy change because there was no "CPT" procedure code to report it. J. Bruce Moseley, personal communication, December 7, 2004.

52. Nelda P. Wray, personal communication, October 8, 2004.

53. The Aberdeen study is available at www.abdn.ac.uk/hsru/news.shtml (October 2004).

54. See Roy K. Aaron and others, "Arthroscopic Debridement for Osteoarthritis of the Knee," *Journal of Bone and Joint Surgery,* vol. 88, no. 5 (2006): 936–43, at 936.

55. Michael J. Solom and Robin S. McLeod, "Surgery and the Randomized Controlled Trial: Past, Present and Future," *Medical Journal of Australia,* vol. 169 (1998): 380–38.

56. J. P. Bunker, D. Hinkley, W. V. McDermott, "Surgical Innovation and Its Evaluation," *Science,* vol. 26 (May 1978): 937–41.

57. The FDA review process is not uncontroversial. Some critics believe that FDA review is too stringent and that it excessively delays the time it takes firms to bring safe and effective drugs to market. Others contend that new drugs should be shown to work better (or most cost effectively) than alternatives, not simply to be superior to a placebo. The lack of *any* meaningful third-party control of the dissemination of surgical procedures is arguably an even more fundamental problem.

58. David H. Spordick, "Numerators without Denominators: There Is No FDA for the Surgeon," *Journal of the American Medical Association,* vol. 232, no. 1 (1975): 35–36.

59. J. E. Frader and D. A. Caniano, "Research and Innovation in Surgery," in *Surgical Ethics,* edited by L. B. McCullough, J. W. Jones, and B. A. Brody (Oxford University Press, 1998), pp. 216–41.

60. In 1959 the *New England Journal of Medicine* published the results of a sham surgery trial that found that a procedure known as internal mammary artery ligation worked no better than placebo. More recently, a placebo-controlled trial of implantation of embryonic neurons in patients with Parkinson's disease found a very strong placebo effect, though those who received the real procedure did experience slightly greater improvement along certain dimensions. See "Should Fusion Surgery Be Compared with a Placebo Operation," *BackLetter,* 19, no. 5 (2004): 51.

61. As Baruch Brody, the ethicist who participated in the arthroscopy study, points out, this ethical conclusion "is not based upon a commitment to a utilitarian philosophy that allows for the mistreatment of subjects if it is sufficiently socially or scientifically valuable." Risks still must be sufficiently minimized, and special steps must be taken to ensure that prospective participants in the trial really understand the nature of the placebo control group. See Baruch A. Brody, "Criteria for Legitimate Placebo Controlled Surgical Trials" (www.bcm.edu/pa/knee-drbrody.htm [October 25, 2004]).

62. Frances G. Miller, "Sham Surgery: An Ethical Analysis," *American Journal of Bioethics,* vol. 3, no. 4 (2003): 42.

63. David H. Spodick," Numerators without Denominators,*"Journal of the American Medical Association,* vol. 242, no. 1 (1975): 36.

64. As a practical matter, this question is not especially relevant to the debate over the use of arthroscopic surgery. Even the proponents of arthroscopic surgery do not justify the surgery based on its placebo benefits, and there is a strong medical ethic against performing interventions that are known to be useless beyond the placebo effects.

65. It might be tempting to argue that surgeons should carry out fake procedures if patients feel better afterward, but this approach would be self-defeating over time. If patients were told that their operations did not involve real medical interventions, they would likely experience a much smaller placebo benefit. Moreover, because all medical interventions likely produce some placebo benefits, the knowledge that placebos were now an accepted course of personal medical therapy might lead to worse patient outcomes in general. Keeping patients in the dark about the use of placebos (outside of control arms in clinical trials) would only create more problems. Such deceptions would inhibit open communication between physicians and their patients and erode trust in the health care system. It would also damage the medical research enterprise, discouraging the identification of procedures with true medical benefits.

66. The problem is not only that too little information is generated about the effectiveness of medical procedures. It is also that available information will tend to be distributed asymmetrically. Although the Internet is an empowering tool, the capacity of ordinary citizens to gain *independent and reliable* information about the risks and benefits of complex medical procedures remains limited at best. In sum, medical providers do not know nearly as much as they should about how well procedures work, and patients generally know only what their physicians tell them.

67. Charles E. Phelps, "Diffusion of Information in Medical Care," *Journal of Economic Perspectives,* vol. 6, no 3 (1992): 23–42. Phelps also notes that although drug companies are often codefendants in medical malpractice trials, even if the performance of

the drug is not a major question, no liability attaches to the use of a surgical innovation except in the particular instance of a single doctor-patient combination.

68. David M. Cutler, *Your Money or Your Life* (Oxford University Press, 2004), p. 82.

69. Because surgical procedures are nonstandardized, the major quality issue for surgery has historically been seen less as a matter of weeding out poor procedures (for example, surgeries that are not effective no matter how well they are performed) than in weeding out less skilled practitioners. In recent years, the focus has been on clinicians who perform certain procedures very infrequently (so-called low-volume surgeons). We owe this insight to Mark Schlesinger.

70. Quoted in Jerry Avorn, *Powerful Medicines: The Benefits, Risks, and Costs of Prescription Drugs* (New York: Knopf, 2004), pp. 378–79.

71. Ibid.

72. On the effects of the distribution of policy costs and benefits on political mobilization, see James Q. Wilson *Political Organizations* (New York: Basic Books, 1973).

73. The history of the Agency for Healthcare Research and Quality illustrates the point. In late 1994 the agency set off a political firestorm when it issued a set of guidelines that argued, in effect, that most back surgeries are unnecessary because back pain disappears by itself in most cases. Angry back surgeons convinced Congress to slash the agency's budget in retaliation. See Neil A. Lewis, "Agency's Report Provokes a Revolt," *New York Times*, September 14, 1995, p. A16.

74. The implication of this argument is that the proposals to strengthen the FDA will split the drug industry. For those companies able to produce effective products, the existence of a respected third party blocking competition and validating efficacy claims is very useful. "Low-quality" companies will tend to oppose a more potent FDA. To be sure, advocates of tighter FDA regulations have at times found it politically expedient to harness broad public pressure as well (as in the case of the famous congressional hearings over the thalidomide drug scandal in 1961). The debate over these reforms, however, would have been far more contentious if drug manufacturers who make useful products had not been prepared to acknowledge the need for governmental intervention in the first place.

75. See www.fda.gov/bbs/topics/NEWS/NEW00732.html (October 2004).

76. Mark Schlesinger, "A Loss of Faith: The Sources of Reduced Political Legitimacy for the American Medical Profession," *Milbank Quarterly,* vol. 80, no. 2 (2002): 1–45.

77. See, for example, Paul M. Sniderman, Richard A. Brody, and Philip E. Tetlock, *Reasoning and Choice: Explorations in Political Psychology* (Cambridge University Press, 1991); John A. Ferejohn and James H. Kuklinski, eds., *Information and Democratic Processes* (University of Illinois Press, 1990); and Arthur Lupia and Mathew McCubbins: *The Democratic Dilemma: Can Citizens Learn What They Need to Know?* (Cambridge University Press, 1998). For a powerful critique of this line of research, see Paul Pierson, "The Prospects for Democratic Control in an Age of Big Government," in Arthur M. Meltzer, M. Richard Zinman, and Jerry Weinberger, eds., *Politics at the Turn of the Century* (Lanham, Md.: Rowman and Littlefield, 2001), pp. 140–61.

78. In 1998 the Australian government funded a pilot study to develop a mechanism for generating data on the efficacy of selected new surgical procedures. One goal was to suggest which procedures are appropriate candidates for randomized control trials. See "Surgery and Evidence-based Medicine," *Medical Journal of Australia,* vol. 198 (1998): 348–49.

79. See John Zaller, *The Nature and Origins of Mass Opinion* (Cambridge University Press, 1992).

80. A discussion of the details of this reform proposal is beyond the scope of this chapter.

81. How soon after their introduction radically new surgical innovations should be made the subject of structured scientific research is a matter of current debate. See, for example, James W. Jones, Laurence McCullough, and B. W. Richman, "Ethics of Surgical Innovation to Treat Rare Diseases," *Journal of Vascular Surgery*, vol. 39, no. 4 (2004): 918–19.

4

Urban Transportation

CLIFFORD WINSTON

Public provision of urban transportation is, in theory, socially desirable.[1] Rail and bus operations exhibit economies of traffic density that could lead to destructive competition in an unregulated market. Highways are traditionally perceived as public goods that require enormous capital and maintenance investments that the private sector is unlikely to finance. Improving the urban mobility of elderly and low-income citizens is an important social goal that should be addressed by government. In their official capacity as regulators, service providers, and investors, however, public officials have generally instituted policies that have led to inefficient and inequitable urban transportation. A case for privatizing urban transport is developing because these actual *government failures* most likely outweigh potential *market failures*.

Governmental involvement in the transportation systems of U.S. cities illustrates the problem. Local governments, with state and federal financial support, are quasi-monopoly providers of urban bus and rail transit. Most U.S. roads and bridges are owned and operated by federal, state, or local governments. How has the public system performed? City roads are jammed at an ever-expanding rush hour, causing infuriating delays. Bus service, never fast, has deteriorated over the years, while real fares have risen. Pressures to expand rail service to outlying suburbs remains strong, even though current rail operations cannot attract enough riders to cover more than a small fraction of their total expenses, including capital costs.

Popular opinion seems to be that the United States can—and should—spend its way out of this mess by building more roads, running more buses, and installing more track. Indeed, since the early 1980s Congress has passed transportation bills that have significantly increased federal support for highways and transit. Currently, highway and transit spending from all sources of government exceeds $100 billion per year.

Many transportation analysts are skeptical of this approach and argue that although more public spending for urban transport may result in some improvements for travelers, its primary effects will be to swell transportation deficits and waste tax revenues. Instead, they suggest that government pursue more "efficient" policies such as charging motorists for the congestion they cause and balancing costs and benefits when deciding transit frequencies, route coverage, and vehicle sizes.

I have come to believe that it is futile to expect public officials to consider such changes, because urban transportation policy is largely shaped by entrenched political forces. The forces that have led to inefficient prices and service, excessive labor costs, bloated bureaucracies, and construction-cost overruns promise more of the same for the future. The only realistic way to improve the system is to shield it from those influences and expose it to market forces through privatization. Preliminary evidence from the United Kingdom and elsewhere suggests that although a private urban transportation sector should not be expected to perform flawlessly, it could eliminate most government failures and allow innovation and state-of-the-art technology to flourish free of government interference. The real uncertainty is what could spur policymakers to initiate change.

The Evolution of the U.S. Urban Transit System

The U.S. government began subsidizing urban transportation in the 1950s, funding urban extensions of the interstate highway system. In the early 1960s, in response both to the deteriorating financial condition of private transit and arguments by big-city mayors that subsidizing transit would be more cost-effective than building highways, Congress passed legislation that helped cities buy their transit companies. Federal operating subsidies followed in the 1970s. Today, most operating assistance comes from state and local governments while Washington shoulders most capital investment.

Figure 4-1. *Heavy and Light Rail and Motor Bus Vehicle Miles, 1950–2002*[a]

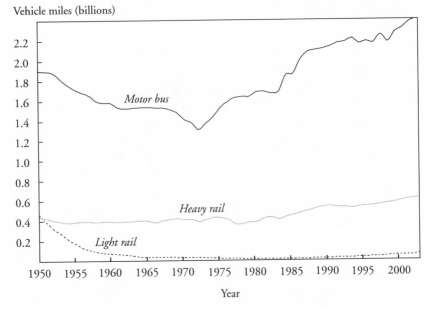

Vehicle miles (billions)

Sources: American Public Transit Association (APTA), *2003 Transit Fact Book* (for 1996–2002); *1997 Transit Fact Book* (for 1984–95); *1991 Transit Fact Book* (for 1975–83); *1974–75 Transit Fact Book* (for 1960–73); *1981 Transit Fact Book* (for 1974); and *1960 Transit Fact Book* (for 1950–59).

a. A number of smaller and rural systems are excluded before 1984.

Growing federal support of mass transit slowed the long-run decline in the use of buses and light rail systems—trolleys and streetcars (figure 4-1). By the late 1970s, federal subsidies had expanded bus and heavy rail capacity.[2] Capacity has continued to increase in the past two decades, but other trends have revealed ominous weaknesses in service.[3] Many cities have cut bus frequency on their core routes to extend service to the suburbs. Many others, including New York, Chicago, and San Francisco, have cut rail-service frequency and raised real fares. Indeed, since 1980 real transit fares per passenger-mile have increased 54 percent.[4] Although federal support of public transit was intended to lure urban travelers from their cars, the share of commuters who use bus and rail has diminished since the 1960s. Suburban sprawl and rising incomes have reinforced commuters' preferences for their automobiles, causing autos' share of work trips to climb to 89.5 percent by 2000 (table 4-1).[5] Between 1960 and 2000, mass transit's share of *all* trips in large urban areas, where transit service should be most attractive, fell from

Table 4-1. *Journey to Work Passengers and Mode Shares in U.S. Urban Areas with Population Greater than 1 Million, 1960–2000*

Mode	1960[a]	1970[a]	1980	1990	2000
Millions of workers					
Privately owned vehicle	17.5	27.6	36.5	49.8	67.4
Bus	3.8	3.3	3.0	2.9	2.1
Subway and rail	2.3	2.2	2.0	2.3	0.71
Walk	3.0	2.7	2.1	2.2	1.8
Other	5.2	1.2	1.7	2.4	3.1
Percentage of workers					
Privately owned vehicle	61.0	74.4	80.4	83.5	89.5
Bus	13.1	9.0	6.7	4.9	2.8
Subway and rail	8.0	5.9	4.5	3.8	1.0
Walk	10.4	7.4	4.7	3.8	2.4
Other	7.5	3.3	3.7	4.0	4.1

Source: Federal Highway Administration, *Journey-to-Work Trends in the United States and its Major Metropolitan Areas 1960–1990, 1993,* from census data; Federal Highway Administration, *Journey-to-Work Trends,* based on 1960, 1970, and 1980 decennial censuses, 1986; *Means of Transportation to Work,* 2000 census; and author's calculations.

a. The category "other" in 1960 and 1970 passenger trips includes walking, taxi, motorcycle, bicycle, and respondents who work at home; this category in other years and in mode share includes these modes except walking. The mode share data for walking in 1960 and 1970 are based on U.S. data rather than major urban area data; the set of major urban areas with population exceeding 1 million changes by decade.

more than 20 percent to less than 3 percent.[6] Transit's high share of empty seats attests to its inefficient operations. In the mid-1990s rail filled roughly 18 percent of its seats with paying customers, buses roughly 14 percent.[7] Since then, the Federal Transit Authority has stopped requiring transit systems to report load factor data.

Public transit's long-run growth in capacity and decline in patronage have helped create deficits that are a serious drain on the public purse. By 2002, transit operating expenses in the United States were about $27 billion a year, more than twice the yearly $13 billion in operating revenues. Continuing capital investments are swelling this deficit (2002 capital subsidies amounted to $9.3 billion).[8] Furthermore, government involvement portends better things for special interests than for travelers. According to Don Pickrell and Douglass B. Lee, as much as 75 percent of federal spending on mass transit ends up in the pockets of transit workers (as above-market wages) or goes to suppliers of transit capital equipment (as higher profits and interest). Just 25 percent is used to improve transit and lower fares.[9]

Long-run trends in transit demand, which are reported in the *National Transit Database,* are ominous as its market share and patronage continue to fall. Nonetheless, with growing government support for transit, cities will find it easier to build new (light) rail systems or extend existing ones, ensuring that transit deficits will grow even larger. Indeed, Houston and Minneapolis recently opened new light rail lines while small, sparsely populated cities such as Sioux City, Harrisburg, and Staunton, Virginia, suggested that they wanted federal funds to help build their systems.

A fundamental problem with rail construction projects is that ridership tends to be grossly overestimated at the planning stage, while capital and operating costs are underestimated. For example, after breaking ground in 1986, the new Los Angeles Red Line (light rail system) finally opened in June 2000. The 17.4-mile system, costing more than $4.5 billion, currently lures only 120,000 riders a day in a county with 10 million residents.[10] The system was originally intended to be much larger and carry more passengers, but after years of construction delays and cost overruns and faced with cost projections of some $75 billion for the next twenty years, Los Angeles voters decided in 1998 to block further use of local sales tax revenue for subway construction. Unfortunately, the ballot measure does not prevent the use of other funds (federal and state) to apply to light rail.

Public transit authorities face growing financial pressures to maintain rail operations as these systems age. For example, the Washington, D.C., Metro subway system, which began service only in 1976, is currently struggling with equipment breakdowns, such as broken escalators and failed relays, and water seepage that is crippling power and communications systems and track infrastructure at an alarming rate. When faced with the likelihood that money would not be available over the next several years to make all necessary repairs and purchase additional equipment, regional planners concluded that far more people will have to drive cars than previously projected.[11]

In retrospect, the U.S. public transportation experiment has been a major disappointment and done little to stem the growth of automobile travel. Policymakers are now confronted with the rising costs of this experiment.

U.S. Urban Highways

The United States has invested hundreds of billions of dollars—primarily from taxes on gasoline—in building and maintaining roads to accommodate auto and truck travel, but, like rail transit investments, the cost of some urban road projects has turned out to be much higher than anticipated. The

Figure 4-2. *Average Annual Traffic Delay in Major Metropolitan Areas, 1982–2001*

Hours of traffic delay per person

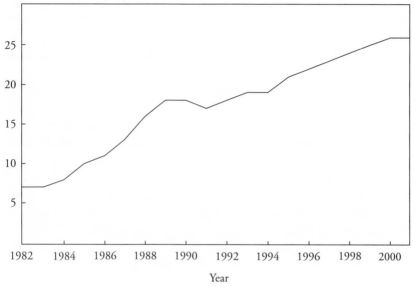

Year

Sources: Texas Transportation Institute.

most glaring example of cost overruns is the so-called Big Dig depression of Boston's central artery, considered to be the largest public works project in U.S. history. Originally projected to cost $2.3 billion in 1984, its total cost approaches $15 billion as it nears completion. On a smaller scale, but indicative of the extent of the problem, transportation officials in the Washington, D.C., region acknowledge that the cost of replacing a major highway interchange known as the "Mixing Bowl" has ballooned from the initial $220 million price tag in 1994 to $1 billion and become the region's most expensive highway project.

The motoring public is less knowledgeable about construction cost overruns than about the increase in urban automobile congestion. Vehicle-miles traveled in urban areas increased 93 percent from 1980 to 2002, while urban road mileage increased only 36 percent.[12] Average annual traffic delay incurred by motorists in major metropolitan areas has more than tripled during the past two decades (figure 4-2). The current annual costs to travelers, mainly in the form of wasted time but also including additional consumption of gasoline and vehicle wear and tear, have been estimated to run as high as $50 billion. Moreover, the annual cost of congestion to truckers, in the form of higher fuel, labor, and maintenance costs, and to shippers, in the form of higher inventories and more (perishable) goods stuck en route, adds considerably to this figure.[13]

Even when roads are widened to keep up with demand, the expanded roads shortly fill to capacity. For example, the Montgomery County, Maryland, transportation director pressed the Maryland state government to widen its Interstate 270 six years ahead of schedule to accommodate growing traffic. Maryland responded with $200 million to widen more than a dozen miles of Interstate 270, up to twelve lanes in some stretches. But fewer than eight years after the project was finished, county officials describe the highway as "a rolling parking lot."[14]

The U.S. road system represents the nation's largest civilian public investment. Nonetheless, congestion appears to have become an intractable problem because public expenditures to expand urban road capacity cannot keep up with growing automobile travel. Indeed, Clifford Winston and Ashley Langer find that one dollar of highway spending in a given year reduces congestion costs to road users only about eleven cents in that year.[15]

Economic Inefficiencies of Current Urban Transport Policy

The traditional theoretical justification for government management and operation of transit is that a private transit market would result in destructive competition.[16] Public transit agencies could maximize social net benefits by setting travelers' fares equal to the marginal cost of their trips and providing service, such as frequency and route coverage, where additional benefits to travelers equal the additional costs.[17] Government ownership and management of roads is justified on the grounds that roads are (for the most part) public goods that require enormous investments. In light of congestion and pavement wear, the public highway authority could maximize social net benefits by charging users for the particular costs they incur and by making investments where marginal benefits equal marginal costs.

Pricing and Service Inefficiencies

Large public transit deficits, low transit load factors, and severe highway congestion and pavement damage suggest that the U.S. public sector is not setting urban transportation prices and service to maximize net benefits. Clifford Winston and Chad Shirley explore this matter empirically by estimating the net benefits from two policies: replacing current transit prices and service frequency with marginal cost transit fares and optimal service frequency and setting marginal cost automobile congestion tolls.[18]

Congestion pricing has been a long-standing recommendation by economists to reduce traffic delays. The basic idea is that a road user delays other motorists when he or she travels on a road whose traffic volume is beginning to approach available road capacity. The cost of the delay that a user imposes on other motorists is based on the value that motorists place on their travel time; thus, an efficient toll would charge a motorist for this cost.

In practice, congestion tolls can be assessed with current technology that does not disrupt motorists' journeys or invade their privacy. Rather than assign a congestion cost to each motorist, the level of the tolls can be determined by a plausible estimate of what users would be willing to pay to save a minute of travel time. Naturally, tolls will be highest during peak travel times and considerably lower during off-peak periods. The higher tolls during congested travel conditions will reduce delays and smooth the traffic flow by encouraging some motorists to either take alternative routes, modify their schedules to travel during less congested times, or shift to public transit. The recent introduction of congestion pricing on high-occupancy-toll (HOT) lanes indicates that some form of road pricing has attained political acceptability.

The policy simulations summarized here are based on an equilibrium model of urban transportation pricing and service where urban commuters choose among alternative modes (auto, bus, rail, taxi, or carpool) and departure times. The effects of the pricing and service policies on consumer benefits and government balances are shown in table 4-2.[19]

The net benefits from implementing only the pricing components of this policy total nearly $8 billion a year. Because optimal pricing means much higher fares and tolls, travelers themselves lose $16 billion.[20] These private losses, however, are more than offset by the reduced public transit deficits and accumulated toll revenues that bring the urban transportation budget into balance. It is, of course, questionable whether the average citizen will see benefits in policies that increase his or her costs, even as they lower public deficits, but voters are demonstrably inclined to support elected officials who reduce government spending,[21] so travelers wearing their hats as taxpayers would likely vote for their enlightened self-interest at the ballot box. In fact, the benefits noted in table 4-2 are understated because they do not account for the cost of raising public funds (excess burden) to cover the transit deficit.

Some policymakers and analysts have tried to justify transit subsidies on second-best efficiency grounds because auto travel is implicitly subsidized—

Table 4-2. *Effects of Efficient Urban Transportation Pricing and Services in the United States*
Billions of 1998 dollars

Assumption and mode	Consumer benefits	Government balances	Net benefits
Efficient pricing only			
Auto, bus, and rail total	−16.0	23.9	7.9
Auto toll	−8.2	12.0	3.8
Bus	−4.3	7.0	2.6
Rail	−2.4	2.8	0.4
Efficient pricing and transit service frequency			
Auto, bus, and rail total	−16.2	29.3	13.0
Bus	−4.3	11.7	7.3
Rail	−2.8	4.3	1.6

Source: Clifford Winston and Chad Shirley, *Alternate Route: Toward Efficient Urban Transportation* (Brookings, 1998).

that is, travelers' costs of using their automobiles do not include the costs of congestion, pollution, and the like. The findings, however, show that overall urban transportation efficiency would improve if *any* mode's prices were aligned with its marginal costs. Current transit fares are so out of line with costs that marginal cost pricing would reduce economic waste, even if the price of using the auto remained unchanged. By the same token, raising the cost of driving to account for congestion without raising mass transit fares would also increase overall urban transportation efficiency.

Net benefits to society would climb to $13 billion a year if service frequency as well as prices were adjusted to maximize net benefits. Current transit frequency is excessive because of low ridership and oversized vehicles. Thus, cutting frequency generates benefits because public deficits are reduced by more than the value of service lost to urban travelers. Benefits would climb still further if transit's route coverage were optimized.

Finally, inefficiencies have arisen because highway charges do not explicitly account for the pavement damage caused by trucks. Road damage depends on a truck's weight per axle (the more axles a truck has for a given load, the less pavement damage) and should be covered by a user charge per mile based on axle weight. Current charges are based on the gas tax, which actually discourages truckers from using more axles because vehicles will get lower fuel economy. Indeed, in some states user charges rise with a vehicle's axles. Kenneth Small, Clifford Winston, and Carol Evans estimate that replacing the gas tax with an axle-weight tax would encourage truckers to shift to vehicles with more axles that do less damage to road pavement, thereby reducing maintenance expenditures and producing annual net welfare gains that currently approach $10 billion.[22] Despite its appeal on economic efficiency grounds, though, axle weight pricing has not been seriously considered by federal policymakers, presumably because it would be opposed by the trucking industry.

Production Inefficiencies

Public authorities have also failed to keep down the cost of urban transit and the road system. The large share of empty bus and rail seats is one indication that transit costs are too high.[23] This excess capacity also prevents transit from realizing its competitive advantage over the auto. Transit's average operating costs per *seat* mile are lower than an auto's, but its empty seats drive its operating costs per *passenger* mile above the auto's.[24] Other indications of transit inefficiency include excessive wages (the typical Washington, D.C., Metrobus driver, for example, is paid twice as much as drivers for the handful of private bus companies in the D.C. area) and declining productivity. Charles Lave estimates that transit productivity has fallen 40 percent since the public takeover in the mid-1960s.[25]

Travel on urban thoroughfares is also not produced at minimum cost. Gabriel Roth argues that highways make inefficient use of their capacity and actually run a substantial deficit when depreciation of highway capital is taken into account.[26] Small, Winston, and Evans found that highway pavement is generally too thin, which raises maintenance costs.[27] Public management of construction projects also raises costs because bureaucratic rules prevent the government from using the latest technologies, causing some investments to need upgrading shortly after completion. Project managers also specify detailed regulations that force contractors to adhere to the letter of the contract instead of seeking higher-quality, efficient alternatives. Finally, the Davis-Bacon Act, which requires that prevailing union wages must be paid on all federal construction contracts, has raised highway labor costs.

The legislative process also encourages waste. At the federal level, transportation bills are loaded with demonstration or "pork barrel" projects to ensure passage. The 1997 Transportation Equity Act for the 21st Century was larded with some $9 billion of pork, and the 2005 Safe, Accountable, Flexible, Efficient Transportation Equity Act (SAFETEA) contains some $24 billion worth of earmarked projects. Perhaps the most notorious example of wasteful spending in the 1997 act is the stretch of Interstate 99 connecting Wolfsburg and Bald Eagle, Pennsylvania. Dubbed the "Bud Shuster Highway" after the influential local congressman, the road carries less traffic in a year than the Washington, D.C., Capital Beltway carries in three days. Nonetheless, Shuster supported extending it to the tune of $400 million. The SAFETEA legislation contains the "bridge to nowhere" that has been subject to considerable attention and controversy given its $300 million price tag to connect an Alaskan island inhabited by fewer than 100 people to the mainland.

For their part, state and city officials tend to prefer urban transportation projects that entail a large federal contribution over those that could yield greater social benefits. In addition, federal legislation in 1991 may have encouraged local officials to understate the potential costs of their projects by requiring that regions craft transportation programs that included only those road and transit projects that had lined up funding. When the true, as opposed to wishful, costs of these projects have become apparent, officials have delayed other projects.

It would be expected that as the road system matures, the payoff from investments in it would decline, but inefficient highway policies also appear to have significantly reduced the rate of return from highway infrastructure investments. Shirley and Winston found that during the 1970s annual returns exceeded 15 percent, but that returns have fallen to less than 5 percent during the 1980s and 1990s.[28]

Until analysts better understand how both mass transit and the auto can benefit travelers, it is premature to say whether a more efficient urban transportation system would shift travelers from mass transit to autos or vice versa. In light of the inescapable reality that the delivery of urban transportation by the public sector is creating substantial allocative and technical inefficiencies, researchers should consider how each mode's operations would improve in a privatized environment. Unfortunately, many analysts are preoccupied with how mode shares would change if policymakers followed their advice on how to design a "better" public urban transportation system. What they fail to recognize is that current inefficiencies in the public sector are not simply a historical accident that can and will be easily corrected, but rather the predictable result of powerful political forces that are unlikely to change.

Political Forces in Urban Transportation

It is no secret that policymakers—appropriately—respond more to political forces than to market forces. Thus, the subsidies that have become a fixture in urban transit largely accrue to powerful interests—higher wages to labor, including managers, operators, and station agents, and higher profits to suppliers of transit capital. A portion, however, does go to keeping fares below cost and expanding service beyond what could be supported without subsidies. Winston and Shirley link much of transit's pricing and service inefficiencies with patrons' political influence: upper-middle-income rail riders benefit from more frequent service and route coverage, lower- and middle-income bus riders get more frequent service, and so on.[29] Indeed, the recent debate about where to put the Red Line and new rapid bus lines in Los Angeles was more about the strength of homeowner groups and less about where the lines best integrate with the city.[30]

Transit inefficiencies might be more easily overlooked if they redistributed income from the well-to-do to the poor, but with the average annual household income of bus commuters approaching $40,000, the average annual household income of rail commuters exceeding $50,000, and with train operators and station agents for the BART system in San Francisco, for example, being paid more than $40,000 a year, the poor are hardly transit's greatest beneficiaries.[31]

Highway spending also responds to strong interest groups, "pork barrel" projects being an obvious example.[32] To maintain political support for a national highway system, the allocation of funds for highway repairs appears to be based on formulas that are biased in favor of (rural) states with relatively low highway use.[33] In some cases, highway construction has been slowed because neighborhoods (in Boston and San Francisco, for example) resist demolitions for expressways that will mostly serve suburban commuting to downtown.

Efforts to implement congestion pricing on public highways have also been held hostage by politics. For example, a dispute between California public agencies and the state legislature over the redistribution of toll revenues prevented a congressionally authorized congestion toll experiment from being implemented on the San Francisco Bay Bridge.[34] In view of the wasteful spending of transportation funds, perhaps a silver lining in the nation's failure to introduce congestion pricing is that the "pot of gold" represented by congestion toll revenues has not materialized in the public sector.

A fundamental question is how much travelers are willing to pay to save travel time by having road authorities set congestion tolls on highways. John Calfee and Winston and Calfee, Winston, and Randolph Stempski suggest that in most metropolitan areas automobile travelers' willingness to pay may be lower than once thought and that most travelers do not appear to value travel time savings enough to benefit substantially from optimal tolls.[35] They contend that travelers with high values of time tend to live close to their workplaces to reduce congestion costs. It is clear in certain congested and very expensive metropolitan areas, however, that auto travelers would be willing to pay considerable sums to travel faster because they are significantly constrained from trading off housing expense for commuting time. For example, Small, Winston, and Jia Yan find that commuters in Southern California exhibit high values of travel time and reliability.[36]

Policymakers' preferred method of combating congestion has been to build more roads. As noted, however, Winston and Langer find that highway spending has been an ineffective way to reduce congestion costs.[37] Policymakers have also tried to reduce congestion by allocating reserved lanes to vehicles carrying two or more people, but recent evidence indicates that these "high-occupancy-vehicle" (HOV) lanes sometimes carry fewer people than general-purpose lanes, attract many family members who would ride together anyway, and shift some travelers from vanpools or buses to low-occupancy carpools.[38]

Recently, some urban areas have tried to fill the reserved highway capacity not used by HOVs with solo drivers willing to pay a toll. These so-called HOT lanes can be found in the Los Angeles, San Diego, Houston, and Minneapolis–St. Paul metropolitan areas. HOT lanes, however, remain questionable on efficiency grounds for two reasons. First, motorists continue to impose high congestion costs on each other because most of the highway is unpriced. Second, the express (reserved) lanes are still underused because a wide price differential exists between the two roadways.[39]

U.S. policymakers at all levels of government have shaped an urban transportation system that benefits specific travelers and suppliers, but whose welfare costs are borne by all taxpayers. As long as transit is provided by the public sector, it is difficult to see how the political forces that contribute to its current allocative and technical inefficiencies could be overcome. Indeed, Winston and Vikram Maheshri have recently estimated that virtually all urban rail transit systems are not even socially desirable—that is, the benefits they provide to users and to motorists, truckers, and shippers by reducing road congestion fall short of their subsidies—but they conclude that these systems will continue to evolve because they enjoy strong support from urban planners, suppliers of transit capital and labor, civic boosters, and city and federal policymakers.[40]

Efforts to improve the efficiency of public roads are also hamstrung by politics. During congressional debates over the SAFETEA legislation, Senator Rick Santorum warned lawmakers "not to get between a congressman and asphalt, because you will always get run over."[41] Apparently, the federal government sees no reason to change matters because recent transportation bills simply enlarge the pot of money available to road and transit interests without imposing any guidelines that would significantly improve efficiency. Privatization is therefore starting to be seen in a different light and is slowly attracting interest among transportation analysts as the only realistic hope for paring the huge inefficiencies that have developed in urban transportation under public management.

Building the Case for Privatization

Privatization and deregulation could transform the U.S. urban transportation system in the same way that deregulation has transformed U.S. intercity transport. Starting in the mid-1970s, deregulation of the railroad, trucking, and airline industries gave each the incentive and ability to become more efficient, innovative, and responsive to customers, generating more than $50 billion in annual net benefits to consumers.[42] In light of deregulation's bipartisan political support, it is puzzling that privatization conjures up ideological connotations among some policymakers instead of hope that it, combined with deregulation, can solve government failures. In fact, there is ample evidence that market forces in urban transit could accomplish a great deal of what public officials have been unable or unwilling to do. A conceptual case for privatizing roads can be made, but empirical analysis is needed.

Urban Transit

It is true that the federal government got involved in urban transit during the 1960s because private transit failed, but Peter Pashigian[43] and George Hilton[44] provide evidence that private bus operations failed because they were weakened by government regulation. John Meyer and Jose Gomez-Ibanez point out that federal policy almost made it mandatory for cities to acquire their private transit companies instead of allowing them to raise fares to become more profitable.[45] In response to those who claim that public transit's vehicle size and scale economies imply competition is unworkable in a private market. A. A. Walters argues that the extent of these economies indicates that public transit's operations are plagued by excess capacity.[46] Such inefficiencies could be substantially eliminated in a private market where operators have the incentive and ability to improve their operations.

Just how would privatization and deregulation reduce transit pricing and service inefficiencies? Winston and Shirley construct a model in which existing bus and rail companies are forced to compete with one another, as well as with automobiles, and set prices and service frequency to maximize profits.[47] They find that the effects of this competitive environment are remarkably similar to the effects of marginal cost transit pricing and optimal service frequency. Society's gains from eliminating transit deficits—private carriers would earn profits—would substantially exceed travelers' losses from higher fares and reduced service. These findings, however, greatly overstate the potential losses to travelers because they do not reflect the improvements in operations, marketing, and service that could be achieved by private transit and the impact that new entrants would have on fares and service.

Deregulation of intercity transportation revealed that regulation had substantially raised carriers' costs and inhibited marketing and service innovations.[48] Given the freedom and incentive to use the latest technologies to improve routing, scheduling, and vehicle design, private transit companies could substantially raise load factors and improve productivity. Greater competition would put downward pressure on labor and capital costs. Indeed, the competition stimulated by deregulation drove railroads', airlines', and truckers' real operating costs more than a third lower than they had been under regulation. It is likely that transit operating costs would decline similarly if bus and rail companies were privatized.[49]

Under deregulation, airlines accelerated development of hub-and-spoke route structures to increase flight frequencies, railroads introduced double-stack trains and made greater use of intermodal (truck-rail) systems to improve service times, and truckers developed high-service megacarriers. Railroads and truckers also contracted with shippers for special services, such as expedited pick-up and delivery to facilitate just-in-time inventory policies. Similar service innovations by privatized bus and rail transit companies would also benefit travelers. Possibilities include new nonstop express van and bus services, specialized scheduled and nonscheduled van services, and door-to-door services.[50] Private bus and rail companies might also find it profitable to offer premium higher-fare service with seat and schedule guarantees. Transit service innovations could also generate improvements in land use, something rarely achieved by public transit.[51]

These innovations go beyond what John R. Meyer characterizes as "transit's streetcar mentality"—scheduled stops by large buses or rail cars along a fixed route under all travel conditions. Transit operators, for example, might improve efficiency and service to travelers by providing looped express bus operations—turning some buses short instead of running all buses the full length of the route—and running minibus operations on the outer (lower density) parts of the route.[52] Indeed, intensive minibus operations have been a beneficial outcome of British bus privatization.

The deregulation experience has also shown that new market entrants, such as Southwest Airlines, often become the most efficient firms in a deregulated industry. In the transit industry, privatization could lead to intense competition supplied by paratransit operations, such as jitneys, and other low-cost operations, such as minibuses. Competition among these new entrants and conventional bus, rail, taxi, and auto modes would ensure that cost reductions would become fare reductions.[53]

Unlike airlines and trucks, railroads were deregulated because of their poor financial performance under regulation. It was expected that in pursuit of greater profitability the deregulated railroad industry would substantially reduce its operations, raise rates on much of its bulk freight, and cede much of manufactured freight to the trucking industry. Railroads have indeed pruned their systems, but they have also become more efficient and responsive to customers—offering lower (contract) rates and better service. Thus, instead of losing market share, deregulated railroads are actually carrying more freight, regaining market share, and increasing their earnings. Depending on the behavior of new entrants and what is done with the established transit authorities, there are numerous possibilities for how a privatized transit industry would supply peak and off-peak service.[54] Nonetheless, the railroads' experience suggests that an efficient transformation of the transit industry's operations, technology, pricing, and service could increase transit use and relieve taxpayers of subsidizing transit's operations.

From a political perspective, deregulation succeeded because its benefits did not accrue to the rich at the expense of the poor. To be sure, some travelers and shippers benefited more than others, but the distribution of benefits generally had a rational economic basis. Public transit authorities have not aggressively pursued, let alone achieved, laudable social goals such as improving the urban mobility of the poor.[55] Thus, a private system would not threaten to undermine any socially desirable income transfers. In fact, a private system may benefit low-income travelers because carriers would have the financial incentive and ability to develop a market for such customers. For example, Queens Van Plan, a private company, developed a highly valued and profitable service for low- to middle-income minority workers in New York's Queens and Nassau counties, who were largely neglected by public transit.[56]

Roads

Public highways are characterized by pricing and design inefficiencies, inflated labor costs and expenditures on new construction and repair, and wasteful projects. Public authorities' delays in adopting technological innovations that could substantially improve the speed and safety of highway travel may also emerge as a large social cost.

At this point, the appeal of highway privatization in U.S. cities and inter-city stretches is conceptual. Empirical evidence on its potential effects is not yet available. Thus, I believe it is premature to recommend privatizing U.S. highways, but it is worth considering how market forces could reduce highway inefficiencies.

Let us begin with pricing. The conventional criticism of current road pricing is that it does not account for congestion. I have presented estimates of the benefits of congestion pricing in the United States based on an average value of travelers' willingness to pay to save travel time. Travelers, however, differ—sometimes greatly—in how much they are willing to pay for transport capacity. For example, in airline travel some business travelers are willing to pay the large costs that airlines incur for making seats available to them when they travel at the last moment. At the other extreme, some pleasure travelers make an effort to get low fares by planning their trips far in advance and being flexible about which day of the week they can travel. Other air travelers have preferences and constraints that fall between these extremes, and their fares are set accordingly. Thus, by offering a range of fares and associated travel restrictions, the deregulated airline industry has greatly improved the use of its aircraft capacity and benefited travelers.

Some highway commuters are willing to pay a great deal to get to work much faster on a particular day, whereas others are not willing to pay much to speed up their trip.[57] Highway capacity could be used more efficiently if motorists were offered a range of prices and service levels (for example, travelers could choose among high-priced lanes with little congestion and lower-priced lanes with more congestion).

As noted, a few U.S. highways have made a start in this direction by introducing HOT lanes that enable solo drivers to pay a toll to use less congested carpool lanes. By varying thoughout the day, the toll more accurately reflects the value the road provides over alternate routes. But as Small points out, second-best pricing distortions may arise in highway travel because one or a few lanes are tolled, but free alternate lanes and routes are close at hand.[58] Small, Winston, and Yan provide an empirical analysis of motorists' behavior on California Route 91 in greater Los Angeles and show that the efficient (first-best) policy is to price all lanes (and alternate highways) in accordance with traffic conditions and travelers' willingness to pay to save travel time.[59] The authors also show that highway tolls could be adjusted to meet political feasibility constraints and, by accounting for differences in motorists' preferences, could still generate significant welfare gains.

Could competition among highways develop and produce efficient tolls? New Zealand is considering a bold first step, called commercialization, where the government turns its roads over to commercial road companies, which would be expected to charge for their use and earn a return on capital while being regulated as public utilities. Such a policy would be problematic in the United States, where government regulation of public utilities is renowned for creating inefficiencies. Others have suggested that the U.S. government franchise highways to private companies, though the devil would still be in the operating and financial constraints that the government placed on franchised companies and whether competition could evolve in light of these constraints.

Intercity deregulation offers a potentially useful analogy for solving this problem. Deregulated carriers have had to compete against each other, and in a certain sense against consumer "organizations." For example, railroads set most of their rates through contract negotiations with shippers. Among other factors, rates are affected by a shipper's traffic volume and competitive options. Shippers can improve their bargaining position by increasing their traffic volume as part of a group of firms that negotiates rates and by playing off one railroad against potential sources of competition. These sources include other railroads in the market, other railroads reasonably close to the shipper, plants that compete with the shipper's plant in the product market, alternative origins from which the receiver could use alternative railroads to receive a product, alternative modes such as truck and barge, and so on. By enhancing their bargaining power, shippers can fully realize the benefits of rail freight competition. Similarly, the benefits of airline competition are enhanced when travelers negotiate as a group to get lower fares or encourage a new entrant to provide service when they are dissatisfied with incumbent carriers.

Could highway users help road competition develop by organizing as bargaining units that negotiate prices and service? Suppose the government distributes roads to commercial companies, as in commercialization, but aims to allocate potentially competitive intercity stretches (for example, California's Highway 101 and Interstate 5) and urban freeways and arterials to different companies. As in the railroad industry, a "contract equilibrium" could develop where private companies negotiate prices (long-term contracts) with private organizations representing motorists, truckers, railroads, private transit companies, and public-sector transport. Public and private users en masse would therefore be able to bring competitive discipline on prices.

What would these prices look like? Customer groups would likely prefer a range of prices and levels of service. For example, FedEx and other time-sensitive companies would want a lane (or even separate roads) to be available at a premium price. And time-sensitive automobile travelers would probably be willing to pay high tolls for travel on a less congested lane. It would take time for private road companies to explore various services that users were willing to pay for and for users' preferences to crystallize. But after that transition, the benefits could be large. Firms, and ultimately consumers, and households would gain from savings of travel time. Out-of-pocket highway travel expenses would increase, especially for those who desire premium uncongested service, but price increases would be mitigated by users, and taxpayers, in general, would benefit from the lower cost of building, maintaining, and operating highways.

Profit-seeking private road companies would have strong incentives to shed the inefficiencies developed over decades in the public sector. Cost-cutting measures would include using axle-weight truck taxes to charge for pavement damage, building stronger pavement, placing much more control over construction and repair expenditures, reducing wages and managerial waste, and eliminating politically motivated projects.

Private road companies could improve the speed and safety of urban (and intercity) highway travel by implementing an intelligent transportation system (ITS). The system could include centrally controlled traffic signals, electronic toll collection, message signs about traffic conditions, and traffic control centers that, as needed, dispatch emergency vehicles, adjust signal timing, and relay important road information to motorists. Under government management, the high-tech promises of this system could be compromised. One only has to think of the Federal Aviation Administration's management of air traffic control to understand how the U.S. government would raise the cost and slow the implementation of ITS.[60]

The possibility of turning U.S. roads over to private companies will seem less far-fetched as the inefficiencies caused by the public sector increase and become more widely known. The best way to implement this experiment and estimates of its economic effects await further research.[61]

Of course, it is not sufficient to make a convincing case that privatization of urban transportation would enhance economic efficiency and expect the policy to be adopted. I have indicated that current urban transportation policy harms taxpayers and benefits certain interest groups such as transit labor and managers, suppliers of transit capital, beneficiaries of pork barrel highway projects, and subsidized users. Privatization may have adverse effects on some of these groups—while benefiting taxpayers and the traveling public—but, most important, privatization would mean that policymakers at all levels of government no longer have a large and steady supply of funds for transportation projects. Indeed, the most important and politically sensitive redistributive effect of privatization may be that it threatens one of the most visible ways that elected officials reward their supporters.

The British Experience with Urban Transport Privatization

Urban transport in the United Kingdom suffers from many of the same economic problems. Prices for all modes fall short of efficient prices,[62] urban bus and rail transit require large subsidies, road congestion is severe, and transit and highway infrastructure is in poor condition, but funds are not available to finance required investments. Unlike the United States, however, the United Kingdom has begun to address some of these problems by privatizing and deregulating part of its urban transport system.

The Transport Acts of 1980 and 1985 largely privatized and deregulated the bus industry in the United Kingdom, with the exception of London and Northern Ireland. Although buses operating within London were not deregulated, individual routes were put out for competitive tender. Under the 1985 act, public or private bus companies could offer virtually any bus service they deemed profitable by giving local authorities forty-two days' (three fortnights') notice. The seventy subsidiaries of the National Bus Company, a nationalized entity, were sold, and the other publicly managed bus companies that had dominated local bus service were reorganized as separate for-profit corporations. Many of these companies were subsequently sold to the private sector while those that remained public could no longer receive direct government subsidies. Local authorities could supplement commercial routes by subsidizing additional services that they felt were justified by social concerns, but these services had to be secured through competitive bidding.

The privatized U.K. bus industry has consolidated to a great extent and is currently dominated by large bus companies such as Stagecoach. Nonetheless, the economic effects of the transport acts have been broadly consistent with the predictions of bus privatization and deregulation in the United States.[63] Peter White found that improvements in labor productivity, lower wages, and lower fuel and maintenance costs for minibuses—a major service innovation—reduced real bus operating costs.[64] David Kennedy found that competitive tendering for bus routes in London also lowered operating costs.[65] As costs have fallen and fares have risen, the government has reduced bus subsidies from £237 million in 1985 to £117 million in 1998. Bus ridership has declined roughly a quarter, but in some areas of the country ridership has increased in response to intensive minibus operations.[66] Just three years after privatization, minibuses providing local service outside of London have grown from a few hundred to nearly 7,000.[67] Minibuses operate at higher average speeds and offer greater frequencies than conventional buses, and their smaller sizes and maneuverability allow some operators to offer "hail and ride" service in which the minibus will stop at any point on the route to pick up and discharge passengers. White and others estimate that travelers have benefited substantially from minibus services that have expanded into suburban areas.[68]

The United Kingdom has not privatized inner-city rail operations, but in March 1998 Deputy Prime Minister John Prescott announced that the London Transport Group (now London Underground Limited) will award three private-sector contracts to maintain and modernize the London Underground. Successful bidders will be responsible for track, signals, and stations, though trains will continue to operate within the public sector. The reform is expected to reduce rail infrastructure costs and the Underground's annual subsidy (now some £100 million). The economic effects of this policy will also depend on the rental charges that the public authority must pay the private companies to use the renewed facilities.

The United Kingdom has taken no steps to privatize roads, but in 2003 under the leadership of Mayor Ken Livingstone, a £5 toll was introduced for motorists who wish to enter London's Inner Ring on weekdays between the hours of 7 a.m. and 7 p.m. By achieving its goals of noticeably reducing traffic and increasing vehicle speeds, the toll has attracted the attention of city officials throughout the world.

Budgetary pressures, rather than concern with allocative and technical inefficiencies created by the public sector, are motivating the United Kingdom's privatization efforts in urban bus operations and rail infrastructure. From a U.S. perspective, the U.K. experience is encouraging because it demonstrates that transit privatization and deregulation can reduce costs and spur innovative services such as minibuses.[69] On the other hand, policymakers in the United States have yet to express much concern about transit deficits, as indicated by recent transportation bills that increase federal spending for transit (and highways). Thus, it is not clear what will induce the United States to pursue privatization.

Final Comments

Intercity deregulation in the United States became politically attractive in the 1970s when the political benefits to policymakers from working in harness with carriers and labor were overwhelmed by the potential political gains from reducing inflation. When policymakers were ready to act, academic research was available to guide their understanding of the likely effects of deregulation.

Similarly, the probability of privatizing urban transport in the United States will increase if the prospect of major political gain becomes clear. Unfortunately, it will not in the near future because policymakers do not appear to be under significant pressure to cut wasteful spending on urban transportation. Indeed, the recent standoff between Congress and the White House over the SAFETEA legislation revolved around how much federal transportation spending would *increase*. Nonetheless, researchers should continue to explore the effects of privatization and provide guidance for how cities can conduct privatization experiments. There is no escaping the evidence that the U.S. government's activity in this area is marked by failure. Research should be available when the promise of political gains beckons policymakers to acknowledge this failure.

Notes

1. This chapter updates an article entitled "Government Failure in Urban Transportation" that was originally published in *Fiscal Studies,* vol. 21, no. 4 (2000): 403–25.

2. It would be preferable to measure bus and rail capacity in terms of seat miles instead of vehicles miles. Information on seat miles, however, is available from the American Public Transit Association only since 1980. On the basis of these data, bus and heavy rail seating capacity has remained relatively constant, while light rail's seating capacity has increased somewhat. Thus, using vehicle miles instead of seat miles understates the recent growth of light rail capacity but does not have much impact on the growth of bus and heavy rail capacity.

3. See Clifford Winston and Chad Shirley, *Alternate Route: Toward Efficient Urban Transportation* (Brookings, 1998).

4. American Public Transit Association, *Transit Fact Book* (various issues).

5. These mode shares are based on decennial censuses.

6. Passenger counts and mode shares for all types of trips are available from the U.S. Federal Highway Administration, *National Household Travel Survey* (Washington, D.C.:

U.S. Department of Transportation, 2001). Because the sample sizes are generally considered small, national estimates derived from these data should be regarded as preliminary. Nonetheless, the data reveal trends and magnitudes that are consistent with those based on reliable samples of work trips.

7. Winston and Shirley, *Alternate Route: Toward Efficient Urban Transportation.*

8. Operating subsidies are from the American Public Transit Association, *2002 Transit Fact Book,* and capital subsidies are from the National Transit Administration, *2004 National Transit Database* (Washington, D.C.: U.S. Department of Transportation, 2004).

9. Don H. Pickrell, "Rising Deficits and the Uses of Transit Subsidies in the United States," *Journal of Transport Economics and Policy,* vol. 19 (September 1985): 281–98; and Douglass B. Lee, *Evaluation of Federal Transit Operating Subsidies,* Transportation Systems Center, U.S. Department of Transportation, 1987.

10. Metropolitan Statistics, Los Angeles, cited in Todd S. Purdum, "LA Subway Reaches End of the Line," *New York Times,* June 6, 2000, p. A1.

11. Alan Sipress, "Transportation Plan Reveals Funding Gap," *Washington Post,* July 13, 2000, p. A1.

12. U.S. Federal Highway Administration, *Highway Statistics,* various years.

13. Estimates of the costs of automobile congestion to motorists are produced by the Texas Transportation Institute at Texas A&M University.

14. This is partly an outcome of Downs's law: on urban commuter expressways, peak-hour traffic congestion rises to meet maximum capacity, because commuters shift from less preferred modes and times of day. See Anthony Downs, "The Law of Peak-Hour Expressway Congestion," *Traffic Quarterly,* vol. 16 (July 1962): 393.

15. Clifford Winston and Ashley Langer, "The Effect of Government Highway Expenditures on Road Users' Congestion Costs," *Journal of Urban Economics* (forthcoming, 2006).

16. Government intervention has also been justified on the grounds of "Hotelling" bunching—competing transit companies would arrive at bus stops or rail stations at the same time. Bunching, however, occurs quite frequently in most public transit systems.

17. If transit companies operate where there are increasing returns to scale, this first-best policy will require some subsidy because marginal costs are below average costs. If no subsidies are available (an unlikely situation in public transit), Ramsey pricing represents the efficient second-best policy where the percentage mark-up of fares above marginal cost is inversely related to travelers' demand elasticities subject to a break-even constraint.

18. Winston and Shirley, *Alternate Route: Toward Efficient Urban Transportation.* Optimal transit frequency is the level of bus and rail frequency that maximizes net benefits, which are composed of the changes in travelers' benefits, congestion toll revenues, bus revenues and costs, and rail revenues and costs.

19. Consumer benefits are measured by compensating variations that are based on the joint choice model of mode and departure time. Changes in government balances are based on changes in bus revenues and costs, rail revenues and costs, and toll revenues.

20. Congestion pricing provides benefits to peak-period auto travelers in the form of shorter travel time. The losses to travelers are net of these benefits.

21. Sam Peltzman, "Voters as Fiscal Conservatives," *Quarterly Journal of Economics,* vol. 107 (May 1992): 327–61; and Clifford Winston and Robert W. Crandall, "Explaining Regulatory Policy," *BPEA: Microeconomics* (1994), pp. 1–49.

22. Kenneth A. Small, Clifford Winston, and Carol A. Evans, *Road Work: A New Highway Pricing and Investment Policy* (Brookings, 1989).

23. Transit's inherent operations—gradually increasing ridership in the primary commuting direction and consistently low ridership for the reverse commute—suggest that even an efficient transit system is unlikely to achieve average load factors that exceed 50 percent. But public transit's average load factor is far below that figure and has been declining for some time. It was 22 percent in 1975, 18 percent in 1985, and 16 percent in 1995.

24. Winston and Shirley, *Alternate Route: Toward Efficient Urban Transportation*.

25. Charles Lave, "Measuring the Decline in Transit Productivity in the U.S.," *Transportation Planning and Technology*, vol. 15 (1991): 115–24.

26. Gabriel Roth, *Roads in a Market Economy* (Hants, U.K.: Avebury Technical, 1996).

27. Small, Winston, and Evans, *Road Work: A New Highway Pricing and Investment Policy*.

28. Chad Shirley and Clifford Winston, "Firm Inventory Behavior and the Returns from Highway Infrastructure Investment," *Journal of Urban Economics*, vol. 55 (March 2004): 398–415.

29. Winston and Shirley, *Alternate Route: Toward Efficient Urban Transportation*.

30. Glenn Gritzner and Katherine Perez, "Something is Missing in this Red Line Picture," *Los Angeles Times*, July 10, 2000, p.1, metro section.

31. Winston and Shirley, in *Alternate Route: Toward Efficient Urban Transportation*, summarize evidence concluding that public transit programs such as reverse commuting, which are designed to give low-income people greater access to suburban jobs, have not met with much success.

32. Diana Evans, "Policy and Pork: The Use of Pork Barrel Projects to Build Policy Coalitions in the House of Representatives," *American Journal of Political Science*, vol. 38 (November 1994): 894–917. Evans shows that the inclusion of highway demonstration projects is important to securing passage of legislation authorizing the nation's highway and transit programs.

33. Ronald N. Johnson and Gary D. Libecap, "Political Processes and the Common Pool Problem: The Federal Highway Trust Fund," working paper, University of Arizona, Department of Economics, June 2000.

34. Stephen Shmanske, "The Bay Bridge Blunder," *Regulation*, vol. 19 (1996): 58–64.

35. John E. Calfee and Clifford Winston, "The Value of Automobile Travel Time: Implications for Congestion Policy," *Journal of Public Economics*, vol. 69 (September 1998): 83–102; John E. Calfee, Clifford Winston, and Randolph Stempski, "Econometric Issues in Estimating Consumer Preferences from Stated Preference Data: A Case Study of the Value of Automobile Travel Time," *Review of Economics and Statistics*, vol. 83 (November 2001): 699–707.

36. Kenneth A. Small, Clifford Winston, and Jia Yan, "Differentiated Road Pricing, Express Lanes, and Carpools: Exploiting Heterogeneous Preferences in Policy Design," in *Brookings-Wharton Papers on Urban Affairs*, edited by Gary Burtless and Janet Rothenberg Pack (Brookings, 2006, forthcoming).

37. Winston and Langer, "The Effect of Government Highway Expenditures on Road Users' Congestion Costs." Similarly, policymakers' preferred approach to reducing road

damage is to repair roads. They have not pursued efficient road wear taxes that would encourage truckers to shift to trucks that do less damage to the roads.

38. See Kenneth Orski, "Carpool Lanes: An Idea Whose Time Has Come and Gone," *TR News*, vol. 214 (May–June 2001): 24–28; and Robert W. Poole Jr. and Ted Balaker, "Virtual Exclusive Busways: Improving Urban Transit While Relieving Congestion," *Reason Foundation Policy Study*, vol. 337 (2005).

39. Kenneth A. Small and Jia Yan, "The Value of 'Value Pricing' of Roads: Second-Best Pricing and Product Differentiation," *Journal of Urban Economics*, vol. 49 (2001): 310–36.

40. Clifford Winston and Vikram Maheshri, "On the Social Desirability of Urban Rail Transit Systems," *Journal of Urban Economics* (forthcoming, 2006).

41. Christopher Lee, "Highway Bill Passes Senate, Faces Opposition From Bush," *Washington Post*, February 13, 2004, p. A4.

42. Clifford Winston, "U.S. Industry Adjustment to Economic Deregulation," *Journal of Economic Perspectives*, vol. 12 (Summer 1998): 89–110.

43. Peter B. Pashigian, "Consequences and Causes of Public Ownership of Urban Transit Facilities," *Journal of Political Economy*, vol. 84 (December 1976): 1239–59.

44. George W. Hilton, "The Rise and Fall of Monopolized Transit," in *Urban Transit: The Private Challenge in Public Transportation*, edited by Charles Lave (Boston: Ballinger Press, 1985), pp. 31–48.

45. John R. Meyer and Jose A. Gomez-Ibanez, *Autos, Transit, and Cities* (Harvard University Press, 1981).

46. A. A. Walters, "Externalities in Urban Buses," *Journal of Urban Economics*, vol. 11 (January 1982): 60–72.

47. Winston and Shirley, *Alternate Route: Toward Efficient Urban Transportation*.

48. See Winston, "U.S. Industry Adjustment to Economic Deregulation," and Steven A. Morrison and Clifford Winston, "Regulatory Reform of U.S. Intercity Transportation," in *Essays in Transportation Economics and Policy: A Handbook in Honor of John R. Meyer*, edited by Jose A. Gomez-Ibanez, William B. Tye, and Clifford Winston (Brookings, 1999), pp. 469–92.

49. Indianapolis is one of the few U.S. cities that has privatized its transit system. See Matthew Karlaftis and Patrick McCarthy, "The Effect of Privatization on Public Transit Costs," *Journal of Regulatory Economics*, vol. 16 (1999): 27–43. Karlaftis and McCarthy estimate that although the system is producing more vehicle miles and passenger miles, its operating costs have declined 2.5 percent annually since privatization. These savings are primarily efficiency gains, not transfers from transit labor.

50. See, for example, Volpe National Transportation Systems Center, *Autonomous Dial-a-Ride Transit*, U.S. Department of Transportation, November 1998.

51. Don H. Pickrell, "Transportation and Land Use," in *Essays in Transportation Economics and Policy*, edited by Gomez-Ibanez, Tye, and Winston, pp. 403–36.

52. See Paul Domenic Kerin, "Efficient Transit Management Strategies and Public Policies: Radial Commuter Arteries," Ph.D. dissertation, Harvard University, 1990.

53. It would be desirable to deregulate taxis as part of a broader strategy to stimulate competition in urban transport. No longer enjoying a secure niche between the private car and the city bus or rail service, taxis would be forced, for example, to compete with vans

that operate like taxis and offer links with rail and bus operations. The increased competition and coordination in the new urban transit system should lower taxi fares, improve service quality, and enable taxi operations to impose some competitive pressure on transit.

54. One strategy transit companies might pursue is to set capacity for off-peak periods and rely on part-time labor to develop peak capacity with extra scheduling and looping. Competition from private jitneys and other services with scheduled bus operations could be gradually introduced following the property rights approach developed by Daniel B. Klein, Adrian T. Moore, and Binyam Rega in *Curb Rights: A Foundation for Free Enterprise in Urban Transit* (Brookings, 1997).

55. Winston and Shirley, *Alternate Route: Toward Efficient Urban Transportation.*

56. Hector Ricketts, "Roadblocks Made Just for Vans," *New York Times,* November 22, 1997, p. A15.

57. Kenneth A. Small, Clifford Winston, and Jia Yan, "Uncovering the Distribution of Motorists' Preferences for Travel Time and Reliability," *Econometrica,* vol. 73 (July 2005): 1367–82.

58. Kenneth A. Small, "Pitfalls of Road Pricing Demonstrations," working paper, University of California, Irvine, Department of Economics, November 2000.

59. Small, Winston, and Yan, "Differentiated Road Pricing, Express Lanes, and Carpools: Exploiting Heterogeneous Preferences in Policy Design."

60. Air traffic control has been criticized for decades for cost overruns and delays in introducing new technology that would make air travel safer and faster. Most recently, it has been under the gun for failing to introduce Global Positioning System technology that could enable air carriers to choose speedier flight paths and to take off and land more quickly.

61. Privatization of roads could (and probably should) be introduced sequentially beginning with bridges and bottleneck thoroughfares and moving to entire highways. Indeed, an important experiment has developed as a private consortium has recently purchased the Chicago Skyway Tollway.

62. John Peirson and Roger Vickerman, "The Environment, Efficient Pricing, and Investment in Transport: A Model and Some Results for the U.K.," in *Transport Policy and the Environment,* edited by David Banister (London: Spon Press, 1998), pp. 161–75.

63. Winston and Shirley, *Alternate Route: Toward Efficient Urban Transportation.*

64. Peter R. White, "The Experience of Bus and Coach Deregulation in Britain and in Other Countries," *International Journal of Transport Economics,* vol. 24 (February 1997): 35–52.

65. David Kennedy, "London Bus Tendering: The Impact on Costs," *International Review of Applied Economics,* vol. 9 (1995): 27–43.

66. Bus ridership had been declining before privatization. In light of this trend, one must be careful about attributing all of the recent decline in ridership to privatization.

67. Jose A. Gomez-Ibanez and John R. Meyer, *Going Private: The International Experience with Transport Privatization* (Brookings, 1993).

68. Peter R. White and others, "Cost Benefit Analysis of Urban Minibus Operations," *Transportation,* vol. 19 (1992): 59–74.

69. Gomez-Ibanez and Meyer, in *Going Private,* support this conclusion based on the privatization experience in several countries, including the United Kingdom.

5

Achieving Fundamental Housing Policy Reform

Edgar O. Olsen

Housing assistance is a major part of the U.S. welfare system. Federal, state, and local governments spend about $50 billion a year on it. The most serious shortcoming of the current system of low-income housing assistance is its excessive reliance on unit-based programs that serve about two-thirds of assisted households. Evidence indicates that recipient-based housing vouchers provide equally good housing at a much lower total cost than any program of unit-based assistance. Therefore, it would be possible to serve current recipients equally well (that is, provide them with equally good housing for the same rent), serve many additional families, and reduce taxes by shifting resources from unit-based to recipient-based assistance. This would involve terminating or phasing out current production programs, disengaging from unit-based assistance to existing apartments as soon as current contractual commitments permit, and avoiding new programs of unit-based assistance. Since almost all individuals who do not receive low-income housing assistance will gain from these reforms because of their concern for assisted households or their lower taxes, and many low-income individuals who have not been offered housing assistance will also benefit from receiving assistance, the question is why these reforms have not been adopted.

The primary purposes of this chapter are to provide answers to the preceding question and suggest how the obstacles to reform can be overcome. Among the surmountable obstacles are widespread ignorance of the evidence on the cost-effectiveness of different types of housing assistance, dispersed congressional oversight of the different programs that provide low-income housing assistance, and the fear of unexpected negative consequences of major reforms.

The chapter is organized as follows. The first section provides an overview of the current system of low-income housing assistance. The second summarizes the evidence on the cost-effectiveness of different housing programs. The third discusses the other major advantage of recipient-based housing assistance. The fourth addresses the main objections to exclusive reliance on recipient-based assistance. The fifth describes concrete proposals for phasing out unit-based housing assistance. The sixth discusses the obstacles to the proposed reforms and suggests practical ways to overcome them. The seventh summarizes the chapter.

Overview of Current System of Low-Income Housing Assistance

The U.S. government provides assistance to live in rental and owner-occupied housing.[1] The most important distinction between rental housing programs is whether the subsidy is attached to the dwelling unit or the assisted household. If the subsidy is attached to a rental dwelling unit, each family must accept the particular unit offered if it is to receive assistance and loses the subsidy when it moves. Each family offered recipient-based rental assistance has a choice among many units that meet the program's standards, and the family can retain its subsidy when it moves. The analogous distinction for homeownership programs is between programs that authorize selected developers to build a limited number of houses to sell to eligible families of their choosing and require eligible families to buy from these builders to receive a subsidy, and programs that provide subsidies to eligible families that are free to buy from any seller.

There are two broad types of unit-based rental assistance—namely, public housing and privately owned subsidized projects. Public housing projects are owned and operated by local public housing authorities established by local governments. The overwhelming majority of projects were newly built for the program. Until 1969, with minor exceptions, federal taxpayers paid the initial development cost of public housing and tenants and local taxpayers paid the operating cost. Now, however, the federal government provides local housing authorities with substantial operating and modernization subsidies. In the public housing program, civil servants make all of the decisions made by private owners of unsubsidized housing in addition to enforcing the program's regulations.

The federal government also contracts with private parties to provide unit-based assistance in subsidized housing projects. The majority of these private parties are for-profit firms, but nonprofit organizations have a significant presence. The largest programs of this type are the Internal Revenue Service's Low Income Housing Tax Credit (LIHTC), the U.S. Department of Housing and Urban Development's (HUD) Section 8 New Construction/ Substantial Rehabilitation and Section 236, and the U.S. Department of Agriculture's (USDA) Section 515/521. Under most programs, these private parties agreed to provide rental housing meeting certain standards at restricted rents to households with particular characteristics for a specified number of years. The overwhelming majority of the projects were newly built under a subsidized construction program. Almost all of the rest were substantially rehabilitated as a condition for participation in the program. It is important to realize that none of these programs provides subsidies to all suppliers who would like to participate. Because subsidies are provided to selected private suppliers, the market mechanism does not ensure that subsidies are passed along to occupants of the subsidized units. If this is to be achieved at all, administrative mechanisms must be used. Without these mechanisms, suppliers would provide a level of housing services so that the marginal occupant of the project would receive no net benefit from the program and no additional eligible families would want to live in the project. Furthermore, suppliers would receive a higher return on their investment of time and money than they could earn in the unsubsidized market.

The federal government has administered two large homeownership programs for low-income households—namely, USDA's Section 502 Single Family Direct Loan Housing Program and HUD's Section 235 Homeownership Program. Section 502 provides recipient-based assistance. The larger component of Section 235 provided assistance tied to construction of particular dwelling units. The smaller existing housing component used a procedure for allocating subsidies that had elements of unit-based and recipient-based assistance. Since their establishment, these programs have subsidized about 2.5 million families.

The federal government also provides funds to state and local governments intended to subsidize the housing of low-income families. The HOME Investment Partnerships Program is a housing block grant that has been used to provide rental and homeownership subsidies. Under the Mortgage Revenue Bond Program, state housing agencies issue bonds whose interest is not subject to the federal individual income tax and use the proceeds to provide below-market-rate loans to low-income, first-time homebuyers. Finally, about a third of the funding of the Community Development Block Grant Program is used to provide housing assistance to low- and moderate-income families. State and local governments operate programs of unit-based and recipient-based assistance with the funding from these programs.

Unit-based rental assistance is the dominant form of direct federal housing assistance to low-income families.[2] The overwhelming majority of recipients receive rental assistance, and more than 70 percent of families served by low-income rental housing programs receive unit-based assistance. HUD provides unit-based rental assistance to more than three million families, the Low-Income Housing Tax Credit provides it to more than a million families, and the USDA's Section 515/521 program houses almost a half million families in subsidized projects. HUD's Section 8 Housing Voucher Program accounts for almost all recipient-based rental housing assistance, and even this program now allows housing agencies to devote as much as 20 percent of their vouchers to unit-based assistance.

Evidence on Cost-Effectiveness of Different Housing Programs

The most important finding of the empirical literature on the effects of different housing programs from the viewpoint of housing policy is that recipient-based housing assistance has provided equally good housing at a much lower cost than any type of unit-based assistance.

Four major studies have estimated both the total cost per unit and the mean market rent of apartments provided by housing vouchers and the largest older production programs, namely, Public Housing, Section 236, and Section 8 New Construction.[3] These studies are based on data from a wide variety of housing markets and for projects built in many different years. Two were expensive studies conducted for HUD by a respected research firm during the Nixon, Ford, Carter, and Reagan administrations. They are unanimous in finding that housing vouchers provide equally desirable housing at a much lower total cost than any of these production programs, even though all of these studies are biased in favor of the production programs to some extent by the omission of certain indirect costs.

The studies with the most detailed information about the characteristics of the housing provided by the programs found the largest excess costs for the production programs. Specifically, Mayo and others estimated the excessive cost of public housing compared to housing vouchers for providing equally desirable housing to be 64 percent and 91 percent, respectively, in the two cities studied and the excessive cost of Section 236 to be 35 percent and 75 percent in these cities. Another study with excellent data on housing characteristics estimated the excessive cost of Section 8 New Construction compared to recipient-based Section 8 Certificates to range from 44 percent to 78 percent.[4]

Recent Government Accountability Office (GAO) studies produced similar results for the major active construction programs—LIHTC, HOPE (Housing Opportunities for People Everywhere) VI, Section 202, Section 515, and Section 811.[5] The excess total cost estimates based on the conceptually preferable life cycle approach range from 12 percent for Section 811 to 27 percent for HOPE VI.[6] These estimates are lower bounds on the excessive cost because some costs of the production programs were omitted. Most notably, the opportunity cost of the land and cost of preparing the site were omitted from the cost of HOPE VI projects. These are real costs to society of HOPE VI redevelopment. Furthermore, some costs of each production program were omitted. For example, some projects under each program receive local property tax abatements. The preceding results ignore this cost to local taxpayers.[7]

It is often argued that production programs work better than recipient-based vouchers in the tightest housing markets. The GAO study contains evidence concerning whether production programs are more cost-effective than recipient-based vouchers in housing markets with low vacancy rates. In addition to the national estimates, the GAO collected data for seven metropolitan areas. The data for the GAO study refer to projects built in 1999. In that year, the rental vacancy rates in the seven metropolitan areas ranged from 3.1 percent in Boston to 7.2 percent in Baltimore and Dallas, with a median of 5.6 percent. The overall rental vacancy rate in U.S. metropolitan areas was 7.8 percent. Thus, all of the specific markets studied were tighter than average. Only five of the largest seventy-five metropolitan areas had vacancy rates lower than Boston's. In each market, recipient-based vouchers were more cost-effective than each production program studied.[8]

Unlike the earlier cost-effectiveness studies, the GAO study did not compare the total cost of dwellings under the different programs that were the same with respect to many characteristics. Instead, it simply compared the average cost of dwellings with the same number of bedrooms in the same metropolitan area or the same type of location (metropolitan or nonmetropolitan). It has been argued that the GAO results overstate the excessive costs of the production programs for providing equally desirable housing because these programs provide better housing than the units occupied by voucher recipients. The available evidence does not support the view.[9]

The difference in cost-effectiveness between recipient-based and unit-based housing assistance has major implications for the number of households that can be served with the current budget. If we compare programs of recipient-based and unit-based assistance that serve recipients equally well—that is, provide them with equally good housing for the same rent—the unit-based programs will serve many fewer families with a given budget. No credible evidence shows that any type of unit-based assistance is as cost-effective as recipient-based vouchers in any market conditions or for any special groups. Therefore, many eligible families and the taxpayers who want to help them will gain if recipient-based assistance replaces unit-based assistance.

The magnitude of the gain from shifting from unit-based to recipient-based rental assistance would be substantial. Even the smallest estimates of the excess costs of unit-based assistance imply that shifting ten families from unit-based to recipient-based assistance would enable us to serve two additional families. Because the federal government provides unit-based rental housing assistance to more than 4.5 million families, a total shift from unit-based to recipient-based assistance would enable us to serve at least 900,000 additional families with no additional budget. The most reliable estimates in the literature imply much larger increases in the number of families served. For example, the Abt study of the Section 8 New Construction Program implies that recipient-based vouchers could have provided all of the families who participated in this program with equally good housing for the same rent and served at least 72 percent more families with similar characteristics equally well without any additional budget.[10]

Other Major Advantage of Recipient-Based Housing Assistance

Recipient-based assistance has another major advantage over unit-based assistance, in addition to providing equally desirable housing at a lower cost. It allows each recipient to occupy a dwelling unit with a combination of characteristics preferred to the specific unit offered under a program of unit-based assistance, without affecting adversely taxpayer interests. With recipient-based assistance, a recipient can occupy any unit meeting the program's minimum housing standards.[11] The program's standards reflect the interests of taxpayers who want to help low-income families with their housing. Units that meet the program's standards and are affordable to assisted families differ greatly with respect to their characteristics, neighborhood, and location. Assisted families whose options are the same under a program of recipient-based assistance are not indifferent toward the units available to them. Each family will choose the best available option for their tastes and circumstances. Because all of these units are adequate as judged by the program's minimum housing standards, restricting their choice further serves no public purpose. Unit-based assistance forces each family to live in a particular unit to receive a subsidy. Thus, it greatly restricts recipient choice among units meeting minimum housing standards without serving any public purpose. If the subsidy is the same, it is reasonable to expect recipients of recipient-based assistance to be significantly better off than they would be with unit-based assistance.

Objections to Exclusive Reliance on Recipient-Based Assistance

Although most participants in housing policy debates favor some role for recipient-based assistance, many see a role, in some cases a large one, for unit-based assistance. The two most common objections to exclusive reliance on recipient-based assistance are that recipient-based assistance cannot be used in markets with the lowest vacancy rates and construction programs have an advantage compared with recipient-based assistance that offsets their cost-ineffectiveness—namely, they promote neighborhood revitalization to a much greater extent. This section addresses these objections to exclusive reliance on recipient-based housing assistance and one argument for eliminating this type of assistance altogether.

Taken literally, the argument that recipient-based housing assistance cannot be used in the tightest housing markets is clearly incorrect in that Section 8 housing vouchers have been used continuously in all housing markets for almost three decades. A more precise version of this argument is that recipient-based assistance will not work well in some markets because they do not have enough affordable vacant apartments that meet minimum housing standards to house all families offered vouchers and hence new construction must be subsidized to serve additional low-income households in these areas. This view is inconsistent with evidence on the performance of the Section 8 Housing Voucher Program. Data on utilization rates in the Voucher Program collected by HUD's Office of Policy Development and Research in 2002 and rental vacancy rates in the seventy-five largest metropolitan areas from the U.S. Bureau of the Census indicate that the voucher utilization rate does not depend on market tightness. Because the Census Bureau does not produce vacancy rates for smaller areas between the decennial censuses and HUD did not collect data on voucher utilization rates for four of the largest seventy-five metropolitan areas, the results are for the largest public housing agencies in seventy-one of the seventy-five largest metropolitan areas. In this year, the average voucher utilization rate was 85.8 percent for housing agencies in metropolitan areas with higher than average vacancy rates and 87.9 percent for housing agencies in metropolitan areas with lower than average vacancy rates. That is, the voucher utilization rate is actually higher in the tightest housing markets, and hence tighter housing markets do not necessitate supply-side programs.

In discussing this matter, it is important to distinguish between a housing authority's so-called success rate and its ability to use Section 8 vouchers. An authority's success rate is the percentage of the families authorized to search for a unit that occupy a unit meeting the program's standards within the housing authority's time limit. Its utilization rate is the fraction of all vouchers in use.

An authority's success rate depends on many factors, including the local vacancy rate. Its success rate, however, bears no necessary relationship to the fraction of the authority's vouchers in use at any point in time. No matter what an authority's success rate, the authority can fully use the vouchers allocated to it by authorizing more families to search for apartments than the number of vouchers available. For example, if an authority has a success rate of 50 percent, authorizing twice as many families to search as the number of vouchers available will result in full utilization of the vouchers on average. If each housing authority adjusted its issuance of vouchers to its success rate in this manner, some agencies would exceed their budget and others would fall short in a given year. The national average success rate, however, would be very close to 100 percent.

The voucher utilization rate depends primarily on the aggressiveness of housing agencies in overissuing vouchers. Public housing agencies have overissued vouchers for many years and thereby achieved high usage rates despite success rates well below 100 percent. They have a reserve fund for this purpose, and current regulations call for penalties on agencies with usage rates below 97 percent.

The reason for the success of the Voucher Program in the tightest housing markets is easy to understand. Many families offered housing vouchers already occupy apartments meeting the program's minimum housing standards. We do not need vacant apartments for these families. They can participate without moving. Other families that are offered vouchers live in housing that does not meet minimum standards. These apartments can, however, be repaired to meet the standards. Similarly, vacant apartments that do not initially meet the minimum standards can be upgraded to meet them. That is, housing vouchers can induce an increase in the number of units meeting minimum housing standards even if they have no effect on new construction. Therefore, new construction is not necessary to increase the number of housing units meeting minimum housing standards.[12]

The second major objection to the exclusive reliance on tenant-based assistance is that new construction promotes neighborhood revitalization to a much greater extent than tenant-based assistance. Evidence on program performance suggests that there is little difference between housing programs in this regard.

The evidence from the Experimental Housing Allowance Program is that even an entitlement housing voucher program will have modest effects on neighborhoods, and the small literature on the Section 8 Voucher Program confirms these findings for a similar nonentitlement program.[13] These programs result in the upgrading of many existing dwellings, but this is concentrated on their interiors.

It is plausible to believe that a new subsidized project built at low density in a neighborhood with the lowest-quality housing and poorest families would make that neighborhood a more attractive place to live for some years after its construction. It is equally plausible to believe that the same project located in an upper-middle-income neighborhood and occupied by poorest families would make that neighborhood a worse place to live. The policy issue is not, however, whether some individual subsidized projects lead to neighborhood improvement or decline. The issue is the magnitude of neighborhood upgrading across all projects under a program over the life of these projects.

If a housing project makes its neighborhood a better place to live, it will increase neighborhood property values. If it makes its neighborhood a worse place to live, it will depress neighborhood property values. The published studies find small positive effects on neighborhood property values on average for some programs and small negative effects for others.[14]

A few participants in housing policy debates have argued for ending HUD's Section 8 Housing Voucher Program, the program that accounts for the bulk of recipient-based housing assistance in the United States, primarily on the grounds that this program brings badly behaved low-income people into middle-income neighborhoods, disrupting the lives of their residents.[15] Although there is little doubt that unruly voucher recipients disturb some middle-income neighborhoods, it is unclear from the few anecdotes reported how common these problems are in the voucher program. Furthermore, it is not clear how the individuals interviewed would know that their unruly neighbors have tenant-based Section 8 vouchers. They may be welfare recipients who receive no housing assistance, or they may receive project-based housing assistance. Evidence on the performance of the voucher program suggests that it is unlikely to create substantial class conflicts because many voucher recipients do not move at all and the voucher families that relocate typically move to neighborhoods that are not markedly different from their initial neighborhoods, possibly because they want to remain close to initial jobs, relatives, and friends.[16] Furthermore, the voucher program has little effect on patterns of racial segregation.[17] Finally, the relevant question for this chapter is not whether the voucher program disrupts some neighborhoods but, rather, whether it disrupts these neighborhoods more than other forms of housing assistance. If we compare a program that subsidizes private projects with a voucher program serving the same number of households, the program of subsidized projects will bring a larger number of low-income families into a smaller number of neighborhoods. It is far from clear that taxpayers would prefer the smaller probability of a subsidized housing project in their neighborhood to a few voucher recipients.

Proposals to Shift Budget from Unit-Based to Recipient-Based Assistance

The available evidence on program performance has clear implications for housing policy reform. To serve the interests of taxpayers who want to help low-income families with their housing and the poorest families who have not been offered housing assistance, Congress should shift the budget for low-income housing assistance from unit-based to recipient-based housing assistance as soon as current contractual commitments permit and should not authorize any new programs involving unit-based assistance.[18] The following concrete steps will achieve these results.

First, the money currently spent on operating and modernization subsidies for public housing projects should be used to provide recipient-based vouchers to public housing tenants, as proposed by the Clinton administration and by Senator Robert Dole during his presidential campaign in 1996. HUD provides housing authorities with between $6 and $7 billion each year in operating and modernization subsidies. This is about a fourth of the total HUD budget for low-income housing assistance. The evidence indicates that we can get more for this money by giving it to public housing tenants in the form of housing vouchers.

The Quality Housing and Work Responsibility Act of 1998 mandates the conversion of public housing projects to recipient-based assistance under certain circumstances and allows it under other circumstances. Congress should, however, go further. It should require housing authorities to offer portable housing vouchers to all public housing tenants.

To enable housing authorities to provide decent housing despite this loss in revenue, they should be allowed to rent their apartments to any household eligible for housing assistance for whatever rent this market will bear. Families with recipient-based vouchers would occupy many of these apartments. Other families eligible for housing assistance would occupy the rest. Housing authorities could raise additional money by taking advantage of the current regulation that allows them to sell projects. At present, they have little incentive to do it. Without guaranteed federal operating and modernization subsidies, many authorities would surely decide to sell their worst projects. These are the projects that would be abandoned to the greatest extent by their tenants with vouchers, and they are the most expensive to operate. If housing authorities are unable to compete with private owners for their tenants, they should not be in the business of providing housing.

Second, contracts with the owners of private subsidized projects should not be renewed. The initial agreements that led to the building or substantial rehabilitation of these projects called for their owners to provide housing meeting certain standards to households with particular characteristics at certain rents for a specified number of years. At the end of the use agreement, the government must decide whether to change the terms of the agreement, and the private parties must decide whether to participate on these terms. A substantial number of projects have come to the end of their use agreements in recent years and many more will come to the end of their use agreements over the next few decades. When use agreements are not renewed, current occupants are provided with other housing assistance, usually recipient-based vouchers. Until this point, housing policy has leaned heavily in the direction of providing owners with a sufficient subsidy to induce them to continue to serve the low-income households in their projects. Instead, we should give their tenants portable vouchers and force the owners to compete for their business.

It is important to realize that for-profit sponsors will not agree to extend the use agreement unless doing so provides at least as much profit as operating in the unsubsidized market. Because these subsidies are provided to selected private suppliers, the market mechanism does not ensure that profits under the new use agreement will be driven down to market levels. If this is to be achieved at all, administrative mechanisms must be used. Unfortunately, administrative mechanisms can err in only one direction, namely, providing excess profits. If owners are offered a lower profit than in the unsubsidized market, they will leave the program. We should leave the job of getting value for the money spent to the people who have the greatest incentive to do it, the recipients of housing assistance.

Third, the construction of additional public or private projects should not be subsidized. This involves terminating or phasing out current production programs and avoiding new production programs.

The Low-Income Housing Tax Credit is the largest active production program. It subsidizes the construction of more units than all of the other active production programs combined. The tax credit program is already the nation's second-largest low-income housing program, and it is the fastest-growing. The GAO results on the cost-effectiveness of the tax credit program, combined with the results of studies of similar earlier programs, argue for no additional construction under the Low-Income Housing Tax Credit program. The money spent on this program is better spent on expanding the housing voucher program.

It might be argued that the GAO results are not sufficiently compelling to justify immediate termination of this program, and the tax credit program is sufficiently different from older production programs to make evidence of their effects of little relevance for this decision; however, this evidence is surely more than adequate to justify rescinding the recent indexing of the tax credit for inflation and immediately launching a careful, independent analysis of the cost-effectiveness of the program. If this research shows that the tax credit program is as cost-effective as recipient-based vouchers, indexing for inflation can be resumed. Otherwise, additional construction under the program should be halted.

Similar remarks apply to other active production programs. For example, no additional money should be allocated to HOPE VI. This program is an improvement over traditional public housing in that it avoids concentrating the poorest families at high densities in projects. The GAO study, however, reveals that it is highly cost-ineffective compared with recipient-based vouchers that also avoid these concentrations.

Finally in this regard, there should be no new production programs. Congress should reject the Bush administration's proposal for a tax credit to selected builders of housing for low-income homeowners modeled after the Low Income Housing Tax Credit.[19] It should also reject the Millennial Housing Commission's proposal to create a new rental production program with a

100 percent capital subsidy. Any additional money for housing assistance should be used to expand the housing voucher program.

Fourth, Congress should declare a moratorium on further unit-based assistance under the housing voucher program until it can consider the results of a study that compares the cost-effectiveness of the already committed unit-based vouchers with recipient-based vouchers.

Obstacles to Fundamental Reform

The primary obstacle to fundamental housing policy reform is the enormous difference between the reality and perception of gains and losses from the reforms on the part of almost all individuals. The extremely small group of people who would lose from the reforms are well aware that they would be hurt. The overwhelming majority who would gain from them have no idea that they would benefit. Among these beneficiaries are many major players in housing policy development. Secondary obstacles to the proposed reforms are the dispersed congressional oversight of the different programs that provide low-income housing assistance and the fear of unexpected negative consequences of major reforms. The remainder of this chapter discusses these obstacles and suggests practical ways to overcome them.

Misperceptions of Gains and Losses from the Proposed Reforms

This section explains why some groups would gain and others lose from the proposed reforms, why most winners fail to perceive their gains, and how perceptions of gains can be brought into line with reality.

WHO GAINS AND LOSES FROM THE PROPOSED REFORMS? The proposed reforms would benefit the overwhelming majority of the population. First, they would benefit millions of the poorest families in the country. These are families eligible for housing assistance but not currently served. Their gains would be achieved without increasing taxes or reducing benefits to current recipients. Second, the proposals would benefit all taxpayers who are not involved in the provision of unit-based housing assistance. Almost all taxpayers are in this category. Some of these taxpayers want to help low-income families. These taxpayers would gain even if we continued to spend the same amount of money on low-income housing assistance because we would be able to serve many additional families while continuing to serve current recipients equally well. They would get more for their money. Even taxpayers who are unconcerned about the plight of the poor would benefit if we reduced the amount spent on low-income housing assistance and used the savings to reduce taxes. Because of the excessive cost of unit-based assistance, it is possible to reduce expenditures on low-income housing assistance and still serve all existing recipients equally well and many additional households by shifting the budget from unit-based to recipient-based assistance. Finally, adoption of the proposals would benefit many people who are involved in the provision of unit-based housing assistance. These people would receive more for their services, and they would gain from the reforms for the same reason that other taxpayers gain.

Because it is often argued that all people involved in the provision of unit-based housing assistance benefit financially from its continuation, it is important to understand why this is not the case. Almost all inputs involved in the provision of unit-based assistance are paid market prices for their services. This includes the workers who build and maintain subsidized projects and the lenders who finance these projects. For example, the maintenance staff in subsidized projects do work that is identical to the work that they would do in unsubsidized housing, and there is no compelling reason to believe that they are better compensated than they would be in the unsubsidized sector. The for-profit firms that own subsidized projects will certainly not pay their workers above-market wages. Another good example of input suppliers earning market prices is the people who buy low-income housing tax credits from the developers who are awarded these credits. The tax credits awarded are sold to the highest bidders in competitive capital markets. The buyers have many alternative investments that are almost as good. Even the owners of construction companies do not necessarily earn excess profits from the current system. Most developers who have been awarded low-income housing tax credits hire a general contractor to build their projects. These contractors earn normal profits.

The financial consequences of the reforms for owners of inputs that are paid market prices depend upon whether the reforms increase or decrease the demands for their inputs. It is reasonable to expect the reforms to increase the demands for the inputs used in the construction, renovation, and maintenance of the housing stock. Current recipients of housing assistance will either continue to live in their current units or want to move to better housing. Many public housing tenants offered vouchers would be in the latter category. Millions of additional families will receive housing assistance. These families will eventually want to move to better housing. Taxpayers who do not receive housing assistance and are not involved in the provision of unit-based assistance will pay the same or lower taxes and hence will either continue to occupy equally good housing or want to occupy better housing. The upgrading of the existing housing stock resulting from the reforms will require many of the same inputs used to build new housing, and some additional new housing will surely be built. Only the few people who make excessive earnings from the current system will have significantly less money to spend on housing and hence occupy worse housing as a result of the reforms. However, because the excessive earnings of these people are only a part of the excessive cost of the current system, this reduction in housing consumption will almost surely be smaller than the preceding increases. As a result, the reforms would increase the demand for almost all inputs used to provide housing and hence the prices of these inputs.

It is virtually impossible to design changes in policy that hurt no one, and the proposed reforms are no exception to this rule. It is important to determine who will lose in order to decide whether some attempt should be made to compensate them for their losses.

The clearest losers are some owners of for-profit firms that would be awarded contracts to develop and operate subsidized housing projects in the future if the current system were continued. They would be deprived of the excess profits associated with these projects. The bribery and influence peddling to get contracts that has surfaced under all major construction programs involving for-profit firms tells us that some of these firms earn excessive profits. If they were not earning greater profits from their subsidized projects than they would earn in the unsubsidized market, they would have no incentive to provide bribes. They would also have no incentive to devote resources to lobbying against the proposed reforms. Some current owners of subsidized projects would also lose because their current contracts would not be extended at above-market rents at the end of their use agreements.

Another larger group that might incur modest losses from the reform consists of individuals involved in the provision of unit-based housing assistance whose job requires specialized knowledge that would not be useful if all housing assistance were recipient-based. For example, some employees of public housing authorities perform functions that are specific to public housing, such as preparing applications for modernization funds.[20] The reforms would make some of their skills obsolete. They would have to learn new skills to operate in the new environment, where housing authorities must compete for the tenants in their projects. The reforms will inconvenience these people. This is not to say, however, that the reforms are contrary to their interests broadly conceived. Some of these individuals have chosen their jobs in part because they are particularly concerned about helping low-income families with their housing. If they realized the advantages of the reforms in this regard, many of these people might support the reforms despite the personal inconvenience.

Another large group that would incur some costs but would receive the same offsetting advantages consists of the employees of the not-for-profit organizations that develop and operate subsidized projects. The staff members of these organizations have specialized knowledge that would not be useful if all housing assistance were recipient-based. Many, however, seem strongly motivated by a desire to help low-income families with their housing.

It is reasonable to believe that some individuals who have skills that would become obsolete as a result of the reforms do not have a particularly strong concern for the housing of low-income families. Their financial losses from the reforms will not be offset to any great extent by the advantages of the reforms to low-income families and other taxpayers. For example, some syndicators of tax credit projects are surely in this category. Syndicators arrange for the sales of tax credits from the developers who receive them to others. They will incur losses as a result of the reforms because they will have to find new jobs. Their job is a consequence of the structure of the tax credit program. Because they tend to be well-educated people with a wide range of skills and good ability to learn new skills, the reforms will have a modest effect on their lifetime prospects. So individual syndicators may have little incentive to oppose the reforms. If the few firms that specialize in tax credit syndication are owned by a small number of individuals, however, these individuals might have a strong financial interest in preventing the reforms.

Some directors of state housing agencies might oppose the proposed reforms even if they fully understood their consequences. The federal government provides state housing agencies with substantial federal tax credits each year to allocate to selected developers of privately owned subsidized projects and allows them to issue multifamily housing bonds whose interest is exempt from federal taxation and whose proceeds are used in part to provide below-market-interest loans to selected developers of such projects. There has been little federal oversight of these activities. Obviously, directors of state housing agencies are delighted to have such large sums of money to allocate with so little federal oversight. Many state housing agencies also receive allocations of Section 8 housing vouchers; however, they might well oppose the proposed reforms even if they are allocated all of the money freed by the termination of tax credits and mortgage revenue bonds to expand their voucher programs. This would involve a massive contraction of their primary activities and massive expansion of their small voucher programs. This involves a much greater adjustment on the part of agency employees than in the case of public housing authorities. Only directors with the strongest commitment to helping low-income families with their housing are likely to support the proposed reforms.

WHY HAVE THE REFORMS NOT BEEN ADOPTED? Because the overwhelming majority of citizens would receive some benefit from these reforms and millions of low-income individuals who have not been offered housing assistance would receive large benefits, the question is why these reforms have not been adopted. One conventional answer to this question is that (1) politicians act to maximize their margin of victory in elections, (2) a small group of people who are involved in the provision of unit-based assistance have so much to gain from the perpetuation of the current system that they have organized themselves to pursue their narrow self-interest through financial contributions to candidates, (3) the many taxpayers who would gain from the reforms would not gain enough to be active in the political process with respect to it, and (4) the millions of low-income individuals who have the most to gain do not have the resources to organize themselves. The simplest version of this explanation assumes that everyone is well informed about how they would be affected by the proposed reforms. The costs and benefits of actions at the individual level lead to political activity by a miniscule fraction of the population and to political inactivity by the vast majority. These arguments have led some to conclude that the current policies are the equilibrium outcome of the political process and it is impossible to change them.

Without question, the preceding arguments provide a part of the explanation for why the proposed policies have not been adopted. If all voters were well informed about these issues, however, it is far from obvious that the votes and financial contributions of the miniscule number of people who would lose from the proposed reforms would have been able to prevent them. The average annual subsidy in the voucher program is about $6,000. Therefore, the reforms would produce a substantial increase in the well-being of millions of potential voters in the additional families that would receive housing assistance. For many of these voters, this would be the most important policy issue affecting their well-being. It would swamp other differences in positions between candidates. The overwhelming majority of voters would receive much more modest benefits from the reforms than voters in newly assisted families. They would be swayed by a candidate's position on this issue only if they were nearly indifferent between candidates on other grounds. Because so many voters receive these modest benefits, however, a significant number might be swayed.

A more realistic version of the conventional argument would recognize that the great majority of voters have so little to gain from improved policy in this area and so little ability to affect policy that they have no incentive to be informed. In light of their rational ignorance of these matters, their votes may be unaffected by a candidate's position on them. Nevertheless, this still leaves millions of voters in the families that would receive housing assistance as a result of the reforms who would vote for the candidate espousing them. This would seem to trump the votes and financial support of about a few thousand developers and owners of private subsidized projects who would reap excess profits from the continuation of the current system.

Even after the simplest explanation for the failure to adopt the proposed reforms is modified to allow for rational ignorance on the part of most voters, it still makes highly unrealistic assumptions about who knows what. It assumes that legislators and the individuals who are most affected by policies in a particular area can easily determine what existing and proposed policies best serve their interests. The truth is that determining the effects of government housing programs is difficult even for the best analysts with access to the best data, and mastering what has been learned about program performance is no mean feat.

Some people take the cynical view that members of Congress are well aware that programs of unit-based assistance provide substantial excess profits to selected developers and that they support these programs in exchange for campaign contributions. It is not clear that even the key members of the relevant committees receive a significant fraction of their campaign contributions from individuals who have a financial interest in low-income housing programs. Furthermore, this cynical view seems inconsistent with many congressional actions. For example, the 1998 Quality Housing and Work Responsibility Act mandated that the GAO conduct a comparative study of the full cost of federal assisted housing programs and the qualitative differences in what these programs provide. In 2000 Congress established the Millennial Housing Commission, whose mandate included a study that examines the effectiveness and efficiency of various possible methods for increasing the role of the private sector in providing affordable housing. It is difficult to imagine that members well informed about the excessive costs of the programs of unit-based assistance and seeking to expand these programs to serve the interests of financial supporters would mandate careful studies comparing the cost-effectiveness of vouchers and production programs. Furthermore, this cynical view cannot explain why Congress has continued to provide operating and modernization subsidies to housing authorities rather than vouchers to their tenants. No one has a strong enough financial interest in preventing this reform to contribute much money or time to the campaigns of congressional candidates. Finally, Congress has made the recipient-based voucher program the country's largest low-income housing program, accounting for about a third of all assisted renters. The cynical view cannot explain the existence of this program.

In addition to exaggerating the knowledge possessed by individuals, the conventional explanation for the failure to adopt the proposed reforms greatly oversimplifies the motives of elected officials. It assumes that their decisions are intended to maximize their margin of victory in elections. In reality, their motivations are more mixed, and this surely leads to decisions that reduce their margin of victory. For example, some elected officials are strongly motivated by a desire to serve their neighbors. They realize that their constituents do not typically have the time to be well informed about most policy issues, and they are willing to incur some loss of votes in the next election to pursue what they perceive to be in the long-term interests of their constituents. Other elected officials seek office in part to pursue their own ideas about what is desirable. Because most congressional incumbents win handily, the necessity of getting elected does not dictate their legislative actions. They are able to pursue their own views about what constitutes a good society to some considerable extent. Like others, their knowledge of the effects of alternative policies is limited, and their misperceptions about these effects surely influence their behavior.

The major impediment to fundamental housing policy reform is that very few people have any knowledge of the evidence that argues for these reforms and many key players are only vaguely aware of it. Information about comparative program performance is essential for understanding the virtues of the proposed reforms. This evidence is not mentioned in the popular press. With rare exceptions, congressional testimony makes no reference to it. The Millennial Housing Commission did not report any comparative evidence on the performance of different types of housing program even though one of its mandates was to conduct a study that examines the effectiveness and efficiency of various possible methods for increasing the role of the private sector in providing affordable housing. Most people who have been involved for some time in housing policy debates have certainly heard references to studies of the excessive costs of unit-based assistance. Only a small minority, however, have any idea of the magnitudes involved, and even fewer know anything about the methods used to produce these estimates and hence are able to judge their credibility. This dearth of relevant information is exacerbated by misinformation that dominates the popular press and congressional testimony.

Why are representatives on the relevant congressional committees not well informed about the evidence on program performance? Some are new members of the committee, and all members are spread thin. They are on committees that oversee many programs, and they have many other activities. They certainly do not have the time to read technical studies about program performance. Indeed, they rarely read the written testimony for their hearings. Their information comes largely from brief memoranda from, and conversations with, their staff, listening to the short oral statements of witnesses at hearings and their answers to questions, and conversations with financial supporters, lobbyists, and a few constituents who are particularly interested in this topic. Congressional staff members are better informed, but they do not have the time to read many technical studies of the performance of housing programs.

Although members of Congress have less information than they should about the performance of different housing programs, ordinary citizens have essentially no accurate information. The reasons for this state of affairs are easy to understand. Low-income housing programs account for less than 2 percent of the federal budget, and individual taxpayers have a very limited ability to affect political outcomes. Therefore, they have little incentive to be informed. Some follow public affairs as a hobby and have an interest in housing issues; however, they must rely primarily on television and newspapers for their information. This is also the primary source of information for the millions of low-income voters who would benefit greatly from the reforms. Unfortunately, low-income housing policy is not a large enough issue to receive extensive coverage. Furthermore, the most important information is not provided at all, and the information provided is highly misleading.

Why is there so much misinformation about housing policy in the popular press? In part, it is because most reporters who write about low-income housing policy are not specialists in this area and have little time to devote to each article. They contact the most obvious sources of information such as program administrators, potential or actual recipients, and representatives of the major organizations that lobby for housing assistance. None of these sources is broadly knowledgeable about the systematic evidence on the performance of alternative programs. The overwhelming majority have no knowledge of it. Even worse, these sources provide misinformation that serves their narrow interests. For example, housing authorities would like to provide voucher recipients in their localities with larger subsidies, in part because it reduces their workload in administering the program. So they misinterpret evidence that they provide to reporters to suggest that federal subsidies are too low in their areas. Organizations that represent the interests of developers of private projects misinterpret the same evidence to suggest that vouchers cannot be used in certain areas and hence subsidized construction is necessary in order to serve low-income households.

Reporters are hard pressed to find sources of objective information about housing policy. Few people are broadly knowledgeable about the systematic evidence on program performance. Many of these people are civil servants at HUD, the Office of Management and Budget (OMB), GAO, and the Congressional Budget Office (CBO) and employees of firms that rely on research grants from government agencies. These people are understandably reluctant to talk with reporters. This leaves a handful of independent housing policy analysts in universities and public policy research firms, and few have made concerted efforts to provide reporters with accurate information.

HOW CAN WE REDUCE MISPERCEPTIONS OF GAINS AND LOSSES? It is difficult to see how the proposed reforms can be achieved unless more individuals realize that they will benefit from them. The question is whether it is possible to overcome this obstacle to reform. The remainder of this section describes some practical solutions for reducing differences between the realities and perceptions of gains and losses.

An important step toward fundamental housing policy reform is for the small number of people who are well informed about evidence on the performance of different types of housing program and who have no financial interests in housing policy, except as ordinary taxpayers, to devote more time to making this information more easily available to their fellow citizens. This would include providing information to journalists and to the key players in housing policy development—namely, Congress members who serve on the relevant committees, their personal staff members who focus on housing policy, the committee staff members, and political appointees and civil servants in the major agencies that administer low-income housing programs (HUD, IRS, USDA) and the major government agencies that analyze program performance (OMB, CBO, GAO). Many of these people welcome short, clearly written, and authoritative papers about program performance and ideas for improving performance.

Improving press coverage requires a few independent housing policy analysts to be active in trying to reach journalists. An excellent first step would be to write a paper for a journalism review that focuses on the most important, persistent misinformation on low-income housing policy that has appeared in the popular press in recent years. Occasional articles of this type, however, are not sufficient. It is important that some independent housing policy analysts follow regularly the major events in housing policy and provide reporters with information and commentary about them. These include legislative proposals, congressional hearings, major government reports, and important proposed regulations. Reporters are always looking for good stories. More relevant and accurate press coverage of housing policy issues will create some public support for the reforms, though it will probably reach only a small fraction of the people who would benefit from them, and the associated change in public opinion alone is unlikely to lead to a major reform of housing policy.

To achieve this goal, it is important to provide information to legislators. Congressional members rarely have the time to interact with housing policy analysts who are not their constituents, except during hearings. They can, however, be reached indirectly through their staff members. Many congressional staff members welcome timely, clear, concise, and reliable information related to their duties. For example, one of their duties is to read the written testimony of witnesses prior to hearings and suggest questions that their congressmen might ask the witnesses. This testimony is sometimes available before the hearings. Many staff members would welcome evidence contradicting the unsupported assertions of witnesses. This would be especially valuable if it is received in time to prepare questions. Evidence on the validity of erroneous assertions is still valuable to congressional staff members, even if it were provided after the hearings, because the same erroneous arguments are used repeatedly in congressional testimony. Lobbyists will continue to use them as long as members of Congress find them persuasive. Congressional staff members will also appreciate brief, clearly written papers that address proposed legislation or summarize the technical literature relevant for their jobs.

In addition to providing information to congressional staff, it would be useful for some independent housing policy analyst to write a paper for fellow analysts that provides a comprehensive evaluation of the erroneous arguments that are commonly used in congressional testimony. Few housing policy analysts read congressional testimony, and they are largely ignorant of the arguments that are heard by the key players in housing policy development. If they were aware of these arguments, they would surely devote more effort to providing evidence concerning their validity.

Another important step in achieving fundamental housing policy reform is to narrow the disagreements among housing policy analysts concerning the effects of different programs. Systematic evidence on program performance will have a greater impact on policy development if independent analysts speak with a similar voice. No housing policy analyst has read all of the important studies of the effects of all major housing programs. Reducing the differences in the views about the effects of different programs among independent analysts might be achieved with a series of conferences dealing with the evidence on each major effect across all major housing programs. The goal of these conferences would be to develop a consensus where the evidence justifies it and a research agenda to resolve differences in other cases. This will make it more difficult for those attempting to influence policy to ignore systematic evidence. Support for these conferences might be sought from foundations with an interest in the plight of low-income families.

One might question the practicality of the preceding suggestions for overcoming the information barriers to fundamental reform. Would independent housing policy analysts have an incentive to undertake the activities needed to increase substantially the knowledge of the key players in the policy process and the public at large? Why have they not undertaken these activities in the past?

In fact, many housing policy analysts do not have an incentive to undertake these activities to any significant extent. Obviously, many would like to help bring about improvements in policy in their area of expertise. Younger academics, however, will want to devote their energies primarily to publishing research in the journals of their profession. This is necessary to attain tenure and promotion. Civil servants and employees of firms that rely on research contracts from government must be circumspect in what they say about housing policy. They are understandably reluctant to say things that undercut the current administration's policy positions or offend any powerful interest group involved in housing policy debates. Nevertheless, some housing policy analysts have both the inclination and incentive to undertake the suggested activities. Some public policy research organizations want their policy analysts to undertake these activities. Furthermore, well-established academics in any discipline can undertake them with little cost, and this would be a valued activity for faculty members in many departments.

Dispersed Congressional Oversight

Fundamental housing policy reform requires action by congressional committees that have responsibilities over different parts of the current system. This creates problems for proposed reforms because these reforms call for the elimination of the IRS and USDA programs and the expansion of HUD's voucher program. Because it may not be possible to persuade the committees that oversee the IRS and USDA programs to terminate their current programs of unit-based assistance so that we can expand HUD's voucher program without spending more in total on low-income housing assistance, it is important to consider reforms that will produce better outcomes without altering the budget under the control of each set of committees. Fortunately, there are some excellent opportunities of this type.

The U.S. Senate Committee on Finance and U.S. House of Representatives Committee on Ways and Means could replace low-income housing tax credits and multifamily housing bonds with a refundable tax credit to all low-income homeowners. Unlike the Bush administration's proposal, this tax credit would be delivered directly to low-income households rather than to selected private developers. Among households living in the same area, the tax credit might be largest for the poorest households of each size and be zero for households with incomes in excess of some amount. Among households with the same income, it might be largest in areas with the highest housing prices.

Replacing low-income housing tax credits and multifamily housing bonds with a refundable tax credit for homeownership directly to low-income households eliminates the excess cost associated with unit-based assistance. It also gives these households considerable choice with respect to their housing. As a bonus, it provides an incentive for homeownership. This offsets the strong bias toward renting in the current system of low-income housing assistance. In the programs that account for the overwhelming majority of units, a household must rent if it is to receive housing assistance. Because there is widespread public support for promoting homeownership among low-income households and recognition that the current income tax system promotes homeownership primarily for middle- and upper-income households, this proposal would have strong political appeal.

USDA has financed the production of few additional units under Section 515 in recent years, and termination of this production program has often been on CBO's list of budget options. USDA has spent considerably more money on rental assistance payments to the owners of existing projects under the Section 521 program. The committees that oversee the USDA programs could contribute to fundamental housing policy reform by using the money devoted to these programs to provide recipient-based vouchers to the families involved.

Fear of Unexpected Negative Consequences

A final obstacle to fundamental housing policy reform is the fear that the changes will have substantial unexpected negative consequences for low-income families. This fear of unexpected negative consequences is likely to be a particularly important obstacle to the proposal to voucher out public housing because the proposal involves major changes in current procedures in the public housing program. Because it is difficult to anticipate all consequences of far-reaching changes in policy, this concern cannot be dismissed out of hand.

A sensible solution is to fund a demonstration program involving innovative public housing authorities willing to experiment with vouchering out some, or all, of their public housing projects. Each tenant in a demonstration project would be offered a portable voucher that could be used for any unit in any demonstration public housing project or in any private unit meeting the voucher program's housing standards. The housing authority would be allowed to (1) rent each apartment in a demonstration project to any family eligible for housing assistance and charge whatever rent this market will bear or (2) sell the project to the highest bidder and use the proceeds to improve their remaining projects or expand their voucher program. This initiative would be funded by reducing the housing authority's operating and modernization subsidies by the fraction of its public housing units committed to the demonstration. These housing authorities would be provided with additional administrative budgets in recognition of the considerable administrative burdens necessary to bring about this radical transformation of public housing. A substantial research budget should be provided to HUD's Office of Policy Development and Research so that we learn from the experiences of these pioneering housing authorities.

Conclusion

In light of the current large budget deficits and the added expense of fighting international terrorism, it is clear that little additional money will be available for housing assistance over the next few years. The question is how we can continue to serve current recipients equally well and serve some of the poorest families who have not yet been offered assistance without spending more money. The answer is that we must use the money available more wisely.

Research on the effects of housing programs provides clear guidance on this matter. It shows that we can serve current recipients equally well (that is, provide them with equally good housing for the same rent) and serve many additional families without any increase in the budget by shifting resources from unit-based to recipient-based assistance. Indeed, we can achieve these outcomes with less money. We should learn from our past mistakes and not heed the call for new production programs. Indeed, we should go further and terminate current production programs and disengage from unit-based assistance to existing apartments as soon as current contractual commitments permit.

A major obstacle to adopting these reforms is that few individuals who would gain from the reforms realize it. Millions of the poorest families would experience large gains. Almost all taxpayers benefit to some extent. The overwhelming majority of these people know little, if anything, about housing policy. They have never heard of the proposed reforms and they have no knowledge relevant for assessing them. Their views on low-income housing policy are based on very inaccurate information in newspaper articles and television reports.

The legislators who are most involved in low-income housing policy are much better informed. They are, however, not sufficiently knowledgeable about the evidence on the performance of different housing programs. In deciding what actions to take on housing policy issues, congressional representatives obviously take account of how these actions will affect the financial support for their campaigns, and this support comes largely from individuals and organizations with substantial financial interests in legislation. Nevertheless, they also take account of public opinion in their district and their own views about desirable states of the world. It is entirely reasonable to believe that legislators are like the people that they represent in caring about many things in addition to their narrow self-interest. Indeed, it is reasonable to believe that they tend to be typical of their constituents with respect to the weight that they attach to these other factors. Information that convinces them that particular housing policy reforms will lead to outcomes that they and their constituents prefer to the current situation will induce some to increase their efforts to achieve these reforms.

This chapter suggests some practical ways that a few well-informed housing policy analysts could promote fundamental reform through improving the information possessed by key players in the policy process and the general public. It also suggests how the other major obstacles to fundamental reform can be overcome.

Notes

1. See Edgar O. Olsen, "Housing Programs for Low-Income Households," in *Means-Tested Transfer Programs in the United States*, edited by Robert Moffitt (University of Chicago Press, 2003), pp. 370–94, for a more detailed description of the system of low-income housing programs.

2. The primary source for the numbers in this paragraph is Millennial Housing Commission, *Meeting Our Nation's Housing Challenges: Report of the Bipartisan Millennial Housing Commission Appointed by the Congress of the United States* (Washington, D.C.: Government Printing Office, 2002), appendix 3.

3. The studies are HUD, *Housing in the Seventies* (Washington, D.C.: Government Printing Office, 1974), chap. 4; Stephen K. Mayo and others, *Housing Allowances and Other Rental Assistance Programs: A Comparison Based on the Housing Allowance Demand Experiment. Part 2: Costs and Efficiency* (Cambridge, Mass.: Abt Associates, 1980); James E. Wallace and others, *Participation and Benefits in the Urban Section 8 Program: New Construction and Existing Housing*, vols. 1 and 2 (Cambridge, Mass.: Abt Associates, 1981); Edgar O. Olsen and David M. Barton, "The Benefits and Costs of Public Housing in New York City," *Journal of Public Economics*, vol. 20 (April 1983): 299–332. Olsen, "Housing Programs for Low-Income Households," pp. 394–99, provides a brief summary of these studies. Edgar O. Olsen, "The Cost-Effectiveness of Alternative Methods of Delivering Housing Subsidies," Thomas Jefferson Center for Political Economy Working Paper 351, December 2000 (www.virginia.edu/economics/downablepapers.htm#olsen [July 22, 2006]), provides a description and critical appraisal of the data and methods used in these studies as well as a summary of their results.

4. Wallace and others made predictions of the market rents of subsidized units based on two different datasets containing information on the rent and characteristics of unsubsidized units. The study did not collect information on the indirect costs of the Section 8 New Construction Program. These indirect subsidies include GNMA Tandem Plan interest subsidies for FHA-insured projects and the forgone tax revenue due to the tax-exempt status of interest on the bonds used to finance state housing finance agency projects. On the basis of previous studies, the authors argue that these indirect costs would add 20–30 percent to the total cost of the Section 8 New Construction Program. The range of estimates reported in the text is based on the four combinations of the two predictions of market rent and the lower and upper limits on the indirect costs.

5. U.S. General Accounting Office [GAO; now Government Accountability Office], *Federal Housing Programs: What They Cost and What They Provide*, GAO-01-901R, July 18, 2001, and U.S. General Accounting Office, *Federal Housing Assistance: Comparing the Characteristics and Costs of Housing Programs*, GAO-02-76, 2002.

6. GAO, *Federal Housing Programs: What They Cost and What They Provide*, p. 3.

7. The authors recognize many of these omissions. See GAO, *Federal Housing Assistance: Comparing the Characteristics and Costs of Housing Programs*, p. 22.

8. GAO, *Federal Housing Assistance: Comparing the Characteristics and Costs of Housing Programs*, pp. 19–20.

9. Edgar O. Olsen, "Fundamental Housing Policy Reform," University of Virginia, Department of Economics, March 2004 (www.virginia.edu/economics/downablepapers. htm#olsen [July 22, 2006]), pp. 13–15.

10. This is based on results in Wallace and others, *Participation and Benefits in the Urban Section 8 Program*, 1981.

11. Recipient-based housing programs often have other standards such as upper limits on the gross rent of the unit occupied. This does not, however, change the essence of the argument. Families offered recipient-based assistance have a much wider range of choice among units that are adequate as judged by the program's minimum housing standards.

12. Olsen, "Fundamental Housing Policy Reform," pp. 22–24, summarizes the evidence from HUD's Section 8 Voucher Program and Housing Assistance Supply Experiment dealing with this matter.

13. See Ira S. Lowry, *Experimenting with Housing Allowances: The Final Report of the Housing Assistance Supply Experiment* (Cambridge, Mass.: Oelgeschlager, Gunn & Hain, 1983), pp. 205–17; and George C. Galster, Peter Tatian, and Robin Smith, "The Impact of Neighbors Who Use Section 8 Certificates on Property Value," *Housing Policy Debate*, vol. 10 (1999): 879–917.

14. See Chang-Moo Lee, Dennis P. Culhane, and Susan M. Wachter, "The Differential Impacts of Federally Assisted Housing Programs on Nearby Property Values: A Philadelphia Case Study," *Housing Policy Debate*, vol. 10 (1999): 75–93; and George Galster and others. *Assessing Property Value Impacts of Dispersed Housing Subsidy Programs: Final Report* (Washington, D.C.: Urban Institute, May 1999). In an excellent unpublished paper entitled "The External Effects of Place-Based Subsidized Housing," Ingrid Gould Ellen and others find more substantial positive effects for subsidized projects in New York City. Time will tell whether these results withstand critical scrutiny and can be replicated elsewhere.

15. See Howard Husock, "Let's End Housing Vouchers," *City Journal*, vol. 10 (Autumn 2000): 84–91; and Heather Mac Donald, "Comment on Sandra J. Newman and Ann B. Schnare's "'. . . And a Suitable Living Environment': The Failure of Housing Programs to Deliver on Neighborhood Quality," *Housing Policy Debate*, vol. 8 (1997): 755–62.

16. See Stephen D. Kennedy and Meryl Finkel, *Section 8 Rental Voucher and Rental Certificate Utilization Study* (HUD, October 1994), p. 15; and Mireille L. Leger and Stephen D. Kennedy, *Recipient Housing in the Housing Voucher and Certificate Programs* (HUD, May 1990), table 4.20.

17. Leger and Kennedy, *Recipient Housing in the Housing Voucher and Certificate Programs*, table 4.25B.

18. See John Weicher, *Privatizing Subsidized Housing* (Washington, D.C.: American Enterprise Institute, 1997), for a detailed analysis of vouchering out unit-based assistance.

19. The Bush administration's American Dream Program to provide a part of the down payment on a house for low-income families is not subject to the same criticisms. Since the argument for subsidizing homeownership is strongest for low-income families and this program is well designed to benefit these families and increase their homeownership rate without creating other distortions, a good case can be made for it.

20. It is also important to realize that many people involved in the administration of public housing perform functions such as determining eligibility and inspecting dwelling units for adherence to housing standards that would be essentially unchanged under the proposed reforms. Indeed, more people would be hired to perform these functions because more families would receive housing assistance.

6

Fixing Special Education

JAY P. GREENE

To produce responsible and effective education for students with disabilities, we must provide schools with a set of balanced incentives that reward good performance while also keeping costs under control, but efforts to put the right kind of incentives into place have been hindered by a lack of understanding that incentives even play a role in this policy area. The strong emotions associated with providing services for students with disabilities clouds many people's thinking about how those services can best be structured to ensure quality while controlling costs. Powerful interest groups, including trial lawyers, special-education advocates, and teachers' unions, exploit and perpetuate these strong emotions, further hindering the adoption of efficient government policies for special education. As a result, the special-education system currently incorporates incentives that serve these interest groups rather than students. Specifically, the system rewards schools for placing more students into special education regardless of whether they are truly disabled; this is detrimental to disabled and nondisabled students alike. Research demonstrates that more efficient arrangements do exist for serving disabled students. Unless political barriers to the adoption of those more efficient policies are overcome, however, education of the disabled will continue to be dominated by costly and ineffective approaches.

A Brief History of the Problem

There is no doubt that the current state of affairs is a significant improvement over the state of education for disabled students before the 1970s. Until Congress passed the Education for All Handicapped Children Act—the predecessor of the current Individuals with Disabilities in Education Act (IDEA)—in 1975, disabled students were frequently denied adequate services by their schools and were sometimes denied services altogether. As the National Council on Disability describes it, "In 1970, before enactment of the federal protections in IDEA, schools in America educated only one in five students with disabilities. More than 1 million students were excluded from public schools, and another 3.5 million did not receive appropriate services."[1]

Before IDEA and its predecessors, the difficulty was not primarily one of ill will toward students with disabilities. Rather, the problem was one of incentives. Disabled students were often expensive to serve and usually did not generate additional revenues for schools. Under those circumstances, serving disabled students necessarily involved diverting resources from the education of other students. Most school districts were unwilling to divert their resources in this way, because doing so would hinder their ability to attract and retain general-education students.

Because school districts are in constant competition for students and the funding those students generate, schools generally could not afford to redistribute resources from less expensive general-education students to more expensive special-education students. Such a policy would tend to attract more special-education students seeking services, pushing up costs further, while also driving away general-education students whose education might be shortchanged, reducing revenues further. This kind of "race to the bottom," as Paul Peterson and Mark Rom describe it in *Welfare Magnets*, is an inherent problem for any redistributive effort by local governments competing for tax base.[2] Special education before IDEA and its predecessors is a classic illustration of this phenomenon.

One solution to the problem of the race to the bottom, Peterson and Rom suggest, is to establish national standards for redistributive policies, thus preventing competitive pressures from undermining the ability of local governments to engage in redistribution. This is exactly what IDEA and previous legislation have done for special education. By mandating that all public schools provide adequate services to disabled students, and by allocating additional funds to help defray the costs, federal special-education legislation has helped ensure that competition among school districts for tax base would not prevent the provision of special-education services.

The Overidentification of Students as Disabled

Although IDEA and its predecessors were an enormous step forward for disabled students, the way in which federal legislation has addressed the education of the disabled has also created very serious problems. One such problem is the overidentification of students as disabled. The percentage of students participating in special education has increased 60 percent since the federal special-education law was first enacted, from 8.3 percent of students in 1976 to 13.3 percent in 2000.[3] Although there is no one definitive measurement of the true rate of disabilities in the population, it simply strains credulity to suggest that more than one in eight students is disabled. At the very least, to claim that so many students are disabled one would have to stretch the meaning of the word "disabled" beyond its common usage and certainly beyond what the authors of the original legislation imagined.

A close examination of different categories of special-education enrollments supports the conclusion that whereas the *identification* of students as disabled has increased, the percentage of students who truly are disabled has remained approximately the same. Almost the entire increase in special-education enrollments since 1976 can be attributed to a rise in one category, called "specific learning disability," which has more than tripled from 1.8 percent of the student population in 1976–77 to 6.0 percent in 2000–01. All other categories of special education combined, including mental retardation, serious emotional disturbance, deafness, blindness, autism, and traumatic brain injury, have increased only slightly, from 6.5 percent to 7.3 percent of the student population, during the same period.[4]

If the true rate of disabilities in the population were really increasing, it should be evident in more than just one disability category. It is highly implausible that something has caused more children to have specific learning disabilities without also causing more mental retardation, serious emotional disturbance, and so forth. It is more likely that the large increase in the category of specific learning disabilities can be attributed to a greater likelihood of children being labeled as having those problems than to a true increase in the incidence of learning disabilities in the student population.

This seems especially likely when we recognize that this high-growth category, specific learning disability, consists of learning problems that are more subjective in their diagnosis and less expensive in their treatment than the other categories of special education. The relative subjectivity of identifying specific learning disabilities makes it possible for an increased propensity to label children as disabled to change the number of children with that diagnosis. The relatively low cost of treating specific learning disabilities may further incline schools and educators to assign that label, especially if the additional funds produced by identifying a child with a specific learning disability exceed the marginal cost of providing that student with relatively minimal services.

The malleability of the "specific learning disability" diagnosis is underscored by the odd way in which disorders in this category are typically identified.[5] To be diagnosed as having a specific learning disability, students must meet two criteria. They must perform significantly worse in a subject area, like math or reading, than is indicated by their cognitive potential, typically measured by an intelligence quotient—or IQ—score. And this mismatch between potential and achievement must be caused by a "disorder in one or more of the basic psychological processes involved in understanding or in using spoken or written language."[6] The problem is that a mismatch between potential and achievement is not always caused by a psychological disorder. For example, it could also result from exposure to ineffective teaching methods. Schools may not be receiving more students with learning problems; in an era of results-based accountability, they may simply be more likely to notice the low performance of students who have been the victims of educational malpractice. And the subjective judgment call of whether a student's mismatch between potential and achievement is caused by a psychological disorder or by bad teaching is usually made by the same school that was responsible for teaching that child in the first place.

Special-education experts, however, do not share this view that true disability rates have remained flat while identification of disabilities has skyrocketed. The common view among practitioners and advocates is that various forces outside of schools have caused a natural increase in disabilities. Consider the arguments advanced by Sheldon Berman and colleagues in their chapter in *Rethinking Special Education for a New Century*. The authors are convinced that "the increases [in special education that] schools have been experiencing have not been caused by school district policy and practice." Instead, they insist, "these cost increases have been primarily due to the increased numbers of children with more significant special needs who require more costly services."[7] In particular, they identify three phenomena that they say have increased the numbers of children with learning problems: improvements in medical technology, deinstitutionalization of children with serious difficulties, and increases in childhood poverty.

All three of these putative causes of greater disabilities have an air of plausibility to them, but they all turn out to be inconsistent with the facts. It is true that improvements in medical technology have saved the lives of more low-birth-weight babies and others with health problems, leading to an increase in children who manifest learning problems later in life because of low birth weight. At the same time, however, other improvements in medical technology, along with other improvements in public health such as reductions in lead paint and safer car seats, have also helped prevent many children from developing disabilities at all and have reduced the severity of disabilities that do occur. Improvements in medical care and public health have led to a net reduction in the number of children with learning difficulties. Berman and colleagues contend that increasing numbers of surviving low-birth-weight babies caused the number of children expected to have mental retardation due to low birth weight to increase from about 4,550 between 1980 and 1985 to 12,375 between 1995 and the present.[8] Overall, however, the number of mentally retarded children in schools actually declined from 961,000 in 1976–77 to 599,000 in 2000–01.[9] Obviously, low-birth-weight babies contribute only a small amount to the total number of children with mental retardation. It appears that any increase in mental retardation attributable to surviving low-birth-weight babies has been more than offset by greater reductions in the number of mentally retarded children attributable to other improvements in medical care and public health.

Berman and his colleagues' claim about deinstitutionalization is no less misleading. Although they provide no numbers, they contend that the deinstitutionalization of mentally retarded children in particular has placed a growing burden on school systems. Yet, as we have already seen, the total number of mentally retarded children served by schools under IDEA has declined steeply. Children with specific learning disabilities were never institutionalized, so deinstitutionalization cannot explain the rise in the one disability category that is driving the growth of special education.

Nor is childhood poverty a plausible explanation for the increase in specific learning disabilities. Poverty among children younger than six is actually about the same now, averaging 18.5 percent in the past five years, as it was in the first five years of federal disability legislation, 18.2 percent.[10] It is true that during the intervening years childhood poverty percentages were sometimes higher because of recessions. But whereas childhood poverty has gone up and down with the business cycle, it has not shown any overall upward trend, and special-education enrollment has steadily increased the whole time.

And this does not even take into account the improvement in the conditions of the poor over the same period. In 1976 the average family in the lowest income quintile earned $12,972 in inflation-adjusted 2001 dollars, compared to $14,021 in 2001.[11] In addition, if poverty were driving specific learning disability diagnoses, this in itself would prove that those diagnoses were not reflecting real disabilities, because the official definition of specific learning disabilities explicitly excludes "children who have learning problems which are primarily the result of . . . environmental, cultural, or economic disadvantage."[12]

Perverse Incentives and Overidentification

If there has not been a natural increase in the rate of disabilities, what is causing this increase in special-education rolls? Although a variety of factors may be at work, including improved awareness and lessened stigmatization of some disabilities, parents increasingly angling for accommodations, and schools seeking to evade accountability for low-performing students, the primary culprit appears to be perverse incentives caused by special-education funding arrangements. Special education is usually funded by providing additional monies to school districts as their special-education enrollment grows. This system, candidly referred to as the "bounty system" by some school finance officials, essentially provides school districts with a financial reward for additional diagnoses. Paying schools more money as they place more students in special education certainly raises the possibility of a perverse financial incentive, swelling special-education enrollments.

Some, however, might object that providing schools with additional funds would not provide them with an incentive to overidentify students as disabled if the costs of serving the disabled equaled or exceeded the additional funds. School officials regularly complain that special-education costs per pupil are far greater than state and federal subsidies, so special education imposes a significant financial burden on schools, not an incentive to overidentify.

This argument embodies a misunderstanding of what truly is and is not a "cost" of placing a child in special education. A true cost is an expenditure that the school would not have made otherwise. Some services that a school would have provided to a particular child no matter what can be redefined as "special-education services" if the child is placed in special education; these services are not truly special-education costs because they would have been provided anyway. For example, imagine that a student is performing substantially below average in reading. The school can choose to help that student by giving him some small-group instruction with a focus on reading fundamentals and simply pay for that as part of its regular education budget. Or the school can say that the student has a specific learning disability (a processing problem in his brain) that is causing his subpar achievement. The intervention that the school would then provide for the student would be essentially the same, some small-group instruction with a focus on reading fundamentals, but under this scenario the school receives subsidies for instructional expenditures that it would have made anyway.

No one in the school system has to consciously or maliciously misidentify a student as disabled for perverse financial incentives to increase special-education enrollments. Well-intentioned teachers and administrators, eager to help students who are behind academically, subtly learn that it is easier to help those students by identifying them as disabled and generating outside subsidies rather than providing the services without special-education status and external resources. The ambiguity of diagnosing specific learning disabilities makes the overidentification of students as disabled possible. The financial bounty attached to additional placement of students in special education makes the overidentification desirable.

Of course, placing a student in special education also generates some additional administrative costs, but in education, even in special education, instructional costs are far greater than administrative costs. In addition, most administrative expenses are fixed costs that do not increase with every new child. Schools need administrators, secretaries, psychologists, speech therapists, and other specialists, whether their special-education caseload is low or high. Placing more students in special education spreads those fixed costs across a larger base of subsidy-generating students.

Overidentification of students as disabled inflicts real harm. First, incorrectly assigning a disability label to a student may alter everyone's expectations about that child's academic potential, hindering his future achievement. Second, swelling special-education rolls do drive up aggregate costs statewide, even if overidentification is in the financial interest of individual schools. Schools and districts have a positive financial incentive to place students in special education as long as the external subsidies exceed a true increase in expenditure, and those external subsidies increase the state's total education spending. Third, shifting large numbers of low-achieving-but-not-disabled students into special education diverts attention and resources away from truly disabled students, depriving them of the quality services they would otherwise receive.

Evidence of Perverse Financial Incentives

The suggestion that financial incentives contribute to increasing special-education enrollment is not just a plausible story. It is supported by three empirical analyses that have examined this question. In one study by Greene and Forster, the role of financial incentives was examined by comparing growth in special education in states with different funding methods.[13] Most states use the "bounty system," in which school districts receive additional funds commensurate with increases in their special-education enrollment. An increasing number of states, however, do not tie funding to the number of students placed into special-education programs. Instead, those states provide districts with a lump sum of money based on their total population, historical special-education enrollments, and demographic characteristics. Except for safety valves provided for the tiny number of severely disabled students who are very expensive to educate, these "lump-sum" states expect that the pool of money allocated to each district should be sufficient. Districts do not get more money for shifting more students to special education.

Greene and Forster compare the growth in special-education enrollments in bounty states to those in lump-sum states during the 1990s. Thirty-three states had bounty funding systems for the entire decade, four states began the decade with lump-sum systems, and twelve switched to a lump-sum system during the 1990s. One state, New Hampshire, did not have any state-level funding of special education until 1999 and was excluded from the analysis. Special-education enrollment under lump-sum systems grew from 10.5 percent in the 1991–92 school year to 11.5 percent in the 2000–01 school year, an increase of 1 percentage point. Meanwhile, special-education enrollment under bounty systems grew from 10.6 percent to 12.6 percent in the same period, an increase of 2 percentage points. Even this simple comparison suggests that special-education growth is much higher when there are positive financial incentives to identify students as disabled. Greene and Forster's analysis estimates that approximately 62 percent of the growth in special-education enrollments in states with bounty funding systems during the 1990s could be attributed to financial incentives, whereas the presence of high-stakes tests had no effect on special-education enrollment.

Greene, Wolf, and Forster subjected these data to a more rigorous analysis to test whether the relationship between funding and enrollment was statistically significant and robust.[14] They organized the information on funding systems and special-education enrollments in each state as a cross-sectional time-series database. Each individual observation was of a particular state in a particular year. They then estimated the effects of lump-sum funding and high-stakes testing on the size of the special-education population while controlling for variation that was specific to particular states and for any general trend over time in special-education diagnoses. Because the special-education enrollments in one state may be influenced by the enrollments in adjoining states—commonly called a "contagion effect"—they used a technique called panel-corrected standard errors to control for such variability. Their statistical analysis finds that special education grew at a significantly faster rate in states that offered positive financial incentives to identify students as disabled. In the average year, states with bounty funding systems had special-education enrollment rates that were higher by 0.555 percentage point. Taking the average total enrollment in bounty-system states across all years in their study and multiplying that by 0.555 percent, they find that this effect is the equivalent of 169,237 extra students assigned to special education because of funding incentives in states that have not reformed their funding systems. The additional spending associated with having that many extra students in special education would be over $1 billion per year.[15]

In a third study, Cullen focused on how changes in special-education financing within a state affected the identification of students as disabled.[16] She studied how school districts in Texas responded to changes in financial incentives arising from court-mandated restructuring of the state education financial system. She found that, after the court order took effect, in districts where the amount of money provided for placing a student in special education went up, special-education enrollment went up faster than in other districts. Specifically, she found that a 10 percent increase in the bounty for placing a student in special education could be expected to produce a 1.4 percent increase in a district's special-education enrollment rate. The relationship between changes in financial incentives and changes in special-education enrollment was strong enough that Cullen found it explained 35 percent of the growth in special education in Texas from the 1991–92 school year through the 1996–97 school year.

Despite this systematic evidence showing a relationship between financial incentives and special-education enrollments, an unwillingness to consider that incentives even play a role causes some people to resist this conclusion. For example, Robert Ervin, the superintendent of schools in Bangor, Maine, reacted to the finding of a relationship between financial incentives and special-education enrollments by telling the *Bangor Daily News* that he could not imagine that "people are sitting in meetings in school on a Thursday afternoon with parents present and they're talking about money."[17] And Perry

Davis, the superintendent of the Dover-Sherborn Schools in Massachusetts, similarly told the *Boston Globe*, "I don't know too many superintendents that are trying to put youngsters into special education to garner more money."[18] School staff, special-education advocates, and others simply have a hard time imagining that financial incentives play a role in labeling students as disabled. Unfortunately, their emotional investment in helping disabled students often blinds them to the possibility that other, less noble motivations can unconsciously and subtly influence decisions about special education even though the evidence clearly indicates that that is the case.

Underserving Disabled Students

In addition to overidentifying students as disabled, the current structure of special education provides incentives to underserve those students who are disabled. Schools do not receive external subsidies based on the quality or extent of services they provide; they get their money simply for placing students in special education regardless of how well those students are served. Even worse, poor accounting and site-based management make special-education monies essentially fungible.

Diverting special-education funds to boost general education is attractive to schools because disabled students are more likely to be captured clientele, whereas the market for general-education students is more competitive. Truly disabled students have extra needs that are more costly to address. Their more expensive needs and the more limited institutions that can effectively serve their needs limit the choices available to the families of disabled students. It is more difficult to find private schools willing to educate more costly students without receiving additional funds. And few families can afford regular private-school tuition, let alone any additional expenses that would be required for disabled students. Choices among public schools are also more limited for disabled students than they are for general-education students because not every public school can address every disability. In addition, all public schools face the same set of perverse incentives to take special-education subsidies while underserving those students.

Even if public schools do not divert funds to general education, they still face inadequate incentives to provide high-quality services with the money they do spend. Because special-education families are more likely to have limited alternatives, their public schools can afford to take them more for granted. Again, no malice on the part of school officials is required for subpar services to be provided to disabled students. The lack of positive financial incentives to serve disabled students well simply undermines, often in subtle and unconscious ways, the motivation of administrators and staff to ensure that disabled students receive the best care.

Disabled students are entitled to free and appropriate education services under the law, and schools that underserve them are potentially subject to lawsuits. Unfortunately, the legal process is an extremely inefficient method of ensuring that students receive complete, quality services. There are significant barriers to families accessing the legal process to obtain quality services. Families have to be aware that they are entitled to certain services, and they have to be aware of the appeals and legal processes by which they could seek those services. Only the most sophisticated families of disabled students are fully knowledgeable about their rights and how to protect them. Hiring legal representation to fight for services often requires money that families are unable or unwilling to spend. Even if families are aware of the quality and type of services they should be receiving, know how to use the legal process to seek those services, and have the resources to do so, families still have to be willing to engage in a legal fight with the same people that take care of their children every day. This is a price that families are often unwilling to pay.

Even before a struggle for services hits the legal arena, families of disabled students are at a distinct disadvantage in seeking fully adequate services. The set of services each student should receive is determined by an individual educational plan (IEP). The IEP is essentially a contract between the school and the family, describing the services and accommodations a disabled student should receive. The IEP is the product of negotiations between school staff and families. In those negotiations, schools have every advantage in seeking to minimize services provided. School officials are much more sophisticated than most parents in negotiating the IEP. School personnel negotiate IEPs almost every day, whereas families do not. Schools know how to craft IEP language to limit their exposure to expensive service mandates in ways that all but the most knowledgeable parents cannot detect. Families can have legal representation at IEP meetings, but all of the barriers to the legal process apply to the use of lawyers in negotiating IEPs as well.

Listening to school officials, however, one might think that militant and lawsuit-happy parents have the edge over schools in the IEP process. Exceptionally sophisticated and active parents extracting expensive services from schools can make for appealing news stories, but this is one of those cases where the plural of "anecdote" is not "data." Families with the knowledge and resources to prevail over the very knowledgeable and very wealthy state are necessarily few in number. Although special-education lawsuits have increased dramatically over the last few decades, they continue to represent a tiny fraction of all students in special education, and their number has begun to level off. Perhaps more important, schools win far more often than school administrators think.[19] Perry Zirkel, who systematically tracks education litigation, finds that "judges increasingly appear to believe that school officials merit the strong benefit of the doubt."[20]

If you doubt that schools work hard to minimize their IEP obligations, consider a satirical skit presented at a 2003 national conference for school disability lawyers. According to the *Washington Post*, the skit's mock newscast "was greeted by abundant laughter" as the anchorman "joked that Cuisinart has come up with the Due Processor, which 'shreds, dices, cuts, blends, frappes and otherwise destroys' unwanted applications for due process hearings. . . . Showing a photo of elated children, he said, 'In Boulder, Colorado, a group of students took to the streets in celebration of their due process victory, where the judges awarded them new sets of parents.'" Perhaps most striking was the skit's frank depiction of how schools manipulate the IEP process: "With a John Madden display of arrows and circles, he gave a play-by-play of how a school system used its skill to deny a family the placement sought for a child." This attack against parents for seeking their IEP rights was so well received that the conference organizers invited the performer—himself a senior special-education attorney for a school district—to deliver it again at the next year's conference.[21]

Evidence of Underserving Disabled Students

As colorful as this anecdote from the *Washington Post* may be, an anecdote does not prove that special-education students are being underserved. In general, because special-education students are often exempt from testing requirements and because other systematic information on the progress of disabled students is difficult to find given privacy concerns, we have less evidence on the question of underservice than we do on the question of over-identification. The evidence we do have, however, supports the plausible theory that the incentives in the current special-education system encourage the underserving of disabled students.

The National Council on Disability has documented widespread problems with the delivery of adequate services to disabled students. In particular it concludes:

Every state was out of compliance with IDEA requirements to some degree; in the sampling of states studied, noncompliance persisted over many years. Notwithstanding federal monitoring reports documenting widespread noncompliance, enforcement of the law is the burden of parents who too often must invoke formal complaint procedures and due process hearings, including expensive and time-consuming litigation, to obtain the appropriate services and supports to which their children are entitled under the law. Many parents with limited resources are unable to challenge violations successfully when they occur. Even parents with significant resources are hard-pressed to prevail over state education agencies (SEA) and local education agencies (LEA) when they or their publicly financed attorneys choose to be recalcitrant.[22]

Although the findings of a disability advocacy group should be taken with a grain of salt, their systematic analyses of compliance and their broad information on reported difficulties with enforcement support the claim that disabled students are seriously underserved.

In addition, Greene and Forster conducted a survey of parents of disabled students who had participated in Florida's McKay Scholarship Program.[23] The McKay scholarship is a voucher that any student with an IEP in Florida can use to attend a different school—public or registered private, within or outside the district. The voucher is worth the entire amount spent on that child in his or her previous public school, so it provides additional dollars for students with more severe disabilities. In that survey, parents were asked whether their public school had provided all of the services that were required by the IEP. Only one-third of parents reported that the schools had provided all required services. In addition, almost half reported that they had conflicts with their public school over the IEP.

Of course, because they were seeking alternative services elsewhere, families who sought a McKay scholarship might be among those who would have the strongest complaints about the quality of services they received. Nevertheless, the fact that almost 4 percent of disabled students were using a McKay scholarship only a few years into the existence of this program suggests that the desire to seek alternative services is not highly exceptional, so their experiences may not be seriously atypical. Even if we assume half as many reports of subpar service from non-McKay families, we would still expect that almost one-third of schools failed to deliver services required by the IEP and almost one-quarter came into conflict with families over the IEP.

Furthermore, these reports of inadequate services would only include incidents where families were sophisticated enough to be aware of the types and quality of services their disabled children should have been receiving.

The Civil Rights Model versus the Market Model

These problems with the overidentification of students as disabled and the underserving of those students who are identified are not inevitable. Failure to devise a special-education system that provides checks and balances to limit the impact of perverse incentives has been facilitated by the modeling of special-education legislation after civil rights efforts. Federal legislation covering the education of the disabled was first adopted in the 1970s on the crest of a wave of civil rights legislation. Measures to ensure an adequate education for disabled students were similar to those adopted to guarantee an adequate education for racial minorities. Legislation explicitly mandated the provision of adequate services with heavy reliance upon the legal system to ensure compliance.

The difficulty with applying the civil rights model to special education is that the barriers preventing adequate services for minority students were different from the barriers preventing adequate services to disabled students. Black students, particularly in the South, were denied services primarily because of irrational racial prejudice. State and local laws reflected those irrational prejudices, legally forbidding school integration and resulting in inferior services. The denial of adequate services to disabled students, however, was not motivated primarily by prejudice or ill will. Instead, the obstacles were largely a matter of finances and incentives. Minority students do not cost more money to educate, but disabled students do.

The civil rights model necessarily relied heavily on enforcement through the courts rather than using market incentives to facilitate the realization of people's preferences, because the problem was irrational racist preferences. Schools could have been provided with financial incentives to integrate and offer better-quality services to minority students, but that approach could not have easily overcome racist preferences. Southern schools could have been offered additional money to admit black students, but schools that integrated would have risked losing many of their white students and the tax revenues those families generated. The only solution was to order integration and ensure compliance through the legal system.

This was not the only solution, nor was it the best solution, for addressing the education of the disabled. Schools could have been offered financial incentives to serve the disabled, and, properly structured, those incentives could have been sufficient to ensure adequate services. Unlike the case of race, people's preferences were not the problem. Rather, the problem was financial and could have been addressed by altering schools' financial incentives.

In particular, special-education legislation should provide additional funds to cover the additional costs associated with educating students given their disabilities, but the funds for special-education students should be in the form of vouchers, not as payments directly to schools. Altering who controls the money students generate has significant implications for how that money affects everyone's behavior. If schools directly receive additional money for placing students in special education, they have an incentive to overidentify students as disabled because there are more rewards than costs to shifting students. In addition, providing additional funds directly to schools regardless of how well disabled students are served provides schools with incentives to take that money while minimizing the quantity of services they offer. Paying schools regardless of how well they serve disabled students also undermines their attention to the quality of the services they do provide.

If every student placed in special education is offered a voucher equal to the entire cost of his education, however, the incentives facing schools are fundamentally changed. Schools would have some reluctance to overidentify students as disabled, because any student placed in special education could take all of the funds he generates for the school and walk out of the door with them. With special-education vouchers, schools put some of their funding in jeopardy when they shift students into special education, placing a check on the financial incentive to overidentify. In addition, giving disabled students vouchers would provide those students with better leverage to obtain full and high-quality services. Rather than having to fight with schools for services in the courts, students could threaten to take their funding elsewhere if they were dissatisfied.

Evidence on the Market Model

The argument for a market approach to special education is not solely theoretical. Evidence from the McKay program in Florida sheds light on what might happen with a broader market model. The McKay program provides a voucher for all students with IEPs from Florida public schools. Disabled students can use the voucher, which is equivalent to the entire amount of money spent on that student in public school, to attend a different public or private school. Families are allowed to supplement the voucher with their own funds to pay tuition if it exceeds the value of the voucher. Private schools can be religious or secular, but they must meet minimal eligibility requirements to ensure financial viability and safety. Private schools receiving McKay students are not required to follow the student's previous IEP, nor are they required to develop a new one. Instead of serving the student by writing a contract that can be enforced through the courts, the McKay program intends to serve students by allowing them to shop for quality services. McKay is essentially a pilot program for switching from the civil rights model to the market model.

Initial results from the McKay program are very encouraging. More than 12,000 disabled students in Florida, representing the full spectrum of disabilities, racial backgrounds, and family incomes, have been able to find seats in private schools, and the evidence suggests that they are being much better served under the market model than they were previously. Also, research has found that the McKay program has begun to reduce the rate of growth in special-education enrollment, limiting the problem of overidentification of students as disabled.

In their evaluation of the McKay program, Greene and Forster found significantly better outcomes for disabled students in private schools with McKay scholarships than in their previous public schools.[24] For example, they found that 86.0 percent of parents of McKay students reported that their private schools provided all promised services, whereas only 30.2 percent reported that their previous public schools had similarly delivered all promised services. McKay students saw class size drop dramatically, from an average of 25.1 students per class in public schools to 12.8 students per class in private schools. Small class sizes may be particularly beneficial to disabled students because addressing their special needs requires higher levels of individualized attention. Disabled students are often more vulnerable to bullying from other students, but McKay students were victimized far less by other students because of their disabilities in private schools. In public schools, 46.8 percent were bothered often and 24.7 percent were physically assaulted because of their disabilities, but in McKay schools 5.3 percent were bothered often and 6.0 percent were assaulted. Higher levels of school follow-through on promised services, smaller classes, and lower levels of victimization contributed to glowing appraisals of the McKay program from the families of disabled students. Almost all (92.7 percent) of McKay participants are satisfied or very satisfied with their McKay schools, compared to only 32.7 percent who were similarly satisfied with their public schools. Even among families that had tried a McKay scholarship and discontinued participating in the program (only 10 percent of all McKay users), almost two-thirds reported being satisfied with the program, and 90 percent said that the program should continue for others.

Despite this success, critics of market approaches to special education, including People for the American Way and the Progressive Policy Institute, have worried that programs such as McKay would make disabled students vulnerable if they have more severe disabilities or come from low-income or racial minority families.[25] The experience with the McKay program, however, suggests otherwise. The distribution of the type and severity of disabilities in the McKay program is roughly representative of the special-education population in Florida public schools. McKay is also roughly representative of the public-school population in its racial and class composition.[26] In addition, it is not entirely clear why low-income and minority disabled children are better protected under the civil rights model, in light of their lower access to the knowledge and resources necessary to protect the right to services through the courts.

These concerns about the McKay program misunderstand why federal legislation has made schools able to serve disabled students. Schools are now able to educate the disabled because they now have the additional funds to provide special-education services. As the experience with the McKay program shows, there are plenty of private schools that, if offered the same additional funds, are happy to serve students with the full range of disabilities. They do not provide those services because they are required by law, documented in an IEP, and enforced by the threat of lawsuits. Private schools accepting McKay students do so because they are paid for their efforts, just as public schools have been for the past three decades. The only difference is that private schools have to earn their payments by providing quality services, whereas public schools only have to do just barely enough to avoid litigation.

Barriers to Fixing Special Education

If the education of the disabled is better structured using a market approach rather than a civil rights approach, why have we not adopted the more efficient policies? First, there is a certain amount of inertia in policy arrangements. Special education was modeled after civil rights legislation in part because of when it was adopted, and it is hard to change approaches once those arrangements have been set.

Second, the civil rights approach has developed powerful constituencies that are reluctant to consider changes. Disability advocates remember the bad days when disabled students were regularly denied adequate services and are grateful for the progress that the civil rights approach has produced. They are understandably cautious about making any changes in the system that realized those gains. The cottage industry of lawyers that has developed around special education is also committed to the civil rights model—not only because their livelihood is dependent upon it, but also because they are more familiar with contracts and litigation than with choice and competition. Public-school officials, including their representatives in the teachers' unions and other professional associations, are also relatively content with the civil rights model. They receive additional funds as students are shifted into special education, and the high costs of enforcing disability rights through litigation make them relatively unaccountable for the quality of services those funds are supposed to support. Of course, the market approach to special education would threaten their funding and increase their accountability for results, making that model particularly unappealing to school officials.

The third and most significant barrier to adopting a market approach to special education is the perceived incompatibility between our emotional commitment to the disabled and the hard incentives of the market model. Students with disabilities rightly deserve our sympathies and emotional support, and thankfully these sentiments are widespread. Nevertheless, people fear that thinking about how incentives operate in special education undermines this emotional support. Will we undermine the notion that people should help disabled students because they need our help if we emphasize the ways in which financial incentives alter the type and quantity of help they receive?

In spite of these barriers, there are also factors that will support policy change. Although reform would create financial "losers"—primarily trial lawyers, special-education staff, and teachers' unions—it will also create "winners." Putting fewer nondisabled students into special education would provide a better education to both disabled and nondisabled students. The former would benefit because special-education programs would no longer be required to serve large numbers of students who are not truly disabled, freeing up the system to serve truly disabled students more efficiently. The latter would benefit because putting a "disabled" label on a student who is not truly disabled harms that student. Parents and teachers of a "disabled" child will have seriously lowered expectations for that child's performance, so many children who could be doing much better academically if only they were served better will languish as low-performing special-education students. Finally, reform would benefit taxpayers, not only by improving the overall efficiency of the system in the ways just described, but also by ending the upward distortion in spending caused by incorrectly labeling students as disabled. Placing a student in special education produces spending mandates that may exceed the amount that would actually have to be spent to address that student's academic needs if they were rightly understood. A more accurate diagnosis of which students are truly disabled and which students are performing poorly because of bad instruction will allow for a more accurate assessment of spending needs.

It is difficult to quantify the inefficiency created by the existing special-education system, but it is possible to at least get a ballpark idea of its size. As noted above, Greene, Wolf, and Forster estimate that 169,237 extra students are assigned to special education in states with bounty funding. This is a very conservative estimate, because it includes only enrollment growth due to funding incentives during the 1990s, whereas funding incentives have actually been driving up special-education enrollment for thirty years. The estimate is also conservative because it includes only states that still have bounty funding, whereas states that have reformed their funding systems still have higher enrollment than they would have had if financial incentives to over-identify had never operated. Special-education subsidies for that many students add up to about $1 billion per year. Not all of that money can be considered lost, of course, because (as we have seen) much of it goes to subsidize services that would have been provided anyway even if those students had not been placed in special education. At least some of that money is wasted, however, because it is spent on disability services that are not truly appropriate for nondisabled students and because placing nondisabled students into special education produces unnecessary administrative costs. If even 20 percent of that money is wasted on inappropriate services and unnecessary costs, the annual loss is considerable.

But this only captures the monetary loss; if the special-education funding system were reformed, it would not only cost less, it would perform better. Disabled and nondisabled students alike would receive a better education. The nation currently spends $400 billion per year on education, a doubling of real per-pupil spending in the past thirty years with no increase in educational outcomes. Any reform that actually provides a better education, and does so while reducing costs, could generate substantial public support.

The only way to overcome the barriers to policy change is to try market approaches in more places, carefully collect information on the consequences of a market approach, and use that evidence to convince people about what will best serve disabled students while controlling costs. This gradual experimentation and persuasion can eventually ease concerns about a tension between hard-headed analysis of incentives and the promotion of compassion. It can also convince disability advocates that the risk of switching to a market approach is less than the benefits it would bring their constituents. Disability lawyers and school officials are going to be the most difficult to persuade, in light of their financial investment in the status quo, but even they can be moved by evidence on what is in the best interest of disabled students. Interests shape people's views, but they do not determine them. If future experiments support a market approach, we might make a second giant step forward in the education of the disabled.

Notes

1. "Back to School on Civil Rights," National Council on Disability, January 25, 2000 (www.ncd.gov/newsroom/publications/2000/backtoschool_1.htm [July 14, 2006]).

2. Paul E. Peterson and Marc C. Rom, *Welfare Magnets: A New Case for a National Standard* (Brookings, 1990).

3. "Digest of Education Statistics," U.S. Department of Education, 2002, Table 52 (http://nces.ed.gov/programs/digest/d02/dt052.asp [July 14, 2006]).

4. "Digest of Education Statistics," table 52.

5. Craig S. Lerner, "'Accommodations' for the Learning Disabled: A Level Playing Field or Affirmative Action for Elites," *Vanderbilt Law Review*, vol. 57, no. 3 (2004): 1058–64.

6. "Digest of Education Statistics," definitions appendix (http://nces.ed.gov/pubs2003/2003060h.pdf [July 14, 2006]).

7. Sheldon Berman and others, "The Rising Costs of Special Education in Massachusetts: Causes and Effects," in *Rethinking Special Education for a New Century*, edited by Chester E. Finn Jr., and others (Washington, D.C.: Thomas B. Fordham Foundation and Progressive Policy Institute, May 2001), p. 183 (www.edexcellence.net/library/special_ed/special_ed_ch9.pdf [July 14, 2006]).

8. Berman and others, "Rising Costs of Special Education in Massachusetts," p. 201.

9. "Digest of Education Statistics," table 52.

10. U.S. Census Bureau, Historical Poverty Tables, Table 20 (www.census.gov/hhes/poverty/histpov/hstpov20.html [July 14, 2006]).

11. U.S. Census Bureau, Historical Income Tables—Families, Table F-3 (www.census.gov/hhes/income/histinc/f03.html [July 14, 2006]).

12. "Digest of Education Statistics," definitions appendix.

13. Jay P. Greene and Greg Forster, "Effects of Funding Incentives on Special Education Enrollment," Manhattan Institute Civic Report 32, December 2002 (www.manhattan-institute.org/html/cr_32.htm [July 14, 2006]).

14. Jay P. Greene and others, "Rewarding Diagnosis: Financial Incentives and the Rise in Special Education," unpublished manuscript, Manhattan Institute, 2003.

15. This cost estimate is based on an estimated additional expenditure per special-education student of $5,918 in the 1999–2000 school year, calculated on behalf of the

U.S. Department of Education by the Center for Special Education Finance. This figure represents spending on special-education students over and above what is spent on regular students. See Jay G. Chambers, Tom Parrish, and Jennifer J. Harr, "What Are We Spending on Special Education Services in the United States, 1999–2000? Advance Report no. 1," Center For Special Education Finance, June 2004 (www.csef-air.org/publications/seep/national/AdvRpt1.pdf [July 14, 2006]).

16. Julie Berry Cullen, "The Impact of Fiscal Incentives on Student Disability Rates," Working Paper 7173 (Cambridge, Mass.: National Bureau of Economic Research, June 1999) (www.nber.org/papers/w7173 [July 14, 2006]).

17. Ruth-Ellen Cohen, "Maine's Special Ed Use among Highest," *Bangor Daily News*, July 16, 2003, p. A1.

18. Shari Rudavsky, "Report Targets Special Needs," *Boston Globe*, December 29, 2002, p. A27.

19. Marjorie Coeyman, "Are Schools More Afraid of Lawsuits Than They Should Be?" *Christian Science Monitor*, May 27, 2003, p. 21.

20. Perry A. Zirkel, "Tipping the Scales," *American School Board Journal*, October 1997 (www.asbj.com/199710/asbj1097.html [July 14, 2006]).

21. Linda Perlstein, "Parents See No Humor in Skit on Special-Ed," *Washington Post*, March 31, 2004, p. B5.

22. "Back to School on Civil Rights."

23. Jay P. Greene and Greg Forster, "Vouchers for Special Education Students: An Evaluation of Florida's McKay Scholarship Program," Manhattan Institute Civic Report 38, June 2003.

24. Greene and Forster, "Vouchers for Special Education Students," 2003.

25. See People for the American Way/Disability Rights Education and Defense Fund, "Jeopardizing a Legacy," March 6, 2003 (www.pfaw.org/pfaw/dfiles/file_167.pdf [July 14, 2006]).

26. Greene and Forster, "Vouchers for Special Education Students," 2003.

III

New Tools for Problem Solving

7

Decision Markets for Policy Advice

ROBIN HANSON

The main cause of bad policy decisions is arguably a lack of information. Decisionmakers often do not make use of relevant information about the consequences of the policies they choose. The problem, however, is not simply that public officials do not exploit readily available information. It is also that they do not take full advantage of creative mechanisms that could expand the *supply* of policy-relevant information. Among the most innovative and potentially useful information-generating mechanisms are speculative markets. Speculative markets produce public information about the perceived likelihood of future events as a natural byproduct of voluntary exchange.

Speculative markets do a remarkable job of aggregating information; in every head-to-head field comparison made so far, their forecasts have been at least as accurate as those of competing institutions, such as official government estimates. Many organizations are now trying to take advantage of this effect, experimenting with the creation of "prediction markets" or "information markets," to forecast future events such as product sales and project completion dates.

This chapter examines the uses and limitations of decision markets. Decision markets are information markets designed to inform a particular policy decision, by directly estimating relevant consequences of that decision. After reviewing the weaknesses of existing institutions, the mechanics of decision markets, and a concrete example, this chapter reviews the requirements, advantages, and disadvantages of decision markets. The chapter also takes a close look at a particular application of this tool—the controversial yet illuminating attempt to establish a "Policy Analysis Market" to forecast the consequences of major U.S. policy choices in the Middle East.

Government Information Failures

There are many ways that governments can fail to achieve good policy outcomes. Some interest groups may have too much power or want the wrong things, or leaders may pursue personal goals that do not have broad public support. Government agencies may also pursue parochial goals or fail to coordinate with each other.

Most of the government failures that we might overcome, however, are arguably due to a lack of information about the consequences of policy choices. Policymakers may have mistaken beliefs about the direct effects of a policy. They may fail to consider an indirect effect or an alternative policy. Or we might fail at a higher level to choose the right institutions to set the context for such judgments and choices. In fact, much of what economists have been doing for the past half century is showing how most social problems are at root caused by such information failures. For example, there is almost no end to the troubles caused by the principal-agent problem—that is, the fact that experts know more than their clients.[1] We rely on doctors, lawyers, teachers, and chief executive officers because they can know more than we do. Government policy similarly relies heavily on expert knowledge, expressed directly via civil servants, contractors, and official boards and commissions, and indirectly via mass media and academic reports and analyses.

We hope that such experts acquire and use their knowledge for our benefit, but we fear that they instead give us the advice that benefits them. Stereo salesmen, for example, may suggest overly expensive stereos, and surgeons may recommend surgery over drug treatments. We cannot trust such experts because of "professional ethics"; if they are trustworthy, it is because their institutional and contractual incentives make them so.

Unfortunately, agency problems in the government-citizen relationship are among the worst, because the chains of delegation are so long, the topic coverage is so broad, and citizens have so little reason to pay attention. Each election, voters, with little expertise or chance of personally influencing the outcome, form judgments about how the policy outcomes they favor relate to the candidates before them. Representatives, anticipating those judgments and any other voter preferences, oversee the agencies that implement government policy. All the way down the long chain of delegation, each official tries somewhat to make his part of government look like what the officials above him want it to look like.

To be sure, voters can try to rely on nongovernmental advisors, such as mass media and organized political groups, but this merely replaces the problem of evaluating candidates with a similar problem of evaluating these advisors and makes the delegation chain even longer. Those who run media firms and organized political groups are professionals, just like politicians and CEOs. They compete with others who could replace them and so mostly do whatever it takes to build their power, prestige, and profit.

Sometimes bad things happen that voters notice that can be attributed to specific actors whom voters can remember to punish in a future election. Sometimes good things happen that voters can similarly notice, identify, and remember to reward. Where voters are willing to act on such clues, government officials have an incentive to avoid these bad things and encourage these good things. Ideally, government officials could be well disciplined if a single entity ran the government over long terms and if each voter only considered whether his life had gone better or worse than expected since the last election.[2]

In fact, however, terms are short, government is divided, and voters do not just consider their own lives.[3] Voters weigh policy effects on distant others and try to distinguish policy influences, and although these strategies may have some advantages, they can make voter information problems far worse. For example, some say the U.S. Food and Drug Administration (FDA) tries harder to avoid bad new drugs than delays in good drugs, because the former are far more noticeable.[4]

Most important, voters have many opinions about the effectiveness of policies and process, and the government naturally caters to those opinions. Policy often seems closer to what public opinion would suggest than to what relevant experts advise.[5] Even when governments apparently rely on expert opinion, they often do so to legitimate predetermined policies, rather than to gain information to help determine policy.[6]

A candidate who cares only about winning the next election should neglect what he knows about good policy and prefer the policies that voters favor.[7] Of course, this is not just a problem with government. A CEO should neglect what he knows about good long-term corporate strategy in favor of whatever will impress stock speculators when that CEO exercises his stock options.[8] This phenomenon is very general. Experts should not even bother to obtain information that their clients will not know when those clients reward the experts.[9]

This problem can, however, be much worse in government. Whereas stock speculators can have a strong personal incentive to think carefully about corporate policy, voters not only have little reason to think carefully about how to vote, but often have positive reasons to be irrational.[10] Yes, voters may need to think about how to deal with the policies that win and may want to sound knowledgeable (and compassionate and loyal and much more) when discussing politics with associates, but these are far weaker than the incentives of serious stock speculators.

What can we do about this policy information problem? We could subsidize voter education, but education is expensive, only somewhat relevant, and it is hard to keep such subsidies politically neutral. We could seek to limit the franchise to the most politically informed, but there is little political support for insulting less informed citizens in this way.

Another approach would be to educate voters to trust and appreciate the benefits of a new policy process. Voters now accept the results of most jury trials not because they have opinions on whether the accused was guilty, but because they believe the process is likely to convict the guilty. Voters also accept most research funding allocations not because they have opinions about which grant proposals should be funded, but because they accept the peer review process in research. The public similarly accepts the results of elections, FDA drug approvals, and exams for driver's licenses, civil service promotion, and college admissions.

All policy processes, however, do not inspire equal confidence. For example, official committee reports are routinely suspected of being biased via the selection of committee members, whereas cost-benefit (and other economic) analyses are often suspected of being biased via method choices. Statistical analyses fare a bit better, but are still often suspect. These cases suggest that voters tend to trust simple informative mechanisms that seem difficult for interested parties to bias.

How Decision Markets Work

Decision markets are a new policy mechanism that we might hope will one day be accepted by the public as especially simple, informative, and difficult to bias. Decision markets are speculative markets that estimate policy consequences.

Speculation takes place when an actor buys or sells something today in the hope of reversing her trade later for a profit. For example, if an actor thinks housing prices are climbing, he might buy a house today in the hope of selling it next year at a higher price. But because it costs so much to buy and sell houses, the actor could lose money even if housing prices did rise. When durable commodities are traded in markets with low transaction costs, however, speculation becomes cheap. These markets are known as *speculative markets*. For example, if you are confident that the price of gold is going up, you are pretty sure to profit from buying gold today in order to sell it tomorrow. And if you are confident that the price of gold is going down, you can profit by selling today in order to buy tomorrow. (If you do not have gold today, you can still sell today by "selling short.")

Speculative markets ultimately do an excellent job of aggregating relevant information. This is because those who think they have information about whether the price is going to go up or down expect to profit by speculating on that information, and by speculating on information, one incorporates that information into the market price. For example, if you think the price is going up, you buy, which tends to raise the price. Speculators thus compete to be the first to profit from any new information relevant to predicting future prices. The net result is that when speculative market prices exist, it is hard to find information that such market prices do not embody. After all, anyone who finds such neglected information can profit by trading on it and thereby eliminating this neglect.[11]

Although the information-collecting abilities of speculative markets are impressive, such markets are usually created for other reasons, such as to allow traders to entertain or insure themselves. One can, however, create new markets specifically to try to take advantage of this information-collecting effect. For example, if one wanted to know whether it would rain here tomorrow (at place *X* and on date *T*), one might create contingent assets that declared "Pays $100 if rain at place *X* on date *T*." If one could get speculators to trade such assets, and if their current market price was $20, one could take this as an estimate that the probability of rain tomorrow is 20 percent. After all, people unconcerned about risk would be buying or selling this asset if they thought the probability of rain was anything other than 20 percent.[12]

Recently some new markets have been created specifically to take advantage of these effects. Called *prediction markets*, information markets, virtual stock markets, artificial markets, or idea futures, these markets are now used to estimate measures such as product sales, project completion dates, or election outcomes.[13] Sponsors have created both public markets, where anyone can trade and learn from the market prices, and private markets, where only a select few can trade or see prices. Sponsors have created both markets where people trade hard cash and markets where they trade "play money" for bragging rights.

Such markets (at least the hard cash versions) have so far done well in every known head-to-head field comparison with other social institutions that forecast. Orange juice futures improve on National Weather Service forecasts, horse race markets beat horse race experts, Academy Award markets beat columnist forecasts, gas demand markets beat gas demand experts, stock markets beat the official NASA panel at fingering the guilty company in the Challenger accident, election markets beat national opinion polls, and corporate sales markets beat official corporate forecasts.[14]

Although more accurate market-based forecasts can be of great value, it seems that market-based policy-conditional forecasts might be of even greater value.[15] Let us now focus on this *decision market* option.

A Concrete Example

Consider the oft-heard proposal to change U.S. health insurance into a single-payer system (SPS), such as many other developed nations use. Many claims have been made in support of such a proposal, but certainly two of the most important claims are that an SPS would improve health and reduce costs. Although media and academic analyses and reports have weighed in on this subject for many decades, the public remains uncertain about whether an SPS would in fact have these consequences.

Let us focus on the health claim, and in particular on whether average lifespan would be increased ten years later if the United States adopted an SPS, relative to if an SPS were not adopted. More specifically, imagine the year is 2008, and people disagree about the consequences of a particular bill before the U.S. Congress, which would implement an SPS starting in 2010.

A decision market approach to this problem would create two speculative markets and then observe two prices. (We explain exactly how below.) One price would represent an estimate of U.S. lifespan in 2020 given that the SPS bill passed, while the other price would represent an estimate of U.S. lifespan in 2020 given that the SPS bill did not pass. The difference between these two estimates would say how much market speculators expected this SPS bill to raise or lower U.S. lifespan.

Once the public accepted such market estimates as good policy estimates, the main remaining tasks for the public, media, and lobbyists would be to monitor the consistency between prices and policy; the policies chosen should seem reasonable given market-specified beliefs.[16] For example, a single-payer health insurance system should not be approved if markets estimate that it would both raise costs and reduce lifespan, at least when these are the main arguments for such a change. Alternatively, we might approve new institutions that more directly put market estimates in charge of decisions.[17]

So how would this work exactly? To get decision market estimates on the SPS question we would first need to define our measures well enough to settle bets. So we might define U.S. average lifespan in 2020 using the official statistics of the U.S. National Vital Statistics System in 2022. We might define SPS adoption to mean that the particular SPS bill, however amended, was signed into U.S. law during 2009. And we might define the assets being bet to be U.S. currency paid in 2022, corrected for officially measured inflation from 2009. Judges would have to be appointed to decide about any remaining unanticipated ambiguities.

Once these measures were defined, one or more financial institutions could create assets to represent the relevant bets. One asset would be "Pays $100 if S," which in 2020 pays 100 inflation-adjusted U.S. dollars if S—that is, if the SPS bill is passed (and nothing otherwise). A second asset would be "Pays $100 if not S." A financial institution would take no net risk by allowing $100 (of inflation-adjusted U.S. dollars in 2020) to be exchanged at any time for the pair "Pays $100 if S" and "Pays $100 if not S."

There would also be no net risk in allowing $100 to be exchanged for the pair "Pays L" and "Pays $(100 - L)$," where L is U.S. average lifespan in 2020 (or 100 in the unlikely case that lifespan were in excess of 100). There would further be no risk in allowing "Pays L" to be exchanged for the pair "Pays L if S" and "Pays L if not S."

Once such assets were available, we could create the two decision markets to trade them. There are many possible market structures. For example, the standard double auction structure supports a single kind of standard trade, such as gold for cash. In the double auction, anyone can at any time post an offer to buy or sell at a chosen price, cancel any previous offer, or accept one of the best current offers.

Another option is a simple automated market maker. Such a market maker always has an offer to buy a standard quantity at some price and a similar offer to sell at some higher price. The market maker sets these prices using a monotonic function of the assets it holds; whenever someone accepts the market maker's sell offer it raises both prices, and whenever someone accepts its buy offer the market maker lowers such prices. As information is revealed, the market maker should lose on average, but a strict bound can be placed on how much it can ever lose, and the gains are given only to those who move the market price toward its ultimate resolution.[18]

Another market structure is a call auction, where offers collect to be matched together at the same price. Call auctions have lower price noise, at the cost of a delay in getting prices. Combinatorial versions of all these structures can support the combined trading of many different related assets. Market structures also include mechanisms for ensuring that traders can and do make good on their offers, and they include choices about who can see what offers and trades.

Whatever the details of the exchange mechanisms, the important thing would be the appearance of two market prices, or trading rates of exchange. In the first decision market we need, people would exchange one asset "Pays L if S" for some chosen fraction of the asset "Pays $100 if S." In the second market, people would exchange one "Pays L if not S" for some fraction of "Pays $100 if not S." These fractions could be taken as market estimates of the conditional expected values $E[L \mid S]$ and $E[L \mid \text{not } S]$, respectively. If the first fraction were higher than the second, market speculators would be saying that they expect U.S. lifespan to be higher if the SPS bill is approved than if not. Such estimates are what we would want to advice SPS policy.

Requirements for Decision Markets

We have good reasons (including formal theory, lab experiments, and field data) to think that decision markets can give accurate estimates. But decision markets are not cure-alls; they require:

Important-enough Claims—There are fixed costs of using this decision market process. You have to set up markets, get traders to pay attention, and so on. Yet if other forecasting institutions are working well, market estimates might only be slightly more accurate than estimates from other institutions. The policy question asked thus needs to be important enough for this added accuracy to be worth the added fixed costs.

Careful thought should be given to what question one wants to pose to market speculators. If you ask the wrong question, the answer you get may not be very useful. For example, if reducing lifespan inequality is as important a benefit of SPS as increasing average lifespan, one might want to ask markets about inequality as well. If one cannot afford to ask about both, one might ask about a weighted average of the two.

Enough Influence—Prices in real markets can contain noise, because of random influences on trader incentives and behavior. So the decision options considered need to have a large enough influence on the outcomes measured for random price fluctuations not to obscure the relevant outcome differences. Decision markets will probably not show how a single act of capital punishment affects the murder rate, for example. Averaging prices over a short time may help, and simple statistical tests can suggest whether a price difference is statistically significant.

Distinct Options—There must be a way after the fact to determine whether a particular decision option was chosen or not. One could not ask markets about the consequences of "progressive reform" or "using quality standards" unless one could define relatively clearly what would count as such a policy. As with the legal system, ambiguities might be dealt with using defaults created by precedents and by using judges who are trusted to be neutral.

Measured Outcomes—There must be a way to create measures of some of the important outcomes of interest after the fact and to identify what those measures will be before the fact. Large measurement errors are not much of a problem, nor are other influences on the measured outcomes. Instead, the problems are correlations between errors and the decision and correlations between errors and efforts to influence the measurement process.

One does *not* need to be able to tell after the fact how much each decision influenced the outcome. Standard decision theory is clear that when you are faced with some options A, and you want to achieve the outcome B, you should choose the option A associated with the maximum value of your expectation E[B | A]. These summary expectations are all that should matter, not the details that produce them.

Decision-insider Trader—Standard decision theory is also clear, however, that the relevant expectations E[B | A] must be calculated relative to the beliefs of the agent who will actually make the decision. Thus, if the people who will actually make the decision have different beliefs from market speculators, a *decision selection* problem can arise.[19] If speculators think that, when the decision is made, decisionmakers will know something important that speculators do not now know, speculators will use the actual decision as a clue about this important hidden information. The market price will then reflect speculators' best guess about how the world would be *given* that decision, rather than their best guess about how the world will be *because* of that decision.

For example, speculators might estimate that on the whole SPS would reduce lifespan, but they may also foresee a small chance that the decision-makers will have surprising information favoring SPS. If this scenario is the main way that the decisionmakers might approve SPS, speculators should estimate that conditional on seeing SPS be approved, SPS would raise lifespan. To avoid this decision selection problem, persons with access to decisionmaker information should be permitted to trade in these markets.[20] Also, the timing of the key decisions should be clearly announced just before such decisions are made so that speculators trading then need not fear the decision will be based on future information.

Enough Informed Traders—Decision markets aggregate information available to their participants, so no minimum number of participants is needed, nor is there a minimum level of participant information. With a subsidized market maker, even a single trader can profit by making the market price express what little he knows. At the other extreme, by inducing more traders to put in more effort, there is often no obvious limit on how accurate prices might become.

Thus, it only makes sense to ask if there are "enough" informed traders relative to some standard of comparison. If anything below a given accuracy is useless, you need traders with enough information to produce that accuracy. If decision markets are being compared with a competing institution, some of the people with the sort of information available to that competing institution must be allowed to trade in the decision markets.

Although the accuracy of some forecasting institutions, such as polls, depends on the information level of the average participant, the accuracy of speculative markets depends more on the most informed participants; the typical person able to trade need not be informed or even rational. Instead, a small group whose members know they are better informed can dominate prices, as long as they have enough resources and if market rules do not artificially limit how much they can trade. Those who know they are less informed tend to back away, and those who do not know that they do not know tend to lose and then back away.

Enough Trader Incentives—Even when people with access to relevant information are able to trade, such people need a reason to bother to trade, relative to the other ways they could spend their time and money. They might trade for insurance, for fun and sport, or because of an irrational overconfidence in their opinions; however, when people expect few others to trade in a market, they may all stay away, and so a market price may fail to exist.

Fortunately, one can ensure market prices exist either via a large enough financial subsidy to fund an automated market maker, or via a large enough chance market prices would influence important decisions. The larger the subsidy or influenced decision, the more incentives traders acquire, and the more accurate prices should be. If individuals vary how much they enjoy trading, or in their cost of trading or acquiring relevant information, prices should also be more accurate when more people are allowed to participate.

There is also the question of whether the assets risked are ordinary highly convertible "real money" assets or "play-money" assets of limited convertibility, where winners mainly win bragging rights. Most of the successes of speculative markets have been for open unlimited mostly anonymous trading of highly convertible assets. But legal barriers are much lower for play-money, and some research has found play-money markets can do as well real-money markets, at least on topics where many people already acquire relevant information for other reasons.[21]

Trader Anonymity—Even when the benefits from trading are large enough to overcome the costs of bothering, threats of retribution could deter participation. Leaders of a government agency, for example, might retaliate against employees who contradicted their official party line in decision markets. Such retaliation can be prevented, however, if people can trade and gain their trading rewards anonymously.

Aggregate-enough Outcomes—Even if prices are accurate reflections of reality, would that accuracy come at the cost of people changing reality, by hurting others to win bets? Such acts of harm might come if people were betting on events small enough for individuals or small groups to influence. Fortunately, it is very difficult for individuals or small groups to have much influence over typical policy aggregates, such as average U.S. lifespan. Furthermore, we do not really see much in the way of attempts to harm in order to profit from trades on the stocks of amusement parks, hospitals, or other companies that individuals or small groups might plausibly effect.[22]

It seems that the sort of people who are willing and able to cause harm do not have access to the capital required to implement such trading strategies; they usually prefer simple extortion. And decision markets should cause far less temptation because they involve far less money than ordinary financial markets. Thus, decision markets should be safe as long as they stay away from estimating parameters that are too easily influenced by individual criminals.[23]

Linear-enough Outcomes—If policymakers look to decision market prices as a guide to policy, others may be tempted to manipulate those prices in order to manipulate policy. Fortunately, the addition of manipulators should *increase* price accuracy. Manipulators are in essence noise traders, because their trades are not correlated with asset value information, and markets with more noise traders generally have more accurate prices, because more informed traders are attracted to profit from the noise traders.[24] This predicted inability of manipulators to hurt price accuracy has been confirmed by lab experiments and in the field.[25]

It is theoretically possible, however, for manipulation to increase the harm from price errors even as it increases price accuracy. For example, a market estimating the probability of some disaster might better estimate the probability of disaster, but do worse at catching the worse disasters. A simple way to avoid this possibility is to trade assets whose payoffs are relatively linear in the relevant harm.

Conditional-enough Outcomes—One important aspect of asking the right question is avoiding self-fulfilling prophecies. For example, imagine that the market estimated that a new ambitious government computer system would be delivered late, and in response the contract was renegotiated to make the system less ambitious so it could be delivered on time. This would punish the market speculators for giving their valuable forecast. A better approach is to ask about outcomes conditional on the relevant policy responses. In this example, one could ask the market about the system delivery date conditional on not changing the contract and then conditional on some change in the contract. This approach would reward speculators for giving good advice.

Intermediate-enough Estimates—Speculative markets sometimes seem to show "long-shot" biases when estimates are extreme. For example, when estimating the probability of an unlikely event, those who want to raise the probability of that event have to spend a lot less in each trade than people who want to lower the probability. This can result in a bias toward less extreme prices, at least when transaction costs are high enough to discourage attempts by other speculators to profit by correcting such biases.

Low transaction costs can reduce this problem, as can allowing combinatorial trading. With combinatorial trading, high probability outcomes can be broken down into lots of low-probability components, so all components traded have a similar probability.

Can Show Prices—It is more difficult (though hardly impossible) for traders to inform prices when they cannot observe recent market prices, but such prices reveal to observers something close to our best estimates at that point in time of the consequences of our choices. If we do not want potential "adversaries" to know these estimates, we may want to limit who is allowed to trade or how recent are the prices they can observe. Such limitations are possible, but probably cost something in the way of price accuracy.

Legal Permission—The cost of following the legal process to gain permission to open a few markets to evaluate a policy must be smaller than the benefits that an interest group might gain from advocating that policy. Otherwise no one will bother to set up markets in the hopes of convincing the rest of us of the value of a proposal. Unfortunately, legal fixed costs are far too high for this condition to hold today, at least for real money markets.

Public Credibility—The policy audience must perceive decision market estimates to be relatively accurate and difficult for interested parties to bias. In a democratic government, this means the public must accept such market processes similar to they way they now accept jury trials as a reliable neutral forum for policy debate. This condition does not yet hold today.

Advantages of Decision Markets

Decision markets can directly advise our important policy decisions, by giving us more accurate estimates of the aggregate consequences of those decisions. Decision market price estimates should be numerical, be precise, respond quickly to new information, be self-consistent across a wide range of issues, and be at least as accurate as other publicly available estimates. They are also relatively democratic in the sense of allowing anyone to participate and yet are relatively difficult for interested parties to bias.

Estimates based on cost-benefit or statistical analyses are often criticized as being out of date, being based on bad modeling assumptions or data sets, misjudging causality directions, or failing to control for relevant parameters. Market estimates are mostly immune to these criticisms. Although the analyses that individual traders use to choose their trades may well have these problems, it is up to traders to make their best judgments to fix them. Anyone who could identify a bias in any aspect of the current market estimates would in effect be offered a financial reward to correct that bias.

The cost of creating decision markets does not vary greatly from topic to topic. Most of the variation is probably based on whether information is spread out among many people and on how many people know any given relevant piece of information. The benefit of creating decision markets varies enormously, however, with the importance of the decision being advised. Thus, the most benefit relative to cost will come from decision markets advising the largest most important decisions, where existing forecasting institutions have serious failings.

Early decision markets attempts, however, tend naturally to be efforts to validate the technology. For validation efforts it makes more sense to look for policy decision contexts in which a status quo institution gives concrete enough forecasts to allow a numerical comparison, where that status quo institution is suspected of serious failings, and where many similar decisions have consequences that will be known within a few years. This is where decision markets have their best chance of clearly demonstrating a superior forecasting accuracy.

Disadvantages of Decision Markets

For now, decision markets have two overwhelming disadvantages. First, decision markets have not yet gained enough credibility in the public mind to be an attractive forum in which to argue for particular policy choices. And second, there are enormous legal barriers preventing the creation of public markets trading hard currency.

If these problems can be overcome, other disadvantages will remain. For example, the public may not always want more neutral and accurate forecasts of the consequences of policy decisions. The public may have self-flattering beliefs, ideologies, and entrenched opinions about policy consequences, and they may not appreciate being contradicted by decision markets; sometimes people do prefer to shoot the messenger. Also, the public may have nonoutcome preferences over the processes that produce their policy estimates and over the people who influence it. Accuracy may not be the only issue the public cares about.

Even when the public truly *does* want more accurate forecasts about policy consequences, more disadvantages will remain. Decision markets have nontrivial costs, such as to carefully define relevant options and outcomes and to induce informed traders to participate. And decision markets have nontrivial limitations, such as needing distinct anticipated options that have enough influence over measured aggregate-enough, linear-enough, and conditional-enough outcomes.

Policy Analysis Market: A Case Study

An interesting and well-publicized decision market was the now-defunct Policy Analysis Market, also known as "terrorism futures" or "terror betting."[26] In 2000 Michael Foster, who ran the National Science Foundation quantum computing research program, convinced DARPA (the Defense Advanced

Research Projects Agency, the blue-sky research arm of the U.S. Defense Department) to fund research on information markets starting in 2001.

This research program was eventually named "FutureMAP," but the first DARPA call for proposals went out under the name "Electronic Market-Based Decision Support." The call basically said, "We've heard this works elsewhere; show us it works for problems we care about." The call went out in May 2001, for proposals due in August, and by December two firms had won SBIR (small business independent research) grants. The first winner was Neoteric Technologies, subcontracting to Martek and professors at the University of Iowa. The second winner was Net Exchange, founded by a Caltech professor and subcontracting to two George Mason University professors, and later also to the Economist Intelligence Unit. The Net Exchange project was later named the "Policy Analysis Market" (PAM).

The plan was for two firms to receive $100,000 for a six-month phase I, after which one of them would be awarded $750,000 to continue phase II over two more years. There was also the possibility of receiving $100,000 for the six months between these phases. More money became available than initially planned, so in fall 2002 both firms were funded to continue to phase II, and Net Exchange applied for and won between-phase funding. Also during 2002, the infamous John Poindexter, convicted in the Iran-Contra scandal, became a DARPA executive. Foster's FutureMAP program was placed within Poindexter's organization, the Information Awareness Office (IAO). In December 2002, DARPA called for proposals for related research, at this point using the name FutureMAP. In summer 2003, a half dozen teams—at Penn State, Metron, Institute for Counter-Terrorism, George Mason University, Sparta, and BBN Technologies —were awarded $100,000 each.

Neotek sponsored an end of phase I conference in June 2002, and showed a few demonstration markets, using their preexisting software, on SARS and the color security threat level. When FutureMAP was canceled, Neotek had still not identified its market topics and had probably spent less than half of its phase II funding. Net Exchange spent about two-thirds of its phase II funding, and the new small projects had spent little of their funding. Michael Foster had asked for, but not received, $8,000,000 more in FutureMAP funding over the next few years.

From the very start, the Net Exchange team began laboratory experiments on price manipulation, as this was a widely expressed concern. Also from the start, they planned to forecast military and political instability around the world, how U.S. policies would affect such instability, and how such instability would influence U.S. and global aggregates of interest.[27] The reasoning behind this choice was that the cost to create markets does not depend much on the topic, but the value of estimates varies enormously with the topic. Thus, the greatest benefit relative to cost would come from the highest value estimates. And what could be more valuable than to inform the largest defense policy decisions?

Charles Polk, Net Exchange president, named this the Policy Analysis Market (PAM). The focus later narrowed to a smaller region, the Mideast, because the Economist Intelligence Unit charged a high price to judge after the fact what instability had actually occurred in each nation.

The final plan was to cover eight nations. For each nation in each quarter of a year (over the two-year final phase), traders would estimate five parameters: its military activity, political instability, economic growth, U.S. military activity, and U.S. financial involvement. In addition, traders would predict U.S. GDP, world trade, U.S. military casualties, and western terrorist casualties, and a few to-be-determined miscellaneous items. (The miscellaneous items were to be decided at the last minute based on suggestions from traders, with approval by the Economist Intelligence Unit.) This would add up to a few hundred base parameters to estimate.

In addition, they planned to let traders predict combinations of these, such has how moving U.S. troops out of Saudi Arabia would affect political stability there, how that would affect stability in neighboring nations, and how all that might change oil prices. Similar trades could have predicted the local and global consequences of invading Iraq, had the markets been ready then.

For many years before PAM, Net Exchange had specialized in combinatorial markets, where buyers and sellers could exchange complex packages of items. So from the start, the plan was to see how far the firm could go in developing combinatorial prediction markets. In phase I, Net Exchange put together a combinatorial market similar to its previous combinatorial markets, and at the end of phase I it ran a complex simulation in which a dozen students traded over a few days for real money. Unfortunately, only about a dozen trades occurred, a serious failure.

In the interim phase, the Net Exchange team prepared for and ran lab experiments comparing two new combinatorial trading mechanisms with each other and with a traditional mechanism. These experiments had three traders set seven independent prices in three minutes, and then had six traders set 255 independent prices in three minutes. They found that a combinatorial market maker was the most accurate.[28] Phase II was mostly being spent implementing a scalable production version of this market maker. Because this mechanism requires a net subsidy to traders, they had budgeted

$50,000 for this subsidy, and individual bets were to be limited to a few tens of dollars.

The PAM team was concerned that they might not attract enough traders in the final phase to achieve a meaningful test. Team members had considered running markets within government agencies, but found strong legal barriers to conditional transfers of money between agencies. In the absence of a single agency strongly interested in collaborating with them, they chose to create public markets.

On May 20, 2003, DARPA reported to Congress on the IAO and described FutureMAP in terms of predicting a bioweapons attack against Israel. In June 2003, the PAM team began to tell people about their webpage and to give talks to drum up interest. Charles Polk created the PAM website, wherein as a backdrop to bold text, there were faint background sample screens. In a small (less than 2 percent) section of two such screens, he included as colorful examples of possible miscellaneous items an Arafat assassination, a North Korea missile attack, and the king of Jordan being overthrown.

In the summer of 2003, the Senate but not the House had canceled IAO funding, which included all FutureMAP support, because of privacy concerns with another IAO project, "Total Information Awareness." Because of this funding uncertainty, the PAM plans then were to start on September 1 with 100 testers, who would each be given $100 to trade with. Online registration of people interested in being testers was to open August 1, and public trading of as many as 1,000 initial traders was to begin January 1, 2004. The fact that the PAM team was acting as an agent of the Pentagon was going to give them legal protection against violating antigambling laws.

On July 28, 2003, Senators Ron Wyden (Democrat, Oregon) and Byron Dorgan (Democrat, North Dakota) released an open letter to John Poindexter in which they complained that the U.S. Department of Defense was planning a "terror market" for people to bet on terrorist attacks.[29] They emphasized PAM's association with John Poindexter, who actually had little involvement with PAM, and described PAM as being "designed to predict terrorist events," when in fact it was focused on geopolitical trends. Their main evidence was those miscellaneous items in the PAM website background screen.

Wyden and Dorgan mainly complained that "terrorists themselves could drive up the market for an event they are planning and profit from an attack, or even make false bets to mislead intelligence authorities." Yet a few tens of dollars would hardly pay for an attack, and the PAM team had already told

DARPA about their lab experiments showing manipulators do not hurt price accuracy.

A media storm immediately ensued. Although five mostly positive media articles mentioning PAM had appeared in the previous few months, fifty mostly negative articles appeared on July 29. DARPA's public relations person was out of town and unreachable when the story broke. So DARPA was silent, and initial media reports were based mostly on the senators' complaint.

On July 29, Deputy Secretary of Defense Paul Wolfowitz told the Senate Foreign Relations Committee that he first heard of PAM reading the newspaper a few hours before and that the project was being terminated.[30] During that crucial previous day, no one from the government asked the PAM team whether the accusations were correct or whether the more offensive aspects could be cut from the project. Many slow wheels of government had begun to turn. For example, the president's Council of Economic Advisers was considering coming out in favor of PAM, but the political decision to abandon PAM was made quickly, at a high level, and based on little information or lower-level input.

On July 30, seventy-eight media articles on PAM appeared, even more negative. That day, Poindexter reportedly resigned, and two months later all IAO research was ended. Over the following days, weeks, months, and years, more than 600 more media articles have mentioned PAM, many at first, and then gradually fading in frequency.

An analysis of more than 500 articles on PAM found that coverage gradually became more positive, and the most recent fifty articles on average give readers a positive impression of PAM. One can collect eleven indicators of how informative the articles about PAM were. These indicators include publication date, citing someone with firsthand knowledge, article length, a news or an editorial style, author anonymity, and the awards, circulation, frequency, and topic specialties of the periodical. All eleven indicators individually predict that more informed articles give readers a more favorable impression of PAM. In a multiple regression model using additional six control variables, including media types, political leaning, and author gender, all six of the clearly significant information indicators predict that more informed articles favor PAM more. The more informed articles were more favorable, and eventually the average article was favorable, but the political decision to cancel PAM seems unlikely to be reversed anytime soon.

Psychological research by Philip Tetlock and others on "taboo tradeoffs" can help us to make sense of this unusual political event.[31] Tetlock and others study how people react upon learning that they, or others, have crossed a moral boundary and traded the sacred for the secular. They find that people are not only outraged at anyone who would cross such a moral boundary, but are almost as outraged at someone who would even think about crossing such a boundary.

For example, people might be given a description of a hospital administrator who is considering cutting costs at the possible risk of patient lives. Such people are then outraged at an administrator who chooses to cut costs, regardless of the financial situation of the hospital or the ratio of money saved to lives risked. Furthermore, they are almost as outraged at an administrator who takes several days to think about the decision, even if he ends up not cutting costs. Apparently someone who would even think of doing such a thing is considered nearly as morally bankrupt as someone who actually does it. Bush had long defended Poindexter against attacks on his "Total Information Awareness" project, widely criticized as an attempt to collect and integrate databases on the public, but defending PAM seemed to have been beyond the pale.

PAM seems to have been accused of crossing a moral boundary, which can be paraphrased roughly as "none of us should intend to benefit when some of them hurt some of us." (Yes, many of us do in fact benefit from terrorist attacks; but we can plausibly argue that we did not intend to do so.) So, by the taboo tradeoff effect, it was morally unacceptable for anyone in Congress or the administration to take a few days to think about the accusation. The moral calculus required an immediate response.

Of course, no one at high decisionmaking levels knew much about a $1 million research project within a $1 trillion government budget. If PAM had been a $1 billion project, representatives from districts where that money was spent might have considered whether to defend the project. But there was no such incentive for a $1 million project (spent mostly in California and London); the safe political response was obvious: repudiate PAM, and all associated with it, especially Poindexter. The Senators appear to have anticipated this outcome, and attacked PAM in order to embarrass the Bush administration via its association with the freshly vilified Poindexter and to taint that administration as being a bit too mad about markets.

Since FutureMAP began under Clinton, it would probably have progressed similarly had Gore beaten Bush in the closest presidential election in U.S. history. Gore would not have appointed Poindexter, and Republicans would not have tried to paint Gore as too mad about markets. Thus, but for an accident of history, PAM might have been tried.

Conclusion

Problems of acquiring and aggregating information on policy consequences lie at the core of most political failures, and these problems are often quite severe. Decision markets are a new policy information process intended to help overcome these problems. If our experience with similar markets is any guide, decision markets would be at least as accurate as any coexisting policy information process. Such markets are also precise, consistent, responsive, difficult to bias, and equalitarian in the sense of allowing broad participation.

Decision markets are not cure-alls, of course. They will not function effectively without the ability to create distinct options that have a measurable influence on relevant aggregate outcomes, and the problem has to be important enough to be worth paying to give traders, some of them insiders, enough incentive to trade. The legal costs of market creation also must be low enough, and the public must see market estimates as credible, accurate, and neutral.

It is these last two conditions that remain the biggest problem for decision markets. Without lower legal costs we will not see many trials, and without successful trials the approach cannot gain enough public credibility. Yet without that public credibility there is not enough political support to pass a bill to lower those legal costs to allow more trials.

The history of the aborted Policy Analysis Market shows that absent such credibility, decision markets can be misrepresented and turned into political poison. This vulnerability of a market mechanism to such an attack should not be too surprising. After all, most familiar financial products, including stocks, insurance, futures, and options markets, were once prohibited by laws against gambling. It took a long time for the relevant industries to convince the public to see each of these products as not "just gambling." Of course, all of these products *are* ways to gamble, but because they serve useful social functions, they have become politically and morally acceptable. Similarly, decision markets can also serve an important social function, especially when applied to government policy. Unfortunately, there is no large industry yet with an interest in lobbying the public to see decision markets as more than gambling. In light of elected officials' fear of making the same political mistake twice, the PAM experience is unlikely to be repeated anytime soon. Nevertheless, decision markets remain a potentially valuable, if still maturing, tool for analysis of complex problems. A revival of decision markets in the public sector will likely have to wait for a new generation of politicians, or perhaps some stunning successes with these mechanisms in the private sector.

But eventually, perhaps after they have repeatedly demonstrated their superior information-producing capacities in relatively uncontroversial contexts, decision markets may yet be allowed to revolutionize the way we make high value policy decisions.

Notes

1. John W. Pratt and Richard J. Zeckhauser, *Principals and Agents: The Structure of Business* (Harvard Business School Press, 1991).

2. Jeffrey S. Banks and Rangarajan K. Sundaram, "Adverse Selection and Moral Hazard in a Repeated Elections Model," in *Institutions, Competition and Representation*, edited by William Barnett, Norman Schofield, and Melvin Hinich (Cambridge University Press, 1993).

3. David Sears and Carolyn Funk, "Self-Interest in Americans' Political Opinions," in *Beyond Self-Interest*, edited by J. Mansbridge (University of Chicago Press, 1990), pp. 147–70.

4. Samuel Peltzman, "An Evaluation of Consumer Protection Legislation: The 1962 Drug Amendments," *Journal of Political Economy*, vol. 81, no. 5 (1973): 1049–91.

5. Avinash K. Dixit, *The Making of Economic Policy: A Transaction-Cost Perspective* (MIT Press, 1997); William Ascher, *Why Governments Waste Natural Resources: Policy Failures in Developing Countries* (Johns Hopkins University Press, 1999); Joseph Stiglitz, "The Private Uses of Public Interests: Incentives and Institutions," *Journal of Economic Perspectives*, vol. 12, no. 2 (1998): 3–22.

6. Anthony Barker and B. Guy Peters, *The Politics of Expert Advice* (University of Pittsburgh Press, 1993).

7. Paul Heidhues and Johan Lagerlof, "Hiding Information in Electoral Competition," *Games and Economic Behavior*, vol. 42 (2003): 48–74; Eric Maskin and Jean Tirole, "The Politician and the Judge: Accountability in Government," *American Economic Review*, vol. 94, no. 4 (2004): 1034–54.

8. Adam Brandenburger and Ben Polak, "When Managers Cover Their Posteriors: Making the Decisions the Market Wants to See," *RAND Journal of Economics*, vol. 27, no. 3 (1996): 523–41.

9. Robin Hanson, "He Who Pays the Piper Must Know the Tune," George Mason University, Department of Economics, May 2003 (http://hanson.gmu.edu/expert.pdf [July 2006]).

10. Bryan Caplan, "Rational Irrationality and the Microfoundations of Political Failure," *Public Choice*, vol. 107, nos. 3/4 (2001): 311–31.

11. Andrew Lo, "Finance: A Selective Survey," *Journal of the American Statistical Association*, vol. 95, no. 45 (2000): 629-635. Koleman S. Strumpf and Paul W. Rhode, "Historical Presidential Betting Markets," *Journal of Economic Perspectives*, vol. 18, no. 2 (2004): 127–41.

12. One also has to assume that this agent's utility does not otherwise depend on which outcome is realized.

13. Justin Wolfers and Eric Zitzewitz, "Prediction Markets," *Journal of Economic Perspectives*, vol. 18, no. 2 (2004): 107–26; Martin Spann and Bernd Skiera, "Internet-Based

Virtual Stock Markets for Business Forecasting," *Management Science*, vol. 49, no. 10 (2003): 1310–26; David M. Pennock, C. L. Giles, and F. A. Nielsen, "The Real Power of Artificial Markets," *Science*, vol. 291 (2001): 987–88; Robin Hanson, "Market-Based Foresight: A Proposal," *Foresight Update* (1990): 1–4; Robin Hanson, "Could Gambling Save Science? Encouraging an Honest Consensus," *Social Epistemology*, vol. 9, no. 1 (1995): 3–33; Robin Hanson, "Idea Futures," *Wired*, vol. 3, no. 9 (1995): 125.

14. Richard Roll, "Orange Juice and Weather," *American Economic Review*, vol. 74, no. 5 (1984): 861–80; Stephen Figlewski, "Subjective Information and Market Efficiency in a Betting Market," *Journal of Political Economy*, vol. 87, no. 1 (1979): 75–88; Pennock and colleagues, "The Real Power of Artificial Markets"; Spencer Jakab, "New ICAP-Nymex Derivatives Have U.S. Gas Market's Number," *Wall Street Journal*, August 4, 2004, p. 1; Michael T. Maloney and J. Harold Mulherin, "The Complexity of Price Discovery in an Efficient Market: The Stock Market Reaction to the Challenger Crash," *Journal of Corporate Finance*, vol. 9, no. 4 (2003): 453–79; Joyce E. Berg and Thomas A. Rietz, "Prediction Markets as Decision Support Systems," *Information Systems Frontiers*, vol. 5, no. 1 (2003): 79–93; Kay-Yut Chen and Charles R. Plott, "Prediction Markets and Information Aggregation Mechanism: Experiments and Application," working paper, California Institute of Technology, Social Science, 1998.

15. Robin Hanson, "Decision Markets," *IEEE Intelligent Systems*, vol. 14, no. 3 (1999): 16–19; Marc Stiegler, *Earthweb* (New York: Baen Books, 1999); Berg and Rietz, "Prediction Markets as Decision Support Systems"; Michael Abramowicz, "Information Markets, Administrative Decisionmaking, and Predictive Cost-Benefit Analysis," *University of Chicago Law Review*, vol. 71, no. 3 (2004); Robert W. Hahn and Paul C. Tetlock, "How Information Markets Could Change the Policy World," AEI-Brookings Joint Center for Regulatory Studies, 2004.

16. The public would also need to monitor and punish any corruption in parameter judging.

17. Robin Hanson, "Shall We Vote on Values, But Bet on Beliefs?" George Mason University, Department of Economics, September 2000 (http://hanson.gmu.edu/futarchy.pdf [July 2006]); Hahn and Tetlock, "How Information Markets Could Change the Policy World."

18. Robin Hanson, "Combinatorial Information Market Design," *Information Systems Frontiers*, vol. 5, no. 1 (2003): 105–19.

19. Robin Hanson, "Designing Real Terrorism Futures," *Public Choice* (forthcoming, 2006).

20. Such insider trades might be subject to disclosure and other rules similar to those used to govern insiders' participation in the stock market.

21. Emile Servan-Schreiber and others, "Prediction Markets: Does Money Matter?" *Electronic Markets*, vol. 14, no. 3 (September 2004): 243–51.

22. No evidence has ever been found connecting the September 11, 2001, terror attacks or the 1982 Tylenol poisoning to such trading. In fact, I have found no record of any such connection between a large harmful act and a price change.

23. Robin Hanson, "Foul Play in Information Markets," in *Information Markets: A New Way of Making Decisions in the Public and Private Sectors*, edited by Bob Hahn and Philip Tetlock, AEI-Brookings Joint Project (AEI Press, 2006).

24. Robin Hanson and Ryan Oprea, "Manipulators Increase Information Market Accuracy," George Mason University, Department of Economics, 2004 (http://hanson.gmu.edu/biashelp.pdf [July 2006]).

25. Robin Hanson, Ryan Oprea, and David Porter, "Information Aggregation and Manipulation in an Experimental Market," *Journal of Economic Behavior and Organization,* vol. 60 (2006): 449–59; Colin Camerer, "Can Asset Markets Be Manipulated? A Field Experiment with Racetrack Betting," *Journal of Political Economy,* vol. 106 (1998): 457–82; Wolfers and Zitzewitz, "Prediction Markets."

26. Charles Polk and others, "The Policy Analysis Market: An Electronic Commerce Application of a Combinatorial Information Market," in *Proceedings of the 4th ACM Conference on Electronic Commerce* (Association of Computing Machinery, 2003), pp. 272–73. An archive of information on PAM can be found at http://hanson.gmu.edu/policyanalysismarket.html (accessed July 2006).

27. It was my job to survey possible application areas and recommend one. I recommended this one.

28. This mechanism is described in Hanson, "Combinatorial Information Market Design." The experiments are described in Robin Hanson, John Ledyard, and Takashi Ishikida, "An Experimental Test of Combinatorial Information Markets," George Mason University, Department of Economics, February 2005 (http://hanson.gmu.edu/testcomb.pdf [July 2006]).

29. Ron Wyden and Byron Dorgan "Wyden, Dorgan Call for Immediate Halt to Tax-Funded 'Terror Market' Scheme," July 28, 2003 (http://wyden.senate.gov/media/2003/07282003_terrormarket.html [July 2006]).

30. Michele Norris and David Welna, "Reaction to Pentagon's Proposed Terror Futures Market," *All Things Considered,* National Public Radio (9 p.m., July 29, 2003).

31. Philip E. Tetlock and others, "The Psychology of the Unthinkable: Taboo Trade-offs, Forbidden Base Rates, and Heretical Counterfactuals," *Journal of Personality and Social Psychology,* vol. 78 (2000): 853–70.

8

An Experimental Basis for Public Policy Initiatives

CHARLES A. HOLT, WILLIAM M. SHOBE,
AND ANGELA M. SMITH

The joining of experimental economics and market-based policy innovations has resulted in a current of activity that promises to provide public leaders with a revolutionary tool for public policy design. In the past, policymakers have often relied on casual empiricism and implicit economic
theorizing to improve their decisionmaking, yet these methods have often
been too crude to shed light on the likely consequences of proposed government interventions. One of the most exciting public-sector developments in
recent years has been the growing reliance on laboratory experimentation to
develop and test new types of economic activity, such as auctions for national
broadcast spectrum, tradable emissions permits, and airport landing slots.
Although individual policymakers' wisdom and experience remain as important as ever, experimental techniques allow government officials to base their
economic decisions on convincing empirical evidence and provide a rigorous
environment in which policy innovations can be tested prior to implementation. The results of well-designed policy experiments may offer valuable, and
often surprising, insights into the behavior of real-world actors.

This research was funded by grants from the National Science Foundation and the University
of Virginia Bankard Fund.

Three factors have encouraged the growing use of experimentation as a tool of policy analysis. First, the regulatory reform movement of the past several decades has led to severe criticism of many traditional command-and-control regulations and propelled a shift toward greater use of market-based policy mechanisms. Experimental results and insights can provide an important cross-check for the analysis of these new policy instruments that might otherwise be evaluated solely in terms of theoretical models and general intuition.

Second, the objective of many recent policy initiatives has been to increase the supply of goods, such as environmental amenities, that are not generally traded in markets. Experimental procedures can be used to gain insights into the economic value of such nonmarket commodities under different conditions. Some policy economists would no longer feel comfortable recommending novel policy designs solely on the basis of a game-theoretical analysis of bidding strategies. Many laboratory experiments are thus designed to help economists provide useful advice to policymakers, or, as Al Roth termed this activity, "whispering into the ears of princes."[1]

Finally, some of the new interest in controlled experiments has been driven by a sense of frustration among public officials who seek to obtain a measure of control over technically complex, politically perilous situations. For example, NASA officials have used experimental methods to simulate the fiscal and managerial challenges associated with large "deep-space" exploration projects. After several failures of Mars expeditions, these officials were worried that the "faster, better, cheaper" approach was not going to work. Although officials of the space agency realized that it is impossible to design a laboratory experiment that exactly mirrors complex activities like the NASA procurement and project management process, they believed that the experiments were worth doing, because even relatively minor insights are significant when such huge investments are at stake. In sum, experimentation does not eliminate policy uncertainty, but it provides a valuable tool for managing it.

This chapter discusses several innovative public policy experiments that are driven by the need to develop and test new economic institutions, which are emerging as a result of regulatory reform and advances in computation and communications technology. The design of new market institutions is a risky business, rather like writing code for a software program, in the sense that small errors and omissions may produce costly and embarrassing mistakes. Experiments can be used to spot problems with proposed market solutions, and they may provide useful information about likely performance comparisons for settings in which there is no prior evidence on which to base an empirical analysis.

Experiments can also provide an instructive function. Many policymakers may have trouble imagining the changes in behavior that can arise from the incentives created by a new policy regime. For example, market participants might adjust their behavior in response to a new rule in ways that greatly reduce the net benefit of the rule. Although such changes can be predicted in theory, they may seem counter-intuitive to policymakers not trained in economics. Laboratory experiments can help convince policymakers of the likely effectiveness of regulatory reform proposals.

Laboratory experiments provide useful information to policymakers for a relatively modest expense. These studies can often be designed and carried out in weeks or months. The results of such studies must be evaluated critically if the context, incentives, and subjects involved call into question the external validity of these experiments for the policy issue under consideration. These validity concerns can be addressed in part with carefully designed field experiments and laboratory experiments that have been enriched by including more relevant subject pools and more natural environments.

This chapter is not a full survey of public policy experiments, but rather a discussion of several key themes on the basis of selected applications. Our main argument, which reflects our experience as both researchers who have designed experiments and as practitioners who have developed and implemented policies on the basis of experiments, is that the use of experimental evidence in the formulation of policy advice packs a dual punch. Such evidence typically provides the advisor or "expert" with the confidence to make a clear recommendation that is less encumbered by qualifying conditions about theoretical assumptions or the continuation of past trends in data. In sum, experiments help experts make themselves intelligible to the people it is their job to help. In addition, experimental evidence assists advisees by giving them a much clearer vision of the probable effects of recommendations, especially when experiments involve at least some real-world contextual elements. In fact, it is often effective to let the policymakers mingle with subjects or even participate in an experiment, as noted by Kenneth Binmore and Paul Klemperer: "We think that their experience in playing the roles of bidders within our experimental software had a significant effect on bolstering the confidence of non-economists on the auction team in the workability of the design. (By contrast, mathematical equations have very little persuasive power.)"[2]

The remainder of the chapter provides a flavor of the range of the applications of experimental methods to governance. Because of space limitations, the descriptions of experimental protocols are abbreviated. The next two sections review cases in which laboratory experiments have been used successfully to select and refine public auction procedures: the 2001 Georgia Irrigation Reduction Auction and the 2004 Virginia NO$_x$ Emission Allowance Auction. The chapter then considers two cases in which the experiments appear to have a more limited effect on public policy dynamics: the implementation of auction-based allocation of airport landing slots and experiments designed to evaluate antitrust litigation of certain "facilitating practices" in the *Ethyl* case. The final section summarizes the advantages and disadvantages of the use of experimental methods in the design of public policies.

The 2001 Georgia Irrigation Reduction Auction

In early 2000, just after the Y2K bug never materialized, much of the southeastern United States was in the grips of a severe drought, which one Atlanta newspaper termed "Dry 2K." Concern over fresh water flow to the oyster fisheries in the Gulf raised the possibility that water would have to be released from sources that provide drinking water for Atlanta. In April 2000, the Georgia legislature passed a law that called for the use of an auction-like process to restrict agricultural irrigation in certain areas of southern Georgia if the director of the Georgia Environmental Protection Department (EPD) announced a drought emergency. The exact nature of the auction was unspecified, which made an ideal situation for laboratory testing of alternative auction methods that might be recommended.

The law focused on the Flint River watershed. This river, which essentially begins from a drainage pipe near the Atlanta Hartsfield Airport, grows to a size that supports barge traffic by the time it reaches the Florida state line and later empties into the Gulf. Most water usage in this river basin is for agricultural irrigation. A typical irrigation system is a circular array for 50–300 acres, covered by a state permit issued at no charge. Water is not metered, and, as a result, it is pumped freely into the fields during dry periods, creating green circles visible from the air, which makes restrictions easy to monitor. The legislature set aside $10 million from the multistate tobacco industry settlement to pay farmers not to use one or more of their irrigation permits for the current growing season. This land would not be planted in the absence of an irrigation permit.

The main idea behind the law was to pay farmers not to irrigate, which would reduce any negative political impact from farmers who typically resented intrusions from the state capital. A secondary effect was that a bidding process that selects low bids for compensation might retire relatively low-use-value land from irrigation, thereby boosting efficiency levels. The primary motivations, however, were environmental and political, not economic, in nature. The goal of the EPD was to eliminate irrigation for as many acres as possible in light of their budget constraint and to minimize adverse reaction.

EPD officials viewed the auction format as being noncoercive, fast, fair, and easy to implement. Speed was important, in light of the short interval of several weeks between the March 1 deadline for the declaration of a drought emergency and the optimal planting time. In addition, bids would have to be collected from farmers in diverse locations, which suggested either the use of mail-in bids or web-based communications between officials at a number of bidding sites. In fact, the law had mentioned a "telecommunications process."

This would be a multiunit auction, because the state could "purchase" many permits by agreeing to compensate permit holders for not irrigating the covered areas for the specified growing season. It became clear early on that bids should be tendered on a per-acre basis to make them comparable. One possible method, a discriminative auction, would have people submitting sealed bids, with the winning low bidders each receiving the amounts that they bid. For example, if the bids were $100, $200, $300, and $400 per acre for four permits, and, if the two lowest were accepted, the low bidder would receive $100 per acre and the second low bidder would receive $200 per acre. This auction is "discriminative" because different people receive different amounts for approximately the same amount of irrigation reduction per acre.[3] A discriminative auction could be run in several ways, as a one-shot, sealed bid auction or as some kind of a multiround auction in which bids can be revised after each round. A multiround auction would have the advantage of providing farmers with some feedback and a chance to learn in an unfamiliar environment. An additional consideration was the desire to find a procedure that would not be significantly affected by collusion among friends and relatives who might share a distrust of Atlanta-based officials.

The initial experiments were run in May 2000, shortly after the law was passed and almost a year before the actual auction.[4] After watching several of the experiments, the EPD officials selected two procedures to submit for public comment: a multiround discriminative auction and a single-stage, sealed bid discriminative auction. Subsequent experiments focused on these two setups. Participants were recruited in groups ranging in size from eight to more than forty-two. Some of the participants were students from Atlanta, and others were farmers and locals from the southern Georgia area. A final field test the following winter involved more than fifty local participants bidding simultaneously at three different locations in southern Georgia to test the software and communication procedures with officials who were watching on-line from Atlanta.

A typical laboratory economics experiment involves a series of interactions in a repetitive *Groundhog Day* setting that permits learning, even if the process is initially difficult to understand. In contrast, an actual irrigation auction would only be run once per year, with participants who would be very unfamiliar with a setting where the low bids are winners. As a result, most sessions began with an unusually long explanation of the auction format, followed by a single auction. It soon became clear from the experiments that a multiround auction would remove much of the uncertainty that bidders would face in such a new situation. The idea was to collect bids in each round, rank them, and post provisional winners. These provisionally accepted bids, however, would not be implemented if the EPD officials decided to request new bids in a subsequent round. To encourage serious bidding from the start, the farmers would not be told in advance how many rounds there would be, and this procedure also provided more flexibility for the auction officials. Bids that were unchanged between rounds would be carried over, but bidders would have the option of lowering or raising their bids, on the basis of the provisional results. This process was intended to allow farmers to find out the approximate cutoff price and then compete at the margin to be included.

Laboratory experiments usually involve intentionally neutral terminology (for example, "units" of some unspecified commodity) to prevent participants from entering with "home-grown values" or preconceived bias. In contrast, a conscious decision was made in these experiments to provide an amount of context ("farmers," "acres," and "permits") that would help subjects understand the situation and the fact that low bids would be accepted. Another unusual procedure was to let participants talk freely, and even make speeches, to simulate the collusion possibilities. The only restriction was that participants were not allowed to block access to the bid submission area during an experiment.

In most sessions, participants were given three permits, each with a specified number of acres and a "use-value" per acre that would determine earnings for that permit if the bid was not accepted. Subjects were told that the use-value would be zero for permits with accepted bids, in which case the earnings would be the per-acre bid times the number of acres covered by the permit. In both the single-round and multiround experiments, bids were collected on bid sheets and ranked from low to high. Then starting with the low bids, the total expenditures would be calculated for adding permits with higher bids, until the total expenditure reached the amount allotted by the auctioneer. For example, if the amount to be spent had been announced to be 500, and if the lowest thirty bids yielded a total expenditure of 495, and a thirty-first bid would take the expenditure above this limit, then only thirty bids would be accepted. This cutoff would determine earnings in the single-round sessions. Earnings equaled the accepted bid or the use-value for a permit with a bid that was not accepted. In the sessions with a multiround setup, the cutoff would be calculated, and the permits with bids below the cutoff would be announced as being "provisionally accepted." Then new bids would be accepted, which would then be ranked, with a new announcement of which tracts had provisionally accepted bids. This process would continue until the experimenter decided to stop the auction, at which time the final acceptance decisions would be announced.[5]

One session that generated prices in excess of the competitive prediction provides a good example of how laboratory experiments can be used to pretest procedures and discover unanticipated problems before they become costly and embarrassing mistakes. In this session (with student subjects), one person asked what would happen if there was a tie at the cutoff bid that exhausted the announced budget and if there was not enough money in the budget to cover all tied bids. This possibility was not explicitly mentioned in the instructions, and the experimenter in charge generously announced that all tied bids would be included as provisional winners, or as final winners if this were the final round. A tie arose at a price about 5 percent above the competitive level, and all tied bids were provisionally included. In the next round, more bids came in at the previous cutoff level, and this accumulation of tied bids at the focal tie point continued in subsequent rounds. In the end, the resulting payments needed to include all tied bids were about twice the budgeted amount, which would be analogous to spending $20 million in the actual auction instead of the $10 million allocated by the legislature! The next session, run on the same day with a different group of students, used the same procedures and parameters, except that it was announced that a random process would be used to decide which bids to accept in the event of a tie at the cutoff. The average of the accepted bids in this session converged to the competitive level, and the budget constraint was satisfied.

Several other procedural changes were adopted as a result of the experiments. In particular, bids that were below the announced cutoff tended to increase in the next round. This tendency is not surprising, because there is less risk if low bidders could figure out about how high they could have gone in the previous round. This observation was the motivation for running some sessions in which only permit *numbers* (but not the actual bids) for the provisional winners were announced at the end of each round. This information change tended to reduce the upward creep of low bids in successive rounds, without reducing the tendency for high bidders to come down in a scramble to be included. These modifications in tie breaking and announcement procedures were adopted by the EPD in the subsequent auction.

The actual auction was conducted in April 2001, with assistance from a number of experimental economists, including one of the authors (Holt).[6] About 200 farmers showed up at eight bidding sites, along with television cameramen, reporters, and spectators. Bids were received on about 60 percent of the acres that were eligible to be retired from irrigation. The procedures matched those that had been implemented in the experiments, except that farmers' subjective evaluations of their own opportunity costs replaced the redemption use-values that had been induced in the experiment. The acreage amounts were those registered with the EPD. Bids were signed contracts and were entered via web-based forms by auction officials, as had been done in the experiments. The bids were collected at eight locations and were displayed to top EPD officials, who met in the Experimental Economics Laboratory at Georgia State University, where most of the experiments had been performed.

Changes in the provisionally released budget caused the cutoff bid to stay roughly the same in the first four rounds, ending up at $125 per acre in round 4. Bids in the $130–$210 range fell round by round, and the number of provisionally included acres therefore increased. The director of the EPD then decided to release more money and raise the cutoff bid to $200 in round 5, after which a termination announcement was made.

If the auction officials had used a fixed budget to determine provisional winners, as had been the case in the experiments, the cutoff bid would have fallen from one round to the next. It is possible that the increasing budgets that prevented the fall in the cutoff price may have discouraged bid reductions at the margin. Moreover, the large budget increase in the final round might have had serious consequences for bidding in a future auction that used the same procedures. Despite these concerns, the 2001 irrigation auction was considered to be a success, with about 33,000 acres taken out of irrigation at an average price of about $135 per acre.

In the following year, the state officials decided to run the auction as a single-round discriminative auction by mail, with a maximum reserve price of $150 per acre. In this second auction, 41,000 acres were removed from irrigation, at an average cost of $143 per acre.[7] This method was less expensive

and easier to administer, and attendance at the auction site was less important, because farmers were already familiar with the low-bids-win feature of
the previous year's auction. The use of mail-in procedures may have
enhanced participation.

The Virginia NO$_x$ Auction

The June 2004 auction of nitrogen oxide (NO$_x$) emission allowances in Virginia provides a fascinating case study of how experiments enabled a government agency to devise a successful procedure under a very tight time constraint.[8] The auction involved 1,855 one-ton emission allowances for each
of two years, 2004 and 2005. These allowances, which represented just over
5 percent of the state's total allotment of allowances, had previously been
held and allocated to new users at no cost. The remaining 95 percent of the
allowances were allocated to large emitters without cost in five-year blocks
based on the measured heat input at the firms' facilities in the previous five-
year period, a process known as "grandfathering." This use-based procedure
has the potentially inefficient side effect of rewarding firms for increasing
fuel input and for shifting pollution-generating activities to states with
grandfathered allowance allocations. Auction-based allocations would not
have these side effects, but the main factor in the state legislature's decision
to authorize an auction was the desire to raise revenue in the midst of a
budget crisis.

Final approval to go ahead with the planning and execution of an
allowance auction did not take place until December 8, 2003, but legislative
authorization for the auction was set to expire on June 30, 2004. This meant
that the process of auction design and implementation had to be collapsed
into a six-month period. Although the Virginia government had substantial
experience selling surplus property at auction, most of those involved felt
that this did not provide a good model for auctioning emission allowances.
In addition, previous emission allowance auctions had not been done for the
purpose of raising revenue. This uncertainty led agency staff to bring in economists from the budget department and to contract for some very quick
research help from economists at George Mason University. These
researchers conducted a series of experiments to evaluate alternative procedures: a sealed bid discriminative auction, two multiround generalizations of
this method, and a "clock"-driven pricing mechanism. This last mechanism
implemented an ascending-bid or "English clock" auction in which the price
is raised in a sequence of steps. At each step, the bidders are asked to indicate

the number of allowances that they are interested in purchasing at that price, and the process stops when the demand falls to a level that equals the number of allowances available.

The experiments were done at George Mason using groups of eight to twelve financially motivated student subjects.[9] These group sizes turned out to be quite reasonable, given that there were seventeen to nineteen bidders in the actual auctions conducted in June 2004. Unlike the irrigation reduction experiments, the instructions for the allowance auction experiments used neutral terminology, to avoid the negative connotations associated with pollution activities. Each group of people was involved in twelve auctions in a single session, three repetitions of each of the four alternative auction types mentioned above. Thus, there was a considerable degree of repetition, which differed from the approach taken in the irrigation reduction experiments in which most groups only participated in one or two auctions to more closely match the fact that the actual auction would only be held once.

The demand-side structure of the market introduced another important experimental issue. One approach is to induce private values; each person is told his or her own values for one or more allowances—for example, 200 for each of the first five allowances, 190 for each of the next five, and so on. An alternative, common-value approach would be to have an unknown allowance value, with each person receiving a partially informative "signal" of the common value. Because the future spot market prices of allowances cannot be known in advance, the common value of the NO_x allowances would not be known with certainty, and there were some key uncertainties regarding the supply of allowances in future years. Allowances not used in a given year could be banked and used at a later time, but if the total number of banked allowances exceeded a certain threshold, then all *banked* allowances would lose half of their value (one-ton allowances would only be good for half a ton). There is certainly a common-value element in this case, but in light of the random-walk nature of the spot prices, it is possible that individuals have approximately the same information about future spot prices, in which case the main value variations across bidders would be due to production capacities and needs, which have largely private-value characteristics. In any case, time constraints precluded designing the experiment software to include common-value elements.

Just as the opportunity "use values" were arrayed into a supply curve in the irrigation reduction auction, the private values assigned to allowance "units" can be arrayed into a demand curve. In the absence of direct empirical evidence on the demands of the bidders, the George Mason team decided to run the experiments under several alternative demand conditions. The spot prices in June 2004 were slightly above $2,000 per ton for 2004 allowances and just above $3,000 per ton for 2005 permits. The experiments used value distributions that corresponded to four ranges of private values across bidders: very narrow, $2,000–$2,100; narrow, $2,000–$2,500; wide, $2,000–$3,000; and very wide, $2,000–$3,500. In all four treatment conditions, the multiround auctions yielded the lowest sales revenues, and the one-round, sealed bid discriminative auction yielded lower revenues than the English clock auction. The increases in revenue associated with the clock auction relative to the one-round discriminative auction baseline were estimated to be 17 percent for the vary narrow value range, 13 percent for the narrow range, 7 percent for the wide range, and 2 percent for the very wide range. These results came as something of a surprise. Initial theoretical analysis had led researchers to the conclusion that the multistage sealed bid and the English clock would both perform better than the "standard" sealed bid auction. This experimental result, however, led to the elimination of multiround sealed bid designs as candidates for selection.

The experiments had been conducted in March 2004 and reported to agency staff in April, but the results had not been publicized outside of Virginia government at the time that the request for proposal for auction brokerage services was published in mid-May. To all agency staff involved, the tight deadline for holding the auction seemed to preclude all but a single-round, sealed bid auction, and all but one of the proposals from brokerage firms, which came back in late May, were limited to this method. The bid from one of the brokerage firms, Amerex Energy, surprised agency staff because it proposed using an English clock auction and presented credible evidence of an ability to implement the auction within the now extremely short time frame.[10] The state officials chose the risky option of using a clock auction in an effort to generate maximum revenue. The final details of the auction were worked out in intensive negotiations over a five-day period. The auction software had to be developed and tested in the following week. Some of the issues were whether to use a discriminative or uniform price auction, whether to use a single-round or multiround auction, and the order in which the 2004 and 2005 allowances would be sold. The state officials decided on a sequential approach, namely, to sell the 2004 allowances before the 2005 allowances. The clock auction would begin with a low price, and each bidder could then submit a quantity demanded at that price. Based on advice from the experimenters, agency staff decided not to reveal the level of excess demand at the end of each round of bidding.

Although the experimental design had involved a simultaneous auction of the two vintages of allowances, with the ability of bidders to bid for combinations of 2004 and 2005 allowances, this design feature was not implemented in the actual auction. The brokerage firm argued against the multivintage design. They had great difficulty in drafting a document explaining the rules of the auction to potential bidders. In the end, the broker strongly advised that the more complicated bidding structure and the obscure mathematics used to select the revenue maximizing set of winning bids would significantly reduce participation in the auction. Thus, the theoretical niceties of combinatorial bidding were scrapped to ensure greater participation. This decision was a difficult one for the academic advisors to accept.

The auction was considered a success in several dimensions. The Internet-based interface was inexpensive to run and worked well. The bidders seemed to understand the rules. Participation was broad; there were nineteen bidders and ten winners in the auction of 2004 permits, and seventeen bidders and five winners in the auction for 2005 allowances. The final price for 2004 allowances was more than 3 percent above the spot market price for these permits. The auction for 2005 allowances, conducted later in the same day, yielded a price that was about 7 percent above the previous spot price. The costs associated with the auction were about $200,000 (including the initial research contract), and the net sales revenue was about $10.5 million, compared to the preauction expectations of around $9 million. This case serves as an example where experimental results concerning auction design played a crucial role in the choices made by the policymakers involved.

One unusual institutional factor played a key role in the implementation of the Virginia NO_x auction. Possibly because of the perceived political risks involved, no one in upper management of state government cared to be involved with this first-of-its-kind auction. After the initial contracting phase, this left one middle manager (Shobe), an economist in a civil service position, with full discretion on auction design and implementation. Such freedom of action in the implementation of a new policy is arguably rare but was, at least in this case, a critically important factor in the selection of a policy based largely on experimental results and not constrained by external political considerations.

Airport Landing Slots

The dramatic increase in air travel has generated considerable congestion and delays, especially at airports with severe capacity constraints due to their urban locations. This overwhelming congestion and other efficiency problems might be due in part to the nonmarket mechanism used to allocate runway time slots that planes need to take off and land. In response, several proposals have recommended a switch in policy to auctions or other market-based methods of allocating landing slots. In fact, experimental studies have been conducted to suggest alternative policies that might increase efficiency and reduce congestion. Although these experiments have had an impact on framing the discussion of policy alternatives, the resulting recommendations have not yet been fully implemented. Moreover, the effect of these experiments might have extended beyond the Federal Aviation Administration (FAA) and inspired experimental evaluations of policies in other contexts by other agencies. This section will focus on these landing-slot allocation experiments and their limited policy influence on the allocation method determined by the FAA, which is in contrast to the direct and immediate impact of the auction experiments discussed in the two previous sections.

Most airports allocate runway time according to a first-come, first-served rule where airlines (or other general aviation craft) pay low weight-based fees, even at peak times. The rationale behind the weight-based fees is that heavier planes inflict more damage on runways. These fees, however, do not represent the value of the runway time, especially for smaller planes during peak hours, which results in inefficient allocations of runway use. Because of congestion created from insatiable demand for runway time under this first-come, first-served rule, especially at large hub airports, a 1968 FAA ruling set quotas on the number of "slots" (takeoffs and landings in a thirty- to sixty-minute timeframe) at four "high-density" U.S. airports (La Guardia, Washington National, John F. Kennedy International, and O'Hare).[11] According to this ruling, slots at these high-density airports were allocated by the unanimous vote of scheduling committees, which included representatives from all certified airlines operating into or out of a given airport. In these meetings, no discussion was allowed concerning any other aspects of airline competition (city-pairs, profitability, fares, and so forth) to prevent anticompetitive actions. If the committee could not reach a unanimous decision, the FAA determined the default allocation according to an unspecified rule.

To address the growing congestion and possible efficiency concerns associated with the unanimity committee procedure, Grether, Issac, and Plott prepared a report for the Civil Aeronautics Board and the FAA in 1979.[12] In this report, they discuss results from experiments conducted to test the effectiveness of the committee allocation method. They ran twenty-three committee experiments with student subjects that varied according to the default allocation, the dependence of payoffs on the outcomes of two consecutive meetings (meant to represent demand interdependencies across airports), the experience level of the subjects, and the number of committee members. The experimenters attended multiple meetings and designed the committee experiments to replicate the observed procedures followed by slot committees, thus adding significant realistic context. The instructions, however, used neutral terminology—that is, colored cards and flags were allocated instead of different time slots at various airports. This commonly applied experimental technique avoids bias due to preconceived values and opinions the subjects might have concerning airport landing slot allocation. Moreover, the size of the experimental committee was either nine or fourteen, a reasonable approximation of the number of airline representatives that attended any given meeting.

On the basis of these committee experiments, Grether and colleagues concluded that outcomes were very sensitive to the threat allocation, which was incorporated into the experiments as either grandfathering (namely, based on initial allocation), completely random, or mixed (where some slots were taken from those with large initial allocations and distributed randomly to individuals with smaller initial allocations). The results also indicated significant efficiency problems with the unanimous committee system of allocation.[13] First, the experimental data showed that even when it was profitable and efficient to do so, large participants failed to expand their capacities, and smaller participants failed to grow large enough. Some very inefficient participants received a number of slots from the committee, thus redistributing slots away from high-value users. Moreover, all entrants, regardless of their underlying costs, exerted a great deal of power because using their veto would mostly likely result in a default under which they were allocated a positive number of slots. Finally, the experimental evidence supported the notion that the committee method was unable to deal effectively with the interdependencies in demand for slots at different airports. That is, demand for landing slots at a given airport depend on the takeoff slots an airline receives at a different airport when they supply service between these two cities.

Grether and colleagues also investigated alternative potential allocation methods that might remedy some of the concerns with the committee mechanism. This second group of experiments focused instead on market-based methods but employed terminology and payoffs similar to those used in the committee experiments. Among some of the markets tested were one-price, sealed bid auctions and discriminative auctions (sometimes followed by secondary aftermarkets) and "open book" markets. The design allowed a direct

comparison, with identical economic parameters and subjects, of the unanimity committee with an initial allocation default (representing "grandfathering") and a competitive auction with secondary markets. The results
indicated a much higher efficiency level with the market process, which the
experimenters attributed mostly to the inability of committees to deal with
the interdependencies of demand. On the basis of these experiments, Grether
and colleagues proposed that the FAA consider one-price, sealed bid auctions
with "aftermarkets." The aftermarkets would allow free purchase and sale of
slot permits acquired from the initial auction to increase efficiency. Grether
and colleagues also noted that the revenues collected should be used to
increase runway capacity and that the market allocation should be introduced gradually.

A few years later, Rassenti, Smith, and Bulfin conducted other laboratory
experiments that compared the auction method suggested by Grether and
colleagues to an alternative that incorporated combinatorial bidding.[14] A
sealed bid combinatorial auction allows airlines to submit contingent bids
for slots or landing and takeoff slot packages across various airports. The
experimental data supported the hypothesis that the primary combinatorial
auction would allocate more efficiently initially and save transaction costs in
aftermarkets.

Although the auction formats suggested by these experimental studies
have not yet been implemented, the FAA did shift the process of slot allocation in the direction of a market-based institution in 1986 with the introduction of a buy-sell program.[15] The need for change became apparent when the
committees were no longer able to reach unanimous decisions. In response,
the buy-sell program initially allocated slots by grandfathering them to existing users and then allowing airlines to purchase and sell the landing slots to
other airlines in an attempt to increase efficiency. This program seemed similar to the aftermarkets described in the previous experimental studies, but
with the initial grandfathering of existing slots, it inherits potential problems
due to entry barriers, anticompetitive behavior, and high transaction costs.

More recently, growing concerns have prompted the FAA to consider
alternative long-term allocation options, including both administrative procedures and market-based institutions such as auctions or congestion fees.
Although some of these processes seem similar to those suggested by previous
experiments, it is not clear why the earlier relevant experimental studies did
not convince policymakers of the positive attributes of alternative allocation
methods that would help ease congestion problems. To the extent current
policy favors large carriers or new entrants, these airlines might be reluctant

to switch allocation methods to an auction where they are likely to become worse off (that is, having to pay for landing slots that are currently allocated to them at no charge). They would be expected to put significant pressure on the FAA to abort this structure. This political dynamic is difficult to capture in a traditional experimental setting because participants are typically unable to affect the design or rules of the game. It is possible, however, to create an experiment design that incorporates the ability of participants to alter the allocation method with varying degrees of success. Another issue, especially with the combinatorial auction, might potentially arise out of the complexity of the "smart" computer-assisted allocation and pricing rules. There could be problems, or even lawsuits, if participants feel they were unjustly denied a slot due to the allocation based on a non-transparent algorithm. Nevertheless, congestion remains a problem, and it will be interesting to see whether previous experimental research is cited or further experiments are performed to test potential new policies.

An Example from Antitrust Policy: The *Ethyl* Case

Many issues in antitrust analysis involve conjectures about alternative business practices or industry structures that cannot be directly observed, because mergers, divestitures, or other intrusive actions generally have irreversible consequences. In such situations, laboratory experiments may provide useful insights about policy alternatives being considered. The interpretation of laboratory results for antitrust purposes, however, is plagued by concerns about external validity due to the "distance" between the laboratory and natural market environments. At a minimum, this distance makes it difficult to take the data to a courtroom or other setting where individual culpability is not the same as theoretical likelihood and where highly paid expert witnesses are eager to point out such problems. This section reviews the use of laboratory experiments in the study of several business practices that were the target of a particularly innovative antitrust case: *Ethyl Corporation* v. *Federal Trade Commission.*

Many economists have a strong intuition that the process of secret price cutting and aggressive discounting will enhance competition, even in relatively concentrated markets. One Federal Trade Commission (FTC) investigation began with a quick review of transactions data collected from a number of producer-goods markets. This "sweep" revealed a nearly uniform practice of buyers' negotiations of discounts from list prices in most markets. In contrast, discounts were not reported in the market for lead-based gasoline additives that were in widespread use at that time. This market attracted attention because of a somewhat unusual combination of sales contract provisions that was standard for such lead-based antiknock compounds.

In particular, contracts for these gasoline additives had a most-favored-customer provision in which the seller promised the buyer the best available price, and that the buyer would automatically receive any discount subsequently offered to another buyer. This provision would obviously be attractive when the buyers are producers who compete with each other in a downstream market, as was the case. The second provision was a "meet-or-release" provision in which the seller promised to meet any lower price that the buyer could obtain, or to release the buyer from the contract. FTC investigators at the time felt that these provisions would deter the discounting, because the seller, who might be willing to grant discount to one buyer under pressure, would resist more forcefully if that discount had to go to all buyers. In addition, discounts designed to attract new business might only have the effect of getting the target buyers to obtain matching low prices from the sellers with which they are currently doing business. If discounts are restrained by these contracts and practices, the remaining problem for sellers is to coordinate on high prices. The FTC officials suspected this might be done through advance notice of price increases, a common practice in this market, whereby one seller would announce an intended price increase in the trade press and then wait to see whether others followed.

One of the authors was a consultant at the FTC at that time, and the discussion in the hallways centered on the conjecture that this combination of business practices might even allow the four sellers in this market to reach and maintain a *perfectly collusive*, joint-monopoly price, without much worry about new entry because the lead-based additives were to be phased out in the future. At the time the litigation began, these discussions were based largely on intuition, verbal arguments, and some very simple theoretical examples. In an effort to get a firmer view of the effects of the practices that were thought to "facilitate" collusion, the FTC arranged for some laboratory experiments to be conducted by David Grether and Charles Plott.[16]

The Grether and Plott experiments showed that prices were near competitive levels in a treatment in which none of the practices were used and prices were negotiated freely between buyers and sellers by phone. In contrast, the effect of all practices together tended to raise prices significantly, though to a level well below the perfectly collusive monopoly price. These experimental results were explained by the theoretical analysis in a 1987 article by Charles A. Holt and David Scheffman.[17]

In the end, the FTC won the case, but the chairman of the commission, James Miller, wrote a persuasive dissent in which he cautioned against antitrust policies that might depend on particular market conditions and combinations of business practices that could have other procompetitive effects.[18] The FTC decision was later overruled on appeal in the federal courts. The experimental evidence was not introduced in the judicial proceedings, because of concerns about how the defendants could counter with external validity arguments.

General Observations

The cases considered in this chapter indicate how experimental methods can be used effectively to help design and adjust public policy. The most obvious benefit is that well-crafted experiments give researchers the confidence to make strong recommendations where appropriate. Perhaps equally important is the use of experiments to help policymakers envision the effects of the options being considered, a process that sometimes involves letting the policymakers participate in experiments themselves. In addition, experiments are relatively quick and inexpensive to run, and treatments can be structured to match novel (even risky) policy proposals that have never been implemented. There are, of course, worries that the nature of the subject pool (typically students), the setting (repeated interactions in a laboratory), and incentives (induced values with low financial incentives) may limit the external validity of these experiments. These restrictions are often dictated by the tight time frame under which policy options are considered and implemented. With sufficient time, it is possible to use relevant professionals (for example, farmers), high incentives, and more natural settings. One point to be made here is that the laboratory setting for auctions and other markets is often quite similar to a field situation, because both may involve the use of web-based interfaces for bid submission and the announcement of results. This distance is much greater for experiments designed to analyze antitrust issues and complicated institutional arrangements, which may explain the fact that experimental work seems to have had a larger effect on auction design than on the implementation of specific antitrust or industrial organization policies.

One common theme that has emerged is that transparency and simplicity are important in designing new policies. The reversal of the original decision in the *Ethyl* case was based in part on concerns about policies that depended on an analysis of combinations of practices under specific industry conditions. The bidding instructions for the Georgia irrigation reduction auction had to be simple enough so that a one-page version could be read aloud at the eight bid sites (in front of television crews and some skeptical farmers). The tentative decision to run simultaneous auctions for 2004 and 2005 NO_x credits was abandoned when it became apparent that the process of deciding which bids to accept was so complicated that the instructions would not fit on a single page.[19]

We expect the role of laboratory experimentation to increase as market-based solutions to policy problems gain support and as web-based communications expand the menu of available market institutions. For example, the Federal Communications Commission (FCC) is actively considering alternative combinatorial auction formats for selling spectrum bandwith. The FCC contracted for laboratory experiments to ensure that complexity issues associated with bidding on combinations of licenses do not interfere with efficiency and revenue generation goals.[20] In addition, laboratory tests of combinatorial bidding in a clock auction indicate that revenue is highest in all treatments, as compared with alternatives such as the simultaneous multi-round auction format currently being used by the FCC.[21] The successful use of a clock-based auction in the NO_x auction and its impressive performance in laboratory experiments make it a leading contender to be used for selling carbon dioxide emissions allowances, as will be required in northeastern states who are a party to the Regional Greenhouse Gas Initiative (RGGI).[22]

This review of the use of economic experiments to guide policy decisions reminds us of the importance of the institutional context of economic decisions. Both private economic agents and policymakers must take their institutional environment into account in every decision. For the laboratory subjects and their counterparts in the nonexperimental setting, there will always be important unobserved, and hence uncontrolled, constraints and margins of substitution. As a result, experiments may best be seen as design tools for engineering incremental improvements in how policies are implemented. At each stage of this process, the economist as policy engineer will experiment at the margin expected to bring about the greatest incremental improvement in policy performance or the greatest expansion in the range of solvable policy problems.

Even in the relatively straightforward area of auction design, big differences will exist between the prototype in the lab and the product in the field. Much room is left for judgment in applying the new tools. In the Georgia irrigation buy-down and the NO_x auction, the policymakers used the plans provided by the economic engineers and modified them as needed to match the evolving information about how potential bidders in the respective auctions were likely to respond in actual practice. In Georgia, design changes were made on the fly to prevent evolving information from giving bidders perverse bidding incentives. In the NO_x auction, the theoretically attractive combinatorial auction, which would have permitted efficient arbitrage across auctions, was scrapped in the face of probable bidder aversion to the difficulty of knowing in advance what bid combinations would be selected by the computer-assisted revenue-maximization program.

From the policymaker's point of view, newly engineered designs broaden the range of available tools or help eliminate the obviously bad alternatives. Managers of the irrigation auction averted a political disaster by incorporating preauction design testing. In addition, experiments may provide proof that certain behavioral margins are or are not important to policy choices. Even in the face of this evidence, policy choices may be constrained away from the optimum by cost, political considerations, equity, or lack of management support.

This view of experimental methods and policy suggests that experimental methods may be easier to apply where policy choices involve repeated incremental trials—that is, the selling of emission allowances, spectrum rights, or irrigation reduction subsidies. In cases involving large discrete changes or irreversible changes, one may expect the uncertainties over the applicability of experimental methods to result in their being given less weight as a factor in the policy decision. Experiments are more likely to have the role of providing information about the importance of various behavioral margins than they are in determining the outcome of the ultimate policy choice. Thus, in the *Ethyl* case, experiments provided information about the potential collusive value of Ethyl Corporation's pricing policies but could not provide specific evidence needed in the judicial proceedings to justify antitrust action against the company.

Economic policy may usefully be viewed as the output of a research and development process where product innovation advances through a series of stages: basic research, engineering, design, and implementation. As with any product innovation, once the product is actually put to use, the infinite variety of constraints and incentives of an actual rather than imagined economy will expose new margins for product improvement. Some of these margins for improvement will be exploited by the policymakers themselves, while others will likely result in another round of policy research and development (R&D). At each stage of the policy R&D process, experimental methods provide an increasingly effective tool for testing and refining ideas and designs. As these methods have become more sophisticated and more generally accepted in the economics profession as a test bed for economic ideas, their use as a guide for the improved design and implementation of public policy has increased dramatically. Laboratory experimentation in economics has clearly come of age as one of the essential tools of policy design.

Notes

1. Alvin Roth, "Laboratory Experimentation in Economics," in *Advances in Economic Theory, Fifth World Congress*, edited by Truman Bewley (Cambridge University Press, 1987), pp. 269–99.

2. Kenneth Binmore and Paul Klemperer, "The Biggest Auction Ever: The Sale of the British 3G Telecom Licences," *Economic Journal*, vol. 112 (March 2002): C74–C96, C85.

3. In contrast, a uniform-price auction would establish a cutoff price and pay all bidders at or below this level an amount that equals the cutoff price. If the cutoff price were $200 in the above example, the two low bidders would each receive $200, even though one bidder was willing to accept a compensation of only $100 per acre. Early discussions with state officials indicated a preference for discriminative auctions, in order to avoid the apparent "waste" of paying someone more than they bid, which would happen in a uniform-price auction in which all bidders would receive the same amount per acre.

4. Ronald Cummings, Charles A. Holt, and Susan K. Laury, "Using Laboratory Experiments for Policy Making: An Example from the Georgia Irrigation Reduction Auction," *Journal of Policy Analysis and Management*, vol. 23, no. 2 (Spring 2004): 341–63.

5. The setup with a fixed budget for permit purchases allows the calculation of a competitive price that can serve as a standard for judging bid levels. The supply function is determined by the use values (opportunity costs) arrayed from low to high, with horizontal segments of a length that is equal to the number of acres with a particular use value. The demand side is determined by the total dollar amount set aside for permit purchases. If B represents the budget available to purchase Q total acres at a price of P per acre, then all money is spent if $PQ = B$, or if $P = B/Q$. The resulting negative relationship between P and Q is graphed as a rectangular hyperbola, and the intersection with the supply function determines a price that would clear the market. The bids, of course, are not all equal, but competition does cause high bidders to come down if they can in an effort to be included. The average of the accepted bids was generally quite close to this prediction.

6. The auction was administered by Professors Susan Laury and Ronald Cummings, of Georgia State University. Other experimental economists assisting included Laura Taylor (Georgia State), Lisa Anderson (William and Mary), and Mark Van Boening (Mississippi).

7. R. McDowell, "Going Once, Going Twice . . . ," *GMDA News*, vol. 2, no. 2 (Fall 2002): 1.

8. William Shobe, "Allowances for Sale: Virginia's NO$_x$ Allowance Auction," paper presented at the fall meetings of the Emission Marketing Association, Toronto, Ontario, September 24, 2004.

9. David Porter and others, "Final Report for Virginia DEQ NO_x Auction Design," working paper, George Mason University, Interdisciplinary Center for Economic Science, 2004.

10. The Amerex proposal was based on their reading of a paper by Cramton and Kerr on the auction of emission allowances. Peter Cramton and S. Kerr, "Tradeable Carbon Permit Auctions: How and Why to Auction Not Grandfather," working paper, University of Maryland, March 1999.

11. More recently, in April 2000, the Wendall H. Ford Aviation Investment and Reform Act of the 21st Century (AIR-21) mandated exemptions from high-density rule operation limits for certain flights either operated by new entrants or by smaller aircraft providing service to small airport communities. The AIR-21 also stated that the high-density rule would be phased out by 2007. As the number of exemptions grew and congestion was compounded, the FAA ruled in November 2000 to limit the number of exemption slots to 159 within a given period of the day and to allocate these slots via a lottery among all eligible flights.

12. David M. Grether, R. Mark Isaac, and Charles R. Plott, "Alternative Methods of Allocating Airport Slots: Performance and Evaluation," prepared for Civil Aeronautics Board and Federal Aviation Administration, Polinomics Research Laboratories, Pasadena, Calif. (1979).

13. David M. Grether, R. Mark Isaac, and Charles R. Plott, "The Allocation of Landing Rights by Unanimity Among Competitors," *American Economic Review*, vol. 71, no. 2 (May 1981): 166–71.

14. S. J. Rassenti, Vernon L. Smith, and R. L. Bulfin, "A Combinatorial Auction Mechanism for Airport Time Slot Allocation," *Bell Journal of Economics*, vol. 13, no. 2 (Autumn 1982): 402–17.

15. See Wayne Brough, Edward Clarke, and Nicholas Tideman, "Airport Congestion and Noise: Interplay of Allocation and Distribution," 1995 (http://clarke.pair.com/ANCW.html [July 2006]).

16. David M. Grether and Charles R. Plott, "The Effects of Market Practices in Oligopolistic Markets: An Experimental Examination of the *Ethyl* Case," *Economic Inquiry*, vol. 24 (October 1984): 479–507.

17. Charles A. Holt and David Scheffman, "Facilitating Practices: The Effects of Advance Notice and Best Price Policies," *RAND Journal of Economics*, vol. 18, no. 2 (Summer 1987): 187–97.

18. William Breit and Kenneth Elzinga, *The Antitrust Casebook* (New York: Dryden Press, 1996), pp. 85–93.

19. In particular, the simultaneous auction process that was used in the NO_x experiments involved a linear-programming procedure to calculate the revenue-maximizing combination of bids across the two markets. This allowed subjects to submit quantity orders for each market. The total quantity could not increase from round to round, but some units could be switched from one market to another, subject to some constraints, which could permit participants to take advantage of arbitrage opportunities that might arise from the fact that 2004 permits could also be banked and used in 2005 under some conditions. The simultaneous auction setup, however, meant that bidders would not know in advance what bids would be accepted at each stage, and any ex post challenges to

the procedures due to misunderstandings might remove one of the main advantages of auctions: speed and finality.

20. Jacob K. Goeree, Charles A. Holt, and John O. Ledyard, "An Experimental Comparison of the FCC's Combinatorial and Non-Combinatorial Multiple Round Auctions," prepared for the Wireless Communications Bureau of the Federal Communications Commission (http://wireless.fcc.gov/auctions/default.htm?job=papers_studies [July 2006]).

21. Christoph Brunner and others, "Combinatorial Auctioneering," paper to be presented at the fall meetings of the Economic Science Association, Tucson, Arizona, September 2006. For a general introduction to combinatorial auction experiments, see Charles A. Holt, *Markets, Games, and Strategic Behavior* (Upper Saddle River, N.J.: Pearson Addison-Wesley, 2006), pp. 265–80.

22. The ten participating states have agreed to require that at least 25 percent of CO_2 emissions allowances be allocated each year by in a manner that produces a public benefit, which essentially means by auction. The economic effects of this initiative are analyzed in Dallas Burtraw, Danny Kahn, and Karen Palmer, "CO2 Allowance Allocation in the Regional Greenhouse Gas Initiative and the Effect on Electricity Investors," *Electricity Journal*, vol. 19, no. 2 (March 2006): 79–90.

PART IV

Political Institutions as Problem Solvers?

9

Can Congress Serve the General Welfare?

SARAH A. BINDER

D oes Congress contribute to effective national problem solving? Does it adopt socially efficient solutions to pressing problems? Ample theory and evidence suggest that Congress is ill equipped to adopt policy solutions with net social benefits. In fact, prevailing theoretical models of congressional behavior *rule out* the possibility that Congress could adopt such policies. As numerous chapters in this volume attest—on housing reform, special education, mass transit, and evaluation of surgical procedures—Congress is prone to resist efficient policy solutions that would improve undesirable social conditions facing the American polity.

Is the case really closed against Congress's capacity to enact efficient solutions? An occasional success story—such as the creation of a market-based emissions-trading program to control the problem of acid rain in the 1990s—suggests that such dour conclusions may be premature. At a minimum, conventional accounts of congressional failure need to be scrutinized. Why is Congress prone to ignore Pareto-improving policy solutions? Under what conditions might Congress pass laws with net social benefits? How do congressional incentives, information, and institutions affect Congress's ability to weigh social costs and benefits and to solve problems in an instrumentally rational way? In this chapter, I consider these questions, with an eye to understanding the ways in which Congress's rules and practices may undermine or improve the institution's capacity to enact socially efficient legislation in the nation's interest.

Socially Inefficient Policy: The Conventional Account

Predictions that Congress is incapable of enacting general welfare legislation and that it is resistant to Pareto-improving policy solutions are based on well-developed theoretical grounds. As suggested in several chapters in this volume and as detailed in chapter 2 by Weimer and Vining, political economy models of Congress leave little theoretical room for expecting that Congress will adopt socially efficient measures. Rather than viewing political solutions as essential to correcting market failures (including the undersupply of public goods and costly externalities), these schools of thought collectively suggest that political intervention aggravates—rather than reduces—market failure.[1] Considering the interaction of legislators' electoral interests, congressional institutions, the geographic character of representation, and the incentives of interest groups, these accounts—explored in greater detail below—provide little basis for predicting that Congress will adopt socially efficient policies.

This now standard political economy account draws together numerous elements of Congress and its policymaking environment. Several key works helped to establish the prevailing wisdom about Congress's preference for socially inefficient solutions. Of seminal importance is economist Mancur Olson's 1965 book, *The Logic of Collective Action*. In this work, Olson questioned the prevailing view of pluralist scholars that individuals with shared goals would naturally form organizations to secure their common interests.[2] The primary reason, according to Olson, is that individuals do not always have to join a group to enjoy the benefits sought by that group. The provision of public goods—from which no one can be excluded from enjoying—creates the incentive for individuals to "free ride" on the efforts of others. Echoing earlier observations of E. E. Schattschneider that "organization is the mobilization of bias," Olson argued that (in the absence of coercion or selective incentives) individuals are more likely to join small groups that pursue concentrated benefits than large groups seeking public goods.[3] According to Olson, small groups are more viable because the costs of organization are less, and each member receives a more substantial portion of the collective good. So long as the cost of organizing are trivial compared to the benefits of organizing, a group is likely to form to press its case for favorable policy outcomes. In contrast, barriers to organization are much higher for larger groups—across which benefits would have to be distributed, thereby altering the balance of costs and benefits—and even larger for groups that would lobby for public goods.

How does this bias against collective action shape the types of policies Congress enacts? If we assume that interest groups are influential in the legislative process, the outcome is that legislators are heavily lobbied by groups to enact policies that provide concentrated benefits, while they hear very little from groups that would represent diffuse social interests. When groups advocate policies that would pay for concentrated benefits by imposing diffuse costs, Congress is unlikely to object. This is especially so, as Weimer and Vining remind us, in light of legislators' electoral incentives and short-term horizons; these forces limit their motivation to seek out solutions that would impose concentrated costs, rather than benefits. As long as legislators are "single-minded seekers of reelection," there are few electoral incentives for legislators to resist policies that dole out particularistic benefits at the expense of the general public.[4] The provision of agricultural subsidies—whose costs are borne by taxpayers and consumers and far exceed the benefits of the policy—is a classic example of a policy program likely to emerge from this combination of forces. Such rent-seeking by groups is the most commonly cited explanation for Congress's appetite for socially inefficient legislation.

The predictions of the received wisdom rely on several institutional features of Congress. The logic of interest group formation alone is insufficient for predicting the production of inefficient policy. First, as suggested above, the electoral system and the incentives it creates reward members for catering to narrow interests—whether organized economic interests or geographically based constituencies. The frequency of House elections, the geographical basis for both House and Senate representation, and the desire for reelection together create the conditions that allow groups to successfully engage in rent-seeking.

Second, the delegation of policy authority to congressional committees with fixed jurisdictions creates an institutional organization highly conducive to securing "gains from trade."[5] Because House and Senate rules explicitly designate the policy jurisdiction, or turf, of each chamber's standing committees, the "gains from trade" account assumes that legislators have an incentive to join those committees that produce legislation of keenest interest to their constituencies. As long as noncommittee members are indifferent to the policy choices of other committees, a system of log-rolling among autonomous and potentially biased committees is maintained. Such log-rolling allows narrow interests to secure concentrated benefits from favored committees while diffusing the costs across the general public.

Despite the near-legend status of political economy models of Congress, greater scrutiny of Congress's capacity for promoting the general welfare is in order on both empirical and theoretical grounds. First, rival theoretical accounts provide a less dire assessment of congressional capacity. Works by Douglas Arnold, Gary Cox and Mathew McCubbins, and Diana Evans each offer alternative accounts of Congress's incentive and capacity to tackle major social and economic problems.[6] Second, Congress is at times able to summon up collective action necessary to impose concentrated costs and to secure diffuse benefits—even (though rarely) adopting market-based and other solutions to resolve intractable problems. Third, and more generally, the prevailing political economy models make numerous assumptions (sometimes explicit, sometimes not) that deserve greater scrutiny. These critical elements of the theory—congressional incentives, information, and institutions— might not foreclose the adoption of legislation that serves the general welfare.

Revisiting Congressional Incentives

Since publication of David Mayhew's *Congress: The Electoral Connection*, scholars and other close observers of Congress have reached the conclusion that legislators can succeed politically by avoiding the tough business of identifying and working to address difficult public problems. Although Mayhew argued that selective incentives would entice some legislators to engage in institutional maintenance and coalition building for nondistributive policies, he recognized that most legislators could succeed with a strategy of position taking, symbolic action, and blame avoidance. Voters were unlikely to reward legislators who imposed visible costs on them, and, as single-minded seekers of reelection, members of Congress were unlikely to do anything to risk those votes.

Congress does, of course, manage to build majority coalitions for major policy change, and it does it for more than just distributive pork and producer subsidies. Few of Congress's policy solutions may meet the strict definition of Pareto-improving, but difficult policy choices are occasionally made. The following examples come to mind: the legislative package to rescue Social Security in 1983, the success in closing obsolete military bases starting in 1988, the introduction of "pay-as-you-go" tax and spending budgeting rules in 1990, and a budget package in 1993 credited with helping to produce budget surpluses by the late 1990s.[7] These and other examples beg some reconsideration of prevailing economic models of congressional action.[8]

Why might Congress at times be able to enact legislation to serve the general welfare? Several alternative perspectives are often cited. The most prominent of these has been Douglas Arnold's argument in *The Logic of Congressional Action*.[9] Arnold suggests that coalition leaders can manipulate the decision-making process to ensure that legislators are willing to cast votes for general interest measures. The logic of Arnold's account begins, like Mayhew's, with the assumption that legislators seek reelection as their proximate goal. But rather than arguing that legislators attend to the fixed preferences of their constituencies, Arnold suggests that legislators anticipate the "potential" preferences of their constituencies. In deciding how to vote, legislators estimate these latent preferences, as well as the likelihood that such preferences might come to shape citizens' votes. Such citizen preferences are based on perceived costs and benefits of new policies and on the causal link between policy choices and policy effects.

The role of coalition leaders is critical in Arnold's account to explaining how election-maximizing legislators might be enticed to vote for measures that impose costs on their constituents and on organized interests. Leaders' task, in short, is to anticipate legislators' electoral calculations and persuade legislators that it would be electorally advantageous (or at least not disadvantageous) to support leaders' proposed measures. Leaders do so by employing tactics (including strategic framing of the debate, exploiting congressional procedures, and manipulating policy design) to limit (or, at times, to enhance) the "traceability" of policy effects. If citizens have a tough time tracing an observed effect back to government action and then back to a legislator's specific contribution, legislators are unlikely to feel the electoral wrath of attentive constituencies (and inattentive publics are likely to remain so). Voting for socially valuable measures is thus perceived by legislators as an electorally "safe" move. The Arnold model can help account for such legislative successes as the Tax Reform Act of 1986, in which leaders designed an omnibus bill, limited amendments, and kept the focus on benefits for the average taxpayer—strategies intended to limit the traceability of legislators' votes that eliminated tax breaks and other targeted benefits.[10]

On balance, Arnold's account is theoretically cogent and rings true empirically, particularly in recent decades as legislative leaders have more aggressively exploited the rules of the game to secure controversial measures (at least in the House, where such aggressive manipulation of the rules is possible).[11] Arnold, however, does set aside the questions of what role political parties might play in coordinating action on general welfare legislation and why and when coalition leaders are likely to emerge. Those challenges are taken up by Gary Cox and Mathew McCubbins in their *Legislative Leviathan*.[12] Cox and McCubbins modify the standard account of the importance of electoral incentives in the following way: In addition to assuming that legislators are motivated to secure reelection, Cox and McCubbins assert that partisans' collective interest in retaining control of the legislature provides sufficient electoral incentive for majority party members to cast votes for policies that contribute to a favorable electoral reputation for the majority party. As long as the public demands new policies that protect the general welfare, congressional majorities would have an incentive to find ways of securing adoption of such measures. Where Arnold's account leaves open questions about why, when, and which policy entrepreneurs are likely to emerge as successful coalition leaders, Cox and McCubbins's account makes room for party leaders' own electoral incentives (both to be reelected to Congress and to retain their leadership posts) to help explain how parties ensure that leaders will emerge to take on the costs of organizing and coordinating action.

One new account of how Congress manages to enact general interest legislation also modifies the standard theoretical accounts' assumptions about legislators' incentives. Diana Evans, in *Greasing the Wheels,* suggests that legislative leaders—motivated by the pursuit of institutional power or good public policy—use pork barrel projects to buy votes for legislation that serves the general interest.[13] Although such tactics run the risk of turning socially efficient legislation into inefficient solutions, assume for now that the costs of distributive pork barreling do not outweigh the diffuse benefits of general interest measures. Evans's account assumes that legislators are motivated by narrow and geographically based electoral interests that can be satisfied by bringing home concentrated economic benefits to the district. As long as those benefits outweigh the legislator's costs of voting for the general interest measure, leaders can exploit the value of pork to secure votes for measures intended to serve the general welfare.[14]

The key in Evans's account is that by introducing an alternative form of incentives (good policy or institutional power), we expect that at times Congress will produce socially beneficial legislation. Unlike Arnold's account, whose coalition leaders modify the substantive terms of the policy to buy votes, Evans's coalition leaders need not alter legislative compromises to secure votes; they buy votes with "off-dimension" pork. What these accounts have in common, ultimately, is their alternative views about legislators' incentives, alternatives that make it more likely that Congress will do more than adopt symbolic and socially inefficient policy solutions.

Of course, the provision of pork to secure votes for Pareto-improving legislation only feeds, rather than curbs, Congress's appetite for inefficient policy solutions. The tougher challenge for Congress in pursuing Pareto-improving policy solutions is to craft legislative measures in which winners compensate losers and are still made better off.[15] Targeting resources at reform losers to permit the passage a Pareto-improving policy is, however, not an easy political task for members of Congress. First, losers—and their congressional sponsors— must be convinced to give up their targeted benefit. In light of a decentralized legislature and Senate rules that empower intense minorities, producer groups have the capacity to block elimination of their concentrated benefits. Second, if direct compensation to losers is made visible to the public, supporters will likely have a harder time securing reform. And, third, losers have little guarantee that their compensation will be continued in the future. For example, as Joseph Stiglitz has argued, the government's inability to make credible commitments to dairy farmers has undermined efforts to reform government milk subsidies in such a way that dairy farmers would be compensated directly.[16] These and other politics of compensation are consequential, because they discourage legislators from weaning themselves from doling out pork to secure general welfare measures. Thus, although legislators' incentives can at times be harnessed to avoid inefficient policy choices, the political challenges of compensation color the effectiveness of Congress's policy solutions.

Revisiting Congressional Information

According to the standard political economy account, the costs of collective action create an imbalance in the field of groups lobbying Congress: Groups organized to demand particularistic benefits are rarely countered by groups organized to promote broader public interests, thus leading to Congress's adoption of producer subsidies and other inefficient policies. Often left implicit in such accounts is the role of information.[17] As John R. Wright makes explicit, such organizational bias means that "there are sufficiently few organizations lobbying on behalf of the broader public interest to convince legislators that it is in their political interests or in the interests of good public policy to vote them [inefficient policies] down."[18] If it is not rational in cost-benefit terms for groups to organize to lobby against certain particularistic benefits, legislators are left with insufficient informational grounds on which to reject inefficient policies. Such "pro-active lobbying," in Wright's terms, can be "quite compelling when there is little or no credible information to the contrary."[19]

Recent work by Kevin Esterling attempts to incorporate the role of information in the selection of inefficient policies.[20] Esterling's argument draws most directly from a theoretical model of Gary Becker, which shows that the relative effectiveness of a group is shaped by the relative efficiency of the policies pursued by the group.[21] According to the Becker model, groups pursuing efficient policies are more likely to invest scarce resources in lobbying for those policies than are groups that would be disadvantaged by the gain in efficiency. Thus, the "intrinsic advantage" of groups pursuing socially efficient policies should lead Congress to select socially efficient policy. Esterling argues that the quality of policy expertise available to lawmakers and groups will affect the likelihood that groups will lobby for socially efficient or inefficient policies, thus shaping the likelihood that Congress will adopt Pareto-improving solutions.

Esterling focuses on the level of ambiguity and uncertainty in available policy information. When ambiguity and uncertainty about the effectiveness of policy solutions are low and when group debate about such consequences is qualitatively informative, Congress is more likely to adopt market-based, efficient solutions. Thus, incentives alone are insufficient to overcome Congress's tendency to ignore the public's interests: transmission of quality information is necessary as well. Edgar Olsen's account in chapter 5 of the public's lack of information about the effects of market-based housing reform nicely illustrates how and why information gaps may matter.

Is policy expertise—effectively conveyed—*sufficient* to secure congressional action that promotes the general welfare? I am skeptical on two accounts. First, other informational models embrace a wider view of the types of information sought out by legislators and provided by groups; policy expertise alone is likely insufficient for generating congressional action. As David Truman argued decades ago, legislators need both technical knowledge and political knowledge.[22] Such political information need not be systematic and objective; Allen Schick argues persuasively that both ordinary knowledge (anecdotal, biased, and often derived from constituents) and research are critical for policy action.[23] More formally, John Wright argues that legislators need and groups provide information to resolve three different types of uncertainties: about legislators' chances of reelection, the legislative process for particular bills, and the policy consequences of proposed measures.[24] Informational imbalances—due to the uneven organization of interests—can affect the balance of information legislators receive from groups on each of these three dimensions.

The implication of Wright's model is that reducing uncertainty and ambiguity only about the effects of policy solutions is insufficient to entice legislators to vote for general interest measures. In view of the electoral risks of imposing concentrated costs to pay for diffuse benefits and legislators' unwillingness to walk the plank for measures unlikely to pass, legislators depend on more than policy expertise. Absent information about the electoral consequences for members who vote for the measure and about the likelihood of the measure's adoption and in what form, legislators are unlikely to vote for measures that promote the general welfare if the costs are visible and likely to be felt by constituents.

Second, my sense is that Congress does not lack the type of information it needs to produce socially efficient legislation. The key challenge is in fact dealing with *excessive* amounts of information, assessing the validity of the information Congress accrues, and using such information in a deliberative manner.[25] Congressional support agencies (Office of Technology Assessment before 1994, Congressional Budget Office, and General Accountability Office, for examples) can aid in evaluating information, but ultimately they are required to remain politically neutral. How best to interpret and apply policy expertise is ultimately a political question that legislators are typically reluctant to delegate.[26]

Are information gaps ever to blame for Congress's appetite for socially inefficient policy? I have no doubt that organizational bias in favor of narrow and parochial interests affects the flow of information to legislators and most often reduces legislators' incentive to vote against producer groups and others seeking particularistic benefits. And when the public and good government reformers can alter how problems are framed and mount an effective lobbying campaign, Congress does at times reverse itself to remove producer benefits.[27] Legislators, however, still need an incentive to be responsive to the information they receive; otherwise, improving the availability of information about policy costs and benefits is unlikely to expand Congress's appetite for socially efficient legislation. Efficiency is one value among competing values, and legislators have ample incentive to weigh such values against each other in selecting policy solutions.

Finally, it is important to remember that most public policies are not easily categorized as conferring advantage to private interests or public interests, as the prevailing political economy models presume. "Most policies," Arnold reminds us, "embrace all types of costs and benefits."[28] As Frances Lee notes, diffuse benefits can flow from concentrated benefits, making it difficult for legislators (and policy analysts) to tally up costs and benefits.[29] Small business tax incentives, Lee points out, may in fact spur job growth—altering calculations about net social costs and benefits. Moreover, the ability of groups to "convert their special-interest claims into convincing public-interest arguments" likely contributes to groups' success in securing benefits.[30] In other words, information about costs and benefits is less "objective" than policy analysts often assume. How information is packaged and interpreted will affect how lawmakers treat competing policy solutions.

Revisiting Congressional Institutions

To what extent do institutional rules and practices account for Congress's failure to adopt Pareto-improving policy solutions? Is Congress's penchant for facilitating rent-seeking by groups simply a consequence of the problem of collective action in the interest group system? Or do congressional rules and practices in some way make legislators more or less likely to enact broad-based policy reforms? The question—"do institutions matter?—is of course a recurring and difficult one for political scientists.[31] Institutional arrangements affect legislators' strategies and thus have an impact on final policy outcomes. Whether such policies would result in the absence of such institutional arrangements is often a challenging question to test. Moreover, if legislators' preferences help to shape the array of prevailing institutions, the independent impact of rules and practices may be difficult to discern. In the discussion that follows, I consider the ways in which institutional arrangements might make a difference in shaping the likelihood of adopting or resisting socially inefficient measures.

Economic models of rent-seeking essentially lay the blame for inefficient outcomes on the logic of collective action. In other words, organizational bias inherent to the interest group system, rather than the legislative process, is said to account for legislators' penchant for particularistic benefits. As suggested earlier in considering the received wisdom, however, rent-seeking by groups is facilitated by congressional institutions—namely, the committee system. At least in theory, both the House and Senate create committees with fixed jurisdictions that allocate agenda control over those issues to committee members. In light of the low salience of other committee domains to non-committee members, the committee system ensures gains from trade across committees. Giant log-rolls dole out benefits to narrow interests at the expense of the broader public. The congressional committee system lies at the heart of Congress's proclivity to enact inefficient policy solutions.

This distributive model of congressional organization is based on what is termed the "textbook" model of Congress, dating to the mid-twentieth century. Numerous changes in Congress since that period suggest that the distributive model may no longer fully capture the dynamics of the contemporary legislative process. Indeed, challenges to the distributive model leave considerable room for Congress's adoption of socially efficient measures. As the discussion above of Cox and McCubbins's partisan model suggested, incentives of party leaders and their rank and file may be sufficient to encourage exploitation of the committee system to adopt policies that impose costs on organized interests—at least organized interests aligned with the minority party. Keith Krehbiel's often-cited informational model also leads to predictions that Congress may be able to adopt Pareto-improving measures.[32] In the Krehbiel model, the organization of the congressional committee system creates incentives for committee members to develop expertise and to devise broad-based policies acceptable to the chamber's median voter.

Our challenge is to determine how legislative institutions may encourage the adoption of general interest measures and under what conditions institutional arrangements are likely to be used in service of securing Pareto-improving measures. Consider three ways in which institutional arrangements might affect whether Congress adopts socially efficient solutions. First, institutions can affect which problems get onto the congressional agenda. Because agenda-setting powers tend to be concentrated within the majority party, collective incentives of the majority party may encourage Congress to take on broad-based reform. Second and related, institutions help shape how public problems are framed and thus considered. Which committees have jurisdiction, for example, can influence the dynamics of the legislative process. Third, as Arnold has suggested, legislative institutions can be manipulated to diffuse legislators' accountability for tough choices.[33]

Consider first the politics of placing issues onto the congressional agenda. In light of the sheer number of legislative initiatives, not all potential policy solutions are considered. And in view of historical evolution of Congress that has handed considerable agenda control to the majority party (at least in the House), issues are more likely to reach the chamber's agenda if they are salient to the majority party.[34] Although Senate rules and practices grant the minority party some influence over the issues debated on the chamber floor, policy problems are not likely to be considered without some endorsement from the majority party.

Nevertheless, to the extent that broad-based measures may help to build the majority's electoral reputation, collective interests of the majority party may facilitate consideration of measures that attend to diffuse interests.[35] Socially efficient policy solutions do have a chance of securing congressional attention if they provoke party attention. Adoption of agricultural reform in 1996—the "Freedom to Farm" bill that decoupled farm payments from crop production and was heralded as a reversal of decades-long farm policy—was due in large part to the new Republican majority's electoral interest in addressing unpopular farm subsidies.[36] Obstructed by Republicans on the Agriculture Committee who refused to vote for the leadership-inspired farm reform, the measure was largely crafted by the House Budget and Rules Committees in the annual "reconciliation" bill that aimed to reduce the federal budget deficit.[37] By including transition payments to farmers and protecting some farm programs from reform, Republican leaders were able to modify the original proposals to make them more palatable to farm groups and rural legislators. Had the issue not been high on the GOP's agenda, the measure surely would have died in the agriculture panel, after four Republican panel members teamed up with Democrats to resist changes to producer subsidies. When reform becomes a party priority, legislative party leaders have institutional resources that can be used to circumvent resistance to socially efficient solutions.

The Freedom to Farm example also highlights the second way in which institutional arrangements may increase the chances of adopting Pareto-improving measures. By affecting the ways in which issues are framed for consideration, congressional institutions offer a means of altering the terms of debate and thus shaping the likelihood of congressional action.[38] In the case of the farm bill, once agricultural reform was framed as a way of reducing the federal deficit, the leverage of the agricultural panels was diminished.[39] To be sure, more than institutional arrangements typically shape the issue context, but to the extent that the issue context is molded by the institutional venue in which issues are considered, the fate of narrow interests seeking concentrated benefits may be affected.

Consider the case of efforts to regulate oleomargarine in the early twentieth century. When legislators from farm regions were able to convince their colleagues that the issue of regulating "oleo" was an agricultural one, jurisdiction over the issue was assigned to the agriculture panels—whose members were predisposed to favor the butter industry. When oleo supporters managed to refer bills to the Ways and Means Committee—arguing that the competition between the two industries was a tax matter for the government—favorable treatment of oleo prevailed at the expense of butter interests.[40] The manipulation of committee jurisdictions to secure protective measures continues today: By assigning jurisdiction of both farm supports and food stamps to the House and Senate Agriculture Committees, a log-roll between supporters of both programs can be sustained (relying on the committees' procedural advantages on the floor).[41] Institutional features work both ways: They can be manipulated to sustain or to challenge policies that cater to private interests over the public welfare.

More generally, the issue context (both the salience of an issue and how it is framed) can be either favorable or unfavorable to interests seeking to preserve concentrated benefits.[42] This is because the issue context appears to shape the visibility of group claims and counter-arguments as well as the perceived legitimacy of such claims. Tobacco subsidies, for example, came under increasing fire in the 1990s when the issue was reframed as a matter of public health and of tobacco companies' cover-up of the addictive power of nicotine. Such reframing is made possible in part by changes in congressional rules since the 1970s. The advent of "multiple referral"—a process in which bills may be directed to multiple committees—has undermined the ability of committees to direct the policymaking process unilaterally. Bills to regulate tobacco may find themselves referred not only to the Agriculture Committee, but to the Ways and Means and Energy and Commerce Committees—venues in which policy-motivated legislators have greater representation compared to the parochial farm panel.

The impact of framing suggests that the objective dimensions of policy problems and solutions are not in themselves sufficient to generate congressional action. This may partially explain why Congress may ignore socially efficient policy solutions such as those outlined by Alan Gerber and Eric Patashnik in chapter 3. As David Mayhew suggests in chapter 10, technical problems and solutions also need to be viewed as political problems and solutions, and they need to be framed in ways that expand and reframe the scope of conflict beyond the groups that normally benefit from a narrow scope of conflict. Prevailing mass transit programs (see chapter 4, by Clifford Winston, in this volume) may be inefficient and could be amended to produce net social benefits. Unless the economic problem of inefficiency can be reframed as a political problem for a broader set of legislators, however, socially efficient solutions are unlikely to attract the attention of legislative leaders or the public.

Institutional arrangements may shape the likelihood of adopting socially efficient solutions in yet a third way: by limiting the "traceability" of legislators' votes for difficult policy choices.[43] Because organized interests are likely to oppose efforts that would impose concentrated costs, legislators have an electoral incentive to limit the ability of citizens to hold their representatives directly responsible for cost-imposing measures. There are two ways in which institutional arrangements come to bear on this challenge. First, coalition leaders may seek policy solutions that delegate responsibility to outside actors, enabling legislators to avoid blame for unpopular decisions.[44] Second, leaders may use institutional means to obscure legislators' votes from an inquisitive public. Both strategies allow legislators to avoid blame for either perceived or real losses.

Congress's and the president's success in closing military bases in the 1980s and 1990s stems from the policy process designed by former House Republican leader Dick Armey (Texas).[45] Rather than requiring an affirmative vote of Congress to close bases—a strategy that had been used to no avail in the previous decades—Armey advocated delegating the selection of bases to an independent commission. Once the bases were selected and confirmed by the Defense Department and the president, all the designated bases were to be closed—unless Congress could muster a majority to strike the entire list and convince the president to sign the legislation killing the list. The process has largely been deemed a success, as legislators in several rounds of closings have been unable to muster a majority to protect individual bases. Delegating the tough choices has allowed Congress to take credit for the economic efficiency said to accrue from closing obsolete military facilities.

Short of delegating responsibility to external commissions, coalition leaders can also make use of legislative strategies to obscure the traceability of tough votes. Often this can be achieved by crafting omnibus bills that contain provisions to impose concentrated costs on narrow interests. As long as legislators can claim that the benefits of the broader package outweigh the costs of particular provisions, legislative packaging makes more likely the adoption of socially efficient measures. The adoption of a market-based system for limiting emissions of sulfur-dioxide from coal-run power plans in the 1990 Clean Air Act Amendments is a valuable example. Proposed by a Republican president and endorsed by a Democratic Congress, the emissions-trading model controls pollutant emissions by granting utilities emission allowances. Excess permits can be sold or leased to create a market for trading permits and giving firms an incentive to lower their emissions. Conceptually, the market enables firms to reach a cost-effective equilibrium, under the overall emissions cap set by the government.

Esterling suggests that the socially efficient policy solution was adopted because of the consensus and certainty of experts about the policy consequences of embracing the market-based system.[46] This may be true, but more than just information seems to have mattered. First, hard-hit midwestern util-ities extracted additional permit credits during the House-Senate conference, the type of "pork-barrel aid" that Evans argues greases the skids for general interest measures.[47] Second, embedded in a broader clean air act, midwestern legislators who might have been disposed to vote against a market trading sys-tem generally voted for the package on the grounds that the overall public benefits were greater than any costs imposed on their region's interests.

Finally, it is important to note that congressional rules and practices can be used to highlight costly parochial bargains, in addition to obscuring efforts to overturn them. This is particularly the case in the Senate, where the rules of the game grant extraordinary leverage to lawmakers in coalitions of one or more. Threatened and actual filibusters can be used not only to secure inefficient concessions to regional interests, but also to expose rent-seeking that imposes substantial costs on other interests. Here, recent debate on a comprehensive energy package comes to mind. Texans and other representa-tives from oil-producing states sought product liability protection for manu-facturers of methyl tertiary butyl ether (MTBE), a fuel additive required pre-viously by Congress to help the gasoline industry comply with clean air laws. Because MTBE caused ground-water contamination in the Northeast, those senators filibustered the energy bill in 2003, successfully killing the bill.[48]

By elevating the salience of their objections and handing the industry and the Republican administration a clear defeat, senators' willingness to exploit the rules of the game altered the strategic situation when Republicans attempted anew to pass the energy measure in 2005. This time, the Senate refused to protect the oil and gas industries in this way, and the industries' House supporters concluded the fight was futile. Granted, the energy reform ultimately enacted in the summer of 2005 included plenty of targeted subsi-dies for producer groups, but it included one less give-away to narrow eco-nomic interests than might have been predicted. Congressional institutions can be exploited either to obscure the imposition of concentrated costs or to expose concentrated benefits.

Conclusions

The rent-seeking model is theoretically appealing, and its empirical predic-tions conform to much of what the public believes about Congress's appetite for wasteful and inefficient policy solutions. There is certainly ample evidence, as found in other chapters in this volume, that Congress has an exceedingly difficult time selecting socially efficient policy solutions. Congress has a seemingly insatiable appetite for showering narrow interests with parochial and concentrated benefits—whose costs are diffused across a generally inattentive public.

My sense, though, is that the conventional account fails to capture the full range of congressional incentives, information, and institutions that can be harnessed to provide for the general welfare. On strictly empirical grounds, even scholars who embrace political economy models have noted that "the precise extent to which the political agenda is dominated by these [particularistic] issues and exactly how they get there is unknown. Much more study is needed of the types of issues that dominate the national political agenda."[49] In other words, although we have a good sense of the incentives and informational contexts that make rent-seeking attractive, we do not truly have a good empirical grasp of the frequency with which such inefficient policies are adopted.

Why might the received wisdom overstate Congress's appetite for particularized benefits? In part, this stems from the context and times in which the rent-seeking model was formulated. Mancur Olson in the 1960s, James Buchanan, Robert Tollison, and Gordon Tullock in the 1970s—these and other scholars' economic works were received by political scientists in an era of decidedly weak political parties.[50] In a decentralized Congress with few centripetal institutional forces to reign in parochial committees, we probably should not be surprised to find that Congress perennially adopted measures that concentrated benefits and dispersed costs. The log-rolling inherent in a strong committee system is prone to produce such outcomes.

As Frances Lee has argued, changes in the ideological makeup and organization of political parties has likely altered legislators' motivations when it comes to the shape of policy choices. Members of Congress "have stronger reasons than in the past to view policy from a national perspective. Both the high level of ideological polarization and the majority's narrow margin of control have raised the policy and partisan stakes."[51] Those national, partisan, and ideological perspectives—and the tight competition between the parties—are important because they raise the possibility that parties will have an electoral incentive to embrace more effective policy solutions.

That may be far too optimistic a view, in light of Morris Fiorina's cogent views in this volume that partisan polarization and competition may be undermining the parties' capacity for responsible behavior. Voters might not want clear choices, and legislators may be unwilling to risk providing them. Moreover, majority parties may be strong enough—and may have sufficient collective electoral incentives—to pass policies that impose large concentrated costs on minority party constituencies, undermining the adoption of Pareto-improving policies. Further, party leaders may be as likely to facilitate, rather than to diminish, distributive politics.[52] Party leaders often have incentive to be responsive to intense minorities within their party, crafting economically inefficient—but politically efficient—policy solutions to secure their support.[53] As Kenneth Shepsle and Barry Weingast remind us, "even an efficient outcome is vulnerable to democratic tinkering."[54]

Still, the rise in ideological cohesion within each party and the willingness of rank and file members to endow leaders with considerable procedural tools at least makes it easier for party leaders in both chambers to exploit the rules of the game to diminish the visibility of tough policy choices.[55] Awash in information, on occasion motivated to secure efficient solutions, and endowed with institutions that increase the chances of adopting such measures, Congress may at times promote the general welfare.

Notes

1. See, for example, Kenneth A. Shepsle and Barry R. Weingast, "Political Solutions to Market Problems," *American Political Science Review*, vol. 78 (June 1984): 417–34.

2. The pluralist school included Arthur Bentley, *The Process of Government* (University of Chicago Press, 1908), David B. Truman, *The Governmental Process* (New York: Knopf, 1962), and Robert Dahl, *A Preface to Democratic Theory* (University of Chicago Press, 1956).

3. See E. E. Schattschneider, The *Semi-Sovereign People* (New York: Holt Reinhardt, 1960).

4. See David Mayhew, *Congress: The Electoral Connection* (Yale University Press, 1974).

5. The argument is advanced by Barry R. Weingast and William J. Marshall, "The Industrial Organization of Congress; or, Why Legislatures, Like Firms, Are Not Organized as Markets," *Journal of Political Economy*, vol. 89 (February 1988): 642–64.

6. See R. Douglas Arnold, *The Logic of Congressional Action* (Yale University Press, 1990); Gary Cox and Mathew McCubbins, *Legislative Leviathan* (University of California Press, 1993); and Diana Evans, *Greasing the Wheels: Using Pork Barrel Projects to Build Majority Coalitions in Congress* (Cambridge University Press, 2004).

7. See Sidney Waldman, "How Congress Does the Difficult," *PS: Political Science and Politics*, vol. 33, no. 4 (December 2000): 803–08.

8. Interest groups, after all, were actively engaged in each of these efforts over the past few decades, and so rent-seeking need not occur each time groups get involved in the legislative process. On other limitations of the rent-seeking arguments based on Olson's collective action logic, see Frances E. Lee, "Interests, Constituencies, and Policymaking," in *The Legislative Branch*, edited by Paul J. Quirk and Sarah A. Binder (Oxford University Press, 2005), pp. 281–313.

9. Arnold, *Logic of Congressional Action*.

10. Applications of Arnold's model to tax reform and other policy areas appears in Arnold, *Logic of Congressional Action*, part II.

11. On the more limited procedural opportunities afforded Senate leaders, see Steven S. Smith, "Party Leadership in the Senate," in *The Legislative Branch*, edited by Quirk and Binder.

12. See Cox and McCubbins, *Legislative Leviathan.*

13. See Evans, *Greasing the Wheels*. On legislators' multiple goals, see Richard F. Fenno Jr., *Congressmen in Committees* (New York: Little, Brown, 1973).

14. The use of pork projects to build majority coalitions for general interest laws is defended in John W. Ellwood and Eric M. Patashnik, "In Praise of Pork," *Public Interest* (Winter 1993), pp. 19–33.

15. The other, rarer, case is when existing policies are so grossly inefficient that it is possible for Congress to pass a reform law that has only winners. This situation precipitously reduces the political challenge for legislators seeking *Pareto*-improvements.

16. See Joseph Stiglitz, "The Private Uses of Public Interests: Incentives and Institutions," *Journal of Economic Perspectives*, vol. 12 (Spring 1998): 3–22.

17. For an explicit treatment of information asymmetries and inefficient policy choices, see Susanne Lohmann, "An Information Rationale for the Power of Special Interests," *American Political Science Review*, vol. 92 (December 1998): 809–27.

18. John R. Wright, *Interest Groups and Congress* (New York: Longman, 2003), p. 180.

19. Wright, *Interest Groups and Congress*, p. 103.

20. Kevin M. Esterling, *The Political Economy of Expertise* (University of Michigan Press, 2004).

21. The model appears in Gary S. Becker, "A Theory of Competition among Pressure Groups for Political Influence," *Quarterly Journal of Economics*, vol. 97 (1983): 371–400.

22. David Truman, *The Governmental Process: Political Interests and Public Opinion* (New York: Knopf, 1951).

23. See Allen Schick, "Informed Legislation: Policy Research Versus Ordinary Knowledge," in *Knowledge, Power, and the Congress*, edited by William H. Robinson and Clay H. Wellborn (Washington, D.C.: CQ Press, 1991).

24. Wright, *Interest Groups and Congress*, p. 182.

25. See Paul J. Quirk, "Deliberation and Decision-Making," in *The Legislative Branch*, edited by Quirk and Binder.

26. Carol H. Weiss, "Comment," in *Knowledge, Power, and the Congress*, edited by Robinson and Wellborn.

27. Gary Mucciaroni, *Reversals of Fortune: Public Policy and Private Interests* (Brookings, 1995).

28. Arnold, *Logic of Congressional Action*, pp. 26–27.

29. See Lee, "Interests, Constituencies, and Policymaking."

30. Mucciaroni, *Reversals of Fortune*, p. 11.

31. See, for example, Bert Rockman and R. Kent Weaver, *Do Institutions Matter?* (Brookings, 1993).

32. See Keith Krehbiel, *Information and Legislative Organization* (University of Michigan Press, 1991).

33. Arnold, *Logic of Congressional Action*. On the diffusion of accountability, see also Lee, "Interests, Constituencies, and Policymaking."

34. Is the House agenda exclusively framed by the majority party? Unlikely, in light of House rules that allow a majority of the chamber to discharge an issue from committee over the objections of majority party leaders. House consideration of the Shays-Meehan campaign finance reform measure in 2002 is perhaps the most salient such example. Such outcomes—driven by the median legislator—are expected under the informational model of legislative organization (see Krehbiel, *Information and Legislative Organization*).

35. On the relevance of party reputations, see Cox and McCubbins, *Legislative Leviathan.*

36. The policy victory was short-lived. Capitalizing on falling farm prices in 2002, a Republican Congress—encouraged by a Republican president—catered to its southern rural base by restoring and expanding producer subsidies. See Jonathan Rauch, "The Farm Bill Is a Bad Joke with a Good Punch Line," *National Journal,* May 18, 2002. On the forces that affect the sustainability of public interest reforms, see Eric Patashnik, "After the Public Interest Prevails: The Political Sustainability of Policy Reform," *Governance,* vol. 16 (2003): 203–34.

37. On the politics of the farm bill in that Congress, see David Hosansky, "Panel Rejects Farm Overhaul In a Rebuke to Leadership," *CQ Weekly,* September 23, 1995, p. 2875.

38. See Frank Baumgartner and Bryan Jones, *Agendas and Instability in American Politics* (University of Chicago Press, 1993).

39. On the framing of agricultural reform as deficit reduction, see Adam D. Sheingate, *The Rise of the Agricultural Welfare State* (Princeton University Press, 2001).

40. On the institutional politics of oleomargarine, see Eric D. Lawrence, "Institutional Effects on Jurisdictional Politics: The Case of Oleomargarine," unpublished manuscript, George Washington University, n.d.

41. See John Ferejohn, *Pork Barrel Politics* (Stanford University Press, 1974).

42. The argument is developed in Mucciaroni, *Reversals of Fortune.*

43. The term is Arnold's in *Logic of Congressional Action.*

44. See R. Kent Weaver, "The Politics of Blame Avoidance," *Journal of Public Policy,* vol. 6 (1986): 371–98.

45. On the politics and process of closing bases through the base closing commissions, see Kenneth Mayer, "Closing Military Bases (Finally): Solving Collective Dilemmas through Delegation," *Legislative Studies Quarterly,* vol. 20 (1995): 393–413.

46. See Esterling, *Political Economy of Expertise,* chap. 6.

47. On the internal deliberations over the permit program, see Richard E. Cohen, *Washington at Work: Back Rooms and Clean Air,* 2d ed. (New York: Allyn and Bacon, 1995). On the use of pork to buy votes, see Evans, *Greasing the Wheels.*

48. See Ben Evans, "MTBE Taken off Table at Sunday Energy Conference, Clearing Way for Final Action," *CQ Today,* July 24, 2005 (www.cq.com [July 25, 2005]).

49. The assessment appears in Wright, *Interest Groups and Congress,* p. 179.

50. See, for example, the essays compiled in James M. Buchanan, Robert D. Tollison, and Gordon Tullock, eds., *Toward a Theory of the Rent-Seeking Society* (Texas A&M University Press, 1980).

51. Lee, "Interests, Constituencies, and Policymaking."

52. The logic of such a party effect is detailed in Shepsle and Weingast, "Political Solutions to Market Problems."

53. See, for example, Kathleen Bawn, "Congressional Party Leadership: Utilitarian versus Majoritarian Incentives," *Legislative Studies Quarterly*, vol. 23 (May 1998): 219–43.

54. Shepsle and Weingast, "Political Solutions to Market Problems," p. 438.

55. On the expansion and manipulation of legislative procedures by majority party leaders in both chambers, see Barbara Sinclair, *Unorthodox Lawmaking* (Washington, D.C.: CQ Press, 2001); and Smith, "Party Leadership in the Senate," in *The Legislative Branch*.

10

Congress as Problem Solver

David R. Mayhew

"U.S. citizens expect Congress to address key policy issues ranging from
health care to education and homeland security. Some critics argue that lawmaking today is mostly a symbolic or rhetorical exercise designed to score
political points rather than a genuine collective effort to promote social welfare. Does the American Congress have the institutional capacity and/or
political incentive to be an effective problem solver? What political or other
factors tend to improve or reduce the quality (along dimensions such as
appropriate priority setting, technical soundness and instrumentality) of
Congress's legislative product?"

That was the assignment posed to me by the editors of this volume. In
addition, the policy areas of housing, education, and criminal justice
were specified as ones in which problems might be solved.

Let me start with a discussion of the ideas of a "problem" and "problem
solving." What is a problem? It is something like an unfortunate or disor-
dered state of affairs to which there might be a "solution." Probably a problem is not quite the same thing as a "puzzle," to which there is always a solution. But in the case of a problem, there is good reason to think that there
might exist a solution, or possibly a family of solutions.

But in whose mind do these considerations reside? It has to be somebody's. Somebody needs to read a state of affairs as posing a "problem" and

219

imply that it might be possible to arrive at a solution. In the case of a sewer overflow on my front lawn, this is a relatively easy undertaking. But in the case of an entire society, where are we? How can we think about "problems" or "problem solving" for an entire society?

Perhaps it will help to distinguish problem solving from other styles of policymaking. Is distributive politics problem solving? Well, it does not look that way. I get a dam, you get a dam, he gets a dam. That does not seem to meet the commonsense meaning of the idea of problem solving. What about policymaking where one ideological side defeats another, or one party simply votes down the other? Are those kinds of enterprises problem solving? They do not seem to be, at least ordinarily. They seem to be exercises of belief system or muscle. It might be a consideration that, in cases like these, a large proportion of the society will insist that a problem is being caused, not solved, by a specified government action. Was the Bush tax cut of 2001 an instance of problem solving?

Problem solving seems to entail a particular, empirically detectable mindset. Some person, or some large or small set of persons, needs to frame a state of affairs as exhibiting a "problem" and to point toward a "solution." Can a whole society, or a large or hegemonic share of one, do this? Possibly the most confident affirmative answer to this question was posed to thinkers and actors of the American Progressive era. For John Dewey, science was isomorphic to democracy.[1] Both are a search for solutions—in the case of democracy a public can arrive at a satisfactory system of governance through seeking and sharing information and ascending a learning curve. In an optimally functioning political system, the public, partly through the work of its elective representatives, comes to agree on what the problems are, perhaps frames general solutions, and then mandates government agencies to work out the details and implement them. "Research bureaus" commissioned by governments or legislatures figured importantly in the Progressive scheme of things. In some areas, where the public interest was obvious, independent commissions could be given open mandates to gather the facts and do the job. Above all, nonpartisanship was to reign.

This is a thoughtful blueprint for societal and governmental action. It is one way for a society to operate, but one quickly has reservations. Partisanship, ideological warfare, and selfish claims will intrude. Also, having a society define something as a "problem" can raise its own horrors. Consider "the Jewish problem" that became a widespread concern in Germany a century ago. Consider Rwanda. One really does need to pause. But let us posit that in a reasonably decently functioning society, where monsters do not lurk, problem solving has attractions as a way of socially constructing reality and making policy. As a definitional matter, it can be said to involve a widespread, shared perception that some state of affairs poses a problem and that policymaking should entail a search for a largely agreed on solution. Consider the Danes.

Now, some may object that we do not really need all this. Experts are all we need for a problem-solving mode to prevail. Let them define, or at least crystallize, the lineaments of the problems, tell us how to solve them, and then solve them. That is the way the Y2K problem was handled, more or less, as the 2000 calendar loomed. Airport inspections have perked up since 2001.

Unfortunately, however, once beyond a realm of technical or semitechnical matters, the recognition of problems and the weaving of causal stories having to do with their origins and possible solutions are in large part a matter of social construction. Often, the citizens of a society will not agree on what a problem is or whether it exists. Consider as possible problems, for example, obesity, the lapsing of Christian faith, obscene Hollywood movies, provision of health care (remember the Republican riposte in 1993–94: "There *is* no health-care crisis"), income inequality, high taxes, capital punishment, the electoral college, the USA Patriot Act, global warming, the Saddam Hussein regime, the budget deficit, immigration, the decline of labor unions, global outsourcing, affirmative action, and lawsuits against physicians. In all these cases, some people would say a problem exists or existed; others would not.

Even if there were agreement on whether a problem exists, the causal stories related to it may differ. If schools are failing, will vouchers help? If crime is rampant, is poverty or just plain bad behavior at the root of it? There is no easy way to get around these difficulties by consulting a natural scientist or an economist. The other side may consult one, too, with an equally impressive degree. Recently, for example, that has happened on the questions of school vouchers and the effects of the minimum wage—striking illustrations of the way disagreements within social science can replicate and bolster disagreements within society. On the evidence to date, the question of what causes crime cannot be settled by expert advice. How about housing, another problem area assigned to me here? At perhaps the chief critical juncture in this issue domain during American history, the close of World War II, when widespread agreement did indeed exist about the existence of a housing shortage, there was also classic disagreement about how to solve it. Should a solution entail government provision or the market? Causal stories clashed. This was not a question resolvable through resort to experts. A similar controversy convulsed Capitol Hill in the late 1970s in the face of a major oil shortage—an indisputable problem of that era. What was the best solution?— rationing and regulation or the operation of the market? Talented experts could be summoned on both sides.

On top of all this, even if agreement can be reached on what a problem is and how to solve it, there remains the formidable question of weighing problems according to their importance in a context of scarce time, attention, and money. Which ones should be tackled and solved? It is a rare society that will leave such weighing to experts.

Even the plainest, seemingly least-asterisked instances of societal problem solving can exhibit aspects like those described above. As an iconic example from fiction, consider the movie *High Noon*. As viewers, we learn that there was a problem. The bad guys led by Frank Miller were coming back to Hadleyville. They posed a threat of disorder, gunplay, violence in general, immorality in general, a decline of law and civic order. The solution was to stop them. Marshal Will Kane (Gary Cooper) did exactly that—indeed, with the help of his wife (Grace Kelly), he killed them all. In short, a problem arose and it was solved. That is the most obvious meaning of *High Noon*. But along the way we learn about the complexities of problem recognition in a democratic setting. There can be a good deal of pluralism. For Mayor Jonas Henderson (Thomas Mitchell) and many others, the real problem was that Marshal Kane might get the town shot up. It was a matter of weighing concerns. And of causal analysis: would the marshal's defensive strategy really work? For one thing, would Kane be able to solve a pressing collective action problem? (Few local citizens were ready to join an armed defense against the scary Frank Miller.) On balance, the mayoral faction concluded, after much chin scratching, would it not be better to have the bad guys back than to risk the damage to life and property needed to keep them away? Perhaps the marshal should just leave town himself. This was an entirely plausible stance. In addition, we learn that the town's saloon dwellers—of whom there were many, and they were citizens, too—saw the marshal himself as the chief problem. He had been a chronic problem. There was too much law and order in Hadleyville. Get rid of the marshal, welcome the bad guys back, and the town would be magnificently wide open again.

In general, a good many complexities familiar to real societal problem solving appear in this *High Noon* story—dissonant problem perception, competing causal analysis, uneasiness about expertise (the marshal was a package of expertise), cacophonous deliberation, the intrusion of public opinion. It is not a simple story.

Hadleyville seems to have lacked a legislature. Add one to the picture and what happens? More specifically, in terms of this chapter, what is, can be, or should be the role of the U.S. Congress in a political realm where, as an ingoing stipulation, problem solving is the aimed-at style of decisionmaking? I mean problem solving in a particular and ambitious sense. Congress is not a research bureau. Nor is it an organization that merely creates and hires research bureaus. It is a representative institution poised in a complicated way between ordinary citizens and specialized bureaucrats. To contribute effectively to societal problem solving, its members need to be able to help define as "problems" the often inchoate fancies, preferences, or demands of society or its elite sectors. The members need to make such definitions widely known and accepted. They need to frame these problems in ordinary, commonsense language so as to bring the public along, yet also frame them in a way that adapts to the instrumental-rationality needs of political executives and bureaucrats. They need to merchandise plausible causal stories to a wide audience, or else the roll-call votes to take action might not be there. Beyond this, they need to probe evidence reasonably hardheadedly in a search for "solutions," and they need to deliberate, bargain, and compromise in a fishbowl setting in a fashion that can swerve both publics and experts toward emergent solutions.

That seems to be what problem solving should amount to in a popularly based legislature. It is a tall order, but as a descriptor of congressional activity it does not refer to a null set. To go back a ways, consider the Missouri Compromise of 1820 or the Compromise of 1850. In both of these cases, the problem was North-versus-South friction, and the solution was a complicated deal arrived at by inventive politicians operating in a context of lengthy deliberation contributed to and monitored by a broad public. Here are some recent instances. In the early 1980s, a projected insolvency of Social Security rose high on the public and congressional agenda courtesy of Senator Daniel Patrick Moynihan and others, who, through extended bargaining and deliberation, crafted a bipartisan $170 million solution of tax increases and benefit cuts. Also in the 1980s, members of Congress took the lead in defining, highlighting, and to some degree solving the "deficit problem" at a time when the Reagan presidency was relaxed about the matter. Thus, for example, the Gramm-Rudman-Hollings Act of 1986 was passed. In the early 1990s, Senators Sam Nunn and Richard Lugar took the lead in defining a "loose nuclear material in the ex-Soviet Union" problem and in crafting an enactment to help solve it. A few years ago, Senator John McCain and others highlighted a "soft money" problem, ran a publicity campaign, worked both sides of the aisle in both houses, spurred a classic debate in the Senate, and kept on driving until Congress passed the McCain-Feingold Campaign Finance Reform Act of 2002. Yes, this statute has its downsides, but the process that generated it is a textbook instance of problem solving.

What kind of attributes does the U.S. Congress or its membership need to possess to engage effectively in problem solving? Assume the American Constitution, as it exists today, that is, and consider secondary attributes. Assume American society as it exists today. I believe that this is an interesting question, and I will attempt here to address it. I will suggest ten such attributes. In discussing some of them, I will offer judgments about how well Congress is performing today compared with past times or with plausible absolute standards. The resulting report card is not very favorable.

Transparency

No legislative body could foster societal problem solving, as I have defined it, without opening its proceedings to the public. Deal making may not need to be open, but the airing of ideas, deliberation, and the cut and thrust of conflict do.[2] Famously, the U.S. Senate met in secret during its very early years and failed to forge much of a connection then to the public. It is fortunate that the Constitution requires each house to "keep a journal of its proceedings, and from time to time publish the same" and stage yea-and-nay roll calls, on the demand of one-fifth of members, which need to be published in the journals. This is vital stuff, although it is taken for granted.[3] This is the basic congressional transparency framework. But there can be angles. C-SPAN is one current favorable angle. Yet there are disturbing recent developments in the processes of the U.S. House of Representatives, as indicated in the following from a long, convincing analysis in the *Boston Globe*, published in 2004:[4]

> The House leadership is changing the way laws are made in America, favoring secrecy and speed over open debate and negotiation. Long-standing rules and practices are ignored. Committees more often meet in secret. Members are less able to make changes to legislation on the House floor. Bills come up for votes so quickly that elected officials frequently don't know what's in them. And there is less time to discuss proposed laws before they come up for a vote. . . . Bills are increasingly crafted behind closed doors. . . . The amount of time spend openly debating bills has dropped dramatically.

And so on.

To be sure, this state of affairs traces back many years through former House Speaker Jim Wright and the previous Democratic ascendancy. It is not just a fancy of Speaker Dennis Hastert and former majority leader Tom DeLay. But we as political scientists seem to have become numbed to it. Focused as we are on parties, roll calls, and members of Congress as allegedly robotic announcers of exogenously induced ideal points, we are forgetting about processes. From the vantage point of societal problem solving, transparency is key.[5]

Visibility

A somewhat different matter is visibility. Even if legislative processes are open, does the public actually tune in to them? One cannot be a romantic about this. It would be an economically unproductive and no doubt crazed public that spent all its days watching C-SPAN. But one does get the sense that Congress's place in American public life may be slipping. The public is much distracted. There is too much otherwise to do, watch, and listen to. *Law and Order* reruns and other attractions are stiff competition. An attribute of the public itself may be at issue here, but visibility is also an attribute of Congress. In various ways, the institution can render itself more engaging or less engaging. C-SPAN certainly engages a small slice of the public. That is all to the good, but there seems to be flagging on other fronts. Why are Senate debates not more engaging to a general audience? Where are the speakers of yore? The Senate's three-week "great debate" on the McCain-Feingold bill in 2001 seems to have drawn attention partly because such enterprises have become so rare. Similarly, in the face of vast U.S. intelligence problems and failures during recent times, neither house has proven capable of staging riveting public hearings on the subject. They booted it—for reasons of partisan wrangling, lack of suitable leadership, or whatever. The task was passed to an extracongressional body—the Kean-Hamilton commission.

Understandability

This is a difficult one. Virtually everything in modern life is becoming more complicated, including laws, which are getting thicker.[6] Congress needs to employ thousands of staffers to compete with the expertise terms of administrative agencies and interest groups. Expanded staff expertise means complexity. All this is true, but it is also true that, from the vantage point of societal problem solving, sizable shares of the public need to be able to grasp what is going on in Washington. Medicare in 1965 can be said to have solved a problem. The Medicare Modernization Act of 2003 possibly did not—at the least (there were other difficulties) because evidently too few people outside Capitol Hill could understand the logic of the ingoing bill or the resulting complicated enactment. In general, increasingly over the years, congressional lawmaking has gotten caught up in several-inch-thick omnibus enactments, many of them budgetary, that are incomprehensible and fall with a thud.[7] There is much to be said for thin, discrete, comprehensible laws.[8] Today, it might be a positive step to abandon the post-1974 congressional budgetary process that contributes to such omnibus clumping and clogging. Just plain abandon it. Even if it is contributing to budgetary management, an iffy question, it may be impairing societal problem solving.

Independence

To participate effectively in problem solving, members of Congress need to be, and to appear to be, adequately autonomous. They cannot be just puppets of interest groups or parties. They need to enjoy, and to be seen to enjoy, the level of discretion called for in an effective problem-solving process—discretion to maneuver, deliberate, persuade, and decide. I do not have much to say about this matter, but campaign finance practices do arise as a consideration. In general, I would guess that the autonomy of members is best served by regulations that rule out big money, channel contributions to individual candidates rather than to parties, and help diversify the money bases of the various members (the greater the variety of money coalitions, the better).

Attentiveness

Being a legislator is among other things a craft. It requires diligence, responsibility, and attention. A disturbing feature of modern congressional life is that members are spending less and less time at their basic tasks. In a recent study comparing the U.S. House of the 1990s with that of the 1960s, Lewis G. Irwin concludes, "There is less time spent on the floor, allowing for fewer professional and personal opportunities for member-to-member contacts."[9] In general, committee activities have deteriorated. House hearings, once often the sites of vigorous, well-attended testimony, have become "dreary, sparsely attended, perfunctory events" marked by "brief, often tedious testimony, followed by tens, if not hundreds, of pages of reports submitted as part of the record."[10]

It is no mystery why this deterioration has occurred. Congress's workload has soared, the availability of plane travel makes it obligatory to go back to Las Vegas or Milwaukee regularly, campaign money needs to be raised, and, in general, modern life is busier for everybody. But there are costs—particularly from the vantage point of Congress as a problem-solving body. A problem-solving mode requires member application. A small proposal: Perhaps media organs like *Congressional Quarterly* could nudge the members' practices a bit by clocking attendance at committee hearings the way they clock attendance at roll calls.[11]

Communality

Attentiveness can breed interaction among members, which can in turn breed a sense of communality. Perhaps especially important can be carefully built-up personal relationships across party lines. In Richard F. Fenno Jr.'s account of House committees of the 1960s and 1970s, the close personal and working relations between chairs and ranking members stand out in one's memory.[12] The House was once characterized as a "cocoon of good feeling."[13] No one would say that today. Now, to be sure, one has to be careful about accepting communality as a good in itself. It is not clear that the legendary "Senate club" of the 1950s was not at least in part a conspiracy against the public interest, but communality in an institution probably does assist a culture of problem solving.

Experience

It seems a good bet that problem solving can benefit from participants who have practiced it. This is one argument against congressional term limits. True, it is not easy to envision the counterfactuals, but as common sense would suggest, there exist many plausible instances of experience evidently counting. In recent times, consider the following senators of veteran vintage who have taken a role in defining problems, getting the definitions across, promoting suitable causal stories, and crafting solutions: Pete Domenici (R-N.M.) on budget deficits, Edward Kennedy (D-Mass.) on education, Bill Bradley (D-N.J.) on tax loopholes, Alan Simpson (R-Wyo.) on immigration, and the aforementioned John McCain (R-Ariz.) on campaign finance,

Daniel Patrick Moynihan (D-N.Y.) on Social Security financing, and Richard Lugar (R-Ind.) and Sam Nunn (D-Ga.) on loose nuclear materials.

Diversity

To draw the ingredients of problems from, and disseminate solutions successfully to, the whole of a society, a representative institution needs to be reasonably representative of that society. This is one advantage legislatures should have over courts. This means diversity in the usual terms of gender, race, religion, and ethnic background. In current Congresses, the scarceness of African Americans in the Senate may be making it difficult to arrange policy solutions that are salable to the African American population. Diversity might also refer to capacity—in the sense of occupational background. People from different occupational backgrounds often have different ways of thinking about things. We need to be more alert to trends in the membership. Congress seems to be losing its ex-military component as World War II recedes into the past. To a marked, perhaps alarming, degree, the contemporary Senate seems to be filling up with ex-House members. Ex-governors seem to contribute a smaller share of the Senate than they once did. Would this latter trend denote a lapse in a kind of problem-solving outlook? Research into occupational backgrounds used to be a staple of congressional scholarship, but it seems to have fallen away.

Instrumental Activity

A downside of elective legislatures is that they may do little at all that is consequential. Electoral incentives may detour members into small-bore distributive politics and feckless position taking.[14] Also, Terry M. Moe and Scott A. Wilson have written, "The transaction costs of moving a bill through the entire legislative process are enormous. . . . The best prediction is that, for most issues most of the time, there will be no affirmative action on the part of Congress at all. The ideal points may logically support a given outcome, but in reality *nothing will happen.*"[15] These considerations do not bode well for problem solving, which can after all require vast time, energy, and application of skill. Pettiness, partisanship, ideological stubbornness, and cognitive chaos, to say nothing of inertia, may need to be overcome. Thus, a legislative body requires a system of incentives, or perhaps a culture, that fosters instrumental activity.[16] The reelection incentive may help, but in Congress there are additional features. Craftsmanship, or an instinct of workmanship as is found in crafts or professions, is probably as important as anything. Consider the career of the late Wilbur Mills.[17] Honor in the larger society is not to be ignored, as with possibly Daniel Patrick Moynihan. Ambition for higher office may play a role, as with possibly John McCain. In today's Congress, there is a disturbing possibility that craftsmanship may be flagging. As one indication, the recent 9/11 commission report found that "the oversight function of Congress has diminished over time. . . . The unglamorous but essential work of oversight has been neglected, and few members past or present believe it is performed well."[18] Such a downslope could have many causes, but one on the House side might be the weakening of the committees vis-à-vis the party leaderships during the last three decades.[19]

Nonpartisanship

Nonpartisanship or bipartisanship is not a sure indicator of successful problem solving. Certainly, it would not be a misuse of language to point to instances where a party "solved a problem" all by itself, or, contrariwise, where the two parties ganged up to do something that did not look at all like solving a problem. Nonetheless, given the nature of problem solving as I have discussed it, we should not be surprised to find a high incidence of nonpartisanship in its successful pursuit. In recent times, of course, congressional politics have gravitated toward being more partisan, often bitterly partisan. One place to troll for that pattern is the following. Consider recent instances of major legislation that cleared Congress under conditions of unified party control (that is, one party could not simply block the other). That means under Clinton during 1993–94 and under George W. Bush in early 2001 and in 2003–04. On virtually every such enactment, in the roll calls on final passage, a majority of one party voted yea in both houses and a majority of the other party voted nay. It was party versus party. That was true of, for example, Clinton's budget in 1993, the North American Free Trade Agreement in 1993,[20] the Family Leave Act of 1993, the Motor Voter Act of 1993, the National Service Act of 1993, the Brady bill regulating handguns in 1993, the omnibus crime act of 1993, the Bush tax cut of 2001, the Bush tax cut of 2003, and the Medicare Modernization Act of 2003.[21]

Perhaps surprisingly, this is a new pattern. In the earlier instances of unified party control since World War II—that is, during the relevant years of the Truman, Eisenhower, Kennedy, Johnson, and Carter presidencies—major enactments ordinarily earned the assent of majorities of both parties in both houses.[22] I would like to search back through all of U.S. history for patterns of roll call voting on final passage of major legislation, but I have not had a chance to do that. Yet it is interesting to spot-check the record for some of the very tall legislative monuments of the 1930s and 1960s. Both of these eras were times of unified party control as well as of high legislative productivity. Here are some enactments that cleared Congress by majorities of two-thirds or better in both houses *and* that majorities of both parties voted for in both houses: the Social Security Act of 1935 (the House and Senate votes on final passage were 372 to 33 and 76 to 6), the Civil Rights Act of 1964 (289 to 126 and 73 to 27), the Voting Rights Act of 1965 (328 to 74 and 79 to 18),[23] and the Hart-Celler Act opening up immigration in 1965 (320 to 69 and 76 to 18).[24] In addition, here are some enactments that cleared Congress by majorities of two-thirds or better in both houses and that majorities of both parties voted for in one house, affording at least some degree of cross-party legitimation: the Wagner Labor-Management Relations Act of 1935 (no record of the vote in the House; 63 to 12 in the Senate), the Fair Labor Standards Act of 1938 (280 to 89, House, with most Republicans voting yea; 56 to 28, Senate), and Medicare in 1965 (307 to 116, House, with most Republicans voting yea; 70 to 24, Senate).

From these earlier times comes at least a smell of problem solving. Something enfolded the minority party members into these enactment coalitions, and perhaps a spirit and practice of problem solving is what did it.[25]

What Can Be Done?

In general, is problem solving wasting away as a style of operation in congressional politics? As I have defined it, perhaps it is. Several of the relevant attributes have possibly been trending down: transparency (on the House side), visibility, understandability, attentiveness, communality, instrumental activity, and nonpartisanship. Of course, problem solving is not the only way in which a political system can operate. In this country, it harks back to a simpler past shadowed by a Progressive-era way of approaching politics, and perhaps those days are going or gone. Partisanship taken straight is perhaps a viable replacement mode. Yet the American system remains replete as ever with formal veto points, as we have been seeing under Clinton and the Bushes. In the past, a problem-solving mode has offered one route past those veto points.[26]

What can be done? To nourish a culture of problem solving on Capitol Hill is at least, albeit far from entirely, a matter of establishing the right kinds of incentives under which members of Congress operate. That means, in the case of members of Congress, not only the obvious reelection incentive, but also considerations of honor, income, and the opportunity to exercise craftsmanship. The authors of *The Federalist*, in discussing the new U.S. elective offices being created two centuries ago, raised all four of these considerations—not just the first. In our own day, political science does not seem to give rich or careful enough attention to background incentives. At the risk of sounding foolish or utopian, I will close by presenting a number of ideas for institutional change that bear on congressional incentives. In all cases my aim is to foster congressional problem solving as I have defined and discussed it above. In general, the tonics I suggest here conjure up the spirit of the Progressive era—a plausible reach given that era's emphasis on problem solving, expertise, effectiveness, accountability, and, in the service of those ends, nonpartisanship.

Open up Congressional Primaries

In the spirit of the particular Progressive reformer Hiram Johnson, it might be wise to move toward nonpartisanizing congressional elections. One design for reform, although it has run into judicial reservations in recent times, would be to open up congressional primaries to all voters regardless of party. The aim would be to generate more congressional "moderates" and thus reduce partisan polarization on Capitol Hill by stirring congressional candidates to appeal to broader coalitional bases in their states and districts. Why do this? In the past, it might be remembered as a caution, strong parties themselves have been routinely urged as a remedy for congressional difficulties—and as a route to societal problem solving.[27] Again, granted, strong partisanship may indeed be a tolerably viable mode of Capitol Hill operation, but on the real-world evidence of the last three decades it is not a great one. Those decades invite another look at standard dictionary etymology with its "*partir*, to divide" and *The Federalist* with its "factions." In a Westminster-type system, strong parties work well enough, but the United States given its separation of powers is not structurally such a system. The last three decades of partisan polarization have not been an impressive lawmaking era. The results of heated partisan showdowns have included the Reagan tax cuts of 1981 bringing on deficits, the crash of Clinton's health care plan in 1993–94, the crash of the Gingrich-Dole budget in 1995–96, and the strange eked-out Medicare reform of 2003.

Restrict Redistricting

In the same vein, it might be wise to cripple partisan gerrymandering and, in general, computer-assisted drawing of U.S. House districts by insisting that districts be compact, contiguous, respectful of lower-level governmental jurisdictions, and reasonably continuous over time. Again, the chief aim here would be to encourage congressional candidates to appeal to constituencies that are less purely partisan based—yet also possibly to spur members of Congress to a greater sense of Capitol Hill independence by tying them to the idiosyncrasies of local communities and making it easier for voters to see who they are and what they are doing.

Encourage Local Funding

In the area of campaign finance reform, it might be wise to require that House or Senate candidates collect, say, half their contributions from home-district or home-state sources. That would cut down on free-flowing national money that may have a standardizing effect—that is, a left-right dualizing effect—on the ideological positioning of members of Congress. Why should both parties' candidates in the Dakotas raise 90 percent of their money from out of state—notably from the East and West coasts?

Assess Party Influence on Capitol Hill

After thirty years of centralization on Capitol Hill through creeping party leadership, it might be time to assess whether this has been a positive development. For their part, political scientists have spent more time and energy explaining this centralization than assessing it. In reality, what are the ends that have been served? What has been lost? In recent times, party leaders have increasingly displaced committee leaders and subcommittee chairs as writers of major bills.[28] Have the bills improved as a consequence? Only an incurable party-government romantic would answer yes. In the long run, the disempowering of committee chairs now combined as it is with term limits in both houses on chair service might be having the overall effect of dimming an institutional commitment to legislative craftsmanship. Why invest in learning tax lore if the job of committee chair is, or, in the mind of an aspiring backbencher, is expected to be, a short one, or if a Speaker of the House might swoop down at any moment and take over?

Streamline Legislation

In the Progressive era there was a drive for the "short ballot." Voters were said to be confused by the conventional bedsheet-long ballots. At stake were comprehensibility and accountability. It was said, Give the voters a short, easy sense of what was going on and who was or would be responsible for what was going on. On Capitol Hill today, for comparable reasons, we could use a drive for the "short bill." As a matter of incentives impinging on members of Congress, clean, comprehensible bills may afford an easier pinpointing of responsibility to a greater number of members than do today's muddled, massive omnibus instruments. Honor, reelection, and an impulse to craftsmanship might be at issue.

Create Academic Landing Pads . . .

Soon after losing his Senate seat in November 2004, Tom Daschle became a Washington lobbyist. That is a familiar story. It is also a tale of a background incentive system widely thought to be perverse. As a member of Congress, why not cater to K Street interests if you wish or may need to work for them eventually? Where else can one go? Question: Why could not the country's 3,000 or so colleges and universities play more of a role as landing pads for former members of Congress? As a matter of incentives impinging on members, both honor and income could be brought to bear. More specifically, why couldn't colleges and universities *compete* for particularly distinguished former members of Congress—such as, say, Tom Daschle and Richard Lugar whenever he retires? Why not have a hiring market? From the standpoint of intellectual environments alone, rare is the American political science department that would not be enhanced by the addition of a distinguished ex-public official—full time, not just to teach a course.

and Provide More Recognition

At my own home university, I have conducted a losing campaign to award honorary degrees to especially distinguished members of Congress or former members. This is a move to inch along—that is all, to be sure—honor as an incentive lining the environments of incumbent members of Congress.

Package C-SPAN

In one sense, C-SPAN is a wonderful achievement, but in another it is a disappointment. Aside from unemployed political junkies who can devote full days, how can C-SPAN be watched effectively? From the standpoint of the average interested citizen, to televise everything from the House and Senate rostrums unrelievedly, wall-to-wall, day after day, is not a great deal better than televising nothing. In my own experience, most times I am reduced to watching the ten-second sight bytes that the regular or cable channels excerpt from C-SPAN. Oddly, as a practical matter, it seems to be easier to get a sense of British parliamentary goings-on from the televised question periods that are available to us than it is to get a sense of American congressional goings on from C-SPAN. What is needed is a secondary market—some organization or set of organizations ready to excerpt and package especially important or interesting congressional debates in watcher-friendly, hour-long or half-hour-long presentations. For members of Congress, considerations with regard to reelection and honors might be incentives. Good member performances should be widely witnessed, as should bad ones.[29]

Encourage More Realistic Ways to Measure Congress Members' Effectiveness

In writing *Congress: The Electoral Connection* three decades ago, I argued that "making up ideological indexes [using roll-call data] is an agreeable enterprise, but from the voter standpoint it ignores . . . other dimensions of considerable importance."[30] Today, the journalistic and academic communities still rely overwhelmingly on roll-call indexes as their summary arithmetic guides to congressional behavior. I believe it is still true that, valuable as such indexes are, they leave out a lot. We do not have good summary measures of the "effectiveness" of members of Congress—to use a reasonably suitable term, though it is imprecise. A list of bills passed per member is not very helpful. Participation in roll-call voting, which *Congressional Quarterly Weekly* has been nicely clocking for quite a while, may have the perverse effect of helping to induce members to show up and vote on Tuesdays, Wednesdays, or Thursdays but lets them get away with not doing much else; no other behavior is being arithmetized in a way that journalists and potential opponents can seize on and use. As I suggested earlier in this chapter, perhaps attendance at committee hearings could be systematically clocked. Obviously, this is a tricky and difficult area. Even so, it is one in which political science might invest. For every hundred or so journal articles based on roll-call behavior, perhaps a few could experiment with new measures of congressional performance. Journalists and congressional staffers often have a good sense of the individual effectiveness of members of Congress. The relevant information is scattered and decentralized, yet it is ample. It could be aggregated and systematized.

Notes

1. John Dewey, *The Public and Its Problems* (Chicago: Swallow Press, 1954).
2. Yet deal making off camera can risk merchandising troubles later on. Consider the Clinton administration's off-camera crafting of its comprehensive plan for health care reform in 1993.

3. Surprisingly, many Latin American legislatures have not been anywhere near as transparent. See John M. Carey, "Recorded Votes and Legislative Accountability in Latin America," paper prepared for the conference "Exporting Congress? The Influence of the U.S. Congress on World Legislatures," at the Jack D. Gordon Institute for Public Policy and Citizenship Studies, Florida International University, Miami, Florida, December 6–7, 2002.

4. Susan Milligan, "Back-Room Dealing a Capitol Trend," *Boston Globe,* October 3, 2004, pp. A1, A23–24.

5. On the decline of congressional transparency, see also Richard E. Cohen and others, "The State of Congress," *National Journal,* January 10, 2004, pp. 83–105.

6. Joel D. Aberbach, *Keeping a Watchful Eye: The Politics of Congressional Oversight* (Brookings, 1990), p. 38.

7. On the rise of omnibus enactments, see Glen S. Krutz, "Getting around Gridlock: The Effect of Omnibus Utilization on Legislative Productivity," *Legislative Politics Quarterly,* vol. 25 (2000): 533–49.

8. See Jeremy Bentham, "Of Promulgation of the Laws and Promulgation of the Reasons Thereof," in *The Works of Jeremy Bentham,* edited by John Bowring (New York: Russell and Russell, 1962), 1: 157–63.

9. Lewis G. Irwin, *A Chill in the House: Actor Perspectives on Change and Continuity in the Pursuit of Legislative Success* (State University of New York Press, 2002), p. 141.

10. Ibid., pp. 146–47.

11. This is a small move toward a regimen of MC monitoring that I once suggested in *Congress: The Electoral Connection* (Yale University Press, 1974). Beyond the familiar ideological indexes based on roll-call voting, "there is, or could be, an 'intentions-effects' dimension, gauging the inclination of congressmen to try to accomplish what they say they are in favor of" (p. 180).

12. Richard F. Fenno Jr., *Congressmen in Committees* (New York: Little, Brown, 1973). See also Nelson W. Polsby, *How Congress Evolves: Social Bases of Institutional Change* (Oxford University Press, 2004), pp. 114–24.

13. Clem Miller, *Member of the House: Letters of a Congressman* (New York: Scribner, 1962).

14. Mayhew, *Congress: The Electoral Connection.*

15. Terry M. Moe and Scott A. Wilson, "Presidents and the Politics of Structure," *Law and Contemporary Problems,* vol. 57 (1994): 26–27 (italics in original).

16. See David R. Mayhew, *America's Congress: Actions in the Public Sphere, James Madison through Newt Gingrich* (Yale University Press, 2000).

17. Julian E. Zelizer, *Taxing America: Wilbur D. Mills, Congress, and the State, 1945–1975* (Cambridge University Press, 1998).

18. *The 9/11 Commission Report: Final Report of the National Commission on Terrorist Attacks upon the United States* (New York: W. W. Norton, 2004), p. 105. See also Helen Fessenden, "Hill's Oversight Role at Risk," *National Journal,* March 27, 2004, pp. 734–37.

19. For a related argument, see Gregory Wawro, *Legislative Entrepreneurship in the U.S. House of Representatives* (University of Michigan Press, 2000), pp. 158–60.

20. On NAFTA, which Clinton favored, majorities of Republicans voted yea in both houses, and majorities of Democrats voted nay.

21. For the record through 2002, see http://pantheon.yale.edu/~dmayhew/dataset_DWG04_roll_calls_1991_2002.xls.

22. See David R. Mayhew, *Divided We Govern: Party Control, Lawmaking, and Investigations, 1946–2002* (Yale University Press, 2005), p. 122.

23. The Civil Rights Act of 1964 and the Voting Rights Act of 1965 were dogged by Senate filibusters, but I have not seen mention that any other enactment discussed in this paragraph was thus dogged.

24. It used to be thought that Medicare, the Voting Rights Act, and the Elementary and Secondary Education Act were the most important enactments of the ambitious Great Society Congress of 1965–66. Now, in the light of long-term consequences, I would guess that most people would nominate the first two of these plus the immigration act.

25. This is not to say that all the major enactments of these years cleared Congress by such expansive majorities. Relatively narrow majoritarianism could prevail. Instances of major laws that were passed by majorities smaller than two-thirds in both houses, and on which majorities of Republicans in both houses voted nay on final passage, include the bitterly contested Public Utilities Holding Company Act of 1935, the Housing Act of 1961, and the establishment of the Department of Housing and Urban Development in 1965.

26. See Mayhew, *Divided We Govern*, pp. 130–31, 134–35.

27. See, for example, Mayhew, *Congress: the Electoral Connection*, pp. 174–77.

28. See Cohen and others, "The State of Congress," pp. 88–91.

29. Senator Joseph McCarthy was brought down by the nationally televised Army-McCarthy hearings. Senator Joseph Montoya of New Mexico is said to have lost his Senate seat in 1976 as a result of a dim performance in the nationally televised Watergate hearings of 1973.

30. Mayhew, *Congress: The Electoral Connection*, pp. 179–80.

11

Parties as Problem Solvers

Morris P. Fiorina

Some twenty-five years ago I wrote an article entitled "The Decline of Collective Responsibility in American Politics."[1] In that article (henceforth referenced as DOCR), I updated the classic arguments for party responsibility in light of which the politics of the 1970s looked seriously deficient. A subsequent article with a similar theme appeared in a 1984 collection edited by Michael Nelson, with a revised version in a second edition four years later, and a final revision in 1990.[2] In brief, these essays noted that in the 1970s party cohesion had dropped to a level not seen since before the Civil War. As a result, national politics had degenerated into a free-for-all of unprincipled bargaining in which participants blithely sacrificed general interests in their pursuit of particularistic constituency interests. The unified Democratic government of President Jimmy Carter that failed to deal with national problems such as runaway inflation and successive energy crises exemplified the sorry state of national politics. Moreover, not only had policy failure become more likely, but because voting for members of Congress increasingly reflected the particularistic activities and personal records of incumbents, members had little fear of being held accountable for their contribution to the failures of national politics. In that light, I sympathetically resurrected the arguments of early to midcentury political scientists who advocated more responsible parties.[3] Although not all problems were amenable to government solution, unified political parties led by strong presidents were more likely to act decisively to meet the challenges facing the country, and when they took their collective performance records to the electorate for ratification or rejection, the voters at least had a good idea of whom to reward or blame.

Looking back at these essays, the 1980s clearly was the decade of party responsibility for me. But, as noted in an epilogue to the final (1990) revision of the essay in the Nelson volume, the prevalence of divided government in the late twentieth century had raised doubts in my mind about the arguments articulated a decade earlier.[4] These doubts cumulated into a change of position explicated at length in *Divided Government* and later writings.[5] In brief, as the parties became more distinct and cohesive during the 1980s, voters seemed to show little appreciation for the changes. Rather than entrust control of government to one unified party, Americans were increasingly voting to split control of government—at the state as well as the national level. And whether that was their actual goal or not—a matter of continuing debate—polls showed that majorities were happy enough with the situation, whatever political scientists thought of the supposed programmatic inefficiency and electoral irresponsibility of divided government. By the early 1990s, I had come to appreciate the electorate's point of view.

Moving from one side of an argument to the other in a decade suggests that the protagonist either was wrong earlier or (worse!) wrong later. But there is another less uncomplimentary possibility—namely, that the shift in stance did not reflect blatant error in the earlier argument so much as changes in one or more unrecognized but important empirical premises, which vitiate the larger argument. I think that at least to some degree such is the case here. To quote from the 1990 epilogue, "I am now less optimistic than when I first wrote this essay that a stronger role for the parties *as presently constituted* would bring about better government" (emphasis in original).[6] For by 1990 I had come to believe that in important respects the parties we were observing in the contemporary era were different in composition and behavior from the ones described in the political science literature we had studied in graduate school. Parties organized to solve the governance problems of one era do not necessarily operate in the same way as parties organized to solve the problems of later eras.[7]

This chapter considers the capacity of the contemporary party system to solve societal problems and meet contemporary challenges. I do so by revisiting DOCR and reconsidering it against the realities of contemporary politics. I begin by briefly contrasting American politics in the 1970s and the 2000s.

Politics Then and Now

DOCR reflected the politics of the 1970s, a decade that began with divided government (then still regarded as something of an anomaly), proceeded through the resignations of a vice president and president followed by the brief administration of an unelected president, then saw the restoration of the "normal order"—unified Democratic government—in 1976, only to see it collapse at the end of the decade in the landslide rejection of a presidency mortally wounded by international humiliation, stagflation, and energy crises. Contemporary critics placed much of the responsibility for the "failed" Carter presidency at the feet of Carter himself—his obsession with detail, his inability to delegate, his political tin ear, and so forth—but I felt then that the critics were giving insufficient attention to larger developments and more general circumstances that would have posed serious obstacles for presidents who possessed much stronger executive and political skills than Carter.[8]

Political Conditions in the 1970s

Not only did Jimmy Carter's 1976 victory restore the presidency to the Democrats, but large Democratic majorities also controlled both the House and Senate.[9] It seemed that the great era of government activism that had been derailed by the war in Vietnam would resume. Such was not to be. After four years of political frustration Carter was soundly defeated, the Republicans captured the Senate with a remarkable gain of twelve seats, and the Democrats lost thirty-three seats in the House. What happened?

Basically, the country faced a series of new problems, and the Democratic Party failed to deal with them in a manner satisfactory to electoral majorities in the nation as a whole and in many states and districts. Gas lines in particular, and the energy crisis in general, were something new in modern American experience, as were double-digit inflation and interest rates near 20 percent. Middle-class tax revolts were a startling development that frightened Democrats and energized Republicans, and a succession of foreign policy setbacks led many to fear that the United States was ill prepared to deal with new challenges around the world. In the face of such developments Democratic majorities in Congress failed to deliver. Indeed, they seemed fixated on old, ineffective solutions like public works spending and trade restrictions. The honeymoon between Carter and congressional Democrats ended fairly quickly, and the partnership was under strain for most of Carter's administration. Members worked to protect their constituencies from the negative effects of the new developments and worried much less about the fate of

Figure 11-1. *The Decline and Resurgence of Party in Government:
Party Unity, 1954–98*

Party unity scores in congressional voting (percent of all voting)

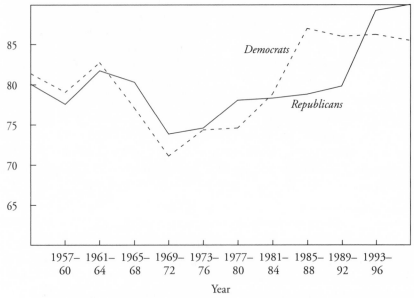

Year

Source: Harold W. Stanley and Richard G. Niemi, eds., *Vital Statistics on American Politics 2005–
2006* (Washington, DC: CQ Press, 2005), table 5.8.

Carter or the party as a whole. As figure 11-1 shows, this was a period of low
party cohesion, and although cross-party majorities were not as common as
in the late 1960s, figure 11-2 shows that they still were common.

The generation of congressional scholars who contributed to the literature
of the 1950s and 1960s had defended the decentralized Congresses of the
period against the centralizing impulses of presidential scholars and policy
wonks. True, Congress did not move fast or efficiently, nor did it defer to
presidential leadership, but most scholars would have characterized this as
pragmatic incrementalism rather than the "deadlock of democracy."[10] Congress reflected and was responsive to the heterogeneity of interests in the
country. No doubt most of the community of established congressional
scholars sympathized with Julius Turner's critique of the 1950 American
Political Science Association (APSA) report.[11]

To a younger generation of scholars, however, the failings of the decentralized Congresses and disorganized parties were cause for concern. Serious
problems faced the country, presidents were held responsible for solving these

Figure 11-2. *The Decline and Resurgence of Party in Government: Party Votes, 1953–98*

Party votes in Congress (percent of all votes)

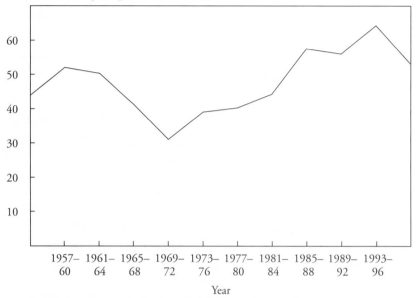

Source: Harold W. Stanley and Richard G. Niemi, eds., *Vital Statistics on American Politics 2005–2006* (Washington, DC: CQ Press, 2005), table 5.7.

problems, but incumbent members of Congress seemingly could win reelection by abandoning their presidents and parties in favor of protecting parochial constituency interests. By emphasizing their individual records, members of Congress had adapted to an era of candidate-centered politics. Historically speaking, they had far less to gain or lose from the effects of presidential coattails, nor need they be very concerned about midterm swings against their president's party.[12] Collective responsibility traditionally provided by the political parties was at low ebb. *Pluribus* was running rampant, leaving *unum* in the electoral dust.

Political Conditions Now

In retrospect, the trends decried in DOCR had already bottomed out by the Carter presidency. The cross-party majorities that passed President Reagan's budget and tax cuts may have obscured the fact, but party unity and party differences already were on the rise and continued rising in succeeding years (Figures 11-1 and 11-2). In a related development, the electoral advantages

Table 11-1. *APSA Report after Forty Years*

Fate of proposal	Democrats	Republicans	System
Full implementation	13	6	5
Partial implementation	7	5	5
De facto movement	8	9	5
No change	3	10	3
Negative movement	2	3	2

Source: Grossly adapted from Denise Baer and David Bositis, *Politics and Linkage in a Democratic Society* (Upper Saddle River, N.J.: Prentice-Hall, 1993), appendix.

accruing to incumbency already were beginning to recede as national influences in voting reasserted themselves.[13] And a new breed of congressional leaders emerged to focus the efforts of their parties in support of or opposition to presidential proposals. In 1993 President Clinton's initial budget passed without a single Republican vote in the House or Senate, and unified Republican opposition contributed greatly to the demise of the administration's signature health care plan.

And then came 1994, when the Republicans finally had success in an undertaking they had sporadically attempted for a generation—nationalizing the congressional elections. In the 1994 elections, personal opposition to gun control or various other liberal policies no longer sufficed to save Democrats in conservative districts whose party label overwhelmed their personal positions. The new Republican majorities in Congress seized the initiative from President Clinton to the extent that he was asked at a press conference whether he was "still relevant." When congressional Republicans overreached, Clinton reasserted his relevance, beating back Republican attempts to cut entitlement programs and saddling them with the blame for the government shutdowns of 1995–96.

At the time, the Republican attempt to govern as a responsible party struck many political scientists as unprecedented in the modern era, but, as Baer and Bositis pointed out, politics had been moving in that direction for several decades. Indeed, a great deal of what the 1950 APSA report called for already had come to pass (table 11-1).[14] Now, a decade later, it is apparent that the Congress elected in 1994 was only the leading edge of a new period in national politics. Party unity and presidential support among Republicans hit fifty-year highs during the first term of President George W. Bush, and in 2002 the president pulled off the rare feat of leading his party to seat gains in a midterm election. After his reelection in 2004, President Bush spoke in terms clearly reminiscent of those used by responsible party theorists. On the basis of a 51 percent popular majority, he claimed a mandate to make his tax cuts permanent and transform Social Security. Moreover, early in 2005 when the president was asked why no one in his administration had been held accountable for mistakes and miscalculations about Iraq, he replied in words that should have warmed the hearts of responsible party theorists: "We had an accountability moment, and that's called the 2004 election. And the American people listened to different assessments made about what was taking place in Iraq, and they looked at the two candidates, and chose me, for which I'm grateful."[15] No president in living memory had articulated such clear statements of collective party responsibility legitimized by electoral victory.

In sum, the collective responsibility DOCR found wanting in the 1970s seems clearly present in the 2000s. Why, then, am I troubled by the operation of something I fervently wished for in the 1970s?

The Problems with Today's Responsible Parties

In 2002 a Republican administration ostensibly committed to free enterprise endorsed tariffs to protect the U.S. steel industry, a policy condemned by economists across the ideological spectrum. Also in 2002 Congress passed and President Bush signed an agricultural subsidy bill that the left-leaning *New York Times* decried as an "orgy of pandering to special interest groups," the centrist *USA Today* called "a congressional atrocity," and the right-leaning *Economist* characterized as "monstrous."[16] In 2003 Congress passed and the president signed a special interest–riddled prescription drug plan that was the largest entitlement program adopted since Medicare itself in 1965, a fiscal commitment that immediately put the larger Medicare program on a steep slide toward bankruptcy. In 2004 congressional Republicans proposed and President Bush supported a constitutional amendment to ban gay marriage, a divisive proposal that had no chance of passing. After his reelection, President Bush declared his highest priority was to avert a crisis in a Social Security system he insisted was bankrupt, by establishing a system of personal accounts, while disinterested observers generally pronounced the situation far from crisis and in need of relatively moderate reform—especially compared to Medicare.[17] In 2005 the Republican Congress passed and President Bush signed a pork-filled transportation bill that contained 6,371 congressional earmarks, forty times as many as contained in a bill vetoed by an earlier Republican president in 1987. Meanwhile, at the time of this writing Americans continue to die in a war of choice launched on the basis of ambiguous intelligence that appears to have been systematically interpreted to support a previously adopted position.

The preceding are only some of the more noteworthy lowlights of public policies adopted or proposed under the responsible party government of 2000–05. All things considered, if someone wished to argue that politics in the 1970s was better than today, I would find it hard to rebut them. Why? Are today's problems and challenges so much more difficult than those of the 1970s that the decentralized, irresponsible parties of that time would have done an even poorer job of meeting them than the more responsible parties of today? Or are today's responsible parties operating in a manner that was not anticipated by those of us who wished for more responsible parties? In the remainder of this chapter, I will focus on the latter possibility.

What Didn't DOCR Anticipate?

With the benefit of hindsight, one potentially negative effect of political competition by cohesive, differentiated parties is to raise the stakes of politics.[18] Certainly, majority control of institutions always is valuable; committee chairs, agenda control, staff budgets, and numerous other benefits go to the majority. But if majority control of the House or Senate means relatively little for policymaking because moderate Republicans and Democrats hold the balance of power, which party formally holds control means less than when policy is decided within each party caucus.[19] Similarly, the knowledge that the president's program either will be rubber-stamped by a supportive congressional majority or killed by an opposition majority makes unified control of all three institutions that much more valuable. The fact that the parties have been so closely matched in the past decade makes the competition that much more intense.

With the political stakes ratcheted upward, politics naturally becomes more conflictual. The benefits of winning and the costs of losing both increase. Informal norms and even formal rules come under pressure as the legislative majority strives to eliminate obstacles to its agenda.[20] Meanwhile, the minority is first ignored, then abused. House Democrats under Jim Wright marginalized House Republicans in the 1980s, and the Republicans have enthusiastically returned the favor since taking control in 1994.[21] Meanwhile Senate Majority Leader Bill Frist threatens the minority Democrats with the "nuclear option"—a rules change that effectively eliminates the filibuster on presidential appointments. In sum, the increasing disparity between majority and minority status further raises the electoral stakes and makes politics more conflictual.

In retrospect, it is probable that the development of more responsible parties was a factor—certainly not the only one—that contributed to the rise of the permanent campaign.[22] With majority status that much more valuable, and minority status that much more intolerable, the parties are less able to afford a hiatus between elections in which governing takes precedence over electioneering. All else now is subordinated to party positioning for the next election. Free trade principles? Forget about them if Pennsylvania and Ohio steel workers are needed to win the next election. Budget deficits? Ignore them if a budget-busting prescription drug plan is needed to keep the opposition from scoring points with senior citizens. Politics always has affected policies, of course, but today the linkage is closer and stronger than ever before.[23]

A second problem with cohesive parties that offer voters a clear choice is that voters may not like clear choices. The APSA report asserted that responsible parties would offer voters "a proper range of choice."[24] But what is "proper"? Voters may not want a clear choice between repeal of *Roe v. Wade* and unregulated abortion, between private Social Security accounts and ignoring inevitable problems, between launching wars of choice and ignoring developing threats. Despite much popular commentary to the contrary, the issue positions of the electorate as a whole are not polarized; voters today remain, as always, generally moderate, or, at least, ambivalent.[25] But candidates and their parties are polarized, and the consequence is candidate evaluations and votes that are highly polarized, which is what we have seen in recent elections.

Even if voters *were* polarized on issues and wished the parties to offer clear choices, they would still be dissatisfied if there were more than one issue and the opinion divisions across issues were not the same. For example, contemporary Republicans are basically an alliance between economic and social conservatives, and Democrats an alliance between economic and social liberals. So, in which party does someone who is an economic conservative and a social liberal belong? An economic liberal and a social conservative? Such people might well prefer moderate positions on both dimensions to issue packages consisting of one position they like a great deal and another they dislike a great deal.

The bottom line is that the majoritarianism that accompanies responsible parties may be ill suited for a heterogeneous society.[26] With only one dimension of conflict a victory by one party can reasonably be interpreted to mean that a majority prefers its program to that of the other party. But with more than one dimension a victory by one party by no means guarantees majority support for its program(s). Indeed, as Anthony Downs noted a half century ago, given variations in voter intensity on different issues, a party can win by constructing a coalition of minorities—taking the minority position on each issue.[27]

American politics probably appeared to have a simpler and clearer structure at the time the APSA report was written. Race was not on the agenda.[28] Social and cultural issues were largely dormant in the midcentury decades, their importance diminished by the end of immigration in the 1920s, the Great Depression, and World War II. A bipartisan consensus surrounded foreign and defense policy.[29] Under such conditions it is understandable that a midcentury political scientist could have felt that all the country needed was two parties that advocated alternative economic programs.[30] For example, in 1962 political historian James McGregor Burns wrote, "It is curious that majoritarian politics has won such a reputation for radicalism in this country. Actually it is moderate politics; it looks radical only in relation to the snail-like progress of Madisonian politics. The Jeffersonian strategy is essentially moderate because it is essentially competitive; in a homogeneous society it must appeal to the moderate, middle-class independent voters who hold the balance of power."[31]

To most contemporary observers the United States looks rather less homogeneous than it apparently did to observers of Burns's era. Compared to 1950, our present situation is more complex with a more elaborate political issue space and less of a tendency to appeal to the moderate voter, as we discuss below.

Burns's contention that majoritarian politics is moderate politics is quite interesting in light of the contemporary discussion of the polarization of American politics. Although the electorate is not polarized, there is no question that the political class—the variegated collection of candidates, activists, interest group spokespersons, and infotainment media—is polarized. And, where we can measure it well, there is little doubt that the political class has become increasingly polarized over the past several decades.[32] Figure 11-3 illustrates the oft-noted fact that moderates have disappeared from Congress: the area of overlap where conservative Democrats and liberal Republicans meet has shrunk to almost nothing, and it has done so at the same time as the parties were becoming more responsible—indeed, figures like these often are cited as indicators of party responsibility.

Figure 11-3. *Polarization of Congress since the 1960s*

Number of members

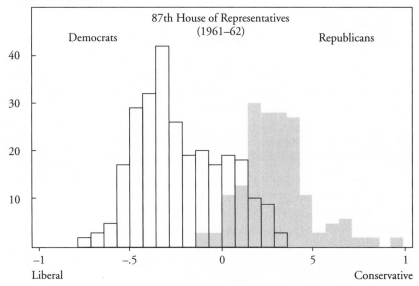

Number of members

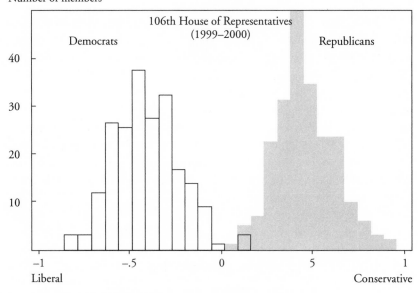

Source: Keith Poole, http://voteview.com/dwnomin.htm.

Why would polarization accompany party responsibility? Logically it need not. Indeed, the APSA report asserted that "[n]eeded clarification of party policy in itself will not cause the parties to differ more fundamentally or more sharply than they have in the past."[33] But as I have argued elsewhere, today's parties are not the same as the parties described in midcentury textbooks.[34] The old distinctions between "amateurs" and "professionals" or "purists" and "professionals" no longer have the same conceptual value because the amateurs have won, or perhaps more accurately, the professionals now are purists. At the time the responsible party theorists wrote, parties nominated candidates on the basis of their service to the party and their connections to party leaders, or, in more competitive areas, their electability. Aside from times when a party was bitterly divided, issue positions were seldom a litmus test of a candidate's suitability.[35] Material motivations—control of offices, patronage—were dominant, but civil service, public sector unionization, conflict of interest laws, social welfare programs, and other developments have lessened the personal material rewards that once motivated many of those active in politics. Today, ideological motivations are relatively more important than previously. Candidates must have the right set of issue stances to attract support, and many of the potential supporters would prefer to lose with a pure ideological candidate than to win with a mushy moderate. Some candidates themselves no doubt feel the same.

These developments have contributed to a basic shift in party electoral strategy in the contemporary United States. At midcentury, the conventional wisdom expressed by Burns was in accord with political science theory—that two-party competition induces parties to move toward the center to capture the median voter.[36] But in the last decade of the century we saw a shift to what now seems to be the prevailing strategy of concentrating on the party base—doing whatever is necessary to maximize loyalty and turnout by core party constituencies. Thus, the aforementioned forcing of a Senate vote on gay marriage was an entirely symbolic gesture toward the evangelical Christian base of the Republican Party. It had nothing to do with governing; it was a costly signal that the Bush administration was on their side.

Seemingly, today's parties no longer strive to maximize their vote, only to satisfice—to get more votes than the other party.[37] At one time a maximal victory was desirable because it would add credibility to the victors' claim that the voters had given them a mandate. But as the previously quoted remarks of President Bush indicate, at least some of today's politicians consider any victory, narrow or not, a mandate.[38]

Parties composed of issue activists and ideologues behave differently from the parties that occupied the political science literature of the mid-twentieth century. At midcentury, each party appealed to a different swath of the American public, Democrats primarily to blue-collar workers and Republicans to middle-class professionals and managers. Because such large social groupings were far from homogeneous internally, the party platform had to tolerate internal heterogeneity to maintain itself and compete across a reasonably broad portion of the country. As Turner put it, "[Y]ou cannot give Hubert Humphrey [liberal Democratic Senator from Minnesota] a banjo and expect him to carry Kansas. Only a Democrat who rejects part of the Fair Deal can carry Kansas, and only a Republican who moderates the Republican platform can carry Massachusetts."[39]

Although both parties continue to have support in broad social groupings like blue-collar workers and white-collar professionals, their bases now consist of much more specifically defined groups. Democrats rely on public-sector unions, environmentalists, prochoice and other liberal cause groups. Republicans rely on evangelicals, small business organizations, prolife and other conservative cause groups. Rather than compromise on a single major issue such as economics, a process that midcentury political scientists correctly saw as inherently moderating, parties can now compromise across issues by adding up constituency groups' most preferred positions on a series of independent issues. Why should conservative mean prolife, low taxes, pro-capital punishment, and preemptive war, and liberal mean just the opposite? What is the underlying principle that ties such disparate issues together? The underlying principle is political, not logical or moral. Collections of positions like these happen to be the preferred positions of groups that now constitute important parts of the party bases.

At one time political scientists saw strong political parties as a means of controlling interest groups.[40] Parties and groups were viewed as competing ways of organizing political life. If parties were weak, groups would fill the vacuum; if parties were strong, they would harness group efforts in support of more general party goals. Two decades ago, I was persuaded by this argument, but time has proved it suspect. Modern parties and their associated groups now overlap so closely that it is often hard to make the distinction between a party activist and an issue activist. As noted above, the difference between party professionals and purists does not look nearly so wide as it once did.

Although more speculative, I believe that unbiased information and policy effectiveness are additional casualties of the preceding developments. The

APSA report asserts, "As a means of achieving responsibility, the clarification of party policy also tends to keep public debate on a more realistic level, restraining the inclination of party spokesmen to make unsubstantiated statements and charges."[41] Recent experience shows just the opposite. Policies are proposed and opposed relatively more on the basis of ideology and the demands of the base, and relatively less on the basis of their likelihood of solving problems. Disinformation and outright lies become common as dissenting voices in each party leave or are silenced. The most disturbing example comes out of congressional passage of the 2003 Medicare prescription drug add-on bill. Political superiors threatened to fire Medicare's chief actuary if he informed Congress that the add-on would be 25–50 percent more costly than the administration publicly claimed. The administration apparently was willing to lie to members of its own party to assure passage of a bill whose basis was mostly political.[42] More recently, President Bush introduced his campaign to add personal accounts to Social Security by claiming that Social Security was bankrupt and that personal accounts were a means of restoring the system to fiscal solvency. Although many experts see merit in the idea of personal savings accounts, most agreed that implementing them would increase Social Security's fiscal deficits in the coming decades. Even greater agreement surrounded rejection of the claim that Social Security was bankrupt. Although politically difficult, straightforward programmatic changes in the retirement age, the tax base, or the method of indexing future benefits would make Social Security solvent for as long as actuaries can reasonably predict.[43]

Moreover, because parties today focus on their ability to mobilize the already committed, the importance of performance for voting declines in importance relative to ideology and political identity. It was telling that in 2004 John Kerry frequently was criticized for not having a plan to end the war in Iraq that was appreciably different from President Bush's. This seems like a new requirement. In 1952 did Dwight Eisenhower have a specific plan to end the war in Korea that differed from President Truman's? "I will go to Korea" is not exactly a plan. In 1968 did Richard Nixon have a specific plan to end the war in Vietnam that differed from President Johnson's? A "secret plan" to end the war is not exactly a precise blueprint that voters could compare to the Johnson policy. Some decades ago voters apparently felt that an unpopular war was sufficient reason to punish an incumbent, regardless of whether the challenger offered a persuasive "exit strategy."

A final consideration relates to the preceding ones. Because today's parties are composed relatively more of issue activists than of broad demographic groupings, they are not as deeply rooted in the mass of the population as was the case for much of our history. The United States pioneered the mass party, but, as Steven Schier has argued, in recent decades the parties have practiced a kind of exclusive politics.[44] The mass-mobilization campaigns that historically characterized American elections gave way to the high-tech media campaigns of the late twentieth century. Voter mobilization by the political parties correspondingly fell.[45] Late-century campaigns increasingly relied on television commercials, and there is some evidence that such ads demobilize the electorate.[46] In a kind of "back to the future" development, the two most recent presidential elections have seen renewed party effort to get out the vote, with a significant impact, at least in 2004. But modern computing capabilities and rich databases enable the parties to practice a kind of targeted mobilization based on specific issues that was more difficult to do in earlier periods. It is not clear that such activities make the parties more like those of yesteryear, or whether they only reinforce the trends I have previously discussed. One-third of the voting age population continues to eschew a party identification, a figure that has not appreciably changed in three decades.[47]

Discussion

In sum, the parties today are far closer to the responsible party model than those of the 1970s, a development that some of us wished for some decades ago, but it would be difficult to argue that today's party system is more effective at solving problems than the disorganized decentralized party system that it replaced. Rather than seek power on the basis of coherent programs, the parties at times throw fundamental principles to the wind when electoral considerations dictate, just as the decentralized parties of the mid-twentieth century did. At other times they hold fast to divisive positions that have only symbolic importance—President Bush reiterated his support for a constitutional amendment to ban gay marriage in his 2005 State of the Union address—for fear of alienating ideologically committed base elements. On issues like Social Security and the war in Iraq, facts are distorted and subordinated to ideology. Mandates for major policy changes are claimed on the basis of narrow electoral victories.

To be sure, I have painted with a broad brush, and my interpretations of recent political history may prove as partial and inaccurate as some of those advanced in DOCR. In particular, I am sensitive to the possibility that unified Democratic government under present conditions might be significantly different from the unified Republican government we have experienced—

Nils Gilman argues that the features of responsible parties discussed above are really Republican features.[48] But even if true, this implies that an earlier generation of political scientists failed to appreciate that Republican and Democratic responsible party government would be significantly different, let alone identify the empirical bases for such differences. What this reconsideration has demonstrated to me is the difficulty of making broad recommendations to improve American politics, even when seemingly solid research and argument underlie many of the component parts, which is the reason I will venture no such recommendations here. It is possible that this paper is as much a product of its temporal context as DOCR was. As Aldrich argues, the political parties periodically reinvent themselves better to deal with the problems they face. That, in fact, is my hope—that the next reinvention of the parties results in organizations that are better than the current models at dealing with the problems our society faces.

Notes

1. *Daedalus,* 109 (1980): 25–45. The article was written for a special issue bearing the title *The End of Consensus?* A number of the articles contained therein discussed the breakdown of consensus in various policy spheres. In light of the contemporary concern with the polarization of American politics, it may be that the fraying of a supposed earlier consensus is a perennial theme.

2. Morris Fiorina, "The Presidency and the Contemporary Electoral System," in *The Presidency and the Political System,* edited by Michael Nelson (Washington, D.C.: CQ Press, 1984), pp. 204–26. A revision titled "The Presidency and Congress: An Electoral Connection?" appeared in Nelson's second edition (1988), pp. 411–34; and a revision with the same title appeared in Nelson's third edition (1990), pp. 443–69.

3. The *locus classicus* is the midcentury report of the Committee on Political Parties of the American Political Science Association (APSA), "Toward a More Responsible Two-Party System," *American Political Science Review,* vol. 44, supplement (1950). For a comprehensive account of the views of responsible party theorists see Austin Ranney, *The Doctrine of Responsible Party Government* (University of Illinois Press, 1962).

4. Indeed, I felt somewhat ambivalent when I learned recently that DOCR still is being reprinted in a widely used law school case book. See Daniel Lowenstein and Richard Hasen, *Election Law: Cases and Materials* (Durham, N.C.: Carolina Academic Press, 2004), pp. 443–59.

5. Morris Fiorina, *Divided Government* (New York: Macmillan, 1992), pp. 126–30 (2d ed. [1996], pp. 173–77).

6. Fiorina, "Presidency and Congress," pp. 465–66.

7. John Aldrich, *Why Parties?* (University of Chicago Press, 1995).

8. For scholarly treatments of the Carter presidency see Erwin Hargrove, *Jimmy Carter as President: Leadership and the Politics of the Public Good* (Louisiana State University Press,

1988); Charles O. Jones, *The Trusteeship Presidency: Jimmy Carter and the United States Congress* (University of Virginia Press, 1988).

9. Carter took office with the Democrats holding 276 of 435 House seats and 59 of 100 Senate seats.

10. James McGregor Burns, *The Deadlock of Democracy* (Upper Saddle River, N.J.: Prentice-Hall, 1963).

11. Julius Turner, "Responsible Parties: A Dissent from the Floor," *American Political Science Review*, vol. 45 (1951): 143–52.

12. Late twentieth-century seat swings were much smaller than in earlier eras. Midterm seat swings sometimes exceeded 90 House seats in the nineteenth century, and even in the New Deal period, the Democrats lost between 55 and 71 seats in three midterms. For a survey of the developments that led to the increased independence of presidential and congressional voting, see the articles in David Brady, John Cogan, and Morris Fiorina, eds. *Continuity and Change in House Elections* (Stanford University Press, 2000).

13. David Brady, Robert D'Onofrio and Morris Fiorina, "The Nationalization of Electoral Forces Revisited," in *Continuity and Change in House Elections*, pp. 130–48.

14. Denise Baer and David Bositis, *Politics and Linkage in a Democratic Society* (Upper Saddle River, N.J.: Prentice-Hall, 1993), appendix.

15. Quoted in Jim VandeHei and Michael Fletcher, "Bush Says Election Ratified Iraq Policy," *Washington Post*, January 16, 2005, p. A1. On electoral mandates generally see Patricia Conley, *Presidential Mandates* (University of Chicago Press, 2001).

16. "Pushing the Limit," *New York Times*, May 19, 2002, p. 14; "While Farmers Milk Public for Billions More," *USA Today*, May 15, 2002, p. 12A; "Bush the Anti-Globaliser," *Economist*, May 11, 2002, p. 14.

17. David Nather and Rebecca Adams, "The Real Crisis Waits Its Turn," *CQ Weekly*, February 21, 2005, pp. 446–51.

18. The APSA report, noted in note 3 above, does recognize the potentially positive effect of higher stakes—increasing popular interest and participation in politics. See, for example, p. 65.

19. At the start of the 109th Congress, Speaker Hastert declared that he would bring no proposal to the floor of the House that did not have a majority in the Republican conference.

20. "Roll call votes on the House floor, which are supposed to take 15 minutes, are frequently stretched to one, two or three hours. Rules forbidding any amendments to bills on the floor have proliferated, stifling dissent and quashing legitimate debate. Omnibus bills, sometimes thousands of pages long, are brought to the floor with no notice, let alone the 72 hours the rules require. Conference committees exclude minority members and cut deals in private, sometimes even adding major provisions after the conference has closed." Norman Ornstein and Thomas Mann, "If You Give a Congressman a Cookie," *nytimes.com,* January 19, 2006.

21. For an overview see Donald R. Wolfensberger, "Pols Apart," *Wilson Quarterly,* vol. 28 (Autumn 2004): 49–59.

22. Norman Ornstein and Thomas Mann, eds., *The Permanent Campaign and Its Future* (Washington, D.C.: American Enterprise Institute and Brookings, 2000).

23. While I was writing this chapter, Karl Rove, President Bush's chief political lieutenant, was appointed deputy chief of staff, a high-level policy post in which he coordinates the work of the Domestic Policy Council, the National Economic Council, the National Security Council, and the Homeland Security Council. According to long-time Washington watchers like Paul Light, "It codifies the fact that policy is politics, and politics is policy." Quoted in Mark Sandalow, "Bush Gives Policy Post to Shrewd Kingmaker," *San Francisco Chronicle*, February 9, 2005, p. A18.

24. APSA, "Toward a More Responsible Two-Party System," p. 1.

25. Morris Fiorina, Samuel Abrams, and Jeremy Pope, *Culture War? The Myth of a Polarized America* (New York: Longman, 2004).

26. Americans may prefer Madisonian supermajoritatianism. Mark Mellman reports a recent poll in which by a two-to-one margin respondents preferred that Supreme Court justices "should have to get the support of at least 60 of the 100 senators" rather than 51. Mark Mellman, "Why Not Require 60 Votes?" *Hill*, March 16, 2005.

27. Anthony Downs, *An Economic Theory of Democracy* (New York: Wiley, 1957). Technically speaking, such a platform is not in equilibrium, but with more than one issue dimension equilibria rarely exist. Parties still have to take positions—out of equilibrium or not.

28. As Baer and Bositis point out, the APSA report was largely silent on race.

29. To be sure, there was the McCarthy episode, but note that McCarthy was censured by a Senate controlled by his own party.

30. Writing about a completely different subject Mayhew also observes that major midcentury political scientists saw American politics largely as a conflict between the economic haves and have-nots. David Mayhew, *Electoral Realignments* (Yale University Press, 2002), pp. 153–56.

31. Burns, *Deadlock of Democracy*, p. 336.

32. Less often noted is that contemporary elite polarization levels resemble those of the late nineteenth century, when politics in the United States also bore some resemblance to responsible party government. See Hahrie Han and David Brady , "A Delayed Return to Historical Norms: Congressional Party Polarization after the Second World War," *British Journal of Political Science* (in press).

33. APSA, "Toward a More Responsible Two-Party System," p. 20.

34. Morris Fiorina, "Parties, Participation, and Representation in America: Old Theories Face New Realities," in *Political Science: The State of the Discipline,* edited by Ira Katznelson and Helen Milner (New York: Norton, 2002), pp. 511–41.

35. Such exceptions would include the fight over silver coinage among late nineteenth-century Democrats and the Regular versus Progressive split among Republicans in the early twentieth century.

36. Duncan Black, *The Theory of Committees and Elections* (Cambridge University Press, 1958); Downs, *An Economic Theory.*

37. Gerber offers an interesting explanation: under some conditions a strategy that maximizes probability of election may produce no gain (indeed, even a loss) of votes. Alan Gerber, "Does Campaign Spending Work?" *American Behavioral Scientist,* vol. 47 (2004): 541–74.

38. Notably, after *losing* the popular vote in 2000, the Republican administration governed as if it had won a mandate.

39. Turner, "Responsible Parties: A Dissent from the Floor," p. 151.

40. As the APSA report comments, "[A] program-conscious party develops greater resistance against the inroads of pressure groups" (APSA, "Toward a More Responsible Two-Party System," p. 19).

41. APSA, "Toward a More Responsible Two-Party System," p. 22.

42. Amy Goldstein, "Foster: White House Had Role in Withholding Medicare Data," *Washington Post*, March 19, 2004, p. A2.

43. See the special issue on social security in the online journal *The Economists Voice* (www.bepress.com/ev/vol2/iss1/).

44. Steven Schier, *By Invitation Only* (University of Pittsburgh Press, 2000).

45. Steven Rosenstone and John Mark Hansen, *Mobilization, Participation, and Democracy in America* (New York: Macmillan, 1993), pp. 162–69.

46. Steven Ansolabehere and Shanto Iyengar, *Going Negative* (New York: Free Press, 1995); and Ted Brader, *Campaigning for Hearts and Minds* (University of Chicago Press, 2006). For other, more skeptical views, see the multiauthor exchange on negative advertising in the *American Political Science Review*, vol. 93 (1999): 851–909.

47. I am unpersuaded by research that purports to show that party in the electorate has resurged to 1950s levels. Morris Fiorina, "Parties and Partisanship: A 40-Year Retrospective," *Political Behavior*, vol. 24 (2002): 93–115.

48. Nils Gilman, "What the Rise of the Republicans as America's First Ideological Party Means for the Democrats," *Forum*, vol. 2 (2004).

12

Taking the Brandeis Metaphor Seriously: Policy Experimentation within a Federal System

MARK CARL ROM

> It is one of the happy accidents of the federal system that a single coura-
> geous state may, if its citizens choose, serve as a laboratory, and try novel
> social and economic experiments without risk to the rest of the country.

> —Louis Brandeis, dissenting opinion in
> *New State Ice Co. v. Liebmann,* 285 U.S. 262, 311 (1932)

The phrase "states as laboratories of democracy" is ubiquitous in the
social science literature.[1] It is often alleged—and rarely denied—that
the American states *are* indeed like laboratories that, through experimentation, learn which policies are effective at remedying public problems and that
these lessons then become more widely adopted across the country.

This wisdom, while conventional, has hardly been demonstrated.
Although many have used the phrase, few appear to have actually asked such
basic questions as how might we interpret the "laboratories of democracy"
metaphor? What would it mean to say these "laboratories" are "effective"?
Why might we expect state "laboratories" to produce good public policy? Do
such laboratories in fact create good policy? Are the successful experiments
emulated, and the failures rejected? Finally, how might we improve the quality of the state laboratories?

This chapter attempts to provide some tentative answers to these questions. First, I assess the key terms in the metaphor: laboratories, experiments, and effectiveness. I emphasize the difference between scientific laboratories and political democracies, between true experiments and policy innovations, and the complexities in determining what we mean by "effective" innovations. Next, I outline three potential institutional arrangements and how these arrangements can promote or inhibit policy innovation; I also discuss the role of nongovernmental actors in policy innovation. The following sections consider the factors that influence state innovativeness and also the role of diffusion in the spread of policy innovations. I offer some examples of innovation in both confederal and federal systems, indicating that confederal systems are not typically successful in developing and spreading effective policies but that federal systems can be effective. Finally, I offer some suggestions for improving our nation's laboratories of democracy.

Laboratories of Democracy

Let us take the metaphor "laboratories of democracy" seriously but not literally.[2] To begin with, the term "laboratories" hardly does justice to what the states actually do. Laboratories conduct experiments within their realm of expertise and determine whether the experiment is successful by generally accepted standards of scientific methods. States must decide whether to experiment or not; they may experiment (or not) over the broadest range of policy domains; they may seek to learn (or not) whether their policy experiments are successful, with success itself a matter of dispute; and they may adopt, reject, or modify the policy experiments of other governments.

Experiments and Innovations

In the laboratory context, an experiment is a systematic attempt to test a hypothesis, determine the efficacy of a treatment, and so forth under strict protocols within a controlled environment. The goal of an experiment is to produce knowledge.

The states rarely experiment in the laboratory sense; rather, the states more typically *innovate*. An innovation is simply "a program or policy which is new to the states adopting it, no matter how old the program may be or how many other states may have adopted it."[3] The goal of a policy innovation is usually not to generate information, but to address some political problem. Policy innovations might involve experimentation, but most often they do not.[4] Policy innovations rarely are designed or implemented in ways resembling laboratory experiments, so the outcomes of the innovation are frequently difficult to assess. This chapter will accordingly focus on policy innovations, discussing policy experiments only when relevant.

Laboratories and Democracies

The states may not be laboratories, but they are democracies. They are, at least, in that the public officials are elected by the citizens (or they are appointed by duly elected politicians), and the laws are enacted through democratic processes. Although it is appropriate to ask "how democratic are the states?" that is not the question addressed here. The states are undoubtedly more or less democratic, depending on how democracy is defined, but in this chapter they all are considered democracies.

That the states are democracies is relevant precisely because this makes them most unlike (scientific) laboratories. Policy innovations in democracies are not designed to learn what works, or on the basis of evidence of what works. Instead, innovations serve the interests of the politicians who design them. It may be that it is in politicians' interests to favor good policy, and many if not most politicians have policy goals they want to accomplish. But the policy itself *is* often the goal. Most politicians have firm commitments to particular types of policies. Conservatives and liberals alike may wish to help the poor—they just see very different policies as being best for doing that.

Politicians might have strong incentives to give the public (or, more accurately, the elements of the public with political resources) what it wants, but there is no particular reason to believe that the public generally agrees on what good policy is or cares much about evidence regarding policy effectiveness.[5] It is reasonable to think that ideology, or tradition, or passion is more important in policy choice than is theory or evidence. When I refer to the states as laboratories in this chapter, I do so only in the metaphorical sense as "a place that produces innovations."

Effectiveness

What makes a laboratory effective? We would call a scientific laboratory effective if it could (1) accurately assess the results of its experiments and (2) conduct experiments that produced beneficial results.[6] For example, an effective pharmaceutical lab would be able to distinguish between drugs that are safe and efficacious and those that are not, and it would also identify drugs with these characteristics. Whether a drug is good is in some ways a matter of judgment, of course, because virtually no drug works for everyone and all drugs have side effects.[7] Still, these criteria of effectiveness are likely to generate little controversy.

Table 12-1. *Political and Policy Laboratories*

Is the innovation effective policy?	Is the innovation effective politically?	
	Yes	No
Yes	Good politics and policy	Good policy but bad politics
No	Good politics but bad policy	Bad politics and policy

The effectiveness of policy laboratories is much more difficult to ascertain for a couple of reasons. First, because policy innovations usually occur in the "real world" (rather than in a controlled setting), it is often difficult to determine the true consequences of the innovation. Second, political actors are concerned about both policy and political effectiveness. An innovation has policy effectiveness to the extent that it remedies a policy problem with minimal harmful side effects. The innovation is politically effective to the extent that it is attractive enough to be adopted, implemented, and sustained over time by democratic institutions. Policy and political effectiveness can vary along a continuous scale, but, to simplify our discussion, let us assume that the answers can be divided into two categories: good (effective) and bad (ineffective).[8] The categories are analytically distinct (good policy might be bad politics, and vice versa), but we might expect to see some correspondence between them.

Table 12-1 shows the analytical possibilities. The heartening results are found along the left-to-right diagonal; the discouraging results along the other. If an innovation is both good politics and good policy, it is likely to be widely adopted; innovations that are unattractive both politically and instrumentally are likely to be rejected. When a programmatic innovation yields political and policy congruence, we should expect the states to work well as laboratories, appropriately sorting out the wheat from the chaff.

The "good-bad" diagonal is less hopeful. Here, innovations that are instrumentally beneficial are politically undesirable, and innovations that have negative policy impacts are nonetheless politically attractive. When these combinations occur, it is generally safe to assume that politics trumps policy: the good policies will be neglected, and the bad ones adopted.

This analysis begs the question: What proportion of innovations is located in each cell? No exact (or, I think, even approximate) empirical answer can be given. The largest cell, by far, certainly involves both bad politics and bad policy. This category contains, literally, an infinite number of possibilities. If such innovations could be imposed by administrative fiat—say, by an authoritarian regime—we might expect to see some large number actually adopted.

One of the greatest blessings of democracy, perhaps, is that these damaging innovations almost never occur. In this sense, democracy itself is likely to generate laboratories that are far more effective than those in nondemocratic polities at solving public problems.

The smallest cell is the one featuring innovations that are both good policy and good politics. This might seem odd because politicians of all stripes routinely proclaim that "good policy *is* good politics." That these outcomes are relatively rare is much less an indictment of democratic politics—or of politicians' aspirations—than a comment on the stringent requirements that must be met for an innovation to fall within this cell. Two requirements are paramount. First, broad political consensus must be achieved regarding the goals of the policy. Lacking such consensus, any innovation will be viewed as beneficial by some ("good policy") and detrimental by others ("bad policy"). Second, evaluation research must clearly demonstrate the innovation's policy effectiveness. Absent compelling evidence, there will be ambiguity as to whether the policy does more good than harm.

The twin barriers of political consensus and evaluation confidence are rarely surmounted. Conflict is inherent to politics: for many issues, individuals will always disagree about what constitutes "good policy" because they have different ideas as to what the good society is.[9] Moreover, politics and policy inherently involve values such as equity, liberty, security, and efficiency. Even though the public might agree that such values are important, these concepts are paradoxical in that any efforts to move closer to them in some respects at the same time move us further away in others.[10] What some see as more equitable will to others seem less equitable. But, as James Madison aptly argued, the only ways to remove political differences of opinion are to destroy liberty or to create uniformity—expedients that are both impractical and unwise.[11]

Why Might State Laboratories Produce Effective Policies?

Before we can assess whether states are effective laboratories, it is fair to ask "effective relative to what?" In this section, I consider alternative institutional arrangements and outline the likely effectiveness of the various scenarios.[12]

Let us begin by considering three hypothetical institutional arrangements, all of which exist simultaneously within the United States: (1) a unitary (or centralized) system, in which the national government has sole authority; (2) a confederal (or decentralized, or "local autonomy") system, in which the states have sole authority over a policy domain; and (3) a federal system, in which federal and state governments share authority.[13] Which, if any, of these arrangements is likely to produce more effective policy experimentation?

Problem Difficulty

The answer depends, in part, on the analytical difficulty of the policy problem.[14] Assume that a fixed set of resources is available to solve the problem. These resources can be pooled or separated. For problems that are only moderately difficult, it appears that dividing the resources into separate pools (the federal approach), which allows for multiple and diverse problem-solving efforts, can lead to optimal solutions. For the most difficult problems, however, divided resource pools may lack the critical mass of expertise necessary for problem solving (the unitary approach).[15] For the simplest problems, neither pooling nor dividing resources is likely to produce more effective policies, because either approach is likely to work.

A key unknown here is how to assess the difficulty of the policy problem. Kollman and colleagues suggest that difficult problems include "curing diseases, constructing welfare policies, or designing computer chips."[16] It is not obvious that centralized systems are better at solving these particular problems than decentralized ones; in fact, many of the successful innovations in these areas have come from smaller units. Although it might be optimal in theory to have unitary governments handle complex problems and decentralized governments address simpler ones, what constitutes complexity in practice is itself difficult to ascertain.

Distribution of Preferences

The effectiveness of institutional arrangements may also depend on the distribution of policy preferences. Preferences may be homogeneous (nationally and thus within the states), heterogeneous across the nation (but identical across the states), or heterogeneous nationally (but homogeneous within each state). This distribution does not influence policy effectiveness, but it does shape political effectiveness, as discussed below.

Unitary Systems

Under a unitary system of government, the central authority is responsible for all policy innovations. The unitary system seems to work best under one main condition.[17] If the policy problem is (analytically) difficult relative to the intellectual and administrative ability to solve it, only the problem-solving capacity of a central authority might be sufficient to find a feasible solution. Even relatively simple problems might still be beyond state remedy, however, if the states' administrative apparatuses are uniformly weak (or motivations low and barriers high). Uniformly weak is an important condition, for even if only a small number of states have adequate capacity and motivation to overcome barriers, the various innovations of these states may prove superior to the single innovation of the national government.

A unitary system could engage in decentralized innovation, with a national department conducting (or funding) multiple experiments within separate geographic locations. In fact, the federal government often does conduct pilot projects in limited geographic areas, though I am unaware of any examples of simultaneously occurring multiple experiments seeking to solve a single problem.[18] In general, we might expect the national government to conduct a single policy innovation at a time for a single policy problem.

Confederal Systems

The states have primary responsibility over a wide variety of policy domains in the United States. There are good reasons to think that when the states do assume authority—that is, when they operate as a confederal system—effective policy innovation will not generally occur. Still, there are countervailing factors that suggest that the states can be quite innovative and that these innovations often will spread across the states.

A confederal system may not be well equipped to produce effective policy experiments, even for moderately difficult problems, for several reasons. First, each state may view itself sui generis, with its own unique history, culture, characteristics, and goals. As a result, the states could be unwilling to learn from the others—after all, what can unique we learn from unique them? Moreover, in a confederal system the states have no particular incentive to innovate, or to share the results of their policy learning with others. This is a classic "public goods" problem: if a state bears all the costs and risks of its experiment, and if other states can easily imitate successful experiments, all states have incentives to let other states experiment. Consequently, little innovation will occur. This would be true even if the states were entirely autonomous (where the innovations of one state have no implications for the other states), but it also seems true if the states were autonomous (in terms of decisions) but integrated (in terms of capital and personal mobility). In the latter case, policy innovations that lead to competitive advantage (that is, developmental policies) are unlikely to be shared; policy innovations that produce competitive disadvantages (that is, redistributional policies) are likely to be avoided.[19] The reluctance to learn, together with the aversion to teach, suggests that successful policy innovations may not easily spread across the governments within a confederal system.

Still, there can be benefits—or at least no disadvantages relative to a unitary system—to a confederal system both in terms of policy innovation and diffusion.[20] Even without concern for the other states, each state has its own reasons to innovate to solve policy problems. Although each state has no special reason to share its innovations, the other states (to the extent that they have common goals and see their problems and environments as similar) do have incentives to emulate policies that they see as effective. The states certainly have easy access to information about the policies of other states through such organizations as the National Governors Association, the National Conference of State Legislatures (NCSL), and countless other specialized professional associations and clearinghouses.[21]

If the distribution of preferences is the same within the states and across the nation, confederal systems should perform no differently than a unitary system in terms of the political effectiveness of policy innovations. Yet if preferences are heterogeneous nationally but homogenous within each state, confederal approaches should have a major advantage over unitary systems regarding political effectiveness.[22] In light of heterogeneous preferences, under confederalism, Michigan can be Michigan and Mississippi can be Mississippi, to the greater satisfaction of both states' residents. Each state can learn what works *for it*, acting as a laboratory for itself, if not for the others.

Federal Systems

I use the term "federal" not to refer to the idea that the states and the national government are each sovereign within some realms, but to the concept that they mutually share power and responsibility over certain policy issues (for example, health, education, welfare, among others). In these circumstances, neither must the states go alone (as under a confederal system) nor does the national government have to devise solutions on its own (as within a unitary system).

Under certain circumstances, a federal system might be superior to both unitary and confederal systems for effective policy innovation. A first condition is that (enough of) the states have sufficient capacity relative to problem difficulty to develop effective innovations. A second condition is that the states have sufficient flexibility to innovate. A third condition is that a clear set of policy goals is established (either by fiat from the national government or by agreement among the states). A final condition is that the states have sufficient motivation (whether through compulsion or inducement) to experiment, learn what works, and adopt effective innovations.[23] Indeed, one way to solve the public goods problem mentioned above is for the national government to reduce the costs and risks of state experimentation through subsidies or other stimulus.

The last two conditions are the key ones that distinguish the federal system from the confederal one and provide the opportunity for more effective innovation. If each state is pursuing the same goal and every state has motivation both to innovate and to adopt the most effective innovations, we might expect more innovation, more learning, and greater policy effectiveness.[24]

Alternative Institutions

Governments—whether in confederal, unitary, or federal systems—need not be the only institutions engaged in policy innovation and, indeed, they are not. Nongovernmental organizations (NGOs) usually, but not always, have also conducted a broad range of policy experiments through governmental contracts.[25]

These nongovernmental experiments have distinct advantages and disadvantages over ones run by governments. One clear advantage is that it is probably easier for NGOs to design, implement, and evaluate the innovations in ways better able to yield knowledge of policy effectiveness. Several NGOs (such as Mathematica, RAND, the Manpower Development Research Corporation [MDRC], and Abt, among others) have strong reputations for conducting high-quality program evaluations, and they are able to remain unbound by political manipulation or partisan commitments.

One set of disadvantages—or, perhaps more appropriately, challenges—the NGOs face is to produce information that is definitive, generalizable, timely, visible, and relevant.[26] As the history of social experimentation has shown, these challenges are real and large. Policymakers, however, are understandably loath to put much stock in the results of NGO experiments unless those challenges have been met. Still, even when the evaluation results do not meet these high standards for information, they can contribute to the "inventory" of potentially useful knowledge.[27]

A second set of challenges concerns the policy environment, or what Carol Weiss calls the I-I-I (ideology-interests-information) model.[28] The central point of Weiss's model is that policymakers often act on the basis of their ideological preferences, the interests they (and their constituents) maintain, and the types of information they possess (with evaluation research being only one, and often not the most important, source of information). If evaluation research conflicts with the ideological predilections of the interests of those in power or the information it provides is merely one element in a complex informational stew, the policy research is unlikely to impact subsequent policy choice; however, when evaluation research supports the dominant ideology and interests, the information it provides can offer a useful tipping point for policy change.

What Factors Influence State Innovativeness?

In view of our definition of policy innovation, there can be no question that the American states are highly innovative. Each time a state enacts a law, issues a regulation, or promulgates a ruling, it can be said to "innovate." At the time they are adopted, all policies are innovations.

Extensive research has been conducted on policy innovation in the American states.[29] One key finding of this literature is that state innovativeness is highly diverse: it varies across place, time, and policy issue.[30] Innovation is not entirely random, however. Whether operating under confederal or federal arrangements, innovation is more likely to occur in states with greater capacity (also known as "resources" or "slack"), higher motivations, and fewer barriers.[31]

Capacity

Researchers have routinely found that states with higher "capacity"—with income, wealth, or urbanization typically serving as proxies for this concept— are more likely to innovate than states with less capacity.[32] Indeed, of all the quantifiable factors associated with policy innovation, these measures of capacity appear to be the most important. Clearly, though, these measures do not directly cause innovation but are apparently associated with unmeasured variables that do produce innovation.

The political capacities of the states are also associated with their innovativeness, though political capacity is difficult to measure. Legislative professionalism is linked to greater innovation.[33] Bureaucratic competence, in turn, is connected with legislative professionalism.[34] Gubernatorial powers vary substantially across the nation, and governors often play a major role in proposing and promoting innovations, though it seems that the innovativeness of the governors has more to do with their personal characteristics and ambitions than with their institutional authority.[35]

If it is true that greater capacity leads to more innovation, then never have the states been in a better position to innovate. The states are wealthier and more urbanized than ever. Most state legislatures are far "more professional today then they were a generation ago" (though perhaps a few have regressed).[36] State bureaucracies are better staffed and better paid (and more diverse).[37] Governors are now often at the forefront of policy innovation, willing and eager to seek and accept additional policy authority from the national government.

Motivation

Motivations are of two sorts. The first concerns the nature of the problem. In general, the more severe the problem—or the political perception that the problem is severe—the greater the stimulus for addressing it. For example, Virginia Gray and colleagues found that the states most likely to have adopted prescription drug programs were those states with the most rapidly escalating drug prices.[38] Kenneth Meier concluded that the stringency of state drug laws increased with the frequency of illegal drug use, whereas James Lester and colleagues found that state hazardous waste regulation is a function of the number of hazardous waste sites.[39]

The second and more complex aspect of motivation concerns the willingness of political actors to innovate. Political actors are more likely to innovate, understandably, when they see it in their best interest to do so. Politicians and public officials have incentives to innovate when public support for innovation is high and the political consequences of not doing so are real. This suggests that innovation will be positively related to both public opinion and electoral competitiveness.

Public opinion influences both the likelihood and direction of innovation. The more united the public is in calling for a policy innovation, the more likely the change is to occur (though note the impact of mobilized minority opinion, discussed below). It should come as no surprise, for example, that during the early 1980s some forty states adopted stiffer mandatory sentences for selling illegal drugs or that thirty-seven states enacted "defense of marriage" laws or constitutional amendments after the mid-1990s, as public opinion strongly favored such legislation.[40] Liberal states, meanwhile, are predisposed to enact liberal innovations; conservative states, conservative policies.[41] Political culture may also be linked to innovation, with the "moralistic" states most innovative and the "individualist" and "traditionalist" states less so.[42]

The electoral nexus is less clear in the literature. The core idea is that when one party dominates a state, it will have weak electoral incentives to innovate (though innovations may nonetheless reflect public opinion). When party competition is intense, however, it might be expected that politicians will offer policy innovations in order to build electoral support. In general, however, there is little systematic evidence that politically competitive states are more innovative than less competitive ones. More broadly, partisan and electoral variables appear to be only weakly connected to innovativeness, if they are at all.

Barriers

Barriers to innovation (namely, policy change) are pervasive in the American political system. The list of potential barriers is vast: the separation of powers, multiple veto points, judicial review, the power of interest groups, and so forth. Determined minorities are usually in a better position to block change than flaccid majorities are to obtain it. For example, the vast majority of Americans have consistently favored tighter gun control laws, which the ardent opponents of such restrictions have usually been able to block, while states with higher proportions of religious fundamentalists are less likely to adopt lotteries.[43]

Policy Diffusion

It is the rare innovation that is adopted entirely de novo. Most policies that are an innovation to the government adopting it have been tried, in some form, somewhere else first. The states often innovate by emulating: after witnessing other states adopt a policy, they do too. Numerous researchers have noted the adoption-emulation pattern.[44] The exact reasons for the emulation are unclear.[45] Perhaps voters in a state, seeing that other states are offering a policy they prefer, demand it; perhaps politicians, noting that other states have found it politically advantageous to provide a policy, supply it. Policy entrepreneurs—those "who seek to initiate dynamic policy change"— undoubtedly play a role.[46] What is clear from the emulation studies is that states tend to be influenced by the policies of their immediate neighbors and that the more neighbors that have adopted a policy the more likely a state is to imitate. Modeling "neighbor policy choice" as an independent variable in state policy adoption studies is now commonplace.

It is less common to study how "nonneighbors" influence policy emulation—that is, the extent to which states adopt policies that have been enacted in states geographically more remote. The major reason for this gap in the literature is statistical: because every state can potentially be influenced by every other state, it is difficult to estimate the impact of any state's policy adoption on every other state's emulation.[47] But in light of the importance of professional networks, it seems likely that the states are aware of—and presumably influenced by—what other states are doing across most policy domains.

The states emulate, but typically do not copy exactly, the policy choices of other states. Some studies have found that later adopters increase the scope of the laws they emulate.[48] Others claim that the states learn about and improve upon the policies of other states through a "social learning process."[49]

One potential benefit of the adoption-emulation process is that it allows the more innovative states—those with greater resources, higher motivations, and fewer barriers—to conduct policy experiments initially, while allowing the less innovative states to build upon these experiments.[50] Indeed, Frances Berry and William Berry argue that prior policy innovations increase resources (information) while reducing barriers (uncertainty).[51]

Unfortunately, there is virtual silence as to whether effective policies are more likely to disperse than ineffective ones or whether successful policies are dispersed more quickly or completely. A (single) notable exception is a paper by Craig Volden that examines states' adoptions of innovations in the State Children's Health Insurance Program.[52] Volden found that "[p]olicymakers tend to adopt policies found in states with similar partisan and ideological leanings, those with similar demographics, and those facing similar budgetary situations" but also that states "tend to emulate those policies that have been shown to be successful at lowering the uninsurance rate of poor children in other states." Although there is little evidence that states emulate effective policies, it does seem clear that at times demonstrably ineffective and even harmful policies have become widely adopted.[53]

Policy Experimentation in a Confederal System

That states in a confederal system do not necessarily—or often—produce effective laboratories of democracy can best be illustrated by examining our nation's election procedures. Election procedures should, in principle, have a single goal: to record accurately the electoral preferences of registered voters.[54] At the voting place, properly registered voters should be able to vote and nonregistered voters should be barred from voting. Ballots should be designed so that voters can identify their candidates of choice and mark their ballots correctly. Ballots should be counted precisely and, if the results are challenged, recounted exactly.

Election processes should be a good test of the laboratories within a confederal system for several reasons. First, recording citizens' preferences accurately is fundamentally important to democratic politics. Second, literally everyone publicly agrees that these preferences *should* be recorded truthfully.[55] Third, election processes are almost entirely decentralized, with state and local governments having virtually entire control over their design and operation. Fourth, the states have had more than 200 years to perfect their election processes, and these processes are tested on a regular basis. Fifth, improving election processes does not require large and complex behavioral changes (as do many other policy domains); improvements are mainly technological and administrative.

The lab results are in, and they are not exactly glowing. In the 2000 presidential election, "a staggering 179,855 votes were "spoiled" (in Florida)— that is, cast but not counted."[56] An estimated 54 percent of these ballots were cast by African Americans, whose ballots were discarded at a rate eight times higher than those of whites.[57] In Florida's Gadsen County, one in eight ballots was spoiled.[58] In that same election, Florida expunged 94,000 voters from the rolls because they were listed as felons, though only 3 percent were later verified as former convicts.[59]

These problems were hardly limited to Florida. Touch-screen computers are now widely used, even though they are more expensive than paper ballots and scanners. In the 2004 elections, roughly three of every ten ballots were cast on touch-screen computers.[60] Yet vote loss is arguably higher from touch-screen computers than from other methods, such as paper ballots combined with optical scanners. The much-maligned "punch card" process was still being used in 2004 in Ohio, Missouri, and elsewhere.[61] Nevertheless, a Congressional Research Service report concluded that "[t]here is no consensus on whether any one technology is best."[62]

It is amazing how much diversity still exists in ballot procedures across and within states.[63] It is possible that the ballot procedures have not really been studied to determine which ones are most effective. If this is true, the implication is that the states have not been very successful laboratories. If this is not true, the implication is that the states have been unwilling to adopt the balloting procedures that have proven to be most effective.

The states nonetheless continue to experiment with their electoral systems. In the year after the 2000 presidential debacle, the NCSL reported that 1,600 electoral reform bills had been introduced, and 130 had thus far been enacted.[64] To their credit, some states took seriously their responsibility for developing better systems. Georgia, for example, enacted legislation requiring the adoption of uniform systems throughout the state by 2004. Rather than mandating the system to be chosen, Georgia established a pilot program to test electronic touch-screen systems for municipal elections (though, as noted above, touch-screen systems have clear problems) as well as an advisory commission to oversee the pilot and advise the states.[65] In fact, the most commonly proposed reform was to establish task forces, commissions, and study committees to consider reforms.

Innovation within a confederal system does not always lead to such infelicitous outcomes, of course; if it did, our national tradition of substantial policy devolution would have little credibility. Later in this volume Roberta Romano argues that state control over corporate charter law has led to an "effective laboratory for experimentation and innovation."[66] By this she means that state chartering laws have maximized firm values, and that because local corporate bars are "a focused, politically connected and unopposed interest group," there is relatively little disagreement as to what constitutes good policy and good politics. Whether this is a special case, or whether other policy areas have similarly effective innovation, remains an open matter.

Policy Experimentation within a Federal System

A federal system can lead to effective policy innovation under certain conditions, but these conditions rarely have been entirely present in the United States. Perhaps the closest parallels exist in welfare policy, though in recent years education policy has also displayed similar attributes.[67]

Since the creation of the Aid to Dependent Children (later, the Aid to Families with Dependent Children, or AFDC) program in 1935, the national government has been the principal source of both finance and authority. Through the 1970s, at least, the national government's priorities came to dominate AFDC, pushing the system toward liberalization, uniformity, and centralization.[68] At times, however, the national government has allowed the states to experiment, and these experiments have influenced both national welfare policy as well as the welfare policies in the various states.[69] State innovations have played an increasingly prominent role in welfare policy since the 1980s and, especially, after AFDC was eliminated and Temporary Assistance for Needy Families was created in 1996 through the Personal Responsibility and Work Opportunity Reconciliation Act (PRWORA).

What are known as "section 1115 waivers" kick-started these state innovations. Authorized in 1962, these waivers allowed states to carry out "any experimental, pilot, or demonstration" projects judged by the secretary of the Department of Health and Human Services "likely to help in promoting the objectives" of AFDC. Any state could apply for a section 1115 waiver, though the waiver process was cumbersome and approval was not guaranteed. Until the 1980s, few waivers were sought, and most consisted of administrative and service delivery innovations.[70] Beginning during the Reagan administration, and with increasing frequency under President Clinton, numerous states used waivers to conduct welfare innovations.

During the Reagan administration, no fewer than sixty-six waivers were granted to states seeking to conduct "welfare-to-work" experiments, which were encouraged through the Omnibus Reconciliation Act of 1982, OBRA.[71] Formal evaluations were often a component of these waivers, increasing the probability that policymakers could learn whether the experiment was actually effective—indeed, for this reason and others these experiments have been called a "watershed in social experimentation."[72] An important element in the success of these experiments—and their evaluation—was the clear line of responsibility often drawn between the states and the evaluators. The states designed and implemented the innovations according to their own goals and priorities, while the evaluators were responsible for designing and implementing the studies according to evaluation standards (for example, by emphasizing random assignment).[73]

The results of the welfare-to-work experiments were generally encouraging. Moreover, as the experiments continued they learned from each other: questions left unanswered by one innovation were addressed in subsequent studies. Although program impacts were typically modest, they did usually show that those in the treatment groups had higher earnings and lower welfare payments, that the innovations reduced the size of the welfare rolls, and that the innovations yielded net social benefits (as well as lower governmental expenditures).[74] The most successful (and influential) experiment (the GAIN program in Riverside County, California) also produced a finding of profound importance for later welfare reform efforts. The GAIN program emphasized a "work-first" approach that sought to move welfare recipients as quickly as possible into the private labor force, even if in low-paying jobs. This was in contrast to other experiments that stressed the "human capital model," which sought to improve the work skills (through education and training) of welfare recipients prior to seeking employment.

In addition to the impacts of the welfare-to-work programs themselves, the waiver experiments also provided valuable political and administrative lessons.[75] First, the states themselves could plan and operate welfare programs that could work in a variety of settings; this suggested that the states could benefit from additional programmatic flexibility. Second, the evaluations could use available administrative data, rather than requiring special (and onerous) new data collection efforts. Third, requiring AFDC participants to engage in work was administratively feasible and, indeed, the recipients viewed such requirements as fair. Finally, at least some of the experiments suggested that there was an upper limit (perhaps 60 percent) of how many welfare recipients actually would be able to comply with mandatory work obligations.

The influence of the welfare-to-work experiments was profound, not least because they generated information addressing concerns of political actors with differing views.[76] The innovations suggested to conservatives that welfare was not bound to fail but that government programs could produce real (however modest) improvements in the (economic) lives of welfare recipients. At the same time, the experiments undermined liberal opposition to work requirements as impractical and unfair. The programs suggested that the states could be competent to design and implement effective programs, increasing the confidence of state policymakers that they could improve welfare and of national policymakers to give them the authority to do so. Finally, the experiments suggested that the work-first approach was preferable to the human capital method of improving the condition of welfare recipients.

The welfare-to-work experiments also changed the way that the federal government evaluated and approved state waiver requests to suggest that it also learned from them. Before 1987, the Reagan administration only approved waiver requests when it approved the substantive content of waiver; after that time, it allowed the states to conduct the experiments that they wanted to conduct.[77] Moreover, after 1987 the federal government showed a clear preference for waivers that included a "random assignment" component to their evaluation plans.

As Greenberg, Linksz, and Mandell argue, "possibly more than any other social experiments, the welfare-to-work experiments have played an important role in policymaking."[78] The state "welfare-to-work" experiments conducted after OBRA "strongly influenced" the Family Support Act (FSA) of 1988.[79] The centerpiece of the FSA was the Job Opportunities and Basic Skills Training (JOBS) program; by all accounts, JOBS was modeled on the welfare-to-work experiments.[80] (JOBS essentially required the states to implement some of the key lessons of the welfare-to-work experiments.) The modeling was not precise, but neither were the experiments the sole cause of reform. The FSA contained measures that had not been demonstrated by the state experiments, and the act was favored by many for more purely political and ideological reasons.

MDRC's role in the welfare-to-work experiments is instructive both on the opportunities NGOs bring and ways that they can overcome the challenges they face. MDRC conducted the best-known and most influential of the welfare-to-work experiments.[81] It is important to note that the states initially did not exactly rush to MDRC seeking high-quality evaluations; instead, MDRC had to sell the idea of such evaluations to the states.[82] (That governments can be reluctant to evaluate their programs should come as no surprise. Evaluations always pose political risks, as they can show that a program does not work—or that it does. Either way, the evaluation results will threaten those with political commitments either in favor of, or opposition to, the program in question.) MDRC was not content with just producing high-quality evaluations, however. It was able to publish, and widely disseminate, its evaluations at the time (1987) that welfare reform was on the national agenda. MDRC representatives repeatedly testified before Congress and briefed staffers.[83] Although the FSA was not built on MDRC's research, the research appears, at the very least, to have affected the act's finishings.

The FSA hardly ended state welfare reform innovations. President George W. Bush further expanded the use of waivers when his administration explicitly called for the "states as labs" to experiment.[84] His administration also made random assignment a criterion for approving waiver requests.[85] These policies further increased the states' abilities to conduct welfare experiments and evaluate whether the experiments actually worked.

Yet the influence of these experiments on national welfare policy actually declined after Bill Clinton became president in 1992. Clinton had famously campaigned on a pledge to "end welfare as we know it," and his administration's "Work and Responsibility Act" built on, and at times departed from, the evidence of the welfare-to-work experiments.[86] But after the Republicans gained control of Congress in 1994, it did not seriously consider the Clinton proposal. Instead, Congress proposed, and Clinton ultimately signed, PRWORA. PRWORA establishes national standards (regarding, for example, work participation rates, time limits for welfare receipt) and generally leaves it up to the states to determine how to meet those standards. It encourages the states to consider innovative ways to address problems (such as how to lower the teenage birthrate without increasing abortion rates, or how to promote marriage). The states now have more authority over welfare than at any time since the presidency of Franklin Roosevelt.

Although the states may benefit from the additional flexibility provided by PRWORA, their ability to learn from their innovations may actually be weakened. Under the waiver system, the states were compelled to evaluate their innovations; now, they are not. In welfare, we have moved away from a federal system toward a confederal one.

Improving the Laboratories of Democracy

How might we enhance the ability of our country to solve policy problems, to make our laboratories more effective? Several approaches might be considered.

One approach would consider the nature of the problem that is to be solved. Some policy issues might be too difficult for the states to resolve through their own efforts. In principle, these issues might be handled more appropriately by the national government. The twin difficulties faced here are (1) deciding which problems are sufficiently difficult for the authority to be assumed by the national government and (2) obtaining political agreement from both the states and the national government that the central authority take on these issues. Although there will be disagreement as to which kind of problems are "difficult," the key undoubtedly is whether the states have sufficient resources—whether technical, administrative, or financial—to solve the problems on their own.

A second approach would consider the distribution of policy preferences. If preferences are (relatively) homogeneous across the nation, determining whether state or national governments should address the policy problem might be done by considering the difficulty of solving the problem. If preferences are heterogeneous, however, then perhaps it is best to allow the states to experiment in ways that can at least meet the aspirations of the individual states' citizens. Although this might not maximize policy effectiveness, it might increase the political effectiveness of the various innovations. One might imagine that this approach is most useful for issues that are not technically difficult, but morally controversial.

A third way, perhaps most suitable when policy goals can be agreed upon but policy methods are uncertain, is to adopt the federal approach to problem solving. When this is the case—as it seems to have been for welfare policy—the federal government can establish standards while providing the states sufficient incentives to experiment, evaluate these experiments, and adopt those that are effective at improving the quality of life in ways that are politically suitable.

Notes

1. Searching scholar.google.com for this phrase produced about 3,400 hits.
2. For an analysis of Brandeis's use of the laboratories metaphor, see G. Alan Tarr, "Laboratories of Democracy? Brandeis, Federalism and Scientific Management," *Publius,* vol. 31 (Winter 2001): 37–67.

3. Jack Walker, "The Diffusion of Innovations Among the American States," *American Political Science Review,* vol. 64, no. 3 (1969): 880–99, quotation on p. 881. A similar definition is provided by Lawrence B. Mohr, "Determinants of Innovation in Organizations," *American Political Science Review,* vol. 63, no. 1 (1969): 111–26, p. 112. This definition of innovation is quite broad, because it is essentially synonymous with "policy change." It is deliberately broad, however, to forestall semantic debates over how "innovative" a policy change must be before it can be labeled an "innovation." For example, consider tax policy. If "innovation" is limited to policies that are truly original, one must conclude that no innovations are occurring, as all changes in the tax code involve setting rates or targets, and these things have been done since the very inception of taxes. So rather than saying that no innovation is occurring, the definition provided here assumes that any policy change is an innovation, at least for the government instituting the change. For convenience, I will use the term "policy" to include both policy and programs.

4. The states may conduct policy experiments, but more often policy experiments are conducted by other governmental or nongovernmental units. The most definitive source of information on policy experiments is contained in David Greenberg and Mark Shroder, *The Digest of Social Experiments,* 3d ed. (Washington, D.C.: Urban Institute Press, 2004).

5. Note that Jacobs and Shapiro argue that politicians do not typically give the public what it wants but use polls to sell the public what the politicians want (Lawrence R. Jacobs and Robert Y. Shapiro, *Politicians Don't Pander: Political Manipulation and the Loss of Democratic Responsiveness* [University of Chicago Press, 2000]).

6. More specifically, a good experiment will correctly identify true positives and true negatives while avoiding both type I and type II errors.

7. Identifying a "good" drug is not entirely straightforward, of course, because all drugs have side effects. Determining whether drugs are effective thus becomes a matter of balancing costs and benefits, with the outcome depending on how costs and benefits are weighted.

8. On virtually no important policy issue is there unanimity regarding what constitutes good policy or good politics, of course: there are always dissenting voices. We might thus deem a policy effective if the "preponderance of evidence" indicates that the policy realizes its goals, while good politics suggests that a solid majority of the relevant public supports the policy.

9. For example, the scientific evidence indicates (with some dissent) that fluoride benefits public health by reducing tooth decay and that fluoridating public water supplies "is the most equitable, cost-effective, and cost-saving method of delivering fluoride to the community" (Centers for Disease Control, "Recommendations for Using Fluoride to Prevent and Control Dental Caries in the United States," *Mortality and Morbidity Weekly Report,* vol. 50, no. RR-14 [2001]: 26). The public nonetheless seems to hold (with some dissent) that water fluoridation is bad policy because it typically opposes the addition of medications to public water supplies (Fluoride Action Network, "Communities Which Have Rejected Fluoridation since 1990" [www.fluoridealert.org/communities.htm {August 2, 2006}]).

10. Deborah Stone, *The Policy Paradox: The Art of Political Decision Making,* rev. ed. (New York: W. W. Norton, 2002).

11. James Madison, "The Federalist Number 10" (www.constitution.org/fed/federa10.htm [August 2, 2006]).

12. I independently developed many of these ideas, but they closely parallel the work by Ken Kollman and colleagues, who formalized and elaborated the model (Ken Kollman, John H. Miller, and Scott E. Page, "Decentralization and the Search for Policy Solutions," *Journal of Law, Economics, and Organization*, vol. 16, no. 1 [2000]: 102–28). Kollman and colleagues distinguish between four institutional arrangements: centralism, local autonomy, "policy laboratories with best adoption," and "policy laboratories with incremental adoption." I use the terms "confederal," "unitary," and "federal." The ideas expressed are my own unless attributed to Kollman and colleagues.

13. Even though the United States has a federal system of government, it contains aspects of all three systems. In some policy domains, the national government has a monopoly over authority (for example, coining money); in others, the states have a (virtual) monopoly (for example, their own tax systems); in yet others, the state and federal governments share authority (for example, health and welfare policy).

14. Kollman and colleagues, "Decentralization," p. 103 and various.

15. The term "critical mass" is used consciously to invoke the efforts of the Manhattan Project.

16. Kollman and colleagues, "Decentralization," p. 103.

17. Kollman and colleagues specify three conditions: problem difficulty, search capacity, and preference heterogeneity ("Decentralization," pp. 103–04). Here I combine the first two conditions and draw differing conclusions regarding the final one. A unitary system might be preferable to a decentralized one in terms of policy equity and efficiency, but because this chapter focuses on innovation, these other values are not considered here.

18. For example, the landmark New Jersey Income Maintenance Experiment was one such federal experiment. See Greenberg and Shroder, *Digest of Social Experiments*, p. 16.

19. For the distinction between developmental and redistributive policies, see Paul E. Peterson, Barry G. Rabe, and Kenneth K. Wong, *When Federalism Works* (Brookings, 1986).

20. Kollman and colleagues argue that, for moderately difficult policy problems, on average decentralized systems will be as effective as unitary systems at identifying optimal policy solutions.

21. For example, the Economic Success Clearinghouse (www.financeproject.org/irc/win. asp [August 2, 2006]) provides substantial information on state welfare policy experiments.

22. Kollman and colleagues assert that unitary systems will innovate more effectively if the states have heterogeneous preferences (p. 103).

23. Kollman and colleagues discuss two possibilities for this condition. Under "best adoption" the states would be required to adopt the current "best policy" innovation on the basis of the experiments. Under "incremental adoption" the states must at least move in the direction of the best policy innovation (p. 105).

24. Kollman and colleagues argue that if all units can experiment, "too much search may take place," in light of the decreasing marginal value of having additional units search, and they suggest ways to limit excessive search (p. 108).

25. See, for example, Greenberg and Shroder, *Digest of Social Experiments*. Greenberg and colleagues report that of the 143 policy experiments they studied, the federal government was the sole funding source for 57 experiments and contributed to 16 percent of the other experiments (David Greenberg, Donna Linksz,, and Marvin Mandell, *Social Experimentation and Public Policymaking* [Washington, D.C.: Urban Institute Press, 2003], p. 37).

26. Greenberg and colleagues, *Social Experimentation*, p. 52.

27. See Martha S. Feldman, *Order without Design: Information Production and Policy Making* (Stanford University Press, 1989).

28. Carol H. Weiss, "Ideology, Interests, and Information," in *Ethics, Social Science, and Policy Analysis*, edited by D. Callahan and B. Jennings (New York: Plenum Press, 1983).

29. See, for example, Walker, "The Diffusion of Innovations"; Virginia Gray, "Innovation in the American States: A Diffusion Study," *American Political Science Review*, vol. 67, no. 4 (1973): 174–85; George W. Downs, *Bureaucracy, Innovation, and Public Policy* (Lanham, Md.: Lexington Books, 1976); Lee Sigelman and Roland Smith, "Consumer Legislation in the American States: An Attempt at an Explanation," *Social Science Quarterly*, vol. 61 (1980): 58–70; James L. Regens, "State Policy Responses to the Energy Issue," *Social Science Quarterly*, vol. 61 (1980): 44-57; Lee Sigelman, Phillip W. Roeder, and Carol Sigelman, "Social Service Innovation in the American States," *Social Science Quarterly*, vol. 62 (1981): 503–15; and Robert L. Savage, "Policy Innovativeness as a Trait of American States," *Journal of Politics*, vol. 40, no. 1, (1978): 212–19, among others.

30. See, for example, John L. Foster, "Regionalism and Innovation in the American States," *Journal of Politics*, vol. 40, no. 1 (1978): 179–87; Savage, "Policy Innovativeness"; and Virginia Gray, "Expenditures and Innovation as Dimensions of 'Progressivism': A Note on the American States," *American Journal of Political Science*, vol. 18, no. 4 (1974): 693–99, among others.

31. Mohr, "Determinants of Innovation in Organizations," p. 114. Regarding the importance of slack resources, see also George W. Downs and Lawrence B. Mohr, "Toward a Theory of Innovation," *Administration and Society*, vol. 10, no. 4 (1979): 379–408; and Everett M. Rogers, *Diffusion of Innovations*, 4th ed. (New York: Free Press, 1995).

32. See the references in notes 34–36.

33. For example, the bivariate correlation between Walker's "innovativeness" index and Grumm's legislative "professionalism" is 0.67. See Scott P. Hays, "Influences on Reinvention during the Diffusion of Innovation," *Political Research Quarterly*, vol. 49, no. 3 (1996): 631–50, quotation on p. 634. See also Walker, "The Diffusion of Innovations," and John G. Grumm, "The Effects of Legislative Structure on Legislative Performance," in *State and Urban Politics*, edited by Richard I. Hofferbert and Ira Sharkansky (New York: Little, Brown, 1971). For a summary of this and other matters concerning state legislatures, see Keith E. Hamm and Gary F. Moncrief, "Legislative Politics in the States," in *Politics in the American States: A Comparative Analysis*, 8th ed., edited by Virginia Gray and Russell Hanson (Washington, D.C.: CQ Press, 2004), pp. 157–93.

34. I calculated the correlation between Squire's "legislative professionalization" ranking of state legislatures and an administrative ranking I created based on state administrative implementation of 'reinvention' as well as average monthly earnings of government employees. The Pearson's correlation coefficient was 0.60. Data on the Squire's ranking came from Hamm and Moncrief, "Legislative Politics in the States," p. 158; data on "reinvention" are provided by Jeffrey Brudney, F. Ted Hebert, and Deil S. Wright, "Reinventing Government in the American States: Measuring and Explaining Administrative Reform," *Public Administration Review*, vol. 59 (1999): 19–30, cited in Richard C. Elling, "Administering State Programs: Performance and Politics," in Gray and Hanson, *Politics in the American States*, pp. 261–289, quotation on p. 270; data on average earnings are found in Elling, "Administering State Programs," p. 273.

35. For a discussion of gubernatorial powers, see Thad Beyle, "The Governors," in Gray and Hanson, *Politics in the American States*, pp. 194–231.

36. Hamm and Moncrief, "Legislative Politics in the States," p. 159.

37. Elling, "Administering State Programs," pp. 271–79.

38. Virginia Gray, David Lowery, Erik K. Godwin, and James Monogan, "Policymaking under Conditions of High and Low Salience: The Adoption and Design of State Pharmaceutical Assistance Programs," paper presented at the State Politics and Policy Annual Research Conference, East Lansing, Michigan, May 7–9, 2005.

39. Kenneth Meier, *The Politics of Sin: Drugs, Alcohol, and Public Policy* (Armonk, N.Y.: M.E. Sharpe, 1994); James P. Lester and colleagues, "Hazardous Wastes, Politics and Public Policy: A Comparative State Analysis," *Western Political Quarterly*, vol. 36 (1983): 257–81.

40. See Families Against Mandatory Minimums (available at www.famm.org/index2.htm) and Human Rights Campaign, "Marriage/Relationship Laws: State by State" (www.hrc.org [August 2, 2006]).

41. For instance, several studies have found that the states with more liberal ideologies, whether measured in terms of public opinion or congressional voting scores, were more likely to favor more generous public assistance policies for health care. See Charles J. Barrilleaux and Mark E. Miller, "The Political Economy of State Medicaid Policy," *American Political Science Review*, vol. 82 (1988): 1089–1107; Colleen Grogan, "Political-Economic Factors Influencing State Medicaid Policy," *Political Research Quarterly*, vol. 74 (1994): 589–622; Charles J. Barrilleaux, Paul Brace, and Bruce Dangremond, "The Sources of State Health Reform," paper presented at the Annual Meeting of the American Political Science Association, August 29–September 1, 1994, New York; Virginia Gray, David Lowery, and Erik Godwin, "Democratic and Non-Democratic Influences in Health Policy: State Pharmacy Assistance Programs as Innovations," paper presented at the Annual Meeting of the American Political Science Association, September 2–5, 2004, Chicago.

42. These political culture categories were proposed by Daniel J. Elazar, *American Federalism: A View from the States*, 2d ed. (New York: Crowell, 1972). Johnson found that Elazar's categories were related to the index of legislative innovations proposed by Gray, but not the index created by Walker. Charles A. Johnson, "Political Culture in the American States: Elazar's Formulation Examined," *American Journal of Political Science*, vol. 20 (1976): 491–509.

43. Robert J. Spitzer, *The Politics of Gun Control*, 3d ed. (Chatham, N.J.: Chatham House, 2003); Frances S. Berry and William D. Berry, "State Lottery Adoptions as Policy Innovations: An Event History Analysis," *American Political Science Review*, vol. 84, no. 2 (1990): 395–415.

44. For example, see Walker, "The Diffusion of Innovations"; Gray, "Innovation in the American States"; Daniel Elezar, *American Federalism* (New York: Thomas Crowell, 1972); Bradley C. Canon and Lawrence Baum, "Patterns of Adoption of Tort Law Innovations: An Application of Diffusion Theory to Judicial Doctrines," *American Political Science Review*, vol. 75, no. 4 (1981): 975–87; Berry and Berry," State Lottery Adoptions as Policy Innovations"; Donald C. Menzel and Irwin Feller, "Leadership and Interaction Patterns in the Diffusion of Innovations Among the American States," *Western Political Quarterly*, vol. 30 (1977): 528–36; Fred W. Grupp Jr. and Alan R. Richards, "Variations in Elite Perceptions of American States as Referents for Public Policy Making," *American*

Political Science Review, vol. 69 (1975): 850–58; Alfred R. Light, "Intergovernmental Sources of Innovation in State Administration," *American Politics Quarterly*, vol. 6 (1978): 147–65; John L. Foster, "Regionalism and Innovation in the American States," *Journal of Politics*, vol. 40 (1978): 179–87; and Robert L. Savage, "When a Policy's Time Has Come: Case Diffusion, 1983–1984," *Publius*, vol. 15 (1985): 111–24, among others.

45. The diffusion literature commonly finds, in quantitative models, that states are influenced by their neighbors but typically does not specify precisely how the influence is manifested.

46. Michael Mintrom, "Policy Entrepreneurs and the Diffusion of Innovation," *American Journal of Political Science*, vol. 41, no. 3 (1997): 738-770, quotation on p. 739.

47. A political reason might also be offered. State politicians might view that they are most like their neighbors and least like the geographically distant, and so they may be more willing to emulate their immediate neighbors. The public may also be more aware of, and responsive to, the policy options offered by the nearest states.

48. Henry Glick and Scott P. Hays, "Innovation and Reinvention in State Policymaking: Theory and the Evolution of Living Will Laws," *Journal of Politics*, vol. 53 (1991): 835–50; Christopher Z. Mooney and Mei-Hsien Lee, "Legislating Morality in the American States: The Case of Pre-Roe Abortion Regulation Reform," *American Journal of Political Science*, vol. 39 (1995): 599–627; but see also Jill Clark, "Policy Diffusion and Program Scope: Research Directions," *Publius*, vol. 15 (1985): 61–70.

49. Everett Rogers, "Re-Invention During the Innovation Process," in *The Diffusion of Innovations: An Assessment*, edited by M. Radnor, I. Feller, and Everett Rogers (Boston: Northeastern University, Center for the Interdisciplinary Study of Science and Technology, 1978); Mooney and Lee, "Legislating Morality."

50. Hays, "Influences on Regulation," pp. 634, 640.

51. Berry and Berry, "State Lottery Adoptions as Policy Innovations," p. 400.

52. Craig Volden, "States as Policy Laboratories: Experimenting with the Children's Health Insurance Program," *American Journal of Political Science*, vol. 50, no. 2 (2006), pp. 294-312.

53. For some examples, see Mark Carl Rom, "Are States Effective Laboratories of Democracy?" paper presented at the annual conference of the American Political Science Association, Washington D.C., September 1–4, 2005.

54. I differentiate election procedures from electoral ones, which include such matters as the structure of primaries, requirements for appearing on the ballot, registration procedures, and so forth.

55. People can and do argue about who should vote, or whether higher turnout is better than lower turnout, but no one argues that those who do vote should have their preferences recorded inaccurately.

56. Greg Palast, "Another Florida," *Harper's,* (November 2004), p. 75.

57. Ibid., p. 75.

58. Ibid., p. 76.

59. Ibid., p. 76. Permanently prohibiting felons from voting, after they have served their sentences, is itself (arguably) bad policy, as it disenfranchises those who have "paid their debt to society."

60. Ronnie Dugger, "No Appeal," *Harper's,* (November 2004), pp. 77–78. For a review of electronic voting machines and other ballot construction issues, see Paul Herrnson and

others, "Early Appraisals of Electronic Voting," unpublished draft paper obtained from the author, and other publications available at the Center for American Politics (www.capc.umd.edu/rpts/VotingTech_par.html [August 2, 2006]). See also Eric A. Fischer, *Election Reform and Electronic Voting Systems: Analysis of Security Issues* (Washington, D.C.: Congressional Research Service, 2003), available at http://fpc.state.gov/documents/organization/31280.pdf (August 2, 2006).

61. Electiononline.org, "Election Reform 2004: What's Changed, What Hasn't, and Why," p. 2 (www.electionline.org/site/docs/pdf/ERIP_AR2004.pdf [August 3, 2006]).

62. Kevin J. Coleman and Erik A. Fischer, *Elections Reform: Overview and Issues* (Washington, D.C.: Congressional Research Service, 2004), p. 2 (http://fpc.state.gov/documents/organization/36746.pdf).

63. Electiononline.org, "Election Reform."

64. National Conference of State Legislatures, "Overview of Election Reform Activity in the States, 2001," appendix E. When this report was written, thirty-two states with 1,100 pending bills were still in legislative session.

65. National Conference of State Legislatures, "Overview of Election Reform Activity in the States, 2001."

66. Roberta Romano, "The States as a Laboratory: Legal Innovation and State Competition for Corporate Charters," present volume.

67. For a discussion of education policy, see Rom, "Are States Effective Laboratories of Democracy?"

68. Martha Derthick, *The Influence of Federal Grants* (Harvard University Press, 1970).

69. See, for example, Keith Boeckelman, "The Influence of States on Federal Policy Adoptions," *Policy Studies Journal*, vol. 20 (1992): 365–75.

70. Shelly Arsenault, "Welfare Policy Innovation and Diffusion: Section 1115 Waivers and the Federal System," *State and Local Government Review*, vol. 32, no. 1 (Winter 2000): 49-60, p. 51.

71. Arsenault, "Welfare Policy Innovation and Diffusion," p. 55. OBRA reflected, in part, a growing national consensus around the twin goals of reducing welfare caseloads and costs. Sheldon Danziger, "Welfare Reform Policy from Nixon to Clinton: What Role for Social Science?" in *Social Science and Policy-Making*, edited by David L. Featherman and Maris A. Vinovskis (University of Michigan Press, 2001), pp. 137–64, p. 143. President Reagan supported the welfare-to-work experiments in part because he had, when a state governor, implemented such an experiment in California. David Greenberg, Donna Linksz, and Marvin Mandell, *Social Experimentation and Public Policymaking* (Washington, D.C.: Urban Institute Press, 2003), p. 217.

72. The most important of the welfare-to-work experiments are summarized, and other information on the elements that made the evaluations helpful is provided, in Greenberg and colleagues, *Social Experimentation*, chap. 8, quotation on p. 214. See also Judith M. Gueron and Edward Pauly, *From Welfare to Work* (New York: Russell Sage Foundation, 1991).

73. Political actors at times opposed random assignment because they are reluctant to withhold a service from people who might benefit from it. Greenberg and colleagues, *Social Experimentation*, pp. 222, 225.

74. For summaries, see Winston Lin, Stephen Freedman, and Daniel Friedlander, *GAIN: 4.5-Year Impacts on Employment, Earnings, and AFDC Receipt* (New York: Manpower Demonstration Research Corporation, 1995); and Daniel Friedlander and Gary

Burtless, *Five Years After: The Long-Term Effects of Welfare-to-Work Programs* (New York: Russell Sage Foundation, 1995).

75. Greenberg and colleagues, *Social Experimentation*, pp. 233–34.

76. Ibid., 235–37.

77. Ibid., p. 237.

78. Ibid., p. 238.

79. Ibid., p. 22.

80. See, for example, Peter Szanton, "The Remarkable Quango: Knowledge, Politics and Welfare Reform," *Journal of Public Policy Analysis and Management*, vol. 10, no. 4 (1991): 590–602; and Erica Baum, "When the Witch Doctors Agree," *Journal of Public Policy Analysis and Management*, vol. 10, no. 4 (1991): 603–15; Greenberg and colleagues, *Social Experimentation*, pp. 240–44.

81. Greenberg and colleagues, *Social Experimentation*, p. 211.

82. Ibid., pp. 218–19.

83. Haskins reports that MDRC testified four times in 1987 and five times in 1988, and gave a total of twelve briefings during those two years. Ron Haskins, "Congress Writes a Law: Research and Welfare Reform," *Journal of Public Policy Analysis and Management*, vol. 10, no. 4 (1991): 616–32.

84. Greenberg and colleagues, *Social Experimentation*, p. 238.

85. By this time, random assignment has also come to be seen as the best way to learn whether the experiments were "cost neutral" to the federal government, as the waivers were required to be.

86. Numerous books have focused on President Clinton's welfare reform efforts. See, for example, R. Kent Weaver, *Ending Welfare as We Know It* (Brookings, 2000).

13

The States as a Laboratory: Legal Innovation and State Competition for Corporate Charters

ROBERTA ROMANO

Corporate law, the legal rules governing relations between managers and shareholders of for-profit corporations, is an arena in which the metaphor of the "states as a laboratory" describes actual practice, and, for the most part, this is a laboratory that has worked reasonably well. The goal of this chapter is to map out over time the diffusion of corporate law reforms across the states. The lawmaking pattern we observe indicates a dynamic process in which legal innovations originate from several sources, creating a period of legal experimentation that tends to identify a principal statutory formulation that is adopted by a majority of states. It is difficult to imagine that such dynamism could be generated by the centralized lawmaking process that exists at the national level.

The development of corporate law has been left to the states with sporadic federal intervention: the New Deal laws regulating the issuance of securities through a mandatory disclosure regime applying to publicly traded corporations (the Securities Act of 1933 and the Securities Exchange Act of 1934),

I would like to thank for helpful comments William Carney, Robert Daines, Marcel Kahan, Ehud Kamar, Jonathan Macey, and participants in the Columbia Law School Contemporary Corporate Law Scholarship Reading Group and the New York University Law School Law and Economics Workshop.

and substantive regulation of the terms of cash takeover bids (the 1968 Williams Act amendments to the 1934 Act), and, most recently, of audit committees and executive loans (in the Sarbanes-Oxley Act of 2002). Federalism has succeeded in this domain because the states have sorted out among themselves who has exclusive jurisdiction over corporate law to minimize conflict, by adopting an "internal affairs" jurisdictional rule in which the governing choice of law rule is the corporation's statutory domicile. This contrasts with other potential conflict rules: physical domicile (the rule in most of continental Europe), or the domicile of the buyer or seller of its securities (the U.S. states' securities law rule, the site of the securities transaction), which would subject firms operating across state lines to multiple legal regimes in the absence of federal regulation.

Accordingly, U.S. corporations can select the legal regime for shareholder-manager relations from among the fifty states and the District of Columbia, by their choice of incorporation state, without having to establish any physical connection to the choice, and without being exposed to extraterritorial restraints on organizational choices. A firm's statutory domicile is established by a simple paper filing in the office of the chosen domicile's secretary of state and by maintaining a surrogate presence through a designated agent for the service of process (typically the lawyer or firm handling the incorporation documents).

The states' agreement on the internal affairs jurisdictional rule has had important consequences for the development of corporate law. The ease of selecting a domicile whose exclusive jurisdiction is legally recognized has resulted in considerable experimentation and innovation in corporate law, as states have sought to retain locally domiciled firms by offering up-to-date codes to meet changing business conditions. The output of this competition has been, for the most part, welfare enhancing,[1] a contention perhaps best illustrated by the fact that consumers of corporate law (investors and managers and their lobbying organizations) have not perceived a need to advocate replacing the states' authority with either the federal government or purely private contracts and self-regulating organizations, despite some academic support for both of those alternatives.

Key Features of U.S. Corporate Law

Three key features that form the backbone of U.S. corporate law provide the context for evaluating the pattern of corporation law innovation that is the subject of this chapter. First, U.S. corporate law is premised on shareholders being the parties in whose interest firms are to be managed. Second, state corporate law is, for the most part, enabling (in contrast to the federal securities laws, which are mandatory in application). Corporation codes consist of default rules that supply standard contract terms for corporate governance where the parties fail to specify alternative arrangements. These defaults can be customized to meet specific organizational requirements (such as increasing the votes required above the statutory default to a supermajority, for a firm with a blockholder who wants to retain veto control). Third and perhaps most important, one state has dominated the market for incorporations of public firms for almost a century. About half of the largest corporations are incorporated in Delaware, the majority of firms going public for the first time are incorporated in Delaware, and the overwhelming majority of firms that change their domicile midstream reincorporate in Delaware.[2]

It is not fortuitous that the dominant incorporation state is a small state by nearly all measures. Because a corporate charter is a relational contract—it binds the state and firm in a multiperiod relationship, in which performance under the contract is not simultaneous—a state needs a mechanism to commit to firms that it will maintain its code and otherwise not undo existing rules to firms' disadvantage, if it is to obtain more than a minimal incorporation fee from firms. As a small state, a substantial portion of Delaware's tax revenue—an average of 17 percent during the past several decades—is derived from incorporation fees.[3] Moreover, as a small state with limited indigenous revenue sources, there is no ready substitute to which Delaware can turn to maintain the level of services it provides its citizens in the absence of a vigorous incorporation business. This financial dependency on incorporation fees has made Delaware highly responsive to the requirements of corporations for an updated legal regime, and, as a consequence, it has enabled Delaware to commit to firms that it will stay the course and maintain an up-to-date code.[4]

In addition to a reputation for responsiveness created by dependence on franchise fee revenues, Delaware has made a substantial investment in assets that have no alternative use at any comparable value beside the corporate chartering business, assets that can be characterized as relation-specific legal capital (that is, legal capital specific to the corporate chartering relation). These assets are a comprehensive body of corporate case law and judicial expertise in administering corporate law assisted by administrative expertise in expedited processing of corporate filings. Because the value of its investment in those assets would be diminished if it were to lose out to another state in the chartering market, Delaware's legal capital functions as an additional credible commitment device.

The Laboratory of State Competition for Charters

Despite Delaware's overwhelming dominance in the chartering market, there is evidence that states respond to changes in the business environment in competition with Delaware, in enacting legal reforms, to maintain their level of local incorporations, which is why this is an area where the metaphor of "the states as a laboratory" is apt. Three principal indicia of state competition have been noted in the literature. First, corporate law innovations diffuse across states in an S-shaped curve (the proportion of adopters increases with time), similar to technological innovations, a pattern that is interpreted in the economic literature as a sign of competition.[5] Second, state franchise revenues are significantly positively related to the responsiveness of a state's corporate legal system to firm demands.[6] Finally, firms migrate from states with low levels of responsiveness (using the same measure or a similar measure of quickness to adopt an innovation) to those with higher levels.[7]

This chapter focuses on the first facet of competition, the diffusion of legal innovation, because it is this dimension of charter competition that best exemplifies the theme of "taking the metaphor [of federalism as a laboratory of democracy] seriously." The diffusion pattern suggests that states can be characterized as if they were searching for the most suitable corporation laws in a changing business environment, so as to induce firms to incorporate locally (the modus operandi for the states' activity, most typically, is corporate lawyers, acting in their self-interest, and not government officials).[8] That is, in light of Delaware's leading position, other states are engaged in what can be best described as a form of "defensive" competition, in which the local bar advocates law reform so as to be able to offer a local domicile choice to its clients.

The Diffusion of Corporate Law Reforms

In the diffusion process of corporation laws, at the outset there is often variation (different states enact different statutes to solve a particular perceived problem), but eventually one of the variations comes to dominate as the preferred solution (it is enacted by the vast majority of states). To illustrate how the corporate law innovation process has operated, two important initiatives will be examined: the "modernization" of corporation codes associated with the 1967 revision of Delaware's corporation code and the adoption of statutes limiting directors' liability in the late 1980s, which began with three distinct approaches to resolving a perceived crisis in the directors' and officers' (D&O) liability insurance market but concluded in an extraordinarily

Table 13-1. *Diffusion of Selected Corporate Law Statutes*

Statute	No. of states	Year first state adopted	Interval (years)
Indemnification	42	1961	20
Merger vote exemption	22	1963	18
Appraisal exemption	26	1967	14
Action by majority without meeting[a]	11	1949	26
Cumulative voting	30	1892	89
Staggered board	45	1887	94
Limited liability charter amendment	46	1986	16

Source: Compiled by author.

a. This count is as of 1975, compared to 1981 for the other initiatives related to the modernization of corporation codes in the late 1960s.

short time frame with virtually all states enacting the approach selected by Delaware.[9]

THE DRIVE FOR GREATER ORGANIZATIONAL FLEXIBILITY AND DELAWARE'S 1967 CODE REVISION. In 1967 Delaware undertook a major revision of its corporation code, which ushered in an era in which many firms reincorporated there from states that tended to lag behind in code-updating.[10] A major feature of the revision was to enhance organizational flexibility, continuing the trend of the earliest statutory innovations in the late nineteenth century, that relaxed strictures on capital structure and corporate combinations and had placed New Jersey at center stage in the corporate charter market.[11] In an earlier publication I traced the adoption of several of the important innovations that appeared in Delaware's 1967 revision across the fifty states. These tended to be provisions that increased organizational flexibility and, in particular, provisions reducing the cost of acquisitions.

Table 13-1 provides information on the diffusion across the states of six statutory innovations associated with modern statutes and the 1967 Delaware revision.[12] The interval over which the spread of the provisions throughout the states was tracked—from the initial state's adoption of the provision through fourteen years after the Delaware code revision—ranges from ninety-six to fourteen years. Table 13-2 indicates where Delaware stood in the innovation process for each provision, and figure 13-1 tracks the diffusion progress of the six statutes from the initial adoption through fourteen years after the Delaware code revision. Two facts are worth noting with regard to these data. First, Delaware is not always the pioneering innovator, but of the more recent innovations, when not first it has been second or third

Table 13-2. *Delaware's Position in the Diffusion Process*

Statute	Year adopted by Delaware	Delaware's rank	Pioneering state
Indemnification	1967	3	New York
Merger vote exemption	1967	2	Ohio[a]
Appraisal exemption	1967	1	Delaware
Action by majority without meeting	1967	2	Nevada
Cumulative voting	1917	9	New York
Staggered board	1898	4	Pennsylvania
Limited liability charter amendment	1986	1	Delaware

Source: Compiled by author.

a. First merger vote exemption statute had higher threshold (1/6) than Delaware, whose threshold was adopted by most other states.

in adopting the initiative. Second, the innovations spread across the states gradually over time, as a few states followed the pioneers early on, but most states responded years later. The path of the diffusion of the statutes follows an S-shaped (ogive) cumulative distribution, similar to other studies of legal innovation.[13]

Delaware's position, which is close to, but not always at, the top of the list as an innovator, in conjunction with the gradual diffusion of provisions, suggests a pattern of experimentation regarding corporate initiatives. More specifically, Delaware would appear to behave, on occasion, as if it waited until another state acted, to calibrate more precisely what the preferred response to changing business conditions ought to be, and that other states followed suit in a more languid fashion, responding after the innovators' legislation proves sufficiently successful to be actively sought by firms.[14]

Of course, the fact that there has been innovation by the states in corporate law does not of itself demonstrate that a national regime would not innovate at a similar rate. William Carney offers some suggestive, relevant data on the issue: he compared the substantive content of the eight European Union (EU) company law directives to U.S. state corporation codes.[15] The EU-level directives are functionally equivalent to a national regime. Carney finds that of 131 provisions, the vast majority (ninety-five) do not appear in any U.S. state code.[16] Most of those provisions are either mandatory terms that have long been abandoned by U.S. states as they adjusted their codes to enhance organizational flexibility at the turn of the nineteenth century or creditor protections that are long gone from, or were never contained in, U.S. codes. Although it is altogether possible that a U.S. centralized regime

Figure 13-1. *Diffusion Process: Six Statutes Associated with the 1967 Modernization of Delaware's Corporation Code*[a]

Number of states (cumulative)

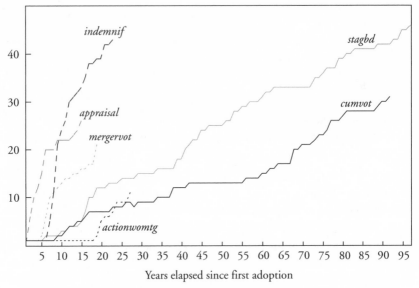

Years elapsed since first adoption

Source: Compiled by author.
a. Last year tracked is 1981 for all statutes, but actionwomtg, which is tracked through 1975.
Indemnif = indemnification clarification and expansion (42 states, first adoption 1961)
Mergervot = merger vote exemption (22 states, first adoption 1963)
Appraisal = appraisal rights exemption (26 states, first adoption 1967)
Actionwomtg = action by majority without a meeting (11 states, first adoption 1949)
Cumvot = cumulative voting not required (30 states, first adoption 1892)
Stagbd = staggered board permitted (45 states, first adoption 1887)

would not replicate the tendency of the EU directives that is at odds with the focus of legal rules adopted in the laboratory of the states, it is, in my judgment, more probable that it would tend in that direction. Lending credence to this conjecture is the fact that the U.S. federal securities laws are closer to the approach of the EU than the states to corporate law: they are mandatory rules that apply to all firms without permitting customization. Most important, where the Securities and Exchange Commission has sought to regulate matters of corporate governance, it has followed a mandatory rather than enabling approach.

THE D&O INSURANCE CRISIS AND LIMITATIONS ON DIRECTORS' LIABILITY. A more telling example of the extent of state-level experimentation and diffusion of innovation in reaction to changing business conditions, which fleshes out the pattern in the 1967 statutory revision data, is the states' response to turbulence in the D&O insurance market in the mid-1980s. By 1984, the market for D&O liability insurance had changed dramatically from the beginning of the decade: firms seeking to renew polices (or enter the market) found premiums skyrocketing at the same time as coverage was shrinking and deductibles increasing. The tight insurance market continued into 1986. Many factors contributed to the market's turbulence, including the expansion of directors' liability.[17] The most important case in this regard was a 1985 Delaware decision, *Smith* v. *Van Gorkom,* that held outside directors had violated their duty of care when agreeing to a merger at a substantial premium without sufficiently informing themselves of the firm's value.[18]

The disruption in insurance markets raised concern that firms would have difficulty retaining quality outside (nonemployee) directors, who many investors, particularly activist institutions, consider a key governance device in constraining managers to act in the shareholders' interest. This concern was magnified by the *Van Gorkom* decision. As a consequence, states sought to mitigate the perceived insurance crisis by limiting outside directors' liability for negligence; the idea was that lowering liability would relieve firms' potential problems in director recruitment created by inadequate or expensive D&O insurance.

By 1987, thirty-five states had modified their corporation codes to reduce directors' exposure to shareholder litigation and the D&O insurance market was beginning to stabilize. The story of how this came about is an excellent case study of the successful operation of federalism as a laboratory for legal reform: early experimentation was followed by most states settling on one solution (the one chosen by Delaware). In the first two years of legislative responses, three different approaches were implemented: reducing the standard of culpability, permitting charter amendments to limit or eliminate liability, and establishing statutory damage caps.[19] But in a rapid diffusion process, the bulk of the states selected the limited liability charter amendment approach as the solution to their common problem.

The first state to respond to the insurance crisis was Indiana, which lowered the standard of care for directors from negligence to willful misconduct or recklessness in April 1986.[20] By changing the statutory standard for a fiduciary breach, Indiana's solution to the insurance crisis applied automatically to all firms incorporated in the state. The Indiana solution is therefore self-executing. In contrast, Delaware left the decision up to individual firms' shareholders, authorizing the inclusion in corporate charters of provisions limiting or eliminating directors' personal liability for negligence.[21] The Delaware approach has not differed much in practical effect from Indiana's, as the vast majority of firms have sought and obtained shareholder approval for a charter provision eliminating directors' liability for negligence.[22]

At the same time that the Indiana and Delaware legislatures were crafting their responses, the American Law Institute (ALI) was promoting a different alternative, a statutory limit on directors' liability that would be commensurate with their compensation.[23] One state, Virginia, adopted the ALI approach a year after Indiana and Delaware acted and capped damages at the greater of $100,000 or the compensation the individual received from the corporation the year before the alleged misconduct.[24] This third approach to the insurance crisis is procedurally self-executing paralleling the Indiana approach but substantively a limited version of Delaware's approach to the problem—namely, a charter provision limiting directors' liability can be cast as a limitation on damages.

Although at the time of enactment some commentators speculated that the Indiana statute would become the template for other states,[25] the Delaware statute turned out to be the model. Within five years, Delaware's charter amendment solution to the perceived D&O insurance market crisis had been adopted by thirty-nine states, whereas the number following one of the other two approaches had risen only to six (and one of those states had also enacted the Delaware statute).[26] Moreover, Virginia amended its statute to include a charter amendment provision, in addition to the statutory damages default provision. The inclusion in 1990 of the Delaware approach in the Model Business Corporation Act no doubt solidified the trend.[27] Today, forty-six of fifty states have a limited liability charter provision (the other four have a relaxed culpability standard). The diffusion of initiatives to limit liability is summarized in tables 13-1 and 13-2 and graphed in figure 13-2.

The diffusion process of the limited liability statute, as evident in figure 13-2, was far more rapid (thus the S-shape is far steeper) than the earlier innovations plotted in figure 13-1. Using the same cut-off as applied to the diffusion of the 1967 Delaware reforms, forty-nine states had enacted one of the statutory forms of limitations on director liability within fourteen years of the first statutory formulation (the remaining state acted two years thereafter). Firms' demand for the limitation of directors' liability was, without question, the impetus for the rapid diffusion: commentaries by practitioners in several states refer to concern that firms would reincorporate if the state did not adopt a limited liability statute similar to the Delaware provision.[28] In addition, the perceived insurance crisis provided a reason for states to respond quickly to that concern, with the easiest response the selection of the leading incorporation state's tried solution. Given that the Delaware statute

Figure 13-2. *Diffusion Process: Statutes Limiting Liability*[a]

Number of states (cumulative)

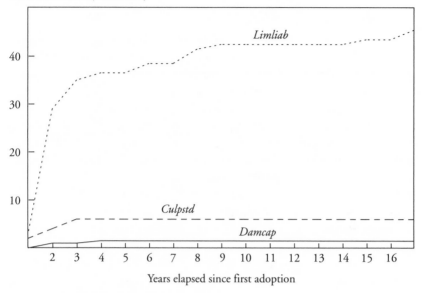

Years elapsed since first adoption

Source: Compiled by author.

a. Connecticut statute permitting damages cap charter amendment allocated across two statutory types, as indicated in note 26.

Limliab = Limited liability charter amendment (45.5 states, first adoption 1986)
Culpstd = Relaxation of culpability standard (6 states, first adoption 1986)
Damcap = Damages cap (1.5 states, first adoption 1987)

offers the greatest flexibility of response, subject to shareholder approval, it is not altogether surprising that it came to dominate state choices. The Delaware approach, in contrast to that of Indiana, leaves the decision on liability to individual firms and investors, not legislators. This characteristic makes it appealing to investors, since their consent is required. Evidence that investors find the solution attractive is that charter amendments limiting liability are uniformly approved by shareholders with the support of institutional investors, though those same investors often vigorously oppose other management initiatives, such as the adoption of takeover defenses.[29] The success of the Delaware approach would not have been predicted by proponents of the view that state competition is a "race to the bottom," that is, that federalism functions to produce laws that entrench managers and exploit shareholders. From that perspective, the self-executing Indiana approach ought to have predominated in the laboratory of state lawmaking because, in contrast to the Delaware statute, it offers directors absolution from liability for negligence immediately upon legislative action, without the need for firms to obtain their shareholders' consent.

Thereafter, several states further refined the Delaware provision, for example, by eliminating some exceptions and expanding coverage to officers.[30] This active shaping of liability limits, producing variety amid a rapid diffusion of an innovative solution to a common problem across the states, is an exemplar of the advantages of federalism. States engaged in efforts to identify, and then hone, an appropriate response to the insurance crisis and in a relatively short time came up with a response offering organizational flexibility and individualization. It is difficult to imagine as rapid a response to a problem in a centralized regime. To provide a straightforward comparison, the Delaware legislature's action, which reversed *Smith* v. *Van Gorkom,* occurred within a year and a half of the decision. Of Delaware code amendments whose legislative history indicated that they were enacted in response to Delaware court decisions, the median interval between legislative response and decision was two years, similar to the reaction to the *Van Gorkom* decision, whereas the average was eight years.[31] By contrast, the average interval for reversals of U.S. Supreme Court decisions involving statutory interpretation in the comprehensive study by William Eskridge of the 1967–90 Congresses was twelve years, with 68 percent of the reversals occurring more than two years after the decision.[32]

Role of the Model Business Corporation Act

An important contributing factor to the diffusion process of corporate law is the activity of the bar in devising, and revising, a model statute, the Model Business Corporation Act, which states can follow in place of, or in addition to, looking to Delaware. The Model Act is a product of the Committee on Corporate Laws of the American Bar Association's (ABA) Corporate and Business Law Section, whose members are, in general, attorneys in large firms whose clients are public corporations. The first Model Act, which was derived from the Illinois statute, was produced in 1950, and there have been several major revisions, most prominently in 1969 and 1984, though incremental changes have been made after each revision.[33] States may follow the Model Act closely, but a state may also modify provisions in the Model Act or adopt only parts of it, and, indeed, some state codes are an amalgam of provisions in the Model Act, the Delaware statute, and other states' codes as well.[34] This affects the diffusion process, for, as would be expected, states differ in the speed with which they respond to changes in the Model Act, which is affected by whether they adopt amendments to the Model Act piecemeal or through complete recodifications, in addition to the fact, as mentioned, that there is some variance across states regarding which provisions of the Model Act are adopted.[35] The drafters currently count thirty-two states as having corporation statutes based on either the 1969 or 1984 Model Act revisions.[36]

The Model Act is a source of statutory innovation, but the degree of originality varies considerably: sometimes the Model Act drafters copy Delaware's innovations (or those of other states) and sometimes in doing so they modify the innovation in response to problems identified ex-post in implementation, while at other times they are indeed the innovator.[37] The statewide pattern of adoption of the four provisions previously identified with the 1967 modernization of the Delaware code (which were not in the Model Act at the time) suggests, however, that even though the Model Act was not the first to adopt the initiatives, it was influential in their diffusion. This is not the case with regard to the states' rapid legislative response to the D&O liability insurance crisis of the 1980s.

THE MODEL ACT AND THE 1967 DELAWARE CODE MODERNIZATION. Of the tracked provisions related to Delaware's 1967 code modernization, the initiatives limiting appraisal rights and clarifying indemnification rights appeared for the first time in the 1969 Model Act revision.[38] By contrast, a merger vote exemption was first included in 1984, and nonunanimous shareholder action without a meeting is still not provided for in the Model Act. The indemnification initiative was, in fact, a joint product of the ABA Corporate Laws Committee and the Delaware Corporate Law Revision Committee, which was created in 1963 by the state legislature to undertake a comprehensive review of the state's corporation code and drafted the 1967 revised code. As a consequence, the language of the Delaware and Model Act revised indemnification provisions was identical.[39] Most of the state adoptions of the two provisions related to Delaware's 1967 code modernization that were included in the 1969 Model Act revision (appraisal rights exemption and indemnification clarification) occurred after 1969 and not after Delaware's action in 1967.[40]

Although not all states mentioned the Model Act as the source of indemnification provisions that tracked the Delaware and Model Act provision in their official statutory comments or annotations, it is plausible to assert that the Model Act's influence on adoption was greater than Delaware's because enactments picked up only after the Model Act revision was published and not immediately following Delaware's legislation. The diffusion pattern of the other three provisions provides further support for the view that the Model Act was influential in the diffusion of the Delaware 1967 reform initiatives. The 1967 initiative absent from the Model Act (nonunanimous shareholder action without a meeting) had few adoptions through the endpoint of the collection of the data in the table (1975). Still, Delaware did influence other states: today the number of states permitting nonunanimous shareholder action without a meeting stands at twenty-four, despite the absence of such a provision in the Model Act.[41]

In addition, there were somewhat fewer states adopting the merger vote exemption than the appraisal exemption in the period before the Model Act was revised to include the merger vote exemption (twenty-two compared to twenty-six states). Currently, however, the totals are thirty-seven and thirty-two states, respectively. That differential provides further evidence of the Model Act's impact on the diffusion process, because the appraisal exemption was removed from the Model Act during this time frame, and the relative rate of its adoption slowed compared to the merger vote exemption provision that was added to the Model Act in the same interval. These data suggest a more subtle role for Delaware's influence on the diffusion process: the Model Act drafters in all probability added the merger vote exemption provision and reintroduced the appraisal exemption provision because they appeared in Delaware's code and had been adopted by a number of states.

THE MODEL ACT AND 1980S INITIATIVES LIMITING DIRECTOR LIABILITY. In contrast with its relation to the 1967 Delaware code initiatives, the Model Act was not a factor in the diffusion of the limited liability reform initiative. A limited liability charter amendment provision was not included in the Model Act until 1990, despite the enactments of the Delaware and Indiana alternatives in 1986 (and a damages cap in Virginia in 1987).[42] The majority of states did not, however, wait for guidance from the Model Act to respond to the issue. Thirty-six states had already adopted the Delaware approach before the Model Act was amended (twenty-one of which were Model Act states), while only nine states did so thereafter.[43] Moreover, all but one of the states enacting one of the other statutory responses to the D&O crisis before the Model Act was revised in 1990 were Model Act states.

The contrasting diffusion pattern of the limited liability statutes could suggest either that the relative importance of the Model Act as a template for state codes has dramatically declined in the 1980s from earlier decades or that the impact of the Model Act on the diffusion process is minimal when business conditions lead local interest groups and elites (managers or the cor-

Figure 13-3. *Diffusion Process: Recent Delaware and Model Act Innovations*

Number of states (cumulative)

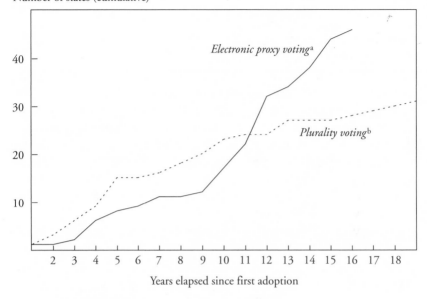

Years elapsed since first adoption

Source: Compiled by author.

a. 46 states, first adoption 1988; includes Texas statute adopted in 2003, although effective date is 2006.

b. 31 states, first adoption 1985.

porate bar) to press vigorously for legislative action.[44] One means of evaluating whether the difference between the diffusion pattern of the 1967 initiatives and the limited liability statutes in the 1980s reflects a new and permanent change in the influence of the Model Act is to examine the diffusion of more recent initiatives that would not have been of intense interest to managers. In an important study of the impact of the Model Act on the diffusion of corporate law reforms, Carney identified a subset of provisions of recent origin related to organizational flexibility, introduced by either Delaware or the Model Act, that meet those requirements.[45] Figure 13-3 updates his data for two of those provisions, a 1990 innovation of Delaware that permitted electronic proxy voting and an innovation in the 1984 revised Model Act that established plurality shareholder voting on matters other than the election of directors. Both of these initiatives are efforts at facilitating institutional flexibility in the shareholder voting process, and the effect of managerial lobbying does not appear to have been a factor in their adoption.[46] In

1996 the Model Act was revised, paralleling the Delaware statute, to permit electronic proxy voting. Delaware has never adopted plurality voting for shareholder action apart from the election of directors and instead retains majority voting (abstentions count as no votes), which was the approach of the 1969 Model Act.

All but four states now have adopted an electronic proxy voting provision, with the bulk of the adoptions coming a few years after the provision's inclusion in the Model Act. Thus, the Model Act's impact here appears to be similar to its relation to the 1967 Delaware initiatives: though not the innovator, it seems to be a catalyst of legislative action (more state codes were modified after the initiative was included in the Model Act). This suggests that the limited liability statutes may be a distinctive statutory setting, and that the Model Act's function as a transmission belt for innovations that enhance organizational flexibility and have no self-evident shareholder-manager conflict has remained relatively intact up to the present.

Of course, this pattern is only suggestive and not conclusive of the Model Act's influence. Because over time there should be an increase in the number of states adopting a provision that is of value to firms, the source of the upswing in the electronic proxy statute adoptions may simply be the passage of time, rather than the Model Act's endorsement.[47] But the facts are not consistent with such an hypothesis: the number of states adopting plurality voting has steadily increased over time, rising to a majority, but it is still far less than the number adopting electronic proxy voting (only thirty-one states, compared to forty-six), whereas the time period over which the diffusion of plurality voting has taken place is over a decade longer. This suggests that more than time (or the Model Act) is necessary to explain a provision's adoption by an increasing number of states: the substantive content in conjunction with the presence of a viable alternative may well matter. In the context of plurality voting, the nonadopting states all follow the same approach to shareholder voting as that followed by Delaware (affirmative majority of votes), which was also the approach of the 1969 Model Act.[48] In my judgment, the differing adoption patterns of these two voting initiatives provide evidence of a "states as laboratory" effect. Although there are some states that adopt Model Act revisions in entirety ("Model Act" states), the many non–Model Act states appear to pick and choose from alternative approaches, and thus the Model Act's interaction with the Delaware statute (sometimes in tune, sometimes out of tune) contributes to experimentation and innovation in corporate law.

Additional support for the laboratory interpretation of the effect of the Model Act can be drawn from further data in Carney's study. Carney examined the diffusion of 142 provisions of the Model Act and found that thirty of them had not been widely adopted (adopted by twenty-five or fewer states). Carney separately examined those provisions to ascertain whether the variation in corporation codes at a given point in time is due to the fact that reforms diffuse across the states slowly, with uniformity being the end product. He concluded that the data were consistent with the view that the limited level of adoption across the states of those thirty provisions was related to their relative newness, because twenty-seven of them were introduced in the 1984 revision of the Model Act or later.[49] Another, not mutually exclusive, explanation for the variation could be related to the content of Delaware's corporation code and the laboratory explanation of Model Act diffusion—namely, to the extent that Delaware's approach is at odds with that of the Model Act, there could be variation across the states not simply due to differential rates of code modernization. Rather, states might not be copying the Model Act to opt for what they consider to be a preferable alternative (that found in Delaware's code, for instance).

To determine the plausibility of the alternative explanation, I checked whether the thirty Model Act provisions that Carney found were not widely adopted were present in Delaware's code. Delaware had, in fact, no analogous provision for twenty-five of the thirty provisions.[50] The absence of most of these provisions from Delaware's code is consistent with the conjecture that their absence from many other states' codes is not solely a matter of timing. Those states could have opted for an alternative approach (Delaware's) to the Model Act.

Although the current count of states with provisions replicating the thirty Model Act provisions is higher by a few more states than the count in Carney's study, most of the provisions are still found in fewer than twenty-six state codes. Three of seven provisions now in the codes of more than twenty-five states also appear in Delaware's code (a circumstance where the laboratory, or competing legal regimes, explanation is inapplicable).[51] One must, however, be cautious when undertaking such a comparison: Delaware may not have a statute identical to a Model Act provision because the subject has already been adjudicated by its courts. In fact, Model Act provisions quite often codify Delaware judicial opinions, because the Model Act is of greatest value as a template for states where there are not a sufficient number of firms for issues to be adjudicated by courts.[52] But there is another datum lending plausibility to the laboratory interpretation that nonwidespread adoption suggests a difference in Delaware's approach: five of the thirty provisions have been eliminated from the Model Act since the Carney study, and none of the eliminated provisions was in Delaware's code. The failure of many states to have copied the Model Act version of, at least, those provisions would not appear to be related to the timing of code updating because many of the states had codes in sync with that of Delaware. The differential numbers of adopters and nonadopters may well have been a contributing factor toward the Model Act's elimination of those provisions.

In sum, the Model Act is a conduit through which innovations in corporate law are introduced and transmitted across the states. Because Model Act initiatives are often reactions to initiatives undertaken by other states (primarily Delaware), the Model Act functions more often as a catalyst of transmission rather than of innovation. A set of states (twenty-five to thirty) use the Model Act as a screen for code updating, as it brings to their local bar and legislature's attention recent statutes devised by more innovative states (or the ABA committee). In this regard, the Model Act would appear to have greater influence on the diffusion of corporate law reforms than Delaware, which would appear primarily to affect the diffusion process by spurring revisions to the Model Act. But the import of the Model Act needs to be placed in a larger context, the structure of the chartering market. Because more publicly traded firms are incorporated in Delaware than in all of the Model Act states put together, Delaware is, without doubt, by far the most important actor, in terms of practical effect, in the making of corporate law.[53]

Conclusion

This chapter has examined the diffusion of corporate law reform initiatives across the states during the past several decades. One observes a typical pattern of initial experimental variation regarding the statutory form thought to be best suited for handling a particular problem, followed by an eventual settling upon one format by a majority of states, ending in relative uniformity across the states. Moreover, the leading domicile state, Delaware, has strong incentives to innovate to maintain its preeminent market position, and it has, in fact, been a consistent innovator (either the pioneer, or one of the earlier adopters, of reform initiatives) in the diffusion process. An additional contributing factor to the diffusion process has been the activity of the national bar association, in producing and publicizing a statutory template, the Model Business Corporation Act, which, in fact, has often incorporated Delaware's solutions to problems.

The dynamic production of corporation laws is an exemplar of how federalism's delegation of a body of law to the states can create an effective laboratory for experimentation and innovation. How transferable this success is to other areas of law, no doubt, depends on whether the states would have incentives to get things right, as they do in the corporate chartering context, where there is a direct financial connection: innovation enhances revenues from charter fees and the income of the local corporate bar—a focused, politically connected, and unopposed interest group in this context—from servicing local clients.[54] This chapter does not have the space to detail how the product of this ongoing innovative process has improved social welfare by maximizing firm value; I refer the reader instead to other work collecting the evidence that supports the proposition.[55]

Notes

1. For a review of the empirical literature indicating that state competition for corporate charters has been, for the most part, shareholder wealth enhancing, see Sanjai Bhagat and Roberta Romano, "Empirical Studies of Corporate Law," in *Handbook of Law and Economics,* edited by A. M. Polinsky and S. Shavell (New York: Elsevier, forthcoming).

2. See, for example, Robert Daines, "The Incorporation Choices of IPO Firms," *New York University Law Rev*iew, vol. 77 (2002): 1559–611, quotation on p. 1571 (IPO firms); Curtis Alva, "Delaware and the Market for Corporate Charters: History and Agency," *Delaware Journal of Corporate Law*, vol.14 (1990): 885–920, quotation on p. 887 (largest firms); Robert Daines, "Does Delaware Law Improve Firm Value?" *Journal of Financial Economics,* vol. 62 (2001): 525–58, quotation on p. 538 (NYSE firms); Roberta Romano "Law as a Product: Some Pieces of the Incorporation Puzzle," *Journal of Law, Economics, and Organization,* vol. 1 (1985): 225–83, quotation on pp. 244, 261 (reincorporating firms and largest firms).

3. Roberta Romano, *The Advantage of Competitive Federalism for Securities Regulation* (Washington, D.C.: AEI Press, 2002), pp. 131–32.

4. This analysis was introduced in Romano, "Law as a Product," and relies on Oliver Williamson's work on transaction-specific assets. For example, Oliver E. Williamson, "Credible Commitments: Using Hostages to Support Exchange," *American Economic Review,* vol. 73 (1983): 519–40.

5. Romano, "Law as a Product," pp. 233–35; William J. Carney," Federalism and Corporate Law: A Non-Delaware View of the Results of Competition," in *International Regulatory Competition and Coordination,* edited by Joseph McCahery and others (Oxford: Clarendon Press, 1996), pp. 153–83.

6. Romano, "Law as a Product," pp. 236–41.

7. Romano, "Law as a Product," pp. 246–47; G. Moodie, "Forty Years of Charter Competition: A Race to Protect Directors from Liability?" Harvard Law School John M. Olin Center for Law, Economics, and Business Fellows' Discussion Paper 1 (2004).

8. Roberta Romano, "Is Regulatory Competition a Problem or Irrelevant for Corporate Governance?" *Oxford Review of Economic Policy,* vol. 21 (2005): 212–31, quotation on pp. 218–21.

9. Another interesting case, not discussed here because of space limitations, is the adoption of statutes making hostile takeovers more difficult during the same time period

(late 1980s), an area in which innovations were rapidly copied but considerable statutory variety still remains. See Roberta Romano, "The States as a Laboratory: Legal Innovation and State Competition for Corporate Charters," Yale Law School Law & Economics Research Paper 310 (2005).

10. See Romano, "Law as a Product."

11. For a description of New Jersey's corporate initiatives in the late nineteenth century, see Christopher Grandy, "New Jersey Corporate Chartermongering, 1875–1929," *Journal of Economic History*, vol. 49 (1989): 677–92, quotation on p. 681.

12. These include three statutory innovations tracked in my prior paper, "Law as a Product," and three additional statutes that I tracked at that time but did not include in the study because the diffusion process for those laws began before the data for that paper's statistical analysis were available: (1) the explicit elaboration of an indemnification standard for directors and officers; (2) the elimination of acquirers' shareholders' vote in mergers involving a specified percentage of the corporation's stock; (3) elimination for publicly traded corporations of appraisal rights (the right to obtain cash, at a price determined by a court, rather than the merger consideration); (4) the right of shareholders to take action without a meeting by a majority vote; (5) the ability to stagger the board of directors into classes for election rather than elect the full board at the annual meeting; and (6) the ability to eliminate cumulative voting (a voting rule for directors that facilitates minority representation on the board by permitting shareholders to cumulate their votes on one candidate rather than spread them evenly across each seat up for election).

13. See, for example, Virginia Gray, "Innovation in the States: A Diffusion Study," *American Political Science Review*, vol. 67 (1973): 1174–85 (education, social welfare, and civil rights); Sharon M. Oster and John M. Quigley, "Regulatory Barriers to the Diffusion of Innovation: Some Evidence from Building Codes," *Bell Journal of Economics*, vol. 8 (1977): 361–77 (building code regulation).

14. The demand for legislative revision is typically communicated by legal counsel. See, for example, Andrew Moore, "State Competition: Panel Response," *Cardozo Law Review*, vol. 8 (1987): 779–82, 780, describing how Delaware legislative reform derives from proposals of the bar; Jonathan R. Macey and Geoffrey P. Miller, "Toward an Interest-Group Theory of Delaware Corporate Law," *Texas Law Review*, vol. 65 (1987): 469–523, emphasizing the importance of the corporate bar in influencing Delaware corporate law; Alva, "Delaware and the Market for Corporate Charters," pp. 898–901, 904–16, detailing the key role of the bar in Delaware's legislative process, and its initiation of legal innovations in the 1980s; and William J. Carney, "The Production of Corporate Law," *Southern California Law Review*, vol. 71 (1998): 715–80, discussing the role of the corporate bar in other states, which he considers less active than the Delaware bar due to reduced incentives and collective action problems.

15. Carney, "Federalism and Corporate Law, " p. 169

16. Carney, "Federalism and Corporate Law." It is possible that the mandatory rules in place in the EU are appropriate for EU firms, which, in contrast to U.S. firms, tend to have more concentrated ownership structures, but that justification has not been advanced as the rationale for the rules that Carney examines (they are not, for example, rules involving the protection of minority shareholders).

17. See Roberta Romano, "What Went Wrong with Directors' and Officers' Liability Insurance?" *Delaware Journal of Corporate Law*, vol. 14 (1989): 1–33.

18. 488 A. 2d 858 (Del. 1985). It should be noted that *Van Gorkom* was decided after the D&O crisis is thought to have begun, so it is best considered a contributing, rather than causal, factor for the market disruption.

19. The classification of experimentation includes only completely new approaches to the problem that entailed limiting liability, as discussed in Romano, "What Went Wrong." It excludes other initiatives that were incremental to existing rules and limits on liability derived from other constituency statutes, which provide boards with discretion to consider non-shareholder interests and are typically limited to decisions regarding control changes. The adoption of other constituency statutes is therefore more appropriately considered in conjunction with the diffusion of state takeover regulation, which is not discussed in this chapter. For classification of all state responses, see James J. Hanks, "Evaluating Recent State Legislation on Director and Officer Liability Limitation and Indemnification," *Business Lawyer*, vol. 43 (1988): 1207–54, quotation on pp. 1209–10.

20. P.L. 149-1986, codified at Ind. Code Ann. section 23-1-35-1(e). The statute became effective April 1, 1986. Leo Herzel and Daniel Harris, "Uninsured Boards Mount Weak Defense," *National Law Journal*, April 21, 1986, p. 19.

21. S. 533, 65 Del. Laws c. 289 (1986), codified at Del. Code Ann. tit. 8, section 102(b)(7). The provision was enacted in June 1986.

22. See, for example, Michael Bradley and Cindy A. Schipani, "The Relevance of the Duty of Care Standard in Corporate Governance," *Iowa Law Review*, vol. 75 (1989): 1–74, p. 62. (From 1982 to 1986, 94 percent of Delaware firms continuously trading on New York or American Stock Exchanges adopted a limited liability charter provisions.)

23. See American Law Institute, *Principles of Corporate Governance: Analysis and Recommendations*, section 7.17 (Tent. Draft No. 7, 1987); and American Law Institute, *Principles of Corporate Governance* (Discussion Draft No. 1, June 3, 1985). The American Law Institute is an organization whose members are practicing lawyers, judges, and legal academics who produce documents for guidance to courts and legislatures. The documents are drafted by academics, with review by the institute's members, and express the drafters' view of the appropriate substantive rules in a field of law.

24. Acts 1987 c. 59, codified at Va. Code Ann. section 13.1-692.1.

25. See, for example, Herzel and Harris, "Uninsured Boards" ("Indiana has just enacted a new corporation statute that may become a model for other states as well").

26. Carney, "Federalism and Corporate Law," p. 181. The Connecticut statute is a hybrid of the Delaware and ALI approach: it permits firms to adopt charter amendments to limit directors' liability for damages to an amount not less than the compensation the individual received from the corporation during the year of the violation. P.A. 89-322, currently codified at Conn. Gen. Stat. Ann. section 33-636(b)(4). Figure 2 therefore counts it as one-half limited liability charter amendment and one-half damages cap.

27. Committee on Corporate Laws, "Changes in the Revised Model Business Corporation Act—Amendment Pertaining to the Liability of Directors," *Business Lawyer*, vol. 45 (1990): 695. The impact of the Model Act on the diffusion process is discussed in part III.B, infra.

28. See, for example, Edgar F. Hansell, Bradford L. Austin, and Gregory B. Wilcox, "Director Liability under Iowa Law: Duties and Protections," *Journal of Corporation Law*, vol. 13 (Winter 1988): 369–429, p. 391 ("The Iowa legislature, in part to avoid corporate flight from Iowa to reincorporate in Delaware and to take advantage of the new limited

liability provisions, adopted legislation that became effective as of July 1, 1987, similar to that of Delaware"); Robert H. Roshe, "Note: New York's Response to the Director and Officer Liability Crisis: A Need to Reexamine the Importance of D&O Insurance," *Brooklyn Law Review*, vol. 54 (1989): 1305–55, p. 1318, n. 81 ("[T]he New York legislature was concerned that legislation was necessary to deter corporations from reincorporating into states which offered laws more favorable to the protectionist needs of directors and officers in light of the corporate liability crisis," citing the New York governor's memorandum in support of proposed legislation in 1987, to adopt Delaware's statute beyond state's prior expansion of indemnification provisions.); Roshe, "Note: New York's Response to the Director and Officer Liability Crisis," p. 1319, n. 81 (quoting California lawyer as stating, in another journal article): "[s]ince July [1987] California corporations have been reincorporating in Delaware at a rapid pace. If the exodus of corporations from California continues, the legislature may consider amending the [California] Corporations Code to follow Delaware's lead"—which it did; *Comment*, S.D. Codified Ann. section 47-2-58.8 (2000): "The [South Dakota] provision contains the same exceptions as Delaware but also authorizes adoption of liability-limiting provisions for the benefit of directors of insurance companies (against policy holders), depository institutions (against depositors), and rural water systems (against members). This is an extraordinary departure from mainstream liability-limiting charter option statutes, and seems like a cynical display of charter-mongering."

29. There is an extensive literature on the subjects of institutional investor activism which indicates that altering directors' limited liability has not been on their agenda. For a literature review see Roberta Romano, "Less is More: Making Institutional Investor Activism a Valuable Mechanism of Corporate Governance," *Yale Journal on Regulation*, vol. 18 (2001): 174–251.

30. See Hanks, "Evaluating Recent State Legislation," pp. 1211–15.

31. Amy Simmerman, an intern at Morris, Nichols, Arsht & Tunnell, compiled the list of amendments. Simmerman, "Amendments to the Delaware General Corporation Law" (internal document, 2005). I would like to thank John F. Johnston of the Morris Nichols Arsht & Tunnell firm for generously undertaking to have such a list compiled for me, in response to communication among John, Bill Allen and myself regarding the relation between a recent code amendment and the Hollinger decision. The list is underinclusive, because not all responses to judicial decisions are identified in the legislative history. The limited liability statute, for example, is not on the list (though I have included it in the calculations in the text and this note). Simmerman's list began with the 1967 code modernization, because it is difficult to document earlier amendments, and identified twenty-eight amendments that were related to specific Delaware cases, including five provisions in the 1967 statute that were responses to decades-old decisions. Of twenty-nine amendments (the twenty-eight identified by Simmerman's research and the limited liability statute), 45 percent were enacted more than two years after the decision; if the five provisions in Delaware's 1967 code modernization are excluded from the calculation, then the respective figures are a third of the statutes were enacted more than two years after the judicial decision, and the average interval between decision and legislation falls to five years (median remains two). It should further be noted that only somewhat more than a third (eleven of twenty-nine) of the statutes appear to have been explicit reversals; the same number (eleven) were characterized as efforts to clarify issues left in confusion or rendered ambiguous, or to resolve questions raised by court decisions. Examining solely

the reversals, the median time to reversal was still two years, but the average reversal took eleven years; this average is closer to the data regarding Congress's reaction to Supreme Court decisions, note 32 infra, but that comparison is misleading as a gauge of responsiveness, which is better measured by the median: only 45 percent of the reversals occurred more than two years after the decision, and the bulk of those were the 1967 statutory changes. If those are excluded, the median time to duration is one year (average of six), and only 25 percent occurred more than two years postdecision.

32. William Eskridge, "Overriding Supreme Court Statutory Interpretation Decisions," *Yale Law Journal*, vol. 101 (1991): 331–455. None of the cases in the study involved the federal securities laws; but consistent with those data, in the Sarbanes-Oxley Act of 2002, Congress overturned a U.S. Supreme Court decision on the statute of limitations for securities violations that had been decided ten years earlier, *Lampf* v. *Gilbertson*, 501 U.S. 350 (1991).

33. See Carney, "Production of Corporate Law," p. 725 The ABA Corporate Law Committee took on the task of drafting a national corporation law in 1940 and upon completing a draft in 1943 turned to drafting a model act for state use, which was published in 1946; the 1950 revision of that draft statute is now considered the first Model Act. Melvin Aron Eisenberg, "The Model Business Corporation Act and the Model Business Corporation Act Annotated," *Business Lawyer*, vol. 29 (1974): 1407–28, quotation on pp. 1407–08.

34. For example, annotations to provisions in the New Jersey statute refer to sources in the Model Act, Delaware and New York state statutes, and annotations to provisions in the Texas statute refer to sources in the statutes of Illinois, Ohio, Oklahoma and New York, among others, as well as the Model Act.

35. For information on when various states have adopted Model Act provisions, and how many states have particular provisions, see Carney, "Production of Corporate Law." The *Model Business Corporation Act Annotated* provides, for each section, a comparison of all state statutes. American Bar Association Section of Business Law, *Model Business Corporation Act Annotated*, 3d ed. (Chicago: Section of Business Law, American Bar Association, 1998, 2000/01/02 & 2005 Supp.), vols. 1–4.

36. *Model Business Corporation Act Annotated*, vol. 1, p. xxvii.

37. For some recent innovations by the Model Act drafters see Carney, "Production of Corporate Law," pp. 747–48. As noted in the text, the limited liability provision in the Model Act was a response to Delaware's innovation.

38. The appraisal rights exemption for publicly traded firms that was included in the 1969 Model Act revision was eliminated in 1978 amendments to the Act, but was reintroduced in 1999. *Model Business Corporation Act Annotated*, vol. 3, pp. 13–29.

39. *Model Business Corporation Act Annotated*, vol. 2, pp. 8–291. It should be noted that the indemnification provision in the original 1950 Model Act was modeled on the provision in Delaware's code at that time, which was selected for its "brevity and simplicity," and was the type found in most state statutes; given its generality, it obviated the need for a specific charter or bylaw provision. American Bar Association Committee on Corporate Law, *Model Business Corporation Act Annotated*, 2d ed. (Chicago: American Bar Foundation, 1971), vol. 1, p. 218.

40. About the same number of states adopted the provisions before 1969 (that is, following Delaware), as did so during 1969 (the Model Act revision was published by the ABA by midyear).

41. *Model Business Corporation Act Annotated*, vol. 2, pp. 7-38–7-39.

42. The Model Act provision refined the language of the statutory exceptions in the Delaware statute and permitted application to inside as well as outside directors. See Committee on Corporate Laws, "Amendment Pertaining to the Liability of Directors." The inclusion of inside directors was not an innovation of the Model Act: several states had already done so, including Louisiana, Maryland and Nevada. See Hanks, "Evaluating Recent State Legislation," p. 1210.

43. Of those nine states, only five are currently identified as Model Act states, but one, Maine, cannot be said to have been affected by the 1990 Model Act revision because it had enacted an Indiana-style culpability statute in 1988 and its adoption of a limited liability charter amendment provision in addition to that statute was in 2002, more than a decade later. In addition, all but one of the states that enacted instead the alternative of a relaxed culpability statute are currently identified as Model Act states, and those states did not repeal their culpability provisions when the Model Act took a different (the Delaware) tack.

44. Carney interprets the more rapid diffusion of takeover and limited liability statutes across the states, compared to the 1967 reform initiatives, as due to their sponsorship by corporate managers (compared to the corporate bar), whom he considers better organized politically because of a greater personal interest in the issues, though he notes that he cannot rule out technological change that improved the spread of information in the 1980s as an alternative explanation. Carney, "Production of Corporate Law," p. 749.

45. Carney, "Production of Corporate Law," pp. 744–48. Carney was interested in testing a hypothesis slightly different from that in this chapter, which his data confirmed: that Model Act initiatives would be more widely adopted than initiatives of a single state.

46. Carney examined two Delaware, one North Carolina, and four Model Act innovations. I use one Delaware and one Model Act initiative of the provisions that Carney examined to facilitate a comparison of relative influence: both of these statutes had similar organizational benefits, improving the efficiency of the voting process by facilitating the accomplishment of a quorum. Carney, "Production of Corporate Law," pp. 745–46; *Model Business Corporation Act Annotated*, vol. 2, pp. 7-157–7-158. It should be noted that Delaware was not actually the pioneer for electronic proxy voting: New Jersey permitted electronic transmissions of proxy votes in 1988. At the time of Carney's study, the Delaware initiative had not been adopted by many states, but he correctly anticipated a future increase because the Model Act had just been amended in 1996 to permit electronic voting, whereas the Model Act initiative had more adoptions, although it was still low for a Model Act provision (fewer than half of the states had adopted plurality voting).

47. I have not tested whether the observed pattern is not random as an indication of the Model Act's influence, because the appropriate benchmark for such a test would be to compare the pattern to a formal model predicting when a state would adopt a provision in the absence of the Model Act.

48. Although the language in three state statutes, "majority of votes cast," could be considered equivalent in effect to plurality voting (if abstentions are not construed to be "cast" votes), this does not appear to be the common interpretation, as the Model Act drafters stated that there was no counterpart in any state code to the Model Act provision when it was introduced. *Model Business Corporation Act Annotated*, vol. 2, p. 7-161.

49. More specifically, he based his conclusion on the fact that when the twenty-seven newer provisions were deleted from his set of provisions, there was a higher degree of

uniformity for the remaining provisions (enacted in 77 percent, rather than 74 percent, of the states). Carney, "Production of Corporate Law," p. 734.

50. The thirty provisions are identified in table 5 of his article. Carney, "Production of Corporate Law," pp. 774–76. I checked both the Delaware statute and the statutory comparison sections in the *Model Business Corporation Act Annotated* for this inquiry. It should be noted that in a few instances, the comparisons in the official annotation to the Model Act stated that there were no analogous provisions in the Delaware code but there were actually similar provisions. For example, two of these instances involved provisions fixing distribution record dates that are part of a larger legal capital scheme in the Model Act that has no counterpart in Delaware's code. Because that larger scheme was the basis for the official statutory comparison, Delaware was reported as lacking the provisions, though it actually has record date provisions with similar effect.

51. I took on face value the counts of adopters that are provided in the official statutory comparisons sections in the *Model Business Corporation Act Annotated* (although a count is not provided for all provisions). The few provisions where the current count for adopters was lower than Carney's count were provisions that had been eliminated from the Model Act since Carney wrote his article but whose presence in state codes was still tracked in the statutory comparisons.

52. See Michael P. Dooley and Michael D. Goldman, "Some Comparisons between the Model Business Corporation Act and the Delaware General Corporation Law," *Business Lawyer*, vol. 56 (2001): 737–66. Although this is clearly true for a few provisions—such as the Model Act provision that officers owe a duty of good faith and care (adopted by thirty states, *Model Business Corporation Act Annotated*, vol. 2, pp. 8-265–8-266)—I did not research whether this is true for others (such as the provision mandating notice to exercise cumulative voting rights). But for six provisions there is explicit statutory language in Delaware's statute at odds with the Model Act language, not counting the Model Act provisions with which the Delaware code differed and that were eliminated after the publication of the Carney study.

53. Lucian A. Bebchuk and Alma Cohen, "Firms' Decisions Where to Incorporate," *Journal of Law and Economics*, vol. 46 (2003): 383–425 (in 1998 more than a majority—3,771—of a sample of 6,530 firms in the Compustat database were incorporated in Delaware); Daines, "Incorporation Choices" (more than a majority of IPO firms incorporated in Delaware); Romano, "Law as a Product" (half of largest firms incorporated in Delaware). The three states with the next largest numbers of incorporations after Delaware (and the only other states with more than 200 domestic incorporations) in Bebchuk and Cohen's sample, California, New York and Nevada, are also not Model Act states.

54. As earlier noted, evidence connecting legal innovation with chartering revenues and with reincorporations and retention of local incorporations is provided in Romano, "Law as a Product," pp. 236–42, 246–47; and Moodie, "Forty Years of Charter Competition." For a discussion of the financial incentives of states to compete for charters see Roberta Romano, "Is Regulatory Competition a Problem or Irrelevant for Corporate Governance?" *Oxford Review of Economic Policy*, vol. 21 (2005): 212–31, quotation on pp. 218–22.

55. Romano, *Advantage of Competitive Federalism*, pp. 64–83.

PART V

Conclusion

14

Two Perspectives on Governmental Underperformance

Eugene Bardach

The chapters in this nicely balanced volume on governmental underperformance fall rather neatly into two classes. One class contains chapters written from a "public choice" or "political economy" perspective, which talks about "government failure." These are written mostly by economists or political scientists trained in economics. The chapter by David Weimer and Aidan Vining nicely summarizes the theoretical ideas in this tradition. The second class contains chapters that talk about the government as a "problem-solver" and assess its performance in terms of "effectiveness." These are written by political scientists (David Mayhew, Morris Fiorina, Jay Greene, Mark Rom, and Sarah Binder).

A reader consuming only the generally excellent chapters in this volume might conclude that both perspectives are valuable and have made roughly equal contributions to the understanding of governmental underperformance. This would be a mistake. Taking the social science literature as a whole, the political economy perspective has contributed far more than the problem-solving perspective. In one sense, this volume represents an effort by the editors, both political scientists who have had graduate training in economics, to encourage political scientists to pay more attention to describing, explaining, and perhaps even prescribing for governmental underperformance.[1]

Why has political science paid relatively little attention to this problem? One possible answer is that they judge government against low expectations. Most political scientists take pride in being realists, not utopians. If Alan Gerber and Eric Patashnik argue that the federal government knowingly spends billions on wasteful arthroscopic knee surgery and cannot stop doing so because of resistance from the providers' lobby, "So what else did you expect?" responds the "realist" political scientist.[2]

Political scientists may also suppose that a close analysis of benefits and costs, which the political economy approach recommends, is rather infra dig when there are grand ideas about matters such as "justice" and "America's role in the world" to worry about. When Clifford Winston observes that the society could save $8 billion annually (in 1996 dollars) by taxing trucks on an axle-weight basis instead of by gas consumption, political scientists, instead of exclaiming "Well, why does that outrage persist?" note, while yawning, that, after all, nobody is aware it is happening.

A misguided protectiveness toward government may also be at work. Students of Aristotle, Locke, and Madison, American political scientists think themselves unusually well equipped to appreciate how fine a human creation is democratic government. And in an era when most Americans hold government in low esteem, the paternalistic instinct comes to the fore.

None of these explanations, if true, counts as an excuse. Those who view the underperformance problem through political economy lenses are surely no less anti-utopian than political scientists. But looking through these lenses often gives them clever, and sometimes politically apt, ideas about what to deregulate or marketize. Airline, railroad, and trucking deregulation have been remarkable successes (Winston). And though it is true that economic efficiency is less sexy than "justice," if justice-seeking political scientists were to think closely about economic efficiency, they would see that in many cases government-created inefficiencies work to the advantage of the better off in society rather than the worse off. They would also see that seemingly minor inefficiencies cumulate to hundreds of billions of dollars annually in excess costs and unrealized benefits, if I may hazard a rough guess. As to the need to protect government from its critics, it is plausible that, in the long run, nothing would legitimize government so much as stripping it of tasks better performed by the private sector and boosting to a high level its performance in its remaining tasks.

But low expectations are only part of the answer as to why political scientists are not more interested in the problem of governmental underperformance. The other main reason is that it is technically difficult to conceptualize "underperformance" and, assuming that is accomplished, theorize regarding its causes (Mayhew) and remedies. This chapter aims mainly to appreciate the contributions of the political economy perspective and develop the problem-solving perspective a little further than has been done till now. I rely mainly, though not exclusively, on the chapters in this book, which are referenced in parentheses without accompanying dates.

I consider ideas in two domains. The first is normative: what should government aim to maximize? The second is diagnostic and prescriptive: what are the origins of underperformance, and what remedies seem to hold promise?

What Is to Be Maximized?

In the political economy framework aggregate utility, or "social welfare," is to be maximized. More pointedly, the maximand is social benefits net of social costs, both benefits and costs being defined in terms of the preferences of the individuals living in the society. This maximand is sometimes called "efficiency" (Weimer and Vining, Binder, Winston) or "the general welfare" (Binder). In the problem-solving perspective, the maximand is less ambitious, is more incrementalist, and defies simple characterization.

Political Economy

Actual performance is to be measured against the potential welfare achievable under ideal conditions. In most cases, the ideal is posited to arise from an effectively competitive private market with sufficiently (not necessarily "perfectly") informed buyers and sellers. In markets beset by information asymmetries, externalities, or other such technical imperfections (Weimer and Vining), appropriate intervention by government (or by its private functional equivalent, such as a professional association) can potentially increase welfare. In such cases, the relevant ideal would be a market in which the appropriate intervention (for example, regulation or subsidy) was installed and working perfectly.

Deviations from the ideal indicate governmental underperformance—for example, ineffective and costly arthroscopic knee surgery (Gerber and Patashnik), preventable traffic congestion (Winston), excessive costs and suboptimal housing for low-income renters (Edgar Olsen).

For evaluating most aspects of government performance, the welfare-maximization test is appropriate and coherent. It is not, however, always easy to apply. It sometimes requires quantification of uncertain benefits and costs as well as a means of comparing utilities across individuals. People's utilities may go up, or down, as a function of how their friends' or their enemies' utilities are affected by a policy. Today's preferences do not very well predict tomorrow's utilities, and preferences can be altered by experience and by discussion with others.[3] These difficulties are in some contexts more troubling than in others. The welfare-maximization framework seems particularly limited with regard to issues that have a heavy symbolic or redistributive component. When that is so, the problem-solving perspective might be more useful.

Problem Solving

The problems to be solved come in many sizes and shapes, from maintaining social stability to creating community to keeping enemies at bay to fixing imperfect markets. On this last point, there is an overlap with the political economy perspective, in that falling short of the welfare-maximization ideal could be framed as a "problem" to be "solved."

Doing so would appear to erase any substantive distinction between the political economy and the problem-solving perspectives. More subtle differences could remain, however, particularly with regard to framing. For instance, as a guide to action, "Maximize welfare!" is usually too global. Something more incremental would be more motivating, for instance, "Take a step toward providing the same services, but find a way to do so at lower cost" or "Assuming your budget stays the same, think of ways to improve the services you offer."[4] Both such prescriptions would fall under the rubric of increasing "cost-effectiveness" subject to certain constraints rather than globally maximizing welfare.

A more significant difference between the welfare-maximization and the problem-solving perspectives concerns who has standing to define either "welfare" or a "problem." The political economy perspective gives the right to define "welfare" unambiguously, and very democratically, to the aggregate of individuals living in the community, and they define "the problem" as some shortfall in their utilities relative to whatever standards these individuals happen to hold, subject to some feasibility constraint. The problem-solving approach, on the other hand, can at least countenance the possibility that the citizenry's understandings and preferences are misbegotten, that responsible elites might sometimes know better.[5]

Welfare-maximization has a far reach, but, in the end, it is limited to policy domains where "welfare," or "utility," is at stake. One might doubt this is so when it comes to matters such as dealing with Iranian nuclear capacity or managing stem cell research, for which preferences are inchoate or are subject to shifts depending on the perceived ebb and flow of opportunities and constraints. Although we can always say that "utility" losses and gains are entailed by any policy, this is so only by definition; and an extension of the concept to these cases stretches it out of all recognition. The vocabulary of "problem solving" seems to fit better.

That vocabulary, unfortunately, does not at present contain a commonly accepted metric for describing degrees of problem resolution. Because problems are rarely solved completely or permanently, such a metric would be useful. Many barriers stand in the way, but the effort to overcome them should be illuminating.

Symbolic and Redistributive Issues

Neither symbolic nor redistributive issues show up in the chapters in this volume. Nor do they appear in the literature on governmental failure or performance generally. Because they are important to citizens, however, and frequently pose political and policy "problems," I sketch a few thoughts about what "good" (never mind "optimal") governmental performance would look like in regard to them.

Symbolic Issues

By "symbolic" I mean issues concerning symbols expressing the identity or character of the political community, such as the pledge of allegiance and holiday displays. Many such issues are two-stage contests: (1) over whether certain categories of acts by the government or by the citizenry are merely private or should be taken as symbolic of the worth, honor, or righteousness of "our community," and (2) if the answer is yes, then, within those categories, which particular expressions count as positive, and which as negative, symbols. Display of the flag, for instance, is taken to count as a largely uncontested expression of community, while exactly how the display is carried out—with what degree of apparent respect or disrespect—remains controversial. Whether abortion is a private act or is community-expressive is contested; hence, stage 2 is never reached. Even when controversial, public art may or may not have a symbolic dimension. When it does not, controversy is simply about whether people like it or not as art, or whether they would prefer different art. When it does, it arouses pleasure or disgust at the prospect that "our community" will be represented by it.

The welfare-maximization framework is inadequate for these community-symbolic issues for two reasons. First, private preferences that exist before the legitimation or delegitimation of a (putative) community symbol have no normative standing, because many participants in the contest believe that the whole point is to find a way to alter such preferences. Flag-wavers and flag-burners are engaged in a battle for each others' hearts and minds. Second, and more important, community-symbolism is in many cases a medium for coercion. Community identity exerts influence on personal identity, and not always benevolently. One faction might value imposing disutility on another if it could get away with doing so, and even if it gave the winners much more utility to win than the losers lost in disutility, we should not necessarily want such an outcome.

The problem-solving schema would be more appropriate. The chief problem, from this perspective, could be thought of as "divisiveness." It has two important aspects, persistence and feelings of alienation and disaffection from the community on the part of the losers.

Redistributive Issues

The chapters in this volume by Olsen (on low-income housing) and Greene (on special education) discuss redistributive programs. They take the objectives and resources of these programs as given and simply compare alternative methods for achieving the objectives and decreasing costs. But we can also ask whether reasonable performance standards can be applied to government's definition of objectives and its allocation of resources in the first place.

Seemingly not, because those matters are highly ideological (Do you like the welfare state, a more egalitarian society, a more self-reliant citizenry?) and even philosophical (What does "justice" require?). The relevant question, however, is not whether a performance standard can be objective in any sense, or even merely consensual. Probably it cannot be either. The issue is whether it is suitable for scholarship to incorporate a concern for any standard at all.

In many contexts, it is suitable. A scholar concerned about what she takes to be the inadequacies of the American welfare state, for instance, could explicitly assert some standard of adequacy and proceed to analyze why it is not achieved. Conversely, the starting point of someone concerned about what is taken to be excessive levels of dependency would be a description of the nature and extent of the problem.[6]

A political economy standard of optimality is available for those redistributive programs that can be construed as a form of insurance. The optimal unemployment insurance program could be viewed as balancing the tax price individuals would be willing to pay for the insurance against the promised benefit package discounted by the improbability of receiving it plus the value attributed to the security from knowing one is covered.

Besides unemployment, the insurance model also to some degree fits disability, old age, and survivorship. John Rawls has implicitly shown how the insurance model can notionally be extended to other conditions, such as being born with genetic endowments unsuited to success in the labor market, provided that people's preferences for an insurance package are formed "behind a veil of ignorance."[7] That is, people must pretend that they do not know their endowments; otherwise, the well-endowed would not vote for very generous packages. In the Rawlsian view, the well endowed, being in the majority, would triumph and leave a minority class of losers to suffer with barely sufficient benefits. In private insurance markets, the analogous practice is called "skimming" the best risks.[8] Government's job therefore is to create a variety of insurance policies—taking into account the "premium," or taxpayer, cost as well as the benefits package—that would come into being were it possible to prevent such skimming.

Whether government performs well in this department according to the political economy standard is difficult to estimate empirically because preferences formed behind the veil of ignorance about managing the risk of low initial endowments are literally impossible to ascertain. The problem-solving perspective, however, may be more congenial. We have had an official "poverty line" since 1969. It was originally based on the costs of food to provide a minimally nutritious diet and is used mainly for statistical purposes. We also have a number of "poverty thresholds" that pertain to eligibility status for various government programs. These have evolved over the years through political and analytical processes. The problem-solving perspective on success against poverty might reasonably mean that 100 percent of the population was above all or some combination of the poverty line and the several poverty thresholds.[9] This proposition would need to be modified somewhat because the defining line and threshold are troubled by technical difficulties and conceptual disagreement.

Causes and Remedies

If government underperformance is the dependent variable, what are the relevant independent variables? What are the relevant causal dynamics?

Political Economy

The political economy tradition starts with ideas deriving directly or indirectly from economics: utility-maximizing agents, utility functions of government officials dominated by private interest, citizens as consumers, and the normative status of welfare-maximization, for instance. It turns them loose on the central institutions of representative government, such as the geographical or other basis for representation, voting rules, legislative logrolling and other coalition-forming dynamics, information-asymmetries and other principal-agent problems, the costs of organizing interest representation, the nature of bureaucratic and monopolistic supply, rent-seeking, and so forth.

The rent-seeking idea is particularly important. It shows up as "interest group politics" in traditional political science, and the phenomenon at issue turns up in one way or another in most of the chapters: orthopedic surgeons protecting arthroscopic knee surgery (Gerber and Patashnik), Washington, D.C., bus drivers pushing their salary to twice the competitive level (Winston), school districts overenrolling and underserving special-education students (Greene), and both for-profit and nonprofit low-income housing developers disposed to protect unit-based subsidies (Olsen).[10]

Among the chapter contributors who are closest to the standard political economy framework, privatization and marketization are the leading reform candidates. These two reforms overlap but are not identical. Marketization is the more general idea. On the supply side, marketization means opening a government monopoly on the provision of some good or service to competitive supply, typically by the private or nonprofit sector. Privatization is often a way to do this, either by selling off assets, contracting out (outsourcing), or, in the domain of social regulation, turning over regulatory responsibility to private organizations, such as professional standard-setting bodies.

But privatization is not the only way. Government can get the benefits of competitive supply by holding an auction among private bidders but allowing participation by public-sector agencies as well. Perhaps the first, and certainly the most documented, case of this last approach was when Indianapolis competed a road-paving contract in 1992; it was won on cost grounds by the city's own Department of Public Works, which found ways to cut its own costs, for the purposes of the competition, by some 25 percent.[11] Roberta Romano's chapter in this volume describes a competitive interstate market in what might be thought of as corporate governance services and that market's beneficial effect on innovation, with Delaware usually at the head of the pack. In a related work, Romano argues that securities regulation would also benefit from a similar competition—just get the Securities and Exchange Commission out of the way!—with investor welfare improved by better disclosure provisions and lower compliance and administrative costs.[12]

On the demand side, marketization means empowering consumers of a good or service to purchase it from competitive suppliers, typically by using a voucher—for example, the low-income housing strategy Olsen reports as being much more cost-effective than a subsidy to housing developers or managers or the McKay program in Florida described by Greene for children in need of special education. This approach not only benefits from competition in supply, but also permits a body of consumers with heterogeneous preferences to shop for different variants of the good or service in question.

In a world of zero transaction or information costs, government failures arising from minority rent-seeking could always be prevented or reversed. This is virtually true by definition, for the loss-bearing majority would not stand for the inefficient result. In the real world, however, where these costs may be very high, entrepreneurial effort—indeed, leadership—may be necessary to mobilize offsetting majorities. The point is made forcefully by Gerber and Patashnik in their chapter on arthroscopic surgery and in their introductory chapter. Binder suggests two especially interesting majority-mobilizing strategies: reframing an issue hitherto salient only to minority rent-seekers as an issue of concern to an opposed and activatable (and perhaps partisan) majority; and using pork barrel side-payments to round out near-majorities. Mayhew offers several ideas to make congressional behavior more transparent, such as "a secondary market . . . to excerpt and package especially important or interesting congressional debates in watcher-friendly hour-long or half-hour-long presentations."

A complementary strategy to mobilizing a majority is demobilizing the rent-seeking minority. Binder notes that Congress can arrange for member votes to be concealed lest they offend special interests and that it can arrange to delegate tough issues, such as military base closures, to outside commissions.

Problem Solving

The political economy view of the policy process is that of a machine that takes in preferences on the front end, mangles and distorts them in the middle, and spits out inefficient policies at the back end. The idea that intendedly rational, forward-looking, problem-solving behavior could be part of the process in the middle is alien, as is the idea that its absence could plausibly figure in any theory explaining government underperformance. From a problem-solving perspective, the potential for such behavior and for its inhibition or degradation should, in my view, be the theoretical starting point.

That said, one must acknowledge that such behavior is protean and probably immeasurable. As a first step, one might look for the *absence* of incentives that would lead to the inhibition or degradation of problem-solving behavior. In a modern mass democracy, this would mean incentives to ignore problems or to reach for policy solutions that are self-delusional or ideological or merely "appearances-maximizing." By this final point, I mean position taking, credit claiming, blame avoiding, and blame assigning.[13] Of course, *all* policy solutions have these characteristics to some degree, and the incentives to choose them are never entirely absent, so absence is a matter of degree. Second, incentives must be *present* for individuals to attend to problems and to work at solving them. It is generally acknowledged that such incentives—to "statesmanship," or "entrepreneurship," so to speak—are sparse and weak. In their introductory chapter, Gerber and Patashnik note some very serious incentive blunters, such as problem-solving time horizons limited by the electoral calendar, public misunderstanding of the problem landscape and of the feasibility of policy solutions, and the proclivity of political rivals to steal one another's issues. Nevertheless, statesmen and policy entrepreneurs are often critical in constructing coalitions of self-interested parties that find they have a stake in the solution to some problem.

If the appropriate incentive structures are known, the next step is to ask what institutions or processes might create them—or, more circumspectly, increase the probability that they will occur. Mayhew has bravely postulated a number of such process features (more transparency, more sophisticated dialogue, fewer incentives to mere posturing), which I would characterize collectively as "democratic deliberation." How often such features support problem solving in large representative bodies can be questioned. Perhaps these features are important but need to be complemented by the clubby norms of cloakroom deal-making. Binder, indeed, suggests that *less* transparency would be helpful rather than more.[14]

Even if all policymakers were highly motivated problem-solvers, their efforts would still fail if they could not act cooperatively to some degree. In this regard, the design of governmental institutions matters. Our own institutions are designed to fragment power; and, as a byproduct, they also fragment policy. Political parties have the potential to integrate power across institutional barriers, but parties are a two-edged sword, for if they integrate across institutions, they also divide across social cleavages. Whether they do more integration than division, or vice versa, depends on a number of conditions, including the degree of hegemony or competitiveness, intraparty factional divisions, the distribution of preferences and loyalties in the electorate, and electoral arrangements.[15]

At the federal level today, the parties are deeply divided, and policy integration across party lines takes a back seat. Mayhew and Fiorina argue that party polarization is the enemy of constructive problem solving, because polarization increases the propensity to maximize appearances and undermines the trust that makes cross-party legislative working relationships possible. In his chapter in this volume, Fiorina eschews offering remedies for this condition. Elsewhere, however, he cautiously endorses some electoral reforms aimed at reducing the influence of party purists in the nominating process, particularly the "blanket primary" and majority-producing run-off elections, and redrawing districts so as to make them more competitive as between parties.[16] This last is only superficially paradoxical, because it is in the less competitive—that is, one-party—districts that incumbents must worry most about primary challenges from the most extreme faction within their own party. Mayhew also endorses a series of electoral reforms: blanket primaries for Congress; finance reforms aimed at reducing dependence on national as opposed to local sources; and reducing partisan gerrymandering. In addition, he mentions changes in Congress to diminish the power of party leaders.

The behavior associated with party polarization is ugly, and certainly it undermines problem-solving efforts that cut across the parties and seek the ideological middle ground. It is not clear, however, that party polarization is worse than interparty consensus building as a way to solve problems or to maximize welfare. Binder, for instance, argues that the opposite may often occur, with the congressional party's image as a successful collective actor hinging on coherent policy thinking and execution. In light of the often-realized potential for policy fragmentation in our complex federal system, overseen by policymakers formally divided by the separation of powers, a strong and occasionally predominant political party might be a good thing. Of course, for those who do not like the (conservative) Republican agenda at the federal level since 2001, the policy record of the past five years may look like highly ineffective problem solving.[17] Indeed, it may look like problem creating, but a fair evaluation of the potentiality for "responsible party government" to solve more problems than it creates is not possible on the fly. Neither Mayhew nor Fiorina pretends that he has done the careful study needed to support a firm conclusion. The question ought to provoke much scholarly analysis.

Enlightenment

Contributors from both the political economy and the problem-solving perspectives suggest that one or another form of enlightenment in high places would help—or at least it could not hurt. Weimer and Vining urge that more policy analysts be hired, that is, people who understand the value of, and the institutions of, economic efficiency; Olsen, that congressional staff allow themselves to be educated by academic and think-tank experts in housing policy; Charles Holt, William Shobe, and Angela Smith, that marketization strategies be supported, when applicable, by auctions designed by economist experts; Robin Hanson, that government stimulate multiple and high-quality analyses of trends by allowing analysts to place bets on their predictions; Rom, that states, long advertised as policy "laboratories," actually take that role seriously and host many policy experiments; Mayhew, that "good . . . performances" by members of Congress be widely covered by C-SPAN, along with poor performances; Gerber and Patashnik, that the evidentiary basis for government decisions in the medical arena be strengthened. From the political economy perspective, enlightenment helps majoritarian mobilization, and from the problem-solving perspective, it gives those with the incentive to look for effective solutions the capacity to do so.

In light of the array of forces massed against welfare-maximizing and/or effective policies, the relatively weaker forces that might favor them—and even including those who do so out of self-interest—need all the help they can get. Enlightenment is a force multiplier, like military intelligence, which affects a variety of missions and assets, both offensive and defensive. Enlightened arguments can help activate diffused beneficiaries of reform and expose weaknesses in the positions of their opponents, but for the very reason that enlightenment is not politically neutral, the same political forces that benefit from government failures or underperformance may try to undermine or destroy (witness the Congressional Office of Technology Assessment) the various embodiments of enlightenment: the people and offices that do analysis, the objectivity-enhancing procedures behind reports, or the channels used to communicate results or ideas.[18]

Enlightenment in regard to public policy institutions and practices may also have cultural and psychological barriers to surmount. The use of markets, analytic tools like cost-benefit analysis, and laboratory and computer simulations is suspect in some quarters, though the first two have made considerable headway. Benefit-cost analysis, its limitations notwithstanding, is a powerful and worthwhile tool and, when done properly, a vehicle for bringing the preferences of *all* affected parties into the weighing of policy options, including those who are poorly organized politically. Ironically, it is sometimes criticized for being "elitist" and "technocratic." Hanson's narrative about the political uproar over the Pentagon-funded Policy Analysis Market is not surprising.

Enlightenment is a tool especially valued by readers of this book (and contributors to it). We would like to think it efficacious. Holt, Shobe, and Smith recount at least two success stories, NOx and irrigation water auctions. The literature contains other examples.[19] Although Olsen does not say so, it would not be surprising if the successes enjoyed by the voucher strategy relative to unit subsidies in helping to house the poorly off were in some degree attributable to the at least partial enlightenment that has spread through the federal housing policy-making network.

More important, from a social point of view, enlightenment is relatively inexpensive and, even if limited in its political influence, almost certainly cost-effective. A well-designed sulfur dioxide trading system, or a deregulated air or truck transport system, saves the society hundreds of billions of dollars over the long run, whereas the cost of the economists and the policy analysts who invented and sold the idea could not possibly be more than 1 percent of such savings.

Conclusion

The political economy perspective on government underperformance has been very successful, as chapters in this collection demonstrate. It is a tradition nurtured largely by economists and their intellectual heirs. However, it leaves gaps that might be filled by work done from a problem-solving perspective, a perspective that ought to be congenial to political scientists (among others). Therefore, I conclude by asking what it would take to persuade political scientists to pay more systematic attention to the problems of, and potential remedies for, governmental underperformance. Here are two admittedly impressionistic and provisional conclusions.

A Lens of One's Own

For professional identity reasons, political scientists need a conceptual scheme that does not simply borrow from economics. All contributors to this volume received nearly identical guidance letters from the editors, and it is striking how systematically the representatives of different disciplines chose to be cued by different phrases. No economist used in his or her chapter "problem solving" or "effectiveness" in preference to "efficiency" or "welfare." In only one case (Binder) did a political scientist make much reference to "welfare" as opposed to problem solving. The political scientists' notion that problem-solving is potentially a useful framework is justified, but for the potential to be realized, a great deal of conceptual and empirical work needs to be done on the details of how "problem solving" actually does or does not occur.[20] It is not likely that economists will rush to take up this labor. Political scientists could have the field to themselves.

Problem Solving and Institutions

The uncertainty, as described above, over whether partisan polarization helps or hurts problem solving is an indicator of just how challenging it is to establish causal linkages between macrolevel institutions and configurations of microlevel behavior. The uncertainty over whether transparency or secrecy in legislatures helps or hurts is the same. It would not be surprising if political scientists, seeing these and other such research difficulties out of the corners of their eyes, have simply eschewed this area of research. Unfortunately, there is no solution to this problem, if it is a problem, except to suggest that those who succeed would be amply rewarded intellectually and professionally.

Notes

1. Gerber holds a Ph.D. in economics, Patashnik, a master's in public policy and a Ph.D. in political science.

2. An epistemological variant of the "realist" defense is: we are social scientists, and we study what is, not what might be.

3. Barry Schwartz, *Paradox of Choice* (New York: HarperCollins, 2004).

4. Karl E. Weick, "Small Wins: Redefining the Scale of Social Problems," *American Psychologist*, vol. 39 (1984): 40–49.

5. Because elites will probably be divided as to what counts as a "problem" anyway (Mayhew), the more democratic approach may in the end be less divisive.

6. Analysis along these lines would require a clear distinction between performance failures *of* government and *by* government. The former defines the performance standard, whereas the latter forms part of the explanation. According to some views, for instance, American federalism—a "failure" of sorts *by* government—partly explains insufficiencies in the American welfare state—a failure *of* government.

7. John Rawls, *A Theory of Justice* (Harvard University Press, 1971), pp. 136–42.

8. Skimming is the opposite of adverse selection. Insurance sellers skim the good risks, but insurance buyers who know themselves to be unusually bad risks select into the insurance market at above-average rates.

9. Other values may be engaged by redistributive policies as well, for example, enabling democratic participation, expressing social solidarity, benevolence. See Robert E. Goodin and colleagues, *The Real Worlds of Welfare Capitalism* (Cambridge University Press, 1999).

10. The other main source of government failure in the political economy tradition, majoritarian domination, does not happen to find its way into the present collection but deserves mention here. The mix and quality of public services provided by government tend to serve the preferences of the median voter. Their hallmarks are standardization and middling quality. Although the presence of competing local, state, and special-district governments is a source of desirable pluralism, it is still hard to find public school curricula based on the philosophy of Rudolf Steiner or public parks that offer nudist enclaves. Even

worse, it is all too easy to find public school districts dominated by white majorities that systematically underserve their black minorities.

11. Howard Husock, *Organizing Competition in Indianapolis: Mayor Stephen Goldsmith and the Quest for Lower Costs (B)* (Cambridge, Mass.: Kennedy School of Government, 1992).

12. Roberta Romano, *The Advantage of Competitive Federalism for Securities Regulation* (Washington, D.C.: AEI Press, 2002). Intergovernmental competition could produce a "race to the bottom" if the competition rewarded the wrong thing. In corporate and securities regulation, however, corporate managers act as proxies for investors, who will prefer to invest in companies that are subject to high-quality regulatory regimes, that is, those that optimize the benefits and costs to investors. These beneficial intergovernmental competitive effects in the regulatory domain are analogous to those in the domain of local public services, classically described by Charles Tiebout, "A Pure Theory of Local Expenditure," *Journal of Political Economy*, vol. 64 (October 1956): 416–24.

13. On credit-claiming in particular, see David R. Mayhew, *Congress: The Electoral Connection* (Yale University Press, 1974).

14. Weaver and Rockman suggest that the congressional vote on a certain type of (proposed but hypothetical) spending rescission plan be by secret ballot so as to "shield legislators from constituency blame if they voted against programs or projects popular in their localities." R. Kent Weaver and Bert A. Rockman, "Institutional Reform and Constitutional Design," in *Do Institutions Matter? Government Capabilities in the United States and Abroad,* edited by R. K. Weaver and B. A. Rockman (Brookings, 1993), pp. 478–79.

15. See the various essays in Weaver and Rockman, eds., *Do Institutions Matter?*

16. Morris P. Fiorina, *Culture War? The Myth of a Polarized America* (New York: Longman, 2005), pp. 106–08.

17. Jacob S. Hacker and Paul Pierson, *Off Center: The Republican Revolution and the Erosion of American Democracy* (Yale University Press, 2005). But see, for the case of health care reform, circa 1993, Weaver and Rockman, eds., *Do Institutions Matter?* pp. 480–81.

18. A colleague and I have recently been struggling with a California state agency over our right to publicize a cost-effectiveness analysis of the agency that put them in a less flattering light than they had expected.

19. Martha Derthick and Paul J. Quirk, *The Politics of Deregulation* (Brookings, 1985); Kevin M. Esterling, *The Political Economy of Expertise: Information and Efficiency in American National Politics* (University of Michigan Press, 2004); A. A. Zagonel and colleagues, "Using Simulation Models to Address 'What If' Questions about Welfare Reform," *Journal of Policy Analysis and Management*, vol. 23 (August 2004): 890–901.

20. The work of Paul Sabatier and his many students and collaborators, however, represents a beginning: Paul A. Sabatier and Hank C. Jenkins-Smith, eds., *Policy Change and Learning: An Advocacy Coalition Approach* (Boulder, Colo.: Westview Press, 1993); and Paul A. Sabatier and Hank C. Jenkins-Smith, eds., *Theories of the Policy Process* (Boulder, Colo.: Westview Press, 1999). This approach looks at macroprocesses involving institutions and elite populations. Esterling, *Political Economy of Expertise*, takes a more micro approach, focusing on the way legislators use evidence in their decisionmaking. The micro approach would benefit from the use of normative benchmarks against which to assess various steps in problem solving such as those in Eugene Bardach, *A Practical Guide for Policy Analysis: The Eightfold Path to More Effective Problem Solving* (Washington, D.C.: CQ Press, 2005).

Contributors

Eugene Bardach
University of California–Berkeley

Sarah A. Binder
Brookings Institution and George Washington University

Morris P. Fiorina
Hoover Institution, Stanford University

Alan S. Gerber
Yale University

Jay P. Greene
Manhattan Institute and University of Arkansas

Robin Hanson
George Mason University

Charles A. Holt
University of Virginia

David R. Mayhew
Yale University

Edgar O. Olsen
University of Virginia

Eric M. Patashnik
University of Virginia

Mark Carl Rom
Georgetown University

Roberta Romano
Yale Law School

William M. Shobe
University of Virginia

Angela M. Smith
University of Virginia

Aidan R. Vining
Simon Fraser University

David L. Weimer
University of Wisconsin–Madison

Clifford Winston
Brookings Institution

Index

AANA. *See* Arthroscopy Association of North America
AAOS. *See* American Academy of Orthopedic Surgeons
ABA. *See* American Bar Association
Abt Associates, 105
Academia, former members of Congress in, 233
Adoption-emulation process, 267–68
AFDC. *See* Aid to Families with Dependent Children
African Americans: in Congress, 228; electoral procedures and, 269; in public education, 141
Aftermarkets, 188
Aggregate outcomes, in decision markets, 161
Agriculture: irrigation reduction in, 177–82; reform in, congressional institutions and, 210–11; subsidies in, 201, 205, 210, 243
Agriculture, U.S. Department of (USDA), housing programs of, 102, 103, 122, 123
Agriculture Committee, House, 210, 211

Agriculture Committee, Senate, 211
Aid to Families with Dependent Children (AFDC) program, 270, 272
Airlines: deregulation of, 13, 87, 88, 89; pricing by, 90, 91
Airport landing slots, policy experimentation on, 185–89
Air traffic control, 92
Alaska, "bridge to nowhere" in, 84
ALI. *See* American Law Institute
Allocation. *See* Market allocation
Ambiguity, in policy information, 206–07
Amerex Energy, 184–85
American Academy of Orthopedic Surgeons (AAOS), 48, 53–54, 55, 56
American Association of Hip and Knee Surgeons, 55
American Bar Association (ABA), 292, 298
American Law Institute (ALI), 290
American Medical Association, 60
American Political Science Association (APSA): *1950* report by, 240, 242, 245, 246, 248, 250; focus of research in, 6

327